Microsoft® SharePoint® Foundation 2010

Step by Step

Olga Londer
Penelope Coventry

PUBLISHED BY
Microsoft Press
A Division of Microsoft Corporation
One Microsoft Way
Redmond, Washington 98052-6399

Library of Congress Control Number: 2011920543
ISBN: 978-0-7356-2726-0

Printed and bound in Canada.

Microsoft Press books are available through booksellers and distributors worldwide. For further information about international editions, contact your local Microsoft Corporation office or contact Microsoft Press International directly at fax (425) 936-7329. Visit our Web site at www.microsoft.com/mspress. Send comments to mspinput@ microsoft.com.

Acquisitions Editor: Kim Spilker
Developmental Editor: Devon Musgrave
Project Editor: Rosemary Caperton
Editorial Production: Custom Editorial Productions, Inc.
Technical Reviewer: Todd Meister; Technical Review services provided by Content Master, a member of CM Group, Ltd.
Cover: Girvin

Body Part No. X17-46527

Contents at a Glance

Contents

What do you think of this book? We want to hear from you!

Microsoft is interested in hearing your feedback so we can continually improve our books and learning resources for you. To participate in a brief online survey, please visit:

microsoft.com/learning/booksurvey

What do you think of this book? We want to hear from you!

Microsoft is interested in hearing your feedback so we can continually improve our books and learning resources for you. To participate in a brief online survey, please visit:

microsoft.com/learning/booksurvey

Acknowledgments

This book is the result of the collective effort of many people. We'd like to start with thanking Kim Spilker and Devon Musgrave of Microsoft Press, who initially approached us about updating the previous version of the book and provided invaluable assistance in getting this project off the ground.

Second, we'd like to thank Neil Salkind from Studio B, our agent, who did an outstanding job resolving contractual issues, making organizational arrangements, and providing great advice at the key points in the project that helped us to make this book a reality.

Next, we would like to thank our contributing authors, Mirjam van Olst, Nikander and Margriet Bruggeman, Kay McClure, and Brett Lonsdale, who stepped in to help us meet the publishing deadlines and whose knowledge and experience significantly added to this book.

At Microsoft Press, Rosemary Caperton, our project editor, oversaw the project with patience and professionalism that ensured that the book was published on time, while always providing us with graceful assistance, for which we are entirely thankful.

We are also grateful to Linda Allen and her team at Custom Editorial Productions, Susan McClung, our copy editor, and Todd Meister, our technical editor, for their professionalism, good humor, and positive attitude to resolving each and every challenge that this project might have presented to them.

Last, but by no means least, we would like to thank our respective husbands, Gregory and Peter, for their boundless support and encouragement, as well as for bearing with us while we worked on this book in the evenings and over the weekends.

Sincerely,

Olga Londer and Penelope Coventry

Features and Conventions of This Book

This book has been designed to lead you step by step through many of the tasks you're most likely to want to perform in Microsoft SharePoint Foundation 2010. If you start at the beginning and work your way through all the exercises, you will gain enough proficiency to be able to create and work with a wide range of SharePoint Foundation features. However, each topic is self contained. If you have worked with a previous version of SharePoint Foundation, or if you completed all the exercises and later need help remembering how to perform a procedure, the following features of this book will help you locate specific information:

- **Detailed table of contents** Search the listing of the topics and sidebars within each chapter.

- **Chapter thumb tabs** Easily locate the beginning of the chapter you want.

- **Topic-specific running heads** Within a chapter, quickly locate the topic you want by looking at the running heads at the top of odd-numbered pages.

- **Detailed index** Look up specific tasks and features in the index, which has been carefully crafted with the reader in mind.

You can save time when reading this book by understanding how the *Step by Step* series shows exercise instructions, keys to press, buttons to click, and other information.

Convention	Meaning
Practice Files	These paragraphs provide information about the practice files that you will use when working through the exercises in a chapter.
SET UP and BE SURE TO	These paragraphs preceding a step-by-step exercise indicate any requirements that you should attend to or actions that you should take before beginning the exercise.
CLEAN UP	This paragraph following a step-by-step exercise provides instructions for saving and closing open files or programs before moving on to another topic.
1 **2**	Blue numbered steps guide you through hands-on exercises in each topic.
1 2	Black numbered steps guide you through procedures in sidebars and expository text.
Important	This paragraph points out information that you need to know to complete a procedure.

Convention	Meaning
Note	This paragraph describes information that merits special attention.
See Also	This paragraph directs you to more information about a topic in this book or elsewhere.
Tip	This paragraph provides a helpful hint or shortcut that makes working through a task easier.
Troubleshooting	This paragraph explains how to fix a common problem that might prevent you from continuing with an exercise.
CTRL+G	A plus sign (+) between two keys means that you must press those keys at the same time. For example, "Press **CTRL+G**" means that you should hold down the **CTRL** key while you press the G key.
Create View	Pictures of buttons appear in the margin the first time the button is used in a chapter.
Black bold	In the hands-on exercises, the names of program elements, such as buttons, commands, windows, and dialog boxes, as well as files, folders, or text that you interact with in the steps, are shown in black bold type.
Blue bold	In the hands-on exercises, text that you should type is shown in blue bold type.
Blue bold italic	Important terms are formatted this way.

Using the Practice Files

Before you can complete the exercises in this book, you need to copy the book's practice files to your computer. These practice files, as well as other information, can be downloaded from the book's catalog page, located at *http://go.microsoft.com /fwlink/?Linkid=206096*.

The following table lists the practice files that are required to perform the exercises in this book.

Chapter	File
Chapter 1: Introduction to SharePoint Foundation 2010	No practice files
Chapter 2: Navigating a SharePoint Site	Chapter02_Starter.wsp
Chapter 3: Creating and Managing Sites	No practice files
Chapter 4: Working with Lists	No practice files
Chapter 5: Working with Libraries	OakChest.docx OakDesk.docx OakEndTable.docx OakNightStand.docx Pjcov.jpg WideWorldInvoice.dcox WideWorldPurchaseOrder.xsn
Chapter 6: Working with Web Pages	Chapter06_Starter.wsp Pjcov.jpg
Chapter 7: Working with List Settings	No practice files
Chapter 8: Working with Library Settings	Contoso Proposal.docx ProposalsTemplate.docx WideWorldImportersLogo.png
Chapter 9: Working with List and Library Views	Chapter09_Starter.wsp
Chapter 10: Working with Surveys and Discussion Boards	No practice files
Chapter 11: Working with Workflows	No practice files
Chapter 12: Working with Workspaces and Blogs	No practice files
Chapter 13: Using SharePoint Foundation with Outlook 2010	Chapter13_Starter.wsp

Chapter	File
Chapter 14: Using SharePoint Foundation with Excel 2010 and Access 2010	ExpImpWideWorldImporters2010.accdb Furniture_Price.xlsx MoveWideWorldImporters.accdb Sales_Figures.xlsx
Chapter 15: Using SharePoint Foundation with InfoPath 2010	Chapter15_Starter.wsp Purchase Order Template.xsn
Chapter 16: Finding Information on the SharePoint Site	Chapter16_Starter.wsp

In addition to the files required to perform the exercises, the following files contain reference information that will enhance your ability to get the most out of this book and Microsoft SharePoint Foundation:

- A comparison of the SharePoint 2010 editions is provided in the file SharePoint2010EditionComparison.xlsx, which is located in the Chapter01 practice folder.

- A SharePoint Foundation 2010 ribbon reference is provided in the file SharePoint_Command_Mapping_Guide.xslx, which is located in the Chapter02 practice folder.

Software Requirements

This section details the software requirements for both your client computer and the server that is running SharePoint Foundation 2010.

Important You must have access to a SharePoint Foundation 2010 installation on the server before performing exercises in this book.

Client Computer

To perform the exercises in this book, your client computer should meet the following requirements:

- Operating system
  - Windows 7 is recommended. However, you can also use Windows Vista, Windows XP, Windows Server 2008, or Windows Server 2003.

- Software

  - ○ Internet Explorer 8 or later is recommended; however, you can use Internet Explorer 7. Other browsers, such as Mozilla Firefox and Safari, can be used with some limitations. For a list of known limitations, refer to *http://technet .microsoft.com/en-gb/library/cc288142.aspx*.

  - ○ Microsoft Word 2010, Microsoft Outlook 2010, Microsoft Excel 2010, Microsoft Access 2010, and Microsoft InfoPath 2010.

- Disk space

  - ○ 10 megabytes (MB) of available hard disk space is recommended for the practice files.

Server Deployment

To perform the exercises in this book, you should have access to a SharePoint Foundation 2010 deployment that can be a single-server installation, a farm deployment, or a hosted service. The server should meet the following requirements:

- Operating system

  - ○ The 64-bit edition of Windows Server 2008 Standard, Enterprise, Data Center, or Web Server with SP2, or the 64-bit edition of Windows Server 2008 R2 Standard, Enterprise, Data Center, or Web Server.

  - ○ Microsoft .NET Framework 3.5.

- Software

  - ○ SharePoint Foundation 2010

See Also For a complete list of hardware and software requirements for SharePoint Foundation 2010, refer to *http://technet.microsoft.com/en-gb/library/cc288955.aspx*.

Important The catalog page for this book does not contain SharePoint Foundation 2010. SharePoint Foundation 2010 is available as a free download from the Microsoft website at *http://go.microsoft.com/fwlink/?LinkId=197422*.

Installing the Practice Files

You need to install the practice files in the correct location on your hard disk before you can use them in the exercises. The default location for the practice files used throughout this book is Documents\Microsoft Press\SPF_SBS.

Important If you install the practice files to a location other than the default, you will need to substitute that path in the instructions for the exercises.

To install the practice files to their default location, follow these steps:

1. On the Windows taskbar, click the **Start** button, and then click **Documents**. Windows Explorer opens.

2. In your **Documents** folder, create a new folder by right-clicking and selecting **New – Folder**. Name the new folder **Microsoft Press**. However, if the Microsoft Press folder already exists, then skip to the next step.

3. Double-click the **Microsoft Press** folder to open it. In the **Microsoft Press** folder, create a new folder and name it **SPF_SBS**.

4. Open your browser and navigate to the book's catalog page: *http://go.microsoft .com/fwlink/?Linkid=206096*.

5. On the book's catalog page, click the **Practice Files** link.

6. On the **Practice Files** page, click **Download the practice files**. The File Download dialog box opens.

7. In the **File Download** dialog box, click **Save**. The Save As dialog box opens.

8. In the **Save As** dialog box, choose **Desktop**, and then click **Save**.

9. Locate the file **SharePointFoundation2010SBS.zip** on your Desktop, right-click it, and select **Extract All.** The Extract Compressed (Zipped) Folders wizard starts.

10. Click **Browse** and navigate to the folder **Documents\Microsoft Press\SPF_SBS** that you created in steps 1–3.

11. Make sure that the option **Show extracted files when complete** is selected, and then click **Extract**. Windows Explorer opens.

12. In Windows Explorer, validate that the chapter-specific folders have been created under **Documents\Microsoft Press\SPF_SBS** and that the practice files have been extracted in the chapter-specific folders.

 **CLEAN UP** Close the browser, and then close Windows Explorer.

Using the Practice Files

The practice files for this book are stored on your hard disk in chapter-specific subfolders under Documents\Microsoft Press\SPF_SBS. Each exercise in a chapter includes a paragraph that lists the files needed for that exercise and explains any preparations needed before you start working through the exercise.

Whenever possible, we start each chapter with a standard SharePoint Foundation Team site, which occasionally must be a top-level team site. If you follow all the exercises in all the chapters in sequence, you do not have to start with a new Team site for every chapter. For most of the chapters, you can just use the same site throughout the book.

However, if you choose to do exercises independently and not in sequence, there are a couple of exercises that depend on other exercises performed earlier in the book. If this is the case, we will tell you where the prerequisite exercise is located in the book so that you can complete the prerequisite exercises. However, you may not want to do the prerequisite exercise, and this is where the starter WSP files will come in handy.

If you have sufficient rights, you can create a new practice site (see the following section titled "Using the WSP Templates") from the chapter's starter WSP file that is provided in the practice folder for the chapter. The starter WSP files contain lists, libraries, files, and pages that you will require during the exercises. The resulting child site will have the prerequisite exercises already completed for you where needed. For chapters that require the creation of a site based on the WSP file, we will tell you at the beginning of the chapter that you need to install the practice site from the starter WSP file for the chapter.

Exercises in some chapters use a subsite in addition to the standard Team site. If this is the case, the practice folder for the chapter contains a WSP file for the subsite.

Using the WSP Templates

To create a practice site for a chapter based on a starter WSP file, perform the following steps:

BE SURE TO verify that you have sufficient rights to upload to the site template gallery of a site collection. If in doubt, refer to the Appendix at the back of this book.

1. In the browser, open the top-level SharePoint site to which you would like to upload the WSP file. If prompted, type your user name and password, and click **OK**.

2. On the **Site Actions** menu, click **Site Settings**. The Site Settings page of the top-level site is displayed.

3. In the **Galleries** section, click **Solutions**. The Solution Gallery – Solutions page is displayed.

4. On the **Solution Gallery – Solutions** page, click the **Solutions** tab on the Ribbon, and then click the **Upload Solution** button. The Solution Gallery – Upload Solution dialog is displayed.

5. In the **Solution Gallery – Upload Solution** dialog, click the **Browse** button.

6. In the **Choose File to Upload** dialog box, navigate to the practice files folder **Documents\Microsoft Press\SPF_SBS\Chapter*NN*** (where *NN* is the chapter number), click the WSP file that you want to use to create the new site, and then click the **Open** button.

7. In the **Solution Gallery – Upload Solution** dialog, click **OK** to complete the upload.

   The **Solution Gallery – Activate Solution** dialog is displayed.

8. In the **Solution Gallery – Activate Solution** dialog, on the **View** tab, click **Activate**.

   The Solution Gallery – Solutions page is displayed. Validate that the practice site WSP file has been uploaded.

You can now create a new practice child site based upon the uploaded WSP template, as follows.

1. Browse to the SharePoint site that you'd like to be the parent of the new practice site.

2. On the **Site Actions** menu, click **New Site**. The Create dialog appears.

3. In the central pane of the **Create** dialog, click the **Chapter*NN*** starter site template that is now available, and then click **More Options**.

4. In the **Title** text box, type a logical name for the new site. You could simply provide the chapter number if you like, such as **Chapter09**.

5. Optionally, in the **Description** text box, type a description, such as **SharePoint SBS Chapter 9 Practice Site**.

6. In the **URL name** text box, repeat the same name that you typed in the **Title** text box.

7. You can leave all the other options as their default values. Click the **Create** button.

   The new practice site has been created and its home page is displayed.

 **CLEAN UP** Close the browser.

Removing the WSP Templates

To remove the chapter starter WSP template from the Solution gallery, perform the following steps.

BE SURE TO verify that you have sufficient rights to delete WSPs from the Solution gallery of a site collection. If in doubt, refer to the Appendix at the back of this book.

1. In the browser, open the top-level SharePoint site where you previously uploaded the WSP files. If prompted, type your user name and password, and click **OK**.

2. On the **Site Actions** menu, click **Site Settings**. The Site Settings page is displayed.

3. In the **Galleries section**, click **Solutions**. The Solution Gallery – Solutions page is displayed.

4. On the **Solution Gallery – Solutions** page, hover the mouse over the template that you wish to remove, and click the arrow that appears on the right to display the context menu. On the context menu, click **Deactivate**.

   The Solution Gallery – Deactivate Solution dialog appears.

5. In the **Solution Gallery – Deactivate Solution** dialog, on the **View** tab, click **Deactivate**.

6. On the Solution Gallery – Solutions page, once again hover the mouse over the template that you wish to remove, and click the arrow that appears on the right to display the context menu. On the context menu, click **Delete**. In the confirmation message box, click **OK** to complete the removal of the site template.

   The Solution Gallery – Solutions page is displayed again. Verify that the practice site template has been removed.

7. Repeat steps 4–6 to remove each practice site template that you no longer require.

 **CLEAN UP** Close the browser.

Deleting a Practice Site

If you created a practice site that you no longer require, you can delete it. Perform the following steps to delete a practice site.

BE SURE TO verify that you have sufficient rights to delete a site. If in doubt, see the Appendix at the back of this book.

1. In the browser, open the SharePoint site that you wish to delete. If prompted, type your user name and password, and click **OK**.

2. On the **Site Actions** menu, click **Site Settings**. The Site Settings page is displayed.

3. In the **Site Actions** section, click **Delete this site**. The Delete This Site confirmation page is displayed.

4. Click the **Delete** button to delete the site.

5. In the message box that appears, click **OK** to confirm the deletion of the site.

The site has been deleted.

 **CLEAN UP** Close the browser.

Removing the Practice Files

After you have completed the exercises for this book, you can free up hard disk space by removing the practice files that were installed from the book's catalog page. This process deletes the downloaded files, as well as the files that you might have created in the chapter-specific folders while working through the exercises. Follow these steps:

1. On the Windows taskbar, click the **Start** button, and then click **Documents**. Windows Explorer opens.

2. In the **Documents** folder, double-click the **Microsoft Press** folder to open it.

3. In the **Microsoft Press** folder, right-click the **SPF_SBS** folder and select **Delete**.

4. In the **Delete Folder** message box, click **Yes** to confirm that you would like to move this folder to the Recycle Bin.

5. If the Microsoft Press folder is not empty and contains practice files for other books, skip to the next step. However, if the Microsoft Press folder is empty, then delete it using instructions in steps 3–4 as a guide.

6. In Windows Explorer, navigate to the **Desktop**. Right-click the compressed folder **SharePointFoundation2010SBS.zip** and select **Delete**. In the **Delete Folder** message box, click **Yes** to confirm that you would like to move this folder to the **Recycle Bin**.

You have removed the practice files for this book.

 **CLEAN UP** Close Windows Explorer.

Accessing Your Online Edition Hosted by Safari

The voucher bound into the back of this book gives you access to an online edition of the book. (In addition to accessing and reading the book online, you can also download the online edition of the book to your computer; download instructions are provided in the next section.)

To access your online edition, perform the following steps.

1. Locate your voucher inside the back cover and scratch off the metallic foil to reveal your access code.

2. Go to *http://microsoftpress.oreilly.com/safarienabled*.

3. Enter your 24-character access code in the Coupon Code field under Step 1.

Note The access code in this image is for illustration purposes only.

4. Click the CONFIRM COUPON button.

   A message will appear to let you know that the code was entered correctly. If the code was not entered correctly, you will be prompted to re-enter the code.

5. In this step, you'll be asked whether you're a new or existing user of Safari Books Online. Proceed either with Step 5A or Step 5B.

   5A. **If you already have a Safari account**, click the EXISTING USER – SIGN IN button under Step 2.

Step ❷

5B. **If you are a new user**, click the NEW USER – FREE ACOUNT button under Step 2.

- ○ You'll be taken to the "Register a New Account" page.
- ○ Complete the registration form and accept the End User Agreement.
- ○ When complete, click the CONTINUE button.

6. On the Coupon Confirmation page, click the My Safari button.

7. On the My Safari page, look at the Bookshelf area and click the title of the book you want to access.

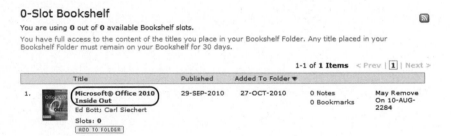

Downloading the Online Edition to Your Computer

In addition to reading the online edition of this book, you can also download it to your computer. First, follow the steps in the preceding section. Then perform the following steps.

1. On the page that appears after Step 7 in the previous section, click the Extras tab.

2. Find "Download the complete PDF of this book" and click the book title.

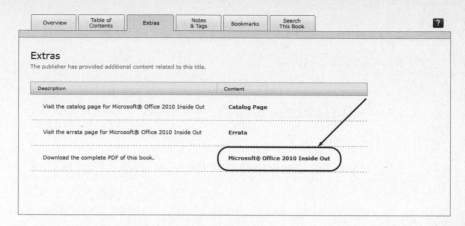

A new browser window or tab will open, followed by the File Download dialog box.

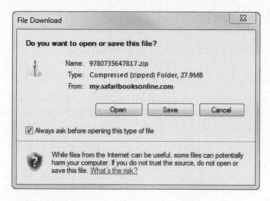

3. Click Save.

4. Choose Desktop and click Save.

5. Locate the .zip file on your desktop. Right-click the file, click Extract All, and then follow the instructions.

Note If you have a problem with your voucher or access code, contact O'Reilly Media, distributor of Microsoft Press books, at mspbooksupport@oreilly.com or call 800-889-8969.

Getting Support and Giving Feedback

Getting Help with This Book and Its Practice Files

The practice files referred to throughout this book are available as web downloads. For more information, see "Using the Practice Files" at the beginning of this book.

Errata

We've made every effort to ensure the accuracy of this book and its companion content. If you do find an error, please report it on our Microsoft Press site at Oreilly.com:

1. Go to *http://microsoftpress.oreilly.com*.
2. In the Search box, enter the book's ISBN or title.
3. Select your book from the search results.
4. On your book's catalog page, under the cover image, you'll see a list of links.
5. Click View/Submit Errata.

Additional Support

You'll find additional information and services for your book on its catalog page at *http://go.microsoft.com/fwlink/?Linkid=206096*. If you need additional support, please email Microsoft Press Book Support at *mspinput@microsoft.com*.

Please note that product support for Microsoft software is not offered through the addresses above.

Getting Help with SharePoint Foundation 2010

If your question is about Microsoft SharePoint Foundation 2010 (not about the content of this book or its practice files), please search Microsoft Support or the Microsoft Knowledge Base at:

http://support.microsoft.com

In the United States, Microsoft software product support issues not covered by the Microsoft Knowledge Base are addressed by Microsoft Product Support Services. The Microsoft software support options available from Microsoft Product Support Services are listed at:

http://support.microsoft.com/gp/selfoverview/

We Want to Hear from You

At Microsoft Press, your satisfaction is our top priority, and your feedback our most valuable asset. Please tell us what you think of this book at:

http://www.microsoft.com/learning/booksurvey

The survey is short, and we read *every one* of your comments and ideas. Thanks in advance for your input!

Stay in Touch

Let's keep the conversation going! We're on Twitter: *http://twitter.com/MicrosoftPress*.

Chapter at a Glance

Locate your SharePoint site, page 3

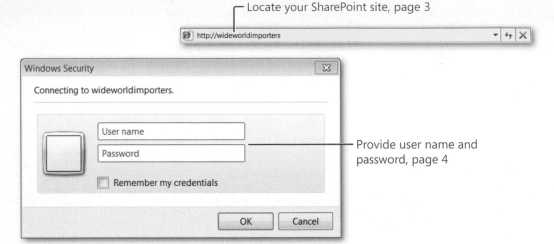

Windows Security

Connecting to wideworldimporters.

User name

Password

☐ Remember my credentials

OK   Cancel

Provide user name and password, page 4

Familiarize yourself with the SharePoint site home page, page 4

Welcome to your site!

Start SharePoint Foundation Help, page 6

Visit Office.com for more help with SharePoint Foundation 2010

Microsoft SharePoint

Categories

- Accessibility
- Co-authoring documents
- Content types
- Getting help

- International environments
- Lists
- Search
- Site and page customization

- Solutions and templates

- Training courses

- Videos
- Web Parts

- Blogs and wikis
- Columns
- Formulas and functions
- Getting started with SharePoint Foundation
- Libraries
- RSS and alerts
- Site and page creation
- Site and site collection management
- Surveys and discussion boards
- Versioning, check-in, and check-out
- Views
- Working with Office programs

1 Introduction to SharePoint Foundation 2010

In this chapter, you will learn

- ✔ What SharePoint Foundation is.
- ✔ How SharePoint Foundation enables team collaboration and sharing.
- ✔ What user permissions are found in SharePoint Foundation.
- ✔ What differences exist between SharePoint Foundation and Windows SharePoint Services.
- ✔ How Office integrates with SharePoint Foundation.
- ✔ What relationships exist between SharePoint Foundation, SharePoint Server 2010, and SharePoint Designer 2010.

In the modern business environment, with its distributed workforce that assists customers at any time and in any location, team members need to be in closer contact than ever before. Effective collaboration is becoming increasingly important; however, it is often difficult to achieve. Microsoft SharePoint Foundation addresses this problem by incorporating a variety of collaboration and communication technologies into a single web-based environment that integrates easily with desktop applications, such as Microsoft Office.

In this chapter, you will learn what SharePoint Foundation is and how it works with Office applications, providing enhanced productivity environments for users and teams. You will also learn the differences between SharePoint Foundation and its predecessor, Microsoft Windows SharePoint Services, as well as the relationships between SharePoint Foundation, Microsoft SharePoint Server 2010, and Microsoft SharePoint Designer 2010 and how to decide which product is right for you.

> **Important** The exercises in this book involve a fictitious business called Wide World Importers. In the scenarios, Wide World Importers is setting up a SharePoint environment for team collaboration and information sharing. There are four people involved in setting up and providing content for this environment: Olga Kosterina, the owner of Wide World Importers; Todd Rowe, her assistant; Bill Malone, the head buyer; and Peter Connelly, the help desk technician.

> **Practice Files** You don't need any practice files to complete the exercises in this chapter.

What Is SharePoint Foundation?

SharePoint Foundation 2010 is a technology that enables organizations and business units of all sizes to improve team productivity and to increase the efficiency of business processes. SharePoint Foundation is provided as a free download and gives you a powerful toolset for organizing information, managing documents, and providing robust collaboration environments.

See Also For system requirements for installing SharePoint Foundation, refer to *http:// technet.microsoft.com/en-gb/library/cc288955.aspx.*

SharePoint Foundation helps teams stay connected and productive by providing an infrastructure that allows easy access to the people, documents, and information that they need. With SharePoint Foundation, teams can create websites to share information and foster collaboration with other users. You can access content stored within a SharePoint site from a web browser and through desktop applications, such as Office.

Team Collaboration and Sharing

SharePoint sites provide places to capture and share ideas, information, communication, and documents. The sites facilitate team participation in discussions, shared document collaboration, blogging, building knowledge bases using wikis, and surveys. The document collaboration features allow for easy check-in and checkout of documents, document version control, and recovery of previous versions, as well as document-level security.

Tip A *blog*, or web log, is an online diary. A blog site allows the diarists, called *bloggers,* to post articles that readers can comment on.

Wiki (pronounced *wee-kee*) is a web environment that allows web browser users to add and edit quickly and easily text and links that appear on the web page. The term *wiki* originates from the Hawaiian word *wikiwiki*, which means "quick." A wiki site can be used, for example, to build a knowledge base, a community resource, or an online encyclopedia, such as Wikipedia.

See Also For more information about blogs, refer to Chapter 12, "Working with Workspaces and Blogs." For more information about wikis, refer to Chapter 6, "Working with Web Pages."

A SharePoint site can have many subsites, the hierarchy of which, on web servers, resembles the hierarchy of folders on file systems—it is a tree-like structure. Similar to storing your files in folders on file systems, you can store your files within SharePoint sites. However, SharePoint sites take file storage to a new level, providing communities for team collaboration and making it easy for users to work together on documents, tasks, contacts, events, calendars, wikis, and other items. This team collaboration environment can increase individual and team productivity greatly.

The collaborative tools provided by SharePoint Foundation are easy to use, so you can share files and information and communicate with your coworkers more effectively. You can create and use SharePoint sites for any purpose. For example, you can build a site to serve as the primary website for a team, create a site to facilitate the organization of a meeting, or create a wiki site to capture team knowledge. A typical SharePoint site might include a variety of useful tools and information, such as shared document libraries, contacts, calendars, task lists, discussions, and other information-sharing and visualization tools.

SharePoint site users can find and communicate with key contacts and experts, both with email and instant messaging. Site content can be searched easily, and users can receive alerts to tell them when existing documents and information have been changed or when new ones have been added. Custom business processes can be attached to the documents. Users can customize site content and layout to present targeted information to specific users on precise topics.

In this exercise, you will locate your SharePoint site and familiarize yourself with its home page.

 SET UP Open the browser.

1. On the browser **Address bar**, type the Uniform Resource Locator (URL), or location, of your SharePoint site: *http://<yourservername/path>*.

   The *yourservername* portion of the URL is the name of the SharePoint server that you will be using for the exercises in this book. The path portion might be empty, or it might include one or more levels in the site hierarchy on your SharePoint server. If you are in doubt about the location of the SharePoint site, check with your SharePoint administrator.

   | http://wideworldimporters | ▾ | ↔ | ✕ |

> **Important** For exercises in this book, we use a site located at the server *wideworldimporters*. Its URL is *http://wideworldimporters*. However, in your environment, you will be using a different site installed on a different server. You will need to use your site location *http://<yourservername/path>* in place of *http://wideworldimporters* throughout the book.

2. If prompted, type your user name and password.

3. Click **OK**.

The home page of your site appears. Although it might look somewhat different from the typical SharePoint Team site that Wide World Importers starts with, it is still likely to include links to a variety of information, as well as the information-sharing tools provided by SharePoint Foundation.

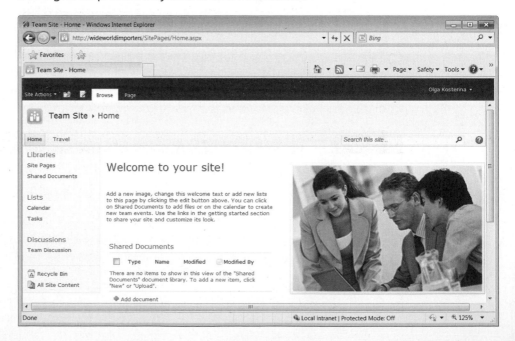

On the left side of the page, you might see links to one or more of the following: Libraries, Lists, and Discussions. This collection of links to frequently used site resources is called a *Quick Launch*. Quick Launch, as the name suggests, enables you to navigate straight to the information and tools that you require.

Below Quick Launch, on the left side of the page, you can see links to Recycle Bin and All Site Content. The panel that contains Quick Launch, Recycle Bin, and All Site Content is referred to as the *left navigation panel*.

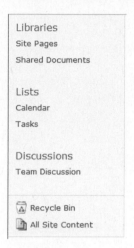

The area at the top of the page is referred to as the *top navigation area*. This area contains a top link bar that appears at the top of each page. It consists of several tabs with links, such as the default Home tab. It may also include other tabs with links to the subsites of this website; for example, the second tab on the left says *Travel*. In our scenario, because the Wide World Importers staff travel extensively worldwide, this links to a subsite that provides Wide World Importers employees with the necessary information and guidelines for arranging business travel.

On the left of the top navigation area, there is a link to a menu called Site Actions. This menu provides access to various actions that allow you to change the site, including site configuration.

Important Your screen might not include links to all parts of the site, such as the Site Actions link, because of the way that security permissions on your server have been set up. SharePoint site users see only the parts of the site that they can actually access: if you don't have access to a part of the site, the link to it is not displayed. To obtain additional access, contact your SharePoint administrator.

4. In the top-right part of the page, click the round Help icon with the question mark. SharePoint Foundation Help opens in a separate window.

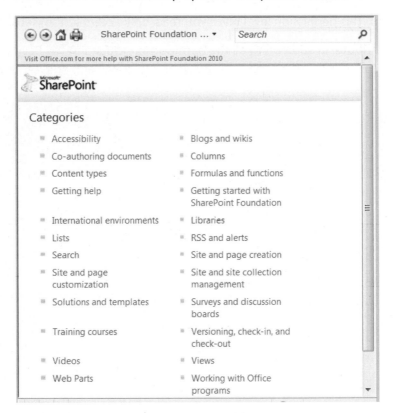

Familiarize yourself with the Help categories and contents, and then close the window.

 **CLEAN UP** Close the browser.

See Also For more information on SharePoint site navigation, refer to Chapter 2, "Navigating a SharePoint Site."

SharePoint Foundation User Permissions

In SharePoint Foundation, access to sites is controlled through a role-based system that uses permission levels. *Permission levels* specify what permissions users have on a SharePoint site. These permissions determine the specific actions that users can perform on the site; in essence, each permission level is a collection of permissions. SharePoint Foundation has five default permission levels:

- **Read** This permission level gives you read-only access to the website.

- **Contribute** In addition to all the permissions included in the Read permission level, the Contribute permission level allows you to create and edit items in existing lists and document libraries.

- **Design** In addition to all the permissions included in the Contribute permission level, the Design permission level allows you to create lists and document libraries, approve items, and edit pages in the website.

- **Full Control** This permission level gives you full control.

- **Limited** The Limited permission level allows access to a shared resource within a site, such as a specific list, document library, folder, list item, or document, without giving access to the entire site.

Important You will need Read or Contribute permission levels for most of the exercises in this book. We will instruct you to verify whether you have a sufficient permission level before introducing exercises, particularly those in which a higher level of access, such as Design or Full Control, is needed. If you are not sure what permissions are set on your SharePoint site, check with your SharePoint administrator.

See Also For more information about permission levels, refer to Chapter 3, "Creating and Managing Sites." A full list of permissions and their associated permission levels is provided in the Appendix at the back of this book.

Versions of SharePoint Foundation

SharePoint Foundation 2010 is an evolution of Microsoft Windows SharePoint Services. Previous versions of this technology include:

- Windows SharePoint Services 3.0
- Windows SharePoint Services 2.0
- SharePoint Team Services

SharePoint Foundation provides many new, enhanced, and updated features in comparison with its predecessors. In particular, it provides a more robust and manageable collaboration platform with a significantly enhanced user interface that includes a new contextual Ribbon. The new features include the following:

● A new user interface that includes the SharePoint Ribbon, which provides a primary command surface and is designed to help you quickly locate the commands that you require. It is similar to the Ribbon in other Office programs such as Microsoft Word, Microsoft Excel, and Microsoft PowerPoint.

● Microsoft SharePoint Workspace 2010 enables you to work offline with SharePoint sites, libraries, and lists. When you are reconnected to your network, the changes are synchronized with the live site automatically.

● The Rich Text Editor allows you to insert and format content directly on wiki web pages and in blog posts.

● The redesigned themes in the Themes Gallery enable you to customize the look and feel of your site, with multiple color options.

● A co-authoring capability allows you to work simultaneously with your team members on the same document.

● Enhanced Calendar functionality, including displaying multiple calendars within a page, inline editing of items, and dragging within the calendar.

● Improved mobile access to your SharePoint site.

In addition, SharePoint Foundation 2010 includes Microsoft Business Connectivity Services (BCS), which enables SharePoint integration with external data, including line-of-business applications. BCS connects SharePoint-based solutions to sources of external data and provides a way to define external content types based on that data. Using the new External list, BCS also allows you to work with external back-end business data offline.

Office Integration with SharePoint Foundation

Office 2010 and SharePoint 2010 are designed to create an integrated productivity environment across the client and the server. They work together to provide you with a set of seamlessly integrated capabilities. In other words, many Office commands, menus, and features are integrated closely with SharePoint Foundation features. You can use SharePoint Foundation functionality not only from a browser, but also from within your Office applications. The new Backstage view feature of Office provides the ability to expose SharePoint 2010 capabilities in the context of Office applications, including access to document libraries and SharePoint sites. For example, you can create a new SharePoint site and save your files to it without leaving your Office client application. A SharePoint site's collaborative content—including documents, lists, events, calendars, task assignments, blogs, wikis, and membership rosters—can be read and edited within Office applications.

To share a particular document or task, SharePoint Foundation provides a specific site environment called a *Document Workspace*. You can create a Workspace site from an Office 2010 application or from a browser. When using Microsoft Word 2010, Microsoft Excel 2010, Microsoft PowerPoint 2010, Microsoft InfoPath 2010, and Microsoft OneNote 2010, users can create Workspaces, post and edit documents, and assign tasks from within Office 2010 applications while working on documents stored in SharePoint sites.

See Also For more information about working with Document Workspaces, refer to Chapter 12.

Office 2010 includes a new SharePoint Workspace 2010 client application, a successor to the Office Groove client. SharePoint Workspace 2010 provides an ability to work offline with SharePoint content and to synchronize the changes when you are reconnected to your network. You can view, add, edit, and delete SharePoint library documents or list items while you are offline. While you are connected to the network, updates to data on your computer and on the network are automatic, providing bidirectional synchronization between your computer and the live SharePoint sites, libraries, and lists.

In addition, SharePoint Foundation 2010 provides integration with Office Web Apps. *Office Web Apps* is a collective name for the online companions to Word, Excel, PowerPoint, and OneNote applications that enable users to view and edit documents using the browser. Office Web Apps services include the Word Viewing Service, PowerPoint Service, and Excel Calculation Services, which run within the context of the services provided by SharePoint Foundation.

Tip Office Web Apps are available to business customers with Office 2010 volume licensing.

Office Web Apps give you a browser-based viewing and editing experience by providing a representation of an Office document in the browser. For example, when you click a document stored in a SharePoint document library, the document opens directly in the browser. The document appearance in the browser is similar to how it appears in the Office client application. While an Office Web App provides lighter editing functionality than the associated Office client application, it provides the user an opportunity to open a document for editing in the associated client application (if an application is installed on the client device) by using a button within the Office Web App page. On a SharePoint site where Office Web Apps have been installed and configured, you can view and edit Office documents in the browser from anywhere you have a connection to your SharePoint site.

See Also For more information on Office Web Apps, refer to *http://office.microsoft.com/ en-gb/web-apps*.

There are different levels of integration between various versions of Office and SharePoint Foundation. The Office 2010 family of products provides a tight, native, rich, built-in integration with SharePoint Foundation. Office 2007 is also well integrated with SharePoint Foundation, providing contextual interoperability between SharePoint and Office client applications. Earlier versions of Office, such as Office 2000 and Office XP, provide some integration, but it is considerably simpler and more basic.

Office 2000 provides a file save integration with SharePoint Foundation. For example, you can open and save files stored on SharePoint sites from your Office 2000 applications and receive alerts in Microsoft Outlook 2000. Office XP provides additional data integration, including interactive access to data stored on SharePoint sites. For example, you can export list data from SharePoint sites to Excel 2002 and view properties and metadata for files that are stored on SharePoint sites. However, Office 2000 and Office XP are not integrated with many other features of SharePoint Foundation. For example, you cannot use Office 2000 or Office XP applications to create Workspace sites.

Tip You can perform these tasks on the SharePoint site by using the browser.

Office 2003 adds more integration features. With Office 2003, you can use SharePoint Foundation to create documents and Workspaces, organize team meetings and activities, and access and analyze data from SharePoint sites. You can also use data integration between Office 2003 and SharePoint Foundation, moving data to and from SharePoint sites and creating databases linked to data stored on SharePoint sites.

Starting with Office System 2007, integration with SharePoint Foundation is enhanced much further. You can interact directly with information stored in SharePoint sites from within Office client applications without manually downloading the content. For example, using Word 2010 and Word 2007, you can create and post to a blog on your SharePoint blog site. Word 2010 and Word 2007 allow you to check documents into and out of a SharePoint library from within Word.

While all Office 2007 and Office 2010 client applications are well integrated with SharePoint Foundation, Outlook provides the closest, most feature-rich integration. With Outlook 2010 and Outlook 2007, you can create and manage sites for sharing documents and organizing meetings. Outlook 2010 and Outlook 2007 provide read and write access to SharePoint items such as calendars, tasks, contacts, discussions, and documents, as well as offline support.

See Also For more information about integration between SharePoint Foundation and Outlook 2010, refer to Chapter 13, "Using SharePoint Foundation with Outlook 2010."

SharePoint Products

SharePoint Foundation 2010, SharePoint Server 2010, and SharePoint Designer 2010—known collectively as SharePoint 2010 Products—facilitate collaboration both within an organization and with partners and customers. However, each of these products has a different set of capabilities.

SharePoint Foundation and SharePoint Server 2010

SharePoint Foundation is a collection of services for Windows Server 2008 that you can use to share information and collaborate with other users. It provides a common framework for document management, a common repository for storing documents of all types, and a platform for collaboration applications.

SharePoint Server 2010 is built on top of SharePoint Foundation. It extends SharePoint Foundation by providing flexible organization and management tools for SharePoint sites and by making it possible for teams to publish information to the entire organization. Because SharePoint Server 2010 requires SharePoint Foundation, all features of SharePoint Foundation are available in SharePoint Server 2010. However, SharePoint Server 2010 provides significant additional enterprise-level capabilities:

- **Sites** capability provides a single infrastructure for all your business websites, both internal and external.

- **Communities** capability delivers powerful collaboration tools—and a single platform to manage them.

- **Content** capability makes content management easy, including compliance features like document types, retention polices, and automatic content sorting.

- **Search** capability provides a unique combination of relevance, refinement, and social cues to help you to find the information that you require and to cut through the clutter.

- **Insights** capability gives you access to the information in databases, reports, and business applications. It also helps you locate the information you need to make decisions.

- **Composites** capability offers tools and components for creating do-it-yourself business solutions without coding, so that you can rapidly respond to business needs.

There are two editions of SharePoint Server 2010: Standard and Enterprise, each of which has a different feature set. To decide whether you need SharePoint Foundation by itself or an edition of SharePoint Server 2010, you need to assess how your requirements are met by the particular features and functionality of these products.

Important A comparison between the feature sets of the different editions of SharePoint Server 2010 and SharePoint Foundation is provided in the SharePoint2010EditionComparison .xls spreadsheet in the Chapter01 folder under Practice Files that can be downloaded from the book's catalog page at *http://go.microsoft.com/fwlink/?Linkid=206096*.

SharePoint Foundation and SharePoint Designer 2010

While SharePoint Server 2010 and SharePoint Foundation 2010 provide the technology and platform, SharePoint Designer 2010 provides the tools with which to tailor SharePoint sites. SharePoint Designer 2010 is an evolution of SharePoint Designer 2007. It is available as a free download and provides tools for the rich customization of sites, as well as the creation of reporting tools and application templates, without writing any code.

See Also For more information on SharePoint Designer 2010, refer to *http://sharepoint. microsoft.com/en-us/product/Related-Technologies/Pages/SharePoint-Designer.aspx*.

Key Points

- SharePoint Foundation provides a powerful set of tools for information sharing and document collaboration.

- SharePoint websites provide places to capture and share ideas, information, knowledge, and documents.

- You can access content stored within a SharePoint site both from a web browser and through client applications, such as Office.

- Access to a SharePoint site is controlled through a role-based system predicated on permission levels. The five default permission levels are Read, Contribute, Design, Full Control, and Limited.

- There are varying levels of integration between different versions of Office and SharePoint Foundation, with Office 2010 having the closest integration.

- SharePoint Server 2010 is built upon SharePoint Foundation. In addition to SharePoint Foundation functionality, SharePoint Server 2010 provides other significant enterprise-level capabilities, including Sites, Communities, Content, Search, Insights, and Composites.

Chapter at a Glance

Navigate the site content tree, page 22

Navigate the Ribbon interface, page 25

Customize the Quick Launch, page 36

Understand Web Parts, page 40

2 Navigating a SharePoint Site

In this chapter, you will learn how to

✔ Navigate the home page and the SharePoint site.

✔ Navigate the site content tree.

✔ Navigate the Ribbon interface.

✔ Browse lists on a SharePoint site.

✔ Browse document libraries.

✔ Customize the top navigation area.

✔ Customize the Quick Launch.

✔ Understand Web Parts.

✔ Use the Recycle Bin.

A typical Microsoft SharePoint Foundation website provides you with an infrastructure where your team can communicate, share documents and data, and work together. Different types of SharePoint sites have different infrastructures, such as a Team site, a blank site, a Document Workspace, a group work site, a Meeting Workspace, and a blog site. The Team site infrastructure includes the following components:

● **Libraries** Document, picture, form, and wiki libraries are collections of files that you share and work on with your team members. A typical Team site includes a built-in document library called Shared Documents. You can create your own document, picture, and form libraries when needed.

● **Lists** With SharePoint lists, you and your team members can work with structured, tabular data on the website. A typical Team site includes four built-in lists: Announcements, Calendar, Links, and Tasks. Other lists are provided by SharePoint Foundation that you can add to your site if required. You can also create custom lists.

- **Discussion boards** Discussion boards provide a forum where you and your team members can post comments and reply to each other's comments. By default, a typical Team site comes with a built-in discussion board named Team Discussion. You can create your own discussion boards when needed.

- **Surveys** Surveys provide a way of polling team members. SharePoint sites don't have a built-in survey, but you can create your own.

- **Recycle Bin** The Recycle Bin allows you to restore items that have been deleted from the site.

In this chapter, you will learn how to navigate the SharePoint site infrastructure. You will start with the home page of a typical SharePoint Team site, and then learn how to browse the site hierarchical structure. You will also learn how to use the Ribbon and customize site navigation, as well as understand the concepts of Web Parts.

> **Practice Files** Before you can complete the exercises in this chapter, you need to (1) download the Chapter 2 practice files from the book's catalog page to the following folder on your computer: Documents\Microsoft Press\SBS_SPF\Chapter02 and (2) install the Chapter 2 practice site using the Chapter02_Starter.wsp file. See "Using the Practice Files" at the beginning of this book for more information.

Important Remember to use your SharePoint site location in place of *http://wideworldimporters* in the exercises.

Navigating the Home Page and the SharePoint Site

A *home page* is the main page of a SharePoint website; it provides a navigational structure that links the site components together. Typically, a home page of a SharePoint site has two main navigation areas: the top navigation area, which is a strip at the top of the page, and the left navigation area, which is a panel at the left of the page.

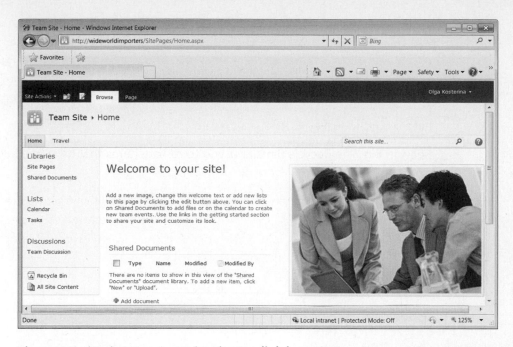

The top navigation area contains the *top link bar,* which consists of the tabs displayed on all pages within the SharePoint site. The top link bar typically includes tabs with the following links:

- **Home** The Home link is usually displayed on the first tab on the left. It opens the home page for a site.

- **Links to the subsites** On a well-organized site, the top link bar contains tabs with links to the subsites of the current site, such as the Travel link on the second tab in our example.

Important If a subsite is configured to inherit a top link bar from the parent site, then the Home tab link on the subsite points to the home page of the parent site.

On the right side of the top link bar, there is a Search box, which allows you to search the current site, and the Help link.

Just above the top link bar, you can see a *content navigation breadcrumb* trail showing the path to the current page within the site. The content navigation breadcrumb helps you keep track of where the current page is located within its site. Components on the breadcrumb trail are links that you can click to open the corresponding pages. The last item on the breadcrumb shows the page title of the current page; it is not a link.

On the top-left area of the screen, you can see the Site Actions link. Clicking this link opens the Site Actions menu, which enables you to edit the current page, synchronize the site to SharePoint Workspace, create a new site or a site component, configure site permissions, and change the settings for your site. The options displayed in the Site Actions menu depend on the permissions that you have on the site: only options applicable to you are displayed.

The View All Site Content link on the Site Actions menu opens the All Site Content page, which lists all the libraries, lists, discussion boards, and surveys on your site. The All Site Content page also provides links to the child sites and Workspaces, as well as the site's

Recycle Bin. This page is your main navigational aid for the site and contains links to all major parts of the site's infrastructure.

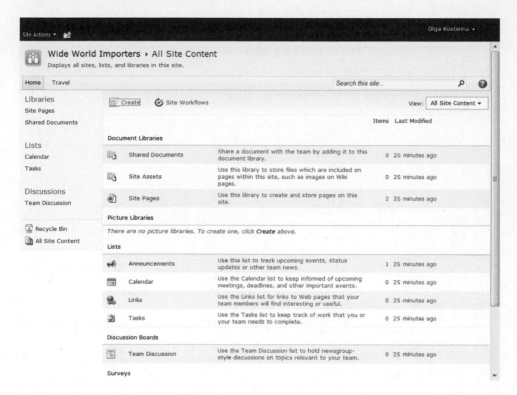

The Site Settings link on the Site Action menu opens the Site Settings page, which enables you to administer and customize your site.

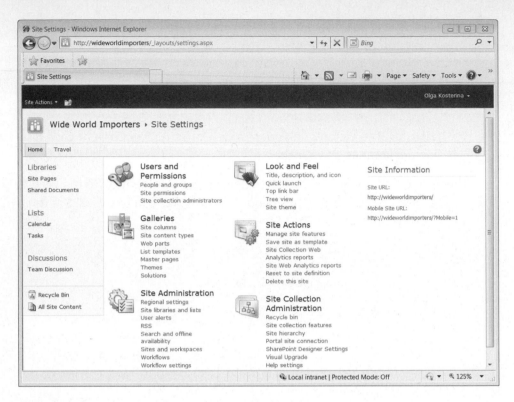

The left navigation panel typically contains a set of *Quick Launch* links, the All Site Content link, and a Recycle Bin.

Depending on the site, the Quick Launch contains one or more links to the subsets of information contained in the All Site Content page. These subsets, referred to as *views*, are created by filtering the information contained within the All Site Content page (for example, to present only lists or only libraries within the current site). The Quick Launch can also contain links to site components created by you and your team members, such as specific document libraries or lists.

Typically, the Quick Launch contains the following links:

● **Libraries** The Libraries link opens a view of an All Site Content page displaying all document, form, and wiki libraries on your site. On a typical Team site, the Quick Launch also provides a second-level link to a Shared Documents library, as well as a Site Pages library.

● **Lists** The Lists link opens a view of an All Site Content page displaying all lists on your site. On a typical Team site, the Quick Launch also provides two second-level links to Calendar and Tasks lists.

- **Discussions** The Discussions link opens a view of an All Site Content page displaying all discussion boards on your site. On a typical Team site, the Quick Launch also provides a second-level link to a Team Discussion board.

- **Sites** The Sites link opens a view of an All Site Content page displaying subsites to your site.

- **Pictures** The Pictures link opens a view of an All Site Content page displaying the picture libraries on your site.

The All Site Content link in the left navigation panel is identical to the View All Site Content link on the Site Actions menu. This link takes you to the All Site Content page, which lists all the libraries, lists, discussion boards, and surveys on your site, as well as the subsites if there are any.

Finally, the left navigation panel contains the link to the Recycle Bin, which opens the site's Recycle Bin.

In addition to the top and left navigation areas, the home page of a typical SharePoint Team site includes the Welcome message, the Getting Started links, and a view of the Shared Documents library that is presented within its own page component, called a *Web Part,* which allows you to work with the documents in this library without leaving the home page.

In this exercise, you will navigate to the All Site Content page, explore its components and views, and then return to the site home page.

 SET UP Open your SharePoint site (for example, *http://wideworldimporters*). If prompted, type your user name and password, and then click OK.

1. In the left navigation panel, click **All Site Content**.

2. Explore the page.

   Notice that the top link bar and the Quick Launch have not changed. However, the breadcrumb trail has changed, showing the path to the current page.

3. Scroll down to the bottom of the page and notice all parts of the site that are listed on the **All Site Content** page, including Document Libraries, Lists, Picture Libraries, Discussion Boards, Surveys, Sites and Workspaces, and Recycle Bin.

   You will now display this page in the Document Libraries view.

4. Scroll up to the top of the page. Open the **View** menu located on the right side of the page, and choose **Document Libraries**.

The Document Libraries view of the All Site Content page is displayed. The main part of the page lists the document libraries available on the site, including the Shared Documents library, which is present on the site by default.

You will now display the All Site Content page in the Surveys view.

5. From the **View** menu, choose **Surveys**.

The Surveys view is displayed. The main part of the page lists the surveys created on the site. The Wide World Importers site has not added a survey yet, so this page doesn't display any surveys.

6. Return to the site's home page by clicking its link on the content navigation bread-crumb located to the left of the **All Site Content** title.

✖ CLEAN UP Leave the browser open if you are continuing to the next exercise.

Navigating the Site Content Tree

A typical SharePoint site contains the following components: lists, libraries, discussion boards, surveys, and web pages. These items are created and maintained by SharePoint Foundation and are linked together within the site infrastructure. In a graphical form, this site infrastructure can be represented as a tree-like diagram.

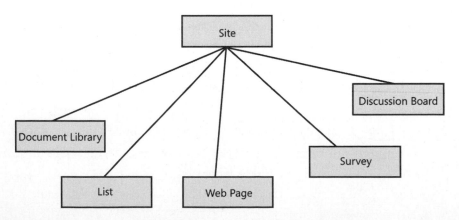

SharePoint Foundation maintains the path in this structure from the site's home page to the currently displayed page. This path is shown on each page as a content navigation breadcrumb, which was introduced in the previous exercise.

In addition to its own components, such as lists and libraries, a SharePoint site can have many subsites. The hierarchy of these subsites, on web servers, resembles the hierarchy of folders on file systems. Sites that do not have a parent site are referred to as top-level sites. Top-level sites can have multiple subsites, and these subsites can have multiple subsites, proceeding downward as many levels as you need. The entire hierarchical structure of a top-level site and all its subsites is called a *site collection*.

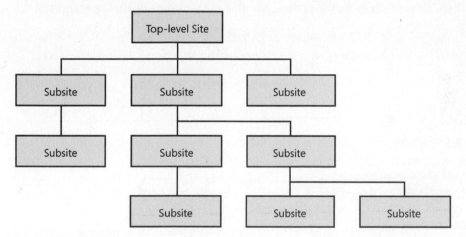

Because the subsites are contained within their parent site, the overall hierarchical structure of a SharePoint site has its own items—such as lists, libraries, discussion boards, and surveys—as well as the child sites. This overall structure can be represented as a *site content tree*.

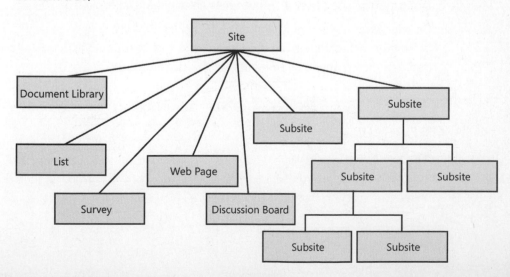

To identify the current page position within the site collection, SharePoint Foundation maintains a global navigation path that shows the trail from the top-level site to the current page. This path is accessible on all pages via the Navigate Up icon located at the top-left area of a page, immediately to the right of the Site Actions menu.

Clicking the Navigate Up icon displays a clickable path from the top-level site to the page that you are currently viewing, so that you always know where you are within the overall hierarchy starting from the top-level site that is represented by the top node on the path. The nodes on the path are links. You can click any node, allowing you to navigate up from the current page within the current site and within the site collection. The last node on the bottom of the path identifies the current page and is not a link.

In this exercise, you will view a list of subsites to your SharePoint site, navigate the site hierarchy, and explore the content navigation breadcrumb and the Navigate Up global path.

 SET UP Open the SharePoint site in which you'd like to view the subsites, if it is not already open. If prompted, type your user name and password, and then click OK.

BE SURE TO verify that you have sufficient permissions to view the subsites. If in doubt, see the Appendix at the back of this book.

1. On the Quick Launch, click **Sites**. The **All Site Content** page in the **Sites and Workplaces** view is displayed.

2. On the **All Site Content** page, under **Sites and Workspaces**, click a subsite where you'd like to go. For example, on the Wide World Importers site, we will go to the Travel subsite.

3. On the subsite's home page, on the Quick Launch, under **Libraries**, click **Shared Documents**. The **Shared Documents** library page is displayed.

   On the Shared Documents library page, notice that the content navigation breadcrumb, located above the top link bar, has changed and is now showing the path from the subsite's home page to the current page.

    Travel ▸ Shared Documents ▸ All Documents ≚
   Share a document with the team by adding it to this document library.

4. On the top left of the page, above the breadcrumb, click the **Navigate Up** icon. The navigation path opens, showing the location of the current page in the site's collection, starting from the top-level site.

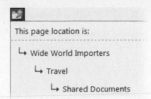

5. Hover your mouse over the top node on the path. The text becomes underlined, showing you that this node is a clickable link. Now, hover your mouse over the bottom node that shows the title of the current page, such as Shared Documents. The mouse pointer changes to the text cursor and the text is not underlined, showing you that this node is not a link.

6. Click the node that points to the parent site. You are taken back to the home page of the site where you started this exercise.

✖ CLEAN UP Leave the browser open if you are continuing to the next exercise.

See Also For more information on working with sites, refer to Chapter 3, "Creating and Managing Sites."

Navigating the Ribbon Interface

In SharePoint Foundation, the Ribbon provides a consistent interface for accessing the commands and tools that you require for the tasks that you want to accomplish. Like the Ribbon in other Microsoft Office programs, such as Microsoft Word and Microsoft Excel, the Ribbon in SharePoint displays many of the most commonly used commands and tools. On a SharePoint site, the Ribbon appears across the top of a web page and is designed to help you quickly locate the commands for performing actions on pages, documents, and lists.

See Also The Ribbon interface is new to this version of SharePoint. In previous versions, commands and tools were located across different menus and toolbars. To find the Ribbon locations of the menu and toolbar commands that you may be used to in previous SharePoint versions, refer to the SharePoint_Command_Mapping_Guide.xslx, located in the Documents\ Microsoft Press\SBS_SPF\Chapter02 folder.

Commands on the Ribbon are organized in logical groups, displayed together under tabs. Each tab relates to a type of SharePoint site component you are working with, such as a document library or a web page. Tabs, groups, and commands on the Ribbon are contextual: the Ribbon commands available to you change depending on the context of what you are doing and where you are on the SharePoint site.

The tabs are displayed at the top of a web page on your site. To use the Ribbon commands, you need to select the tab that corresponds to the kind of task you want to perform. The currently selected tab is highlighted. Each tab provides a specific set of commands depending on the actions that you would like to do.

The Browse tab, as the name suggests, allows you to browse the current page. It is selected when you open a page, providing you with the ability to view the page in the browser. The top link bar and the content breadcrumb are displayed on the Browse tab. This tab does not have Ribbon-based tools associated with it.

Depending on the page that you are viewing, other tabs become available. For example, the home page of the Team site provides a Page tab that allows you to modify this page and its settings.

Commands on the Ribbon are represented as buttons, drop-down lists, and other controls. To make it easier for you to locate the necessary commands, they are grouped together into several sections on the Ribbon by common functionality. The names of the groups are shown at the bottom of the Ribbon. For example, on the Page tab, the Edit group contains commands that provide you with the ability to edit the page, while the Manage group contains commands that allow you to manage the page.

In addition to the Browse tab, a list page provides two tabs that are grouped together in the List Tools tab set. The first tab, Items, provides a set of commands for working with the individual list items. The second tab, List, provides the commands for working with the list as a whole. Similarly, a library page provides two tabs—Documents and Library—that are grouped together in the Library Tools tab set.

The number and types of commands that are available to you under each tab depend not only on the context of where you are and what you are doing, but also on your permission level and the configuration of your site. Some commands on the Ribbon may be unavailable because you do not sufficient permissions to use them or because they have not been enabled for your site. In other cases, to enable a command, you may need to select an object. In a document library, for example, you must first select a document in the library to enable the Ribbon commands for working with the document.

When the Ribbon is displayed, the breadcrumb and the top navigation bar are not visible. On all pages with the Ribbon, you can use the following navigation aids for moving to other pages within the site and the site collection:

● A Navigate Up icon, which provides you with the clickable path from the current page to the top-level site in the site

● A Browse tab, which displays the content breadcrumb and the top link bar

● A View All Site Content link on the Site Actions menu, which takes you to the All Site Content page

In addition, on the pages with the Ribbon where the left navigation panel is available, you can use the Quick Launch and the All Site Content link.

In the following exercise, you will explore the Ribbon on the home page of a SharePoint Team site.

SET UP Open a site where you would like to explore the Ribbon, such as *http:// wideworldimporters,* if it is not already open. If prompted, type your user name and password, and click OK.

BE SURE TO verify that you have sufficient rights to edit the home page of this site. If in doubt, see the Appendix at the back of this book.

1. On the top of the screen, locate the **Browse** tab. Notice that this tab is currently selected and that the content breadcrumb and the top link bar are displayed in the top navigation area.

2. To the right of the **Browse** tab, click the **Page** tab.

   The Ribbon appears. It displays the commands that allow you to work with a web page. The Ribbon is contextual, and the commands that are not available to you at this point in time are dimmed.

   Explore the Ribbon and notice that the commands are grouped into sections on the Ribbon. The name of each group can be found at the bottom of the Ribbon.

Edit

3. In the **Edit** group, click the **Edit** button. The **Editing Tools** tab set appears to the right of the **Page** tab. It contains two tabs: the **Format Text** tab, which is selected, and the **Insert** tab. The **Format Text** tab displays the buttons and the drop-down lists that allow you to change and format the text on the page, as well as its markup.

Notice the Ribbon groups on this tab. For example, the Font group allows you to modify the text formatting on the current page and looks very similar to other Office applications, such as Word or Excel.

4. In the **Editing Tools**, click the **Insert** tab. The set of commands on the Ribbon changes to show the buttons for inserting different objects into the current page. The type of objects to be inserted is identified by the name of a Ribbon group, such as Tables or Links.

5. Click the **Page** tab to open it. Notice that the **Edit** button in the **Edit** group has been replaced with the **Save & Close** button. Because the Ribbon is contextual, it provides you with a command that is appropriate to you at this point in time based on your previous actions.

6. Click **Save & Close**. The **Page** tab closes, and the current page returns to the **Browse** tab, which displays the content breadcrumb and the top link bar in place of the Ribbon.

✖ **CLEAN UP** Leave the browser open if you are continuing to the next exercise.

Browsing Lists on a SharePoint Site

SharePoint lists are web-based, editable tables. SharePoint lists provide you and your team with the ability to work with structured data. As we have discussed, the typical Team site provides four default lists:

● **Announcements** The Announcements list is a place to post information for the team.

- **Calendar** The Calendar list is a place to maintain information about upcoming events.

- **Links** The Links list displays hyperlinks to web pages of interest to team members.

- **Tasks** The Tasks list provides a to-do list for team members.

Tip Links to the Calendar and Tasks lists appear by default on the Quick Launch of the Team site.

In addition to these default lists, you can create your own lists when necessary. When creating a new list, you can choose to place a link to this list on the Quick Launch.

See Also For more information on working with lists, refer to Chapter 4, "Working with Lists." For more information on configuring lists, refer to Chapter 7, "Working with List Settings."

In this exercise, you will view a list of all SharePoint lists that exist on your site. You will navigate to a list, explore its Ribbon, and then return to the home page.

 SET UP Open the SharePoint site in which you'd like to view the existing lists, if it is not already open. If prompted, type your user name and password, and then click OK.

1. On the Quick Launch, click **Lists**.

   The All Site Content page is displayed in the Lists view. This view shows links to all existing lists in your site.

2. Click a list, such as **Announcements**.

   The Announcements page appears. On the top of the screen, notice the Browse tab, which displays the content navigation breadcrumb and the top link bar. To the right of the Browse tab, notice the contextual List Tools tab set, which contains two tabs: Items and List.

3. On the **Announcements** page, view the list items. The team members of Wide World Importers have not put any additional announcements on this list yet, so only the default announcement is displayed.

4. Hover your mouse over the list item and click the check box that appears on the left of the item's title to select it.

When you select an item on the list, SharePoint opens the Items tab, which displays the Ribbon with the commands for working with list items.

Explore the Ribbon and notice the Ribbon groups, such as New, Manage, Actions, Share & Track, and Workflows.

5. In the **List Tools** tab set, click the **List** tab. The List tab opens and displays the commands on the Ribbon that allow you to configure the list.

Explore the Ribbon and notice the Ribbon groups, such as View Format, Datasheet, Manage Views, Share & Track, Connect & Export, and Settings.

6. To return to the site's home page, click the **Browse** tab on the top of the screen and then click the **Home** tab on the top link bar.

✖ **CLEAN UP** Leave the browser open if you are continuing to the next exercise.

Browsing Document Libraries

A SharePoint library is, in essence, a list of files. However, SharePoint libraries not only store files, but they provide a flexible collaboration environment for you and your team to work on these files.

A SharePoint library page lists each file in the library, as well as its properties, and provides a link to each file. By default, the Team site comes with a built-in document library named Shared Documents that is listed on the Quick Launch.

In addition to the Shared Documents library, you can create your own document, picture, form, and wiki libraries when necessary. When creating a new library, you can choose to place a link to this library on the Quick Launch.

See Also For more information on working with documents in document libraries, refer to Chapter 5, "Working with Libraries." For more information on configuring document libraries, refer to Chapter 8, "Working with Library Settings."

In this exercise, you will view a list of all SharePoint libraries that exist on your site. You will then navigate to a Shared Documents library, explore its Ribbon, and then return to the home page.

 SET UP Open the SharePoint site in which you'd like to view the list of existing libraries, if it is not already open. If prompted, type your user name and password, and then click OK.

1. On the Quick Launch, click **Libraries**.

   The All Site Content page opens in the Document Libraries view. This view shows links to all existing libraries.

2. Click a link, such as **Shared Documents**. The Shared Documents library page appears.

   On the top of the screen, notice the Browse tab, the content navigation breadcrumb, and the top link bar. To the right of the Browse tab, notice the contextual Library Tools tab set, which contains two tabs: Documents and Library.

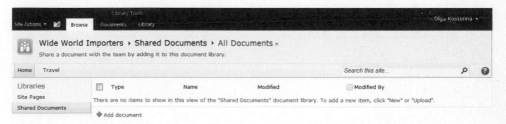

3. On the **Shared Documents** page, view the list of files in this library.

   In this example, the team members of Wide World Importers have not put any documents in this library yet.

4. Click the **Documents** tab, which displays the Ribbon with the commands for working with documents stored in the library.

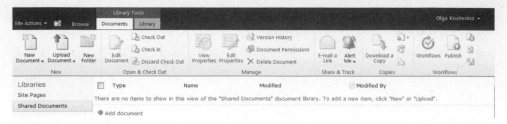

Explore the Ribbon and notice the Ribbon groups, such as New, Open & Check Out, Manage, Share & Track, Copies, and Workflows.

5. In the **Library Tools** tab set, click the **Library** tab, which opens and displays the commands on the Ribbon that allow you to configure the library.

Explore the Ribbon and notice the Ribbon groups, such as View Format, Datasheet, Manage Views, Share & Track, Connect & Export, Customize Library, and Settings.

6. To return to the site's home page, click the **Navigate Up** icon on the top of the screen, and then, in the navigation path that appears, click the node with your site's name, such as Wide World Importers.

 CLEAN UP Leave the browser open if you are continuing to the next exercise.

Customizing the Top Navigation Area

On a SharePoint Foundation site, you can customize both the top and left navigation areas. In the top navigation area, in addition to the links maintained by SharePoint Foundation, you can configure the top link bar to contain links of your own choosing and select the order of their appearance on the bar. In the following exercise, you will create and position a new tab on the top link bar and then delete it.

SET UP Open the top-level site (such as *http://wideworldimporters*) from the address bar of your browser, if it is not already open. If prompted, type your user name and password, and click OK.

BE SURE TO verify that you have sufficient rights to manage the site. If in doubt, see the Appendix at the back of this book.

1. On the **Site Actions** menu, click **Site Settings**. The Site Settings page is displayed.

2. In the **Look and Feel** section, click **Top link bar**.

   The Top Link Bar page is displayed. It shows the links that appear in the top link bar of the site. In our example, two links are already showing: Home and Travel. These links represent the top-level site and the Travel subsite.

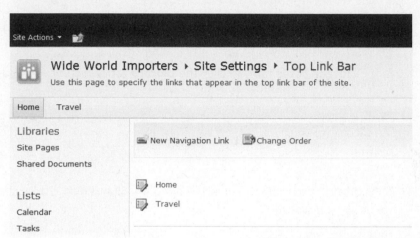

3. Click **New Navigation Link** on the top of the page to display the **New Navigation Link** page.

4. On the **New Navigation Link** page, in the **URL** area, in the **Type the Web address** box, type **http://www.microsoft.com/sharepoint**. Then, in the **Type the description** box, type **SharePoint Home**.

5. Click **OK**. The new link is added to the top link bar and is listed on the **Top Link Bar** page.

6. To test the link, click the new tab to open the SharePoint Products home page at the Microsoft website.

Important You need Internet access to view a page at the external website, such as the Microsoft site.

7. On the top of the browser window, to the left of the address bar, click the down arrow button to display the list of recent sites. Click **Top Link Bar** to go back to the page.

You will now reorder the tabs on the top link bar.

8. On the **Top Link Bar** page, click **Change Order**. The **Reorder Links** page appears.

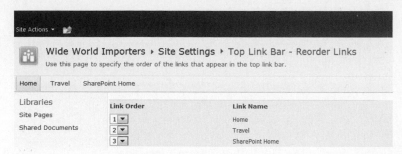

9. From the **Link Order** drop-down list to the left of the **SharePoint Home** link, choose **1**.

The list of the links is reordered automatically. The Link Order for the Home link has changed to 2, and the Link Order for the Travel link has changed to 3.

10. Click **OK**. The tabs on the top link bar have been reordered, and you are taken back to the **Top Link Bar** page.

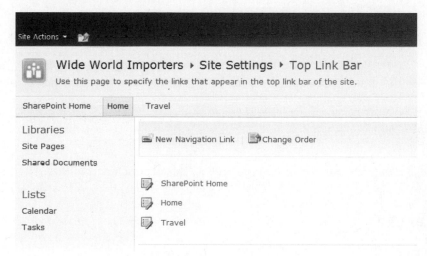

You will now delete the link from the top link bar.

11. On the **Top Link Bar** page, click the **Edit** icon to the left of the link you'd like to delete, such as **SharePoint Home**.

12. On the **Edit Link** page, click **Delete**.

13. Click **OK** in the confirmation message box when it appears.

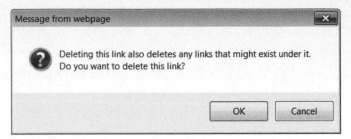

You are back at the Top Link Bar page. Notice that the link has been deleted.

14. On the breadcrumb, click the first link on the left, such as **Wide World Importers,** to return to the home page of your site.

 CLEAN UP Leave the browser open if you are continuing to the next exercise.

Customizing the Left Navigation Panel

There are many options available for customization of the left navigation panel. Similar to the top link bar, you can change the Quick Launch. You can add new links, edit and reorder existing links, and delete those links that you no longer require. You can even hide the entire Quick Launch if you don't need it anymore. In addition, you can display a graphical representation of the site components as a tree view.

Important You cannot remove the All Site Content and Recycle Bin links from the left navigation panel.

In this exercise, you will add a link to the Quick Launch and also reorder the Quick Launch links.

SET UP Open the top-level site (such as *http://wideworldimporters*) from the address bar of your browser, if it is not already open. If prompted, type your user name and password, and click OK.

BE SURE TO verify that you have sufficient rights to manage the site. If in doubt, see the Appendix at the back of this book.

1. On the **Site Actions** menu, click **Site Settings**.

2. On the **Site Settings** page, in the **Look and Feel** section, click **Quick launch**. The Quick Launch page appears.

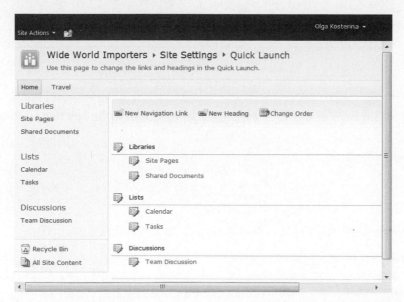

3. On the **Quick Launch** page, click **New Heading**. The **New Heading** page appears.

4. In the **URL** section, in the **Type the Web address** box, type **http://office .microsoft.com/en-us/sharepoint-foundation-help**. In the **Type the description** box, type **Help**, and then click **OK**. You have created a link called Help on the Quick Launch that points to the online help for SharePoint Foundation.

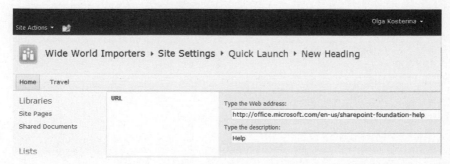

Tip If you'd like to create a heading on the Quick Launch that is not a link but a section heading for a collection of links, type # in the Web Address box. You can then add links to the new section using the New Navigation Link command on the Quick Launch page.

Back on the Quick Launch page, notice the Help link has appeared at the bottom of the page. You will now move the Help link to the first position on the Quick Launch.

5. Click **Change Order** on the toolbar. The Reorder Links page appears.

6. From the drop-down list to the left of the **Help** link, choose the number **1**.

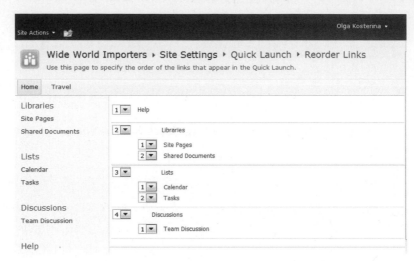

All the other links are reordered.

Tip Links within the sections can be reordered independently of the section headings.

7. Click **OK** to save the new order. The Quick Launch page appears, with the Help link displayed at the top.

8. Return to the site's home page by clicking the **Home** tab on the top link bar.

On the home page, the new Help link is displayed in the left navigation panel on top of the Quick Launch.

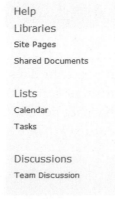

Clicking the new Help link takes you to the SharePoint Foundation online help page.

 CLEAN UP Leave the browser open if you are continuing to the next exercise.

While the Quick Launch represents the frequently needed links, it is sometimes useful to see the full structure of the site visually, in a graphical representation. In this exercise, you will modify the left navigation panel to display the tree view of the site's structure.

SET UP Open the SharePoint site in which you'd like to modify the left navigation panel, if it is not already open. If prompted, type your user name and password, and then click OK.

BE SURE TO verify that you have permissions to manage the site. If in doubt, see the Appendix at the back of this book.

1. On the **Site Actions** menu, click **Site Settings**. The Site Settings page is displayed.

2. In the **Look and Feel** area, click **Tree View**.

3. On the **Tree view** page, select the **Enable Tree View** check box. Click **OK**.

You are taken back to the Site Settings page.

4. Return to the site's home page by clicking the **Home** tab on the top link bar.

The left navigation panel on the home page has changed. Below the Quick Launch, it now displays the Site Content panel, which shows the parts of the site, as well as subsites, in a tree view. In the Site Content panel, notice the difference in the icons that represent different parts of the site's infrastructure, such as the Travel subsite, the Shared Documents document library, the Announcements list, the Calendar list, the Links list, the Tasks list, and the default discussion board.

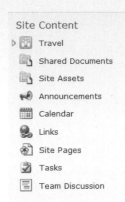

5. Using steps 1-4 of this exercise as a guide, on the **Tree view** page, disable the Quick Launch. Verify that the left navigation panel displays the Site Content but does not display the Quick Launch.

   You will now bring the left navigation panel back to its original configuration, in which it displays the Quick Launch but does not display the Site Content.

6. Using steps 1-4 of this exercise as a guide, on the **Tree view** page, disable the Tree View and enable the Quick Launch. Return to the home page to verify that the left navigation panel displays the Quick Launch.

✖ CLEAN UP Leave the browser open if you are continuing to the next exercise.

Understanding Web Parts

In addition to text, images, and lists, a web page on a SharePoint site can contain one or more Web Parts. A *Web Part* is an independent component that can be reused, shared, and personalized by all users who have permission to access it. Web Parts are the basic building blocks of a page; each Web Part occupies its own rectangular area within the page.

For example, the home page of a newly created Team site contains a Web Part that displays the content of the Shared Documents library.

Web pages can contain several Web Parts that can be connected if necessary. SharePoint Foundation provides built-in Web Parts for all lists and libraries on the current site that you can insert in a web page. By using Web Parts, you can organize disparate information and consolidate data (such as lists and charts) and web content (such as text, links, and images) into a single web page.

See Also For more information on web pages and Web Parts, refer to Chapter 6, "Working with Web Pages."

In this exercise, you will add a Web Part for the Announcements list to the home page of the Team site.

SET UP Open the SharePoint site home page, such as *http://wideworldimporters*, if it is not already open. If prompted, type your user name and password, and then click OK.

BE SURE TO verify that you have sufficient rights to edit the home page of this site. If in doubt, see the Appendix at the back of this book.

1. On the top of the screen, click the **Page** tab.

Edit

2. In the **Edit** group on the Ribbon, click the **Edit** button.

   The page is redisplayed in Edit mode, with the content areas of the page that you can modify outlined.

3. Position your cursor where you would like the Web Part to be inserted. For example, click below the **Welcome** message and above the **Shared Documents** title.

4. In the **Editing Tools** tab set, click the **Insert** tab.

Existing
List

5. In the **Web Parts** group, click the **Existing List** button.

   The Web Parts pane appears below the Ribbon.

6. In the **Web Parts** pane, make sure the **Announcements** list is selected, and then click **Add**.

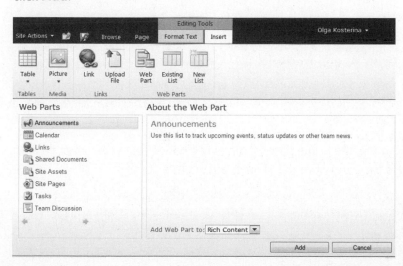

7. The **Announcements** Web Part has been added to the web page at the location of the cursor. It displays the items in the Announcements list.

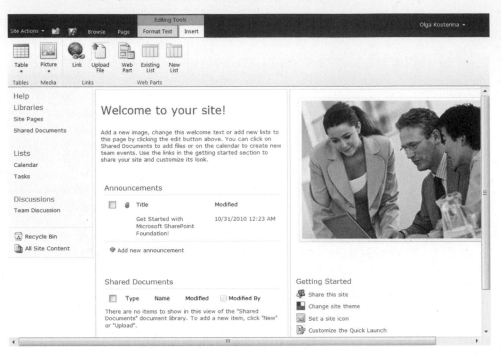

8. On the top of the page, click the **Page** tab, and then, in the **Edit** group on the Ribbon, click the **Save & Close** button.

Save & Close

The changes to the home page have been saved, the Page tab with the Ribbon has been closed, and the home page is redisplayed on the Browse tab.

9. In the **Announcements** Web Part, hover the mouse over any list item and click the check box that appears on the left of the item's title to select it. The Items tab in the List Tools tab set appears and displays the same Ribbon as the list page, providing you with the ability to work with the list items from within the Web Part without leaving the current page and navigating to the list page.

10. In the **Announcements** Web Part, clear the check box on the left of the item's title. The Items tab with the Ribbon closes, and the page is redisplayed on the Browse tab for viewing.

✖ **CLEAN UP** Leave the browser open if you are continuing to the next exercise.

Using the Recycle Bin

The Recycle Bin in SharePoint Foundation provides two-stage protection against accidental deletions. When you delete a document or other item from the SharePoint Foundation site, it is deleted from the site and moved to the site's Recycle Bin, where it can be restored if needed. If you then delete this item from the site's Recycle Bin, it is moved to the site collection's Recycle Bin. From there, the document can be either restored to its original location or deleted permanently.

Important By default, the site's Recycle Bin holds the items for 30 days before deleting them permanently. Your SharePoint administrator can modify this setting.

In this exercise, you will delete and restore a document from the Recycle Bin.

 SET UP Open the SharePoint site in which you'd like to delete and restore the document, if it is not already open. This exercise uses the *http://wideworldimporters/ travel* site, but you can open any site that you want. If prompted, type your user name and password, and then click OK.

BE SURE TO verify that you have permissions to delete and restore items on this site. If in doubt, see the Appendix at the back of this book.

1. On the site home page, select the **Shared Documents** Web Part by hovering your mouse over the Web Part title and clicking the check box that appears on the right of the title.

   The Documents tab opens and displays the Ribbon on the top of the page.

2. In the **Shared Documents** Web Part, select a document that you would like to remove by hovering your mouse over its name and selecting the check box that appears on the left of the name.

✕ Delete Document   3. In the **Manage** group on the Ribbon, click **Delete Document**.

4. Click **OK** in the confirmation message box when it appears.

The document has been deleted from the Shared Documents library. You will now restore this document from the site's Recycle Bin.

5. At the bottom of the left navigation panel, click **Recycle Bin**. The **Recycle Bin** page appears.

6. On the **Recycle Bin** page, select the document that you just deleted by clicking the check box to the left of its name. Then, to restore the document to its original location, click the **Restore Selection** option on the top of the page.

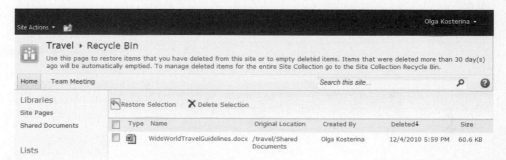

7. Click **OK** in the message box to confirm that you would like to restore this document.

The document has been restored.

8. Return to the site's home page by using either the link on the content navigation breadcrumb or the tab on the top link bar. Verify that the document has been restored and is displayed in the Shared Documents Web Part.

 **CLEAN UP** Leave the browser open if you are continuing to the next exercise.

If an item has been deleted accidentally from the site's Recycle Bin, it can be restored from the Recycle Bin of the site collection. In this exercise, you will restore the document that has been removed from the site and its Recycle Bin.

SET UP Open the SharePoint site in which a document to be deleted and restored is residing, if it is not already open. If prompted, type your user name and password, and then click OK.

BE SURE TO verify that you have permissions to manage the top-level site. If in doubt, see the Appendix at the back of this book.

1. Using steps 1-5 from the previous exercise as a guide, delete a document from the **Shared Documents** library, and then go to the site's **Recycle Bin** page.

2. On the **Recycle Bin** page, select the document by clicking the check box to the left of its name. Then, click **Delete Selection** on the top of the page.

3. Click **OK** in the confirmation message box when it appears. The document has been deleted from the site's Recycle Bin.

4. On the top of the page, click the **Navigate Up** icon, and go to the top-level site by clicking the top node on the path.

5. On the home page of the top-level site, on the **Site Actions** menu, click **Site Settings**.

6. On the **Site Settings** page, in the **Site Collection Administration** section, click **Recycle bin**.

7. On the **Site Collection Recycle Bin** page, in the left navigation area, under **Select a View**, click **Deleted from end user Recycle Bin**.

8. Select the document that you just deleted by clicking the check box to the left of its name, and then clicking **Restore Selection**.

9. Click **OK** in the confirmation message box when it appears. The document has been restored to its original location.

10. Using the top link bar, navigate to the home page of the subsite from where the document was removed and verify that it has been restored.

 **CLEAN UP** Close the browser.

Key Points

- The infrastructure of a typical SharePoint Team site includes the following components: libraries, lists, discussion boards, surveys, and a Recycle Bin.

- A home page of a SharePoint site has two main navigation areas at the top and left areas of the page. The top navigation area contains the top link bar, the content breadcrumb, and the Navigate Up icon. The left navigation panel contains the set of Quick Launch links, the All Site Content link, and the Recycle Bin link.

- The top link bar provides navigation between the sites, while the left navigation panel provides navigation within the current site.

- Both the top link bar and the Quick Launch can be customized to include the links of your choice.

- The All Site Content page that is linked from the left navigation panel displays all the libraries, lists, discussion boards, and surveys on your site. It also provides links to child sites and Workspaces. You cannot delete the All Site Content link from the left navigation panel.

- A SharePoint site can have many subsites. The hierarchy of these subsites, on web servers, resembles the hierarchy of folders on file systems.

- Sites that do not have a parent site are referred to as *top-level sites*. Top-level sites can have multiple subsites, and these subsites can have multiple subsites, proceeding downward as many levels as you need.

- The Ribbon interface is new to SharePoint Foundation. The Ribbon is contextual and is designed to help you quickly locate the commands for performing actions on pages, documents, and lists.

- Commands on the Ribbon are organized in logical groups, displayed together under tabs. Each tab relates to a type of SharePoint site component you are working with, such as a document library or a web page.

- The home page of a typical SharePoint site contains one or more Web Parts.

- A Recycle Bin provides two-stage protection against accidental deletions.

Chapter at a Glance

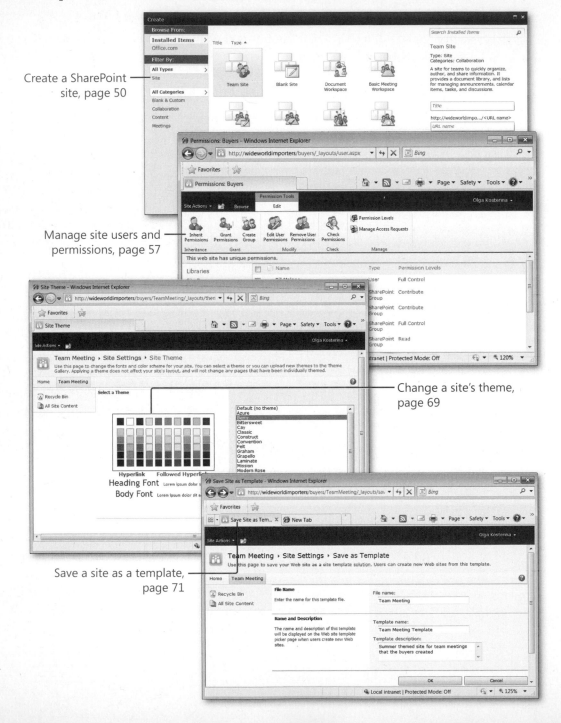

Create a SharePoint site, page 50

Manage site users and permissions, page 57

Change a site's theme, page 69

Save a site as a template, page 71

3 Creating and Managing Sites

In this chapter, you will learn how to

- ✔ Create sites.
- ✔ Manage site users and permissions.
- ✔ Create a child Workspace.
- ✔ Change a site's theme.
- ✔ Save and use a site template.
- ✔ Manage site features.
- ✔ Manage site content syndication.
- ✔ Delete a site.

Microsoft SharePoint Foundation *sites* and *Workspaces* are containers for the web pages, lists, document libraries, child sites, and other elements, as well as features and settings, that provide the site's functionality. *Lists* contain structured, tabular data, while *document libraries* contain unstructured binary documents. You can use any site as a single container for your data, or you can create as many child sites as you need to make your data easier to find and manage. You will also frequently find yourself creating sites to secure a place for a given group of people to collaborate on its contents. For example, you might create a site to manage a new team or project, collaborate on a document, or prepare for and follow up on a meeting. As a container, sites can be used to secure their contents.

As we discussed in Chapter 2, "Navigating a SharePoint Site," sites and Workspaces are organized hierarchically within a *site collection*. There is always one top-level site, and there can be one or more child sites as well. Typically, top-level sites are created for an entire team and therefore have many visitors (that is, people who only read), a few members (that is, people who can create and update content), and one or two owners. But as child sites and grandchild sites are created, the total number of users typically decreases, while the number of people designated as members increases.

Workspaces function just like sites except that they can be created from within Microsoft Office clients, such as Microsoft Word and Microsoft Outlook, their expected lifetime is short relative to a site, and child sites and Workspaces are not allowed. Similar to clearing off a desk to work specifically on a given project, you could create a SharePoint Foundation Workspace to work on a specific document or meeting. When the given project is completed, you would likely keep the results of the project and throw away all the other scraps. Similarly, once you are finished with a Workspace, you publish the results and throw away the container.

Site templates are used in SharePoint Foundation as a blueprint to jump-start a new site's usefulness by autogenerating lists, document libraries, and web pages, prepopulated with Web Parts that likely will be most useful in a given situation. In this chapter, you will learn how to create a site using one of the site templates available from a default installation, as well as the steps necessary to manage a site. You may want to differentiate a site by the way it is presented to the user, so you will also learn how to apply a *theme* to your site.

> **Practice Files** You don't need any practice files to complete the exercises in this chapter.

Important Remember to use your SharePoint site location in place of *http://wideworldimporters* in the following exercises.

Creating Sites

The catalyst for organizing your data into different site containers will often be the same catalyst for creating multiple subdirectories on the file system. You may have too much information to use a single container and still locate your information easily. If all your files were kept in the root of the hard drive along with the operating system files and other program files, the list of files would be difficult to sort through, work with, and manage. Just as you would create subdirectories to organize your file system data, you likely will create child sites to help organize your SharePoint Foundation data in logical ways.

The initial site created in a SharePoint Foundation site collection is called the *top-level site*. Top-level sites are created from within *SharePoint Central Administration* because they don't have a parent site. Although the top-level site is functionally the same as its child sites, it includes administrative links on its Site Settings page to manage site collection functionality.

To create a child site, you must navigate to the Create page of the would-be parent site by selecting the New Site option from the Site Actions menu. When Silverlight is installed on the client, selecting the New Site option displays the Silverlight Create dialog that has an improved, intuitive user interface in comparison with the Create page, while providing the same choice of options.

Tip Alternatively, you can navigate to the site's Create page directly from the browser's address bar. See the sidebar entitled "Layouts Directory," which follows, for details on how to gain direct access to the destination directly from the browser's address bar.

Layouts Directory

The administrative pages of SharePoint Foundation sites are kept in a common folder called _layouts. By using the website address in the address bar of your browser, you can navigate quickly to administrative pages that are buried relatively deep within a site's administrative links.

The following table displays examples that are typically found on the home page of every SharePoint Foundation site.

Website Address (URL)	Administrative Page
http://[site]/_layouts/viewlsts.aspx	All Site Content
http://[site]/_layouts/settings.aspx	Site Settings
http://[site]/_layouts/create.aspx	Create Page

The following table displays the same examples for a child site.

Website Address (URL)	Administrative Page
http://[site]/[childsite]/_layouts/vIewlsts.aspx	All Site Content
http://[site]/[childsite]/_layouts/settings.aspx	Site Settings
http://[site]/[childsite]/_layouts/create.aspx	Create Page

Note that the suffix for each website address is the same no matter how deeply you delve into the site hierarchy.

While the Create page provides the same functionality as the Silverlight Create dialog, the Silverlight dialog provides a better user experience because of its intuitive user interface. Silverlight is a free client add-on, and the link to its installation is provided on the top of the Create page. For better experience with using SharePoint Foundation, it is recommended that you install Silverlight on your computer, if it is not already there.

When you initially create objects like sites, Workspaces, lists, and libraries in SharePoint Foundation, you are establishing two name values: the display name, usually labeled Title or Name, and the Uniform Resource Locator (URL) name, also known as the *internal name.* Typically, as is the case with sites, there is an option to provide the URL name separately. Comply with the best practices outlined in the sidebar entitled "Naming a URL," which follows, when specifying the URL name.

Naming a URL

Follow these best practices when initially establishing a URL for objects in SharePoint Foundation. For example, providing a URL name of Todd Rowe for a new child site would result in the following website address in the browser's address bar: *http://wideworldimporters/Todd%20Rowe*. Subsequently, providing a URL name of "My Cool Docs" for a new document library within that site would result in the following website address in the browser's address bar: *http://wideworldimporters/Todd%20Rowe/My%20Cool%20Docs*. Notice that replacing the spaces with underscores improves the appearance of the website address: *http://wideworldimporters/Todd_Rowe/My_Cool_Docs*.

The best practices for naming URLs include the following:

- The URL name should be descriptive, intuitive, and easy to remember.
- The URL name should be concise. There is a limit on the number of total characters available for the entire website address, so you will eventually encounter problems if you consistently use long URL names.
- The URL name should not contain spaces. Spaces in the address bar are replaced with %20 and take up three characters each. Spaces also make the website address difficult to use in an email and difficult for others to read. To reduce frustration and improve readability, an underscore can be used in place of a space.
- The URL name should be used consistently. By default, tasks are found in a list called Tasks, contacts in a list called Contacts, and so on. Similarly, if you frequently create a document library to house proposals, consistently using a name such as Proposals will help others to locate that content. Of course, you cannot have two lists with the same name in a site. Therefore, you may need to differentiate them by putting a prefix on the name, such as Customer_Proposals and Product_Proposals.

When creating a list or column, the field—generically labeled Name—is used to populate both the display name and the URL name. Because best practices can be initiated for a specific organization, it is wise to establish your own naming conventions as early as possible. This should help prevent unintuitive, verbose, space-laden, and inconsistent objects from being created.

From the Create dialog or page, you can choose to provision your site initially using one of the 10 built-in site templates. Each site template provisions lists, document libraries, and web pages prepopulated with Web Parts that use the navigation best suited for the purpose of the site template.

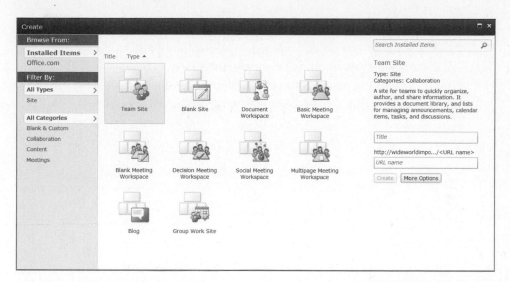

Team Site, Document Workspace, Group Work Site, and Blank Site have the same latent capabilities and *Quick Launch* navigation. The *Team Site* template provisions a Shared Documents library and four lists: Announcements, Calendar, Links, and Tasks. The Shared Documents library is made more visible by placing a Web Part for it on the site's default home page. The *Document Workspace* template provisions the same document libraries and lists as the Team Site, but places a Members Web Part on the default home page. In addition to the same basic lists and libraries as the Team Site, the *Group Work Site* template provisions four lists: Circulations, Phone Call Memo, Resources, and Whereabouts. Instead of a Calendar list, the Group Work Site provides the Group Calendar list that is placed on the site's default home page, together with the Whereabouts list displayed in their associated Web Parts. The *Blank Site template*, as you might surmise, has no lists or document libraries.

The *Blog* site template provides a way to publish a type of journal known as a *web log* or just a *blog*. The blog owner creates posts on which other users can comment. Each post is a separate content page, and a rollup summary of these pages is typically presented in reverse chronological order (with newest entries listed first) on the home page of the blog site. Blogs are commonly used as news sites, journals, and diaries. A blog focuses on one or more core competencies of the author and is sometimes used as a soapbox for the blog owner to state an opinion. Blogs can also be used as a one-way communication tool for keeping project stakeholders and team members informed.

Tip Blog site content can be syndicated using a Really Simple Syndication (*RSS*) *feed*. RSS feed-aggregating software allows people to subscribe to the content they are interested in and have new and updated posts delivered to them. Using these tools, people can aggregate the content from many blogs (or any SharePoint Foundation list) into one common reader where posts from selected authors can be sorted, filtered, and grouped. Microsoft Outlook 2010 can aggregate RSS feeds; there are also many vendors that give away or sell RSS feed–aggregating software.

The five *Meeting Workspace* templates provided by SharePoint Foundation are variations on a theme. Unlike all the previously described site templates, they don't have a Quick Launch or a left navigation area. In addition to the traditional lists and libraries, such as Document Library, Picture Library, Tasks, and Discussion Board, they can provision unique lists, such as Agenda, Attendees, Decisions, Objectives, and Things To Bring.

See Also For more details on Meeting Workspaces and blogs, refer to Chapter 12, "Working with Workspaces and Blogs."

Tip The 10 built-in templates are actually *configurations* of the underlying site definitions. Additional configurations, and even alternate site definitions, can be created in the underlying files by the managers of your web servers. Built-in configurations can also be removed or altered.

You will likely focus, at least initially, on using these built-in site templates that are based on the underlying site definitions. However, it is possible to save the websites you create as custom site templates that you and others can then choose from the Create dialog as a foundation for a new site. When you save the website as a template, a custom *web template* is created by SharePoint Foundation and saved as a file with a .wsp extension. This is done by using the Save Site As Template link in the Site Action section of the Site Settings page of any site. Custom web templates saved in this way are initially available only in the same site collection in which they are saved. The section entitled "Saving and Using a Site Template," later in this chapter, will explain how to copy a saved web template into another site collection. All alterations except security-related settings are retained on those sites provisioned by using saved custom web templates.

When creating a new site, there are two obvious permission options available. The default option, Use Same Permissions As Parent Site, checks the parent site's permission every time the user visits the child site to determine what the user is allowed to do on that site. As the permissions on the parent site change over time, the permissions on the child site also reflect those changes. The other option is to Use Unique Permissions. When you click this option as the site's creator, you are initially the only user with access to the site and are then associated with the Administrator permission level.

Important If you choose Use Same Permissions As Parent Site, it is possible to have the right to create a new site but not have the right to delete it. However, if you choose Use Unique Permissions, you are the site's administrator and, as such, will always have the right to delete the new site.

You have two other options for assigning permissions to a new site that are less obvious. If you initially choose Use Unique Permissions, you are the only user with access to the site and can make any changes you wish. You can then switch to Use Same Permissions As Parent Site, whereby everyone who has access to the parent site (including you) will subsequently have access to the child site using the permissions assigned on the parent site. If you initially choose Use Same Permissions As Parent Site, the parent site's permissions will be used. Yet, if you subsequently switch to Use Unique Permissions, all the permissions of the parent site are copied to the child site. This can save a great deal of time if most of the people who have access to the parent site also need access to the child site.

Three navigation options can be specified when creating a new site. The first two deal with the visibility of the child site being created within the navigation of the parent site. You can choose to show the child site on either the Quick Launch or the top link bar of the parent site. The former defaults to No, and the latter defaults to Yes. Conversely, you can specify whether the top link bar of the parent site should display on the top link bar of the created child site. The default is No.

See Also See "Using the Practice Files," at the beginning of this book, for more information about using the practice site templates provided for chapters in this book.

In the following exercise, you will create a child site that the buyers at Wide World Importers will use for collaboration. As a team, the buyers need a centralized place to consolidate their announcements, links, and general discussions, as well as to track the status of their purchases and the list of current suppliers. You will use the Team Site template to provision the new child site.

 SET UP Open the top-level, would-be parent site from which you'd like to create the new site. The exercise will use the *http://wideworldimporters* site, but you can use whatever site you wish. If prompted, type your user name and password, and click OK.

BE SURE TO verify that you have sufficient rights to create a site. If in doubt, see the Appendix at the back of this book.

1. On the **Site Actions** menu, click **New Site** to display the **Create** dialog.

2. Select **Team Site** from the available templates in the middle pane, and then click **More Options** in the right pane. The Create dialog for Team Site appears.

Tip If you have installed the practice sites from the book's catalog page, you will also see the book's practice site templates at the bottom of the list.

3. In the **Title** text box, type **Buyers** to establish a display name for the new site.

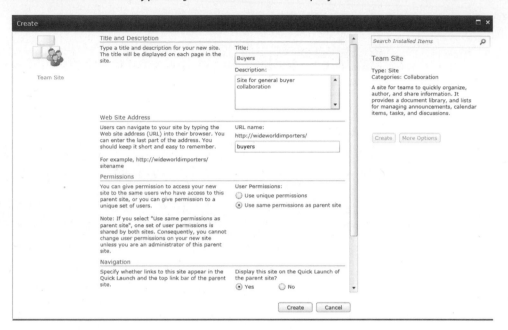

4. In the **Description** text box, type a description, such as **Site for general buyer collaboration,** to help users understand the purpose for the new site.

5. In the **Web Site Address** section, in the **URL name** text box, type **buyers**.

This determines the value in the browser's address bar that users will see when they visit the site. Refer to the sidebar entitled "Naming a URL," earlier in this chapter, for best practices regarding naming conventions.

6. Click the option button that defines the type of permissions that you want to use on the site initially. For the Buyers site, use the default permission **Use same permissions as parent site**.

7. In the **Navigation** section, define whether the links to this site will appear on the Quick Launch and the top link bar of the parent site. Click **Yes** for the link to this site to be displayed on the Quick Launch of the parent site, and keep the default **Yes** option for the link to this site to appear on the top link bar of the parent site.

8. In the **Navigation Inheritance** section, define whether this site will use the top link bar from the parent site or have its own. For the Buyers site, keep the default **No** option for this site to have its own top link bar.

9. Scroll down to the bottom of the dialog and click **Create**.

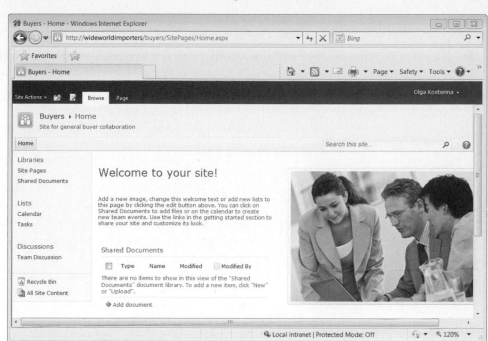

The new Team site with a default set of lists, document libraries, and web pages has been created and is displayed in the browser.

Important Clicking Cancel returns you to the template selection in the Create dialog and will not create the new site.

 CLEAN UP Leave the browser open if you are continuing to the next exercise.

Managing Site Users and Permissions

Information in SharePoint Foundation is secured at one of four levels, as follows: site level, list or document library level, folder level, and list item level. By default, all lists inherit the permissions of the site that contains them; all folders inherit the permissions of the list that contains them; and all list items inherit the permissions of the folder that contains them.

See Also For deeper discussion about list, folder, and list item security, refer to Chapter 7, "Working with List Settings."

Selecting the default option, Use Same Permissions As Parent Site, provides permissions inheritance from the parent site to a newly created child site. SharePoint Foundation checks the parent site's permission every time the user visits the child site.

When creating a new site, if you select the Use Unique Permissions option, SharePoint Foundation initially categorizes users of a site into three SharePoint groups, as follows:

- **Visitors** People or groups who only need to be able to read content on a site

- **Members** People or groups who need to be able to create and edit content, but not create lists or manage site membership

- **Owners** People who are responsible for all aspects of managing and maintaining a site

The Use Unique Permissions option initially specifies you as the site's creator, with sole access to the new site as its owner. After you click Create, you are presented with the Set Up Groups For This Site page to add users to the three groups to provide them with access to the newly created site.

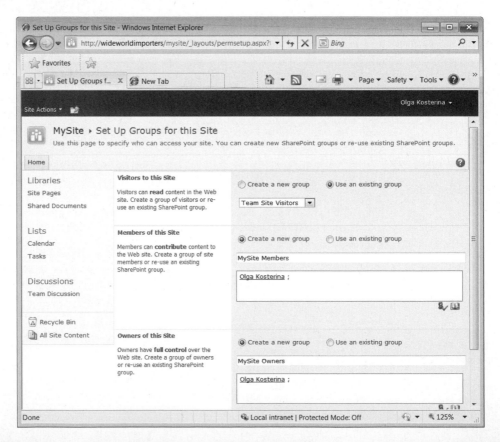

A site can be toggled between inherited permissions and unique permissions using its Permissions page, which you navigate to by clicking Site Permissions on the Site Actions menu. Once on the Permissions page, choosing Inherit Permissions on the Ribbon of a site using unique permissions allows you to toggle the site to have inherited permissions. Choosing Stop Inheriting Permissions on the Ribbon of a site inheriting permissions allows you to toggle the site to have unique permissions. A warning message will display, asking you to confirm your action.

A site using unique permissions has no tie to the parent site, so you are allowed to add and remove users from the site regardless of whether they have permissions on any other site. When users are added to a site, they must be added to a *SharePoint group* or associated with at least one *permission level*.

SharePoint groups are maintained at the site collection level and represent a collection of users or groups with a defined set of one or more permission levels and a few governing attributes. When new users or groups are added to a SharePoint group, they are granted the permissions of that group in any site.

Think of permission levels as a named collection of permissions that can be assigned to SharePoint groups or individual users. Five permission levels are made available by SharePoint Foundation on every site, as follows:

- **Read** The user can only view site content.

- **Contribute** The user can view, add, update, and delete site content.

- **Design** The user can view, add, update, delete, approve, and customize site content.

- **Full Control** The user has full control over site content.

- **Limited** The user has no permissions to the site in its entirety, but only to specific lists, document libraries, folders, list items, or documents when given explicit permission.

The list of individual permissions and the permissions levels they are included in by default is shown here.

Permission Levels

	Full Control	Design	Contribute	Read
Add and Customize Pages	✓	✓		
Add Items	✓	✓	✓	
Add/Remove Personal Web Parts	✓	✓	✓	
Apply Style Sheets	✓	✓		
Apply Themes and Borders	✓	✓		
Approve Items	✓	✓		
Browse Directories	✓	✓	✓	
Browse User Information	✓	✓	✓	✓
Create Alerts	✓	✓	✓	✓
Create Groups	✓			
Create Subsites	✓			
Delete Items	✓	✓	✓	
Delete Versions	✓	✓	✓	
Edit Items	✓	✓	✓	
Edit Personal User Information	✓	✓	✓	
Enumerate Permissions	✓			
Manage Alerts	✓			
Manage Lists	✓	✓		
Manage Permissions	✓			
Manage Personal Views	✓	✓	✓	
Manage Web Site	✓			
Open	✓	✓	✓	✓
Open Items	✓	✓	✓	✓
Override Check Out	✓	✓		
Update Personal Web Parts	✓	✓	✓	
Use Client Integration Features	✓	✓	✓	✓
Use Remote Interfaces	✓	✓	✓	✓
Use Self-Service Site Creation	✓	✓	✓	✓
View Application Pages	✓	✓	✓	✓
View Items	✓	✓	✓	✓
View Pages	✓	✓	✓	✓
View Usage Data	✓			
View Versions	✓	✓	✓	✓

See Also   For more details on the individual permissions and permission levels, refer to the Appendix at the back of this book.

The initial SharePoint groups on a site with unique permissions have the following permission levels:

- The Visitors group has the permission level of Read.

- The Members group has the permission level of Contribute.

- The Owners group has the permission level of Full Control.

Not only can you associate existing SharePoint groups and individual users with permission levels, but you can also associate *Windows groups* (including *Active Directory groups,* and *Local Machine groups*) with permission levels. This is a very practical approach to providing tight security with minimal maintenance. However, you may not have control over the Windows groups defined in your organization.

Although you can create your own permission levels and even alter all permission levels except for Full Control and Limited, you will likely find these built-in levels to be adequate for most business scenarios. You may also want to provide all users with some level of access to the data on your site.

Tip If anonymous access has been enabled for Web application in SharePoint Central Administration and has not been denied via the Anonymous User Policy, anonymous users can be granted some access, either to the entire site or to individual lists on a case-by-case basis. This provides the central administrator with the option to decide whether to grant anonymous access for each Web application before its site administrators can begin to turn on this option.

Tip You will also find an option to provide all authenticated users with site access on each site's Permissions page using the Grant Permissions command. The topic of adding users is covered later in this section.

After all users and groups are assigned to various permission levels, it is possible—even likely—that someone will be associated with more than one permission level. Rather than enforcing the most restrictive permission level, all associated rights are aggregated, and the cumulative list of unique rights applies. This can be overridden only by policies created in SharePoint Central Administration.

In the following exercise, you will change the permissions for a child site from inheriting permissions from its parent site to using unique permissions. You will then add users representing Wide World Importers buyers to the child site with the Contribute permission.

 SET UP Open the Buyer child site created in the first exercise (*http:// wideworldimporters/buyers*) from the address bar of your browser, if it is not already open. If prompted, type your user name and password, and click OK.

BE SURE TO verify that you have sufficient rights to alter the site's permissions. If in doubt, see the Appendix at the back of this book.

1. On the **Site Actions** menu, click **Site Permissions.**

2. The **Permissions: Buyers** page is displayed, showing permission levels that have been assigned to the groups associated with this site. There is a yellow bar across the top of the page stating that this website inherits permissions from its parent. Because this child site is inheriting permissions from its parent, you see the SharePoint groups from the parent site listed.

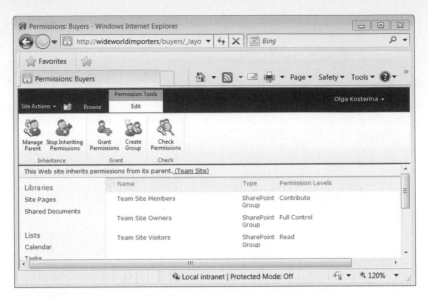

3. On the Ribbon, click **Stop Inheriting Permissions** to establish unique permissions for this site.

4. Click **OK** in the message box that appears to confirm the change.

   Notice how this page has changed. You now have check boxes next to each group, and there are additional commands on the Ribbon that allow you to modify the permissions. The yellow bar across the top of the page now states that this website has unique permissions.

   Tip You would select the Inherit Permissions command to return to using the permissions of the parent site.

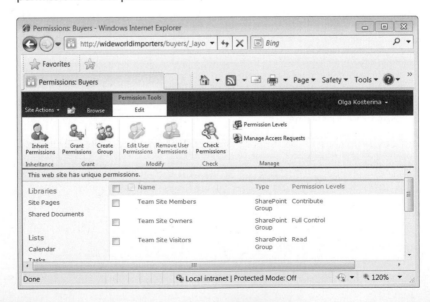

Important Editing a SharePoint group affects the membership of all sites, lists, folders, and items that are using that SharePoint group.

Create
Group

5. On the Ribbon, click **Create Group** to display the **Create Group** page.

6. Type a name, such as **Buyers Members**, into the **Name** text box.

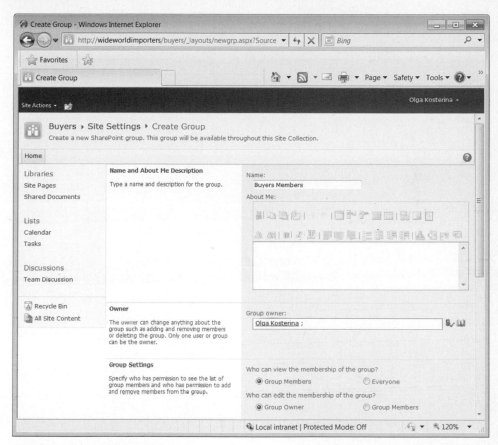

7. If you want, type a description of the new group in the **About Me** text box.

8. Select the user or group that will own this group. It defaults to you; this example uses Olga Kosterina.

9. Leave the default settings for **Group Settings** and **Membership Requests**.

10. Scroll down to the **Group Permissions for this Site** section and click the **Contribute** check box to grant your new group the Contribute permission level on the Buyers site.

11. Click **Create.** The new group has been created and added to the *People and Groups* page for the Buyers Members group.

For the Buyers site, everyone in a Windows group called Buyers needs to be added and associated with the Contribute permission level. You will now add a Windows group to the new SharePoint group.

12. On the **New** menu at the top of the page, click **Add Users** to display the **Grant Permissions** dialog.

13. In the **Users/Groups** text area, type the name of a group to whom to grant Contribute permissions, such as **Buyers**.

Important Typically, you add users and Windows groups by using a format such as *domainname\username* or *domainname\groupname*, but your computer name cannot be anticipated here. Fortunately, SharePoint Foundation searches your computer for users and Windows groups that match even if the proper naming convention isn't provided.

14. Click **OK**. The Buyers Windows group has been added to the Buyers Members SharePoint group.

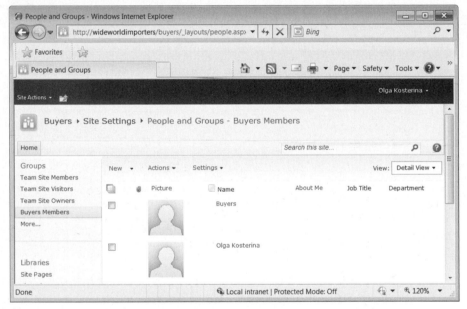

15. On the **Site Actions** menu, click **Site Permissions.** Verify that the **Buyers Members** group is listed on the site Permissions page with **Contribute** permissions.

Bill Malone, who is Wide World Importers' head buyer, needs to be associated with the Full Control permission level for the Buyers site. You will now grant Bill the Full Control permission level.

Grant
Permissions

16. On the Ribbon, click **Grant Permissions**. The **Grant Permissions** dialog opens.

17. In the **Users/Groups** text area, type the name of a user account to whom to grant Full Control. This exercise uses **Bill Malone**.

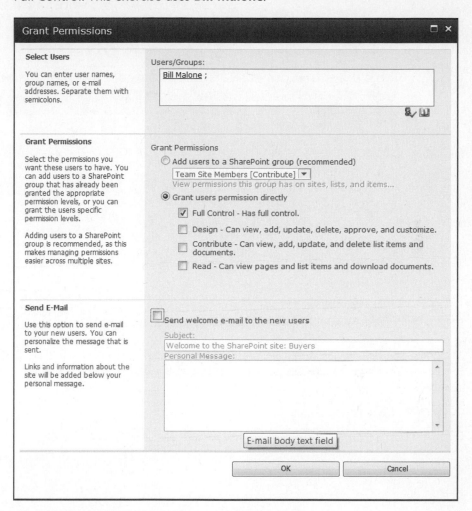

18. Click the **Grant users permission directly** option.

19. Select the **Full Control** check box. If email has been enabled for your SharePoint installation, you have the option of sending a message to Bill to notify him that he now has Full Control of this site. For this exercise, clear the **Send E-Mail** check box.

20. Click **OK** to add the permissions for this user (Bill, in this case) to the site. The user permissions have been added and are shown in the site Permissions page.

No other SharePoint group needs permissions on the Buyers site. You will now remove all other groups.

21. Select the three parent site SharePoint groups by clicking the check boxes to the left of their names.

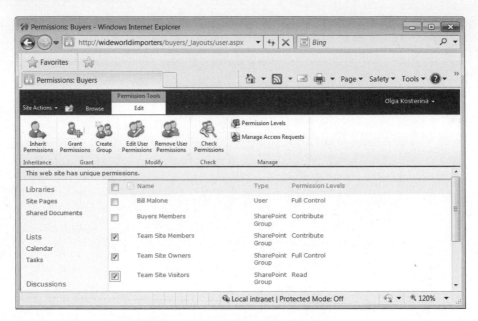

Remove User Permissions

22. On the Ribbon, click **Remove User Permissions**.

23. In the confirmation message box, click **OK** to apply the change. The groups have been removed. Only the Buyers Members group and Bill Malone have permissions on the site.

> **Tip** It is wise to associate every user in the various child sites in a site collection with at least the Read permission level in the top-level site. Users might be unable to use custom site templates and list templates imported into a site collection unless they are associated with one of the built-in permission levels in the top-level site.

CLEAN UP Close the browser.

Creating a Child Workspace

SharePoint Foundation makes it easy to navigate from a parent site to a child site. Because the Buyers child site was created with navigational links on both the top link bar and the Quick Launch of the parent site, navigating to the child site from the top-level site is easy: you simply click the link on the Buyers tab. However, how would you find the Buyers child site if this navigation wasn't included? In the following exercise, you will create a Meeting Workspace as a child site of the Buyers child site. Because you must already be in a site to create a child site, you will first see how to navigate to the Buyers child site from its parent. You will then view the site hierarchy of the entire site collection from the top-level site.

 SET UP Open the top-level site from the address bar of your browser: *http://wideworldimporters*. If prompted, type your user name and password, and click OK.

BE SURE TO verify that you have sufficient rights to create a new site. If in doubt, see the Appendix at the back of this book.

1. In the left navigation area, click **All Site Content** to see all lists, document libraries, sites, and Workspaces that have been created on the **All Site Content** page of this site.

2. In the **Sites and Workspaces** area near the bottom of the page, click **Buyers** to navigate to the child site. This link would appear even if there weren't a link to this child site in the top link bar or the Quick Launch of the parent site.

   Tip Alternatively, you can type the entire site hierarchy directly into the browser's address bar. This suggestion may seem a bit odd at first, but Internet Explorer memorizes the places that you type often, which can be a real time saver over clicking through the user interface. To see the child sites of the current site, complete the current site's website address with */_layouts/mngsubwebs.aspx*.

3. In the **Buyers** site, click **Site Actions** and select **New Site** to display the **Create** dialog.

4. Select **Basic Meeting Workspace**, and then click **More Options**.

5. In the **Create** dialog for Basic Meeting Workspace, as in the earlier example, type a **Title** and **URL name**, such as **Team Meeting** and **TeamMeeting**, respectively. Remember to follow the best practices concerning naming conventions that are found in the sidebar entitled "Naming a URL," earlier in this chapter.

6. Optionally, in the **Description** text box, type a description, such as **Site for monthly team meeting details**, to help users understand the purpose for the new site.

7. Keep the default permissions that are set on **Use same permissions as parent site**.

8. Keep the default navigation settings so that the link to the new Workspace is displayed on the top link bar of the Buyers site, but not on its Quick Launch. In the **Navigation Inheritance** section, click **Yes** so that the new Workspace uses the top-link bar of the Buyers site.

9. Click **Create** to create and display the new Meeting Workspace.

   Notice that Meeting Workspaces differ in appearance from Team sites. There is no Quick Launch, and the Site Actions menu has the Add Pages and Manage Pages options that were not there for the Team site.

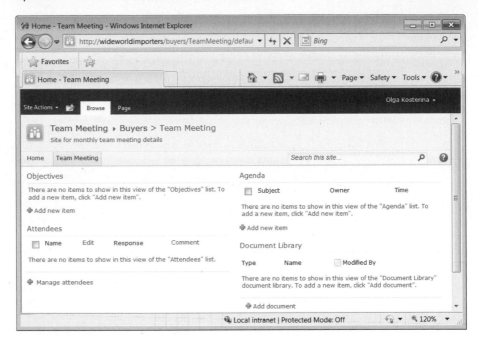

10. You will now navigate up to the top-level site and then view the entire hierarchy of child sites. To return to the top-level site, in the top navigation area, click the **Navigate Up** icon and then click the top-level site. In our scenario, the top-level site is Wide World Importers.

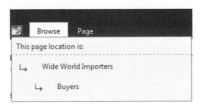

11. On the home page of the top-level site, click **Site Actions** and select **Site Settings**.

12. On the **Site Settings** page, in the **Site Collection Administration** section, click **Site hierarchy** to display the **Site Hierarchy** page.

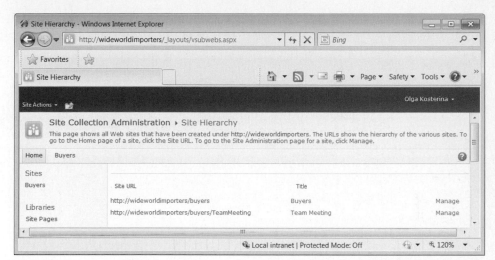

This page shows all the fully qualified, flattened-out child sites in the entire site hierarchy. You can click a site name to display the site or click the Manage link to display the Site Settings page for the associated child site.

✖ **CLEAN UP** Leave the browser open if you are continuing to the next exercise.

Changing a Site's Theme

These blue SharePoint sites are all right initially, but they eventually blur together and start to look too similar. Thankfully, SharePoint Foundation provides us with the ability to apply themes to our sites. Themes can radically affect display items such as colors, graphics, text, banners, and borders. Numerous built-in themes are available from which to choose.

Tip With Microsoft SharePoint Designer, you can gain even more control over how themes are applied to your site. You can choose to apply a theme to only specific pages, or even create your own custom themes.

Each SharePoint Foundation site can have its own theme, or you can set several sites so that they all have a common theme and are related visually.

Tip Because of many changes in the user interface in SharePoint Foundation, the themes created in Windows SharePoint Services 3.0 are not compatible with SharePoint Foundation 2010. You can create new themes in SharePoint Foundation 2010 and apply them to your existing sites. Alternatively, if necessary, you can use Visual Upgrade to continue to use existing sites with the old user interface.

Perhaps the buyers at Wide World Importers want to create a theme for their Team Meeting child site so that it stands out from other sites. In this exercise, you will navigate to the Team Meeting site and apply a theme.

SET UP Open the top-level site (*http://wideworldimporters*) from the address bar of your browser, if it is not already open. If prompted, type your user name and password, and click OK.

BE SURE TO verify that you have sufficient rights to set a site's theme and view the site hierarchy. If in doubt, see the Appendix at the back of this book.

1. On the top-level site, navigate to the **Site Hierarchy** page (if it is not displayed already) by selecting **Site Settings** from the **Site Actions** menu, and then, on the **Site Settings** page, in the **Site Collection Administration** area, clicking **Site hierarchy**.

2. Click the **Manage** link to the far right of the **Site URL** (*http://wideworldimporters/buyers/TeamMeeting*) for the **Site Settings** page of the **Team Meeting** child site to display.

3. In the **Look and Feel** section, click **Site theme** to display the **Site Theme** page.

4. On the **Select a Theme** list, click **Berry**. Note the color scheme and the hyperlinks and font preview displayed on the left of the screen, and then click **Summer**. The color scheme and font preview changes to reflect the selected theme. Browse through the available themes and select the one that you like most.

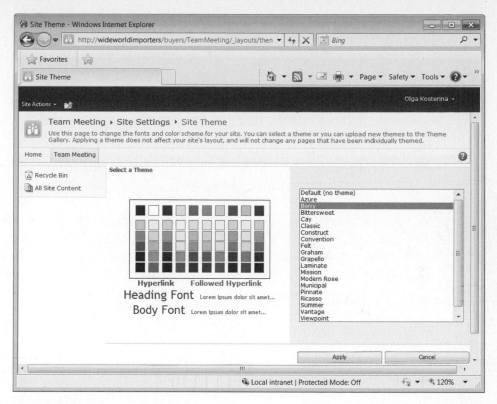

5. Click **Apply**. The changes have been processed, and the new theme is applied to the Workspace site.

6. On the **Site Settings** page, on the breadcrumb, click **Team Meeting** to go to the home page of the **Team Meeting** site. Verify that the new theme has been applied.

✖ **CLEAN UP** Leave the browser open if you are continuing to the next exercise.

Saving and Using a Site Template

After working with a site, you may want to save it just the way it is so that it can be re-created over and over again. SharePoint Foundation facilitates this action by allowing anyone with a Design permission level to save a site as a custom web template. Custom web templates provide a way of packaging up a set of changes to an underlying site definition and making that package available as a template for new sites. Web templates behave in much the same way as built-in templates, in that they provision lists, document libraries, and web pages prepopulated with Web Parts that are best suited for the purpose of the template. In fact, everything in a website except security-related information is saved in a custom web template, including its theme and navigation.

Every custom web template is based on an underlying site definition and saved as a file with a .wsp extension in the Solutions Gallery of the site collection.

Tip Because custom web templates are based on existing sites, they continue to depend, throughout their life cycle, on the site definition that is their ultimate foundation. Therefore, the first site in any SharePoint Foundation deployment must be based on a site definition, not a web template.

Once saved, a web template is made immediately available throughout the entire site collection in which it is saved. When creating a new child site, any user associated with one of the default permission levels (excluding the Limited permission level) in the top-level site can see the saved web template as an option in the Create dialog. Web templates can be downloaded and redeployed to other site collections.

Tip The .wsp files on this book's catalog page that are used to create the practice sites for exercises are actually custom web templates saved to a file.

Important Both custom web templates and custom site definitions can be used to create site templates in SharePoint Foundation. Using a web template is recommended because it maximizes the chances that your solution will be compatible with future versions of SharePoint Foundation. However, in some scenarios, you might need to create the custom site definition to preserve specific site functionality. For more information, refer to "Deciding Between Custom Web Templates and Custom Site Definitions," at *http://msdn.microsoft.com/ en-us/library/aa979683.aspx*.

Let's assume that the unique look that the buyers of Wide World Importers created for their Team Meeting site has caught on, and they want to be able to use it repeatedly. In the following exercise, you will save the Team Meeting site as a web template and then use it to create another meeting site as a child of the Buyers child site.

 SET UP Open the Team Meeting site (*http://wideworldimporters/buyer/TeamMeeting*) from the address bar of your browser, if it is not already open. If prompted, type your user name and password, and click OK.

BE SURE TO verify that you have sufficient rights to save a site template and create a new site. If in doubt, see the Appendix at the back of this book.

1. On the **Site Actions** menu, click **Site Settings**.

2. On the **Site Settings** page, in the **Site Actions** section, click **Save site as template** to display the **Save as Template** page.

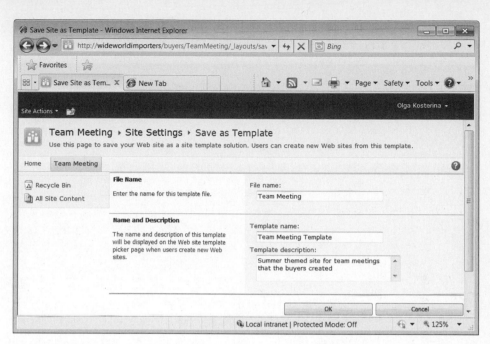

3. In the **File name** text box, type **Team Meeting** to establish a name for the .wsp file.

4. In the **Template name** text box, type **Team Meeting Template**.

5. In the **Template description** text box, type a description, such as **Summer themed site for team meetings that the buyers created**, to help site creators understand the intended purpose of this custom web template.

6. Click **OK** to create the custom web template file, save it in the Solution Gallery, and activate the template within the site collection. When the **Operation Completed Successfully** page is displayed, click **OK**.

    Tip If you want to see where the custom web template is placed, you can click the Solution Gallery link on the Operation Completed Successfully page.

7. You will now create a new child site for the Buyers site that will be based on the site template that you've just created. On the top link bar, click **Home** to display the Buyers site.

8. On the **Site Actions** menu, click **New Site** to display the **Create** dialog.

9. In the central pane of the **Create** dialog, click the **Team Meeting** template, which is now available, and then click **More Options**.

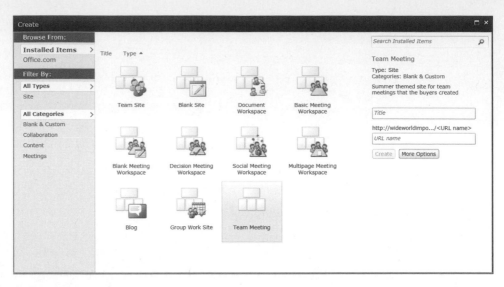

10. In the **Title** text box, type **Important Meeting** to establish a display name for the new Meeting Workspace site.

11. In the **Description** text box, type a description, such as **Site for that important meeting**, to help users understand the purpose for the new site.

12. In the **URL name** text box, type **ImportantMeeting** as the website address. (Remember the naming conventions listed in the sidebar entitled "Naming a URL," earlier in this chapter, when naming URLs.)

13. Keep the default permissions that are set on **Use same permissions as parent site**. Keep the default navigation and navigation inheritance options.

14. Click **Create** to create the new Workspace site.

    The new Important Meeting site is displayed. It is identical to the original Team Meeting site.

✖ CLEAN UP Close the browser.

Managing Site Features

SharePoint Features group together chunks of custom functionality that developers and administrators can activate to make this combined functionality available at one of four scopes, as follows:

- **Farm level** These Features are activated for all sites in the entire SharePoint Foundation farm and are managed by the farm central administrators.

- **Web Application level** These Features are activated for all sites where the web address is the same. For instance, all sites that start with *http://wideworldimporters* would be managed under the same Web application. These Features are also managed by farm central administrators.

- **Site Collection level** These Features are activated only for sites within a given site collection. Management of these Features is accomplished from the top-level site of the site collection and is typically distributed to department-level administrators.

- **Site level** These Features are activated only for the site in which the activation is performed. Management of these Features may be done by anyone with Administrator privileges on the site.

Features encapsulate a combination of custom functionality, such as the following:

- Customizing the Ribbon, including creating new buttons and other controls, groups, and tabs.

- Adding or removing links in the SharePoint Foundation user interface, including the Ribbon controls, the Site Actions menu, the Site Settings page, the Content Type Settings page, and Web Application Settings pages in SharePoint Central Administration.

- Registering a computer program that converts documents from one format to another when uploaded to a document library.

- Adding new application and administration web pages or any other physical documents, including site and list templates, images, or other technical files.

- Defining the style and behavior of a new list of your choice from the Create page.

- Creating a new list.

- Defining a new site column that could be used in lists, document libraries, or content types.

- Defining an entire content type that could be associated with a list or document library subsequently.

- Adding a custom workflow that could dictate the order of tasks that must be accomplished for a list item to move from one state to another.

- Registering a computer program that runs custom code when you interact with items in a list or document library. Adding new items, modifying an existing item, checking out, checking in, or even undoing a checkout of an item or deleting an item are all examples of interactions that can cause this custom code to run.

A Feature must be installed in a scope on your SharePoint Foundation server farm before you can begin working with it. When you created a custom web template for the Team Meeting site in the previous exercise, the Web Template Feature for this template that provided its functionality was created and activated in the site collection. For example, it is this Feature that provides the display of the new template in the Create dialog.

In the following exercise, you will work with the Web Template Feature. You will first deactivate this Feature and verify that the Team Meeting template is no longer available for new site creation. You will then activate this Feature to restore the Team Meeting template in the Create dialog.

SET UP Open the top-level site from the address bar of your browser: *http://widewordimporters*. If prompted, type your user name and password, and click OK.

BE SURE TO verify that you have sufficient rights to manage Features. If in doubt, see the Appendix at the back of this book.

1. On the **Site Actions** menu, click **Site Settings**.

2. On the **Site Settings** page, in the **Site Collection Administration** area, click **Site collection features.** Notice that the **Web template feature of exported web template Team Meeting** has been activated in this site collection; its status is shown as Active.

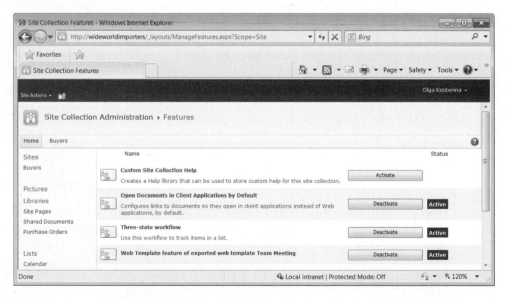

3. To the right of the **Web template feature of exported web template Team Meeting**, click **Deactivate**.

4. A warning page is shown, asking you to confirm that you really want to deactivate this Feature. Click the **Deactivate this feature** link.

5. On the **Features** page, verify that the Feature is no longer shown as Active.

   Because this Feature has been deactivated, the associated site template is no longer available for new site creation. You will now validate that the template has been removed from the **Create** dialog.

6. On the **Site Actions** menu, click **New Site**. In the **Create** dialog, verify that the **Team Meeting** site template that was previously there has been removed, and then close the **Create** dialog by clicking the **Close** icon in the upper-right corner.

   You will now activate the Web Template Feature to restore the Team Meeting template in the Create dialog.

7. On the **Site Actions** menu, click **Site Settings** one last time, and then, on the **Site Settings** page, in the **Site Administration** area, click **Site collection features**.

8. To the right of the **Web template feature of exported web template Team Meeting**, click **Activate** to add the site template back to the **Create** dialog.

9. On the **Site Actions** menu, click **New Site** again to verify that the site template has been restored and is available from the **Create** dialog.

 **CLEAN UP** Close the Create dialog. Leave the browser open if you are continuing to the next exercise.

Managing Site Content Syndication

RSS is a standard way to make new or modified content available to readers of a SharePoint Foundation list or document library. Once you subscribe to an RSS feed (the XML emitted from a web request), you can use an RSS aggregator running on your desktop to check for new or modified content as often as you choose.

Tip Outlook 2010 can be used as an aggregator. This topic is discussed in Chapter 13, "Using SharePoint Foundation with Outlook 2010."

The aggregator gathers all updates into a common pool of data that can be searched, sorted, filtered, and grouped by the aggregator as directed. RSS content is sometimes described as being "pulled" by the subscribers, for they can easily unsubscribe from a feed at any time. This can be a fabulous way to roll up data entered into a SharePoint list. By default, every Web application in SharePoint Foundation is configured to allow RSS feed for all site collections that they contain.

Site collection administrators can specify whether RSS feeds are allowed on lists in the sites within the site collection; they are allowed by default. Each site can then subsequently specify whether RSS feeds are allowed on lists in the site; they are also allowed by default. If sites do allow feeds, several attributes can be defined that will be included in every feed. In the following exercise, you will verify that RSS is allowed on both the site collection and the top-level site and specify the optional attributes.

See Also Consuming the RSS feed for a library is discussed in Chapter 5, "Working with Libraries," while using the RSS feed for a list is covered in Chapter 7, "Working with List Settings."

SET UP Open the top-level site (*http://wideworldimporters*) from the address bar of your browser, if it is not already open. If prompted, type your user name and password, and click OK.

BE SURE TO verify that you have sufficient rights to administrate a site. If in doubt, see the Appendix at the back of this book.

1. On the **Site Actions** menu, click **Site Settings** to display the **Site Settings** page of a top-level site, if not already displayed.

2. On the **Site Settings** page, in the **Site Administration** section, click **RSS** to display the **RSS** page.

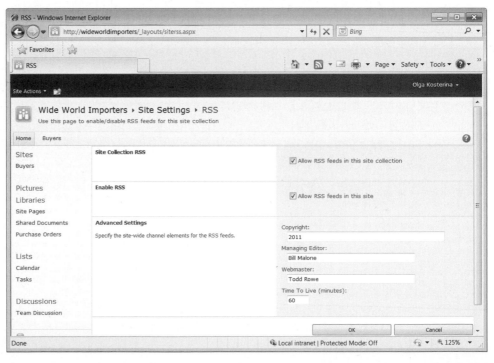

If you are on the top-level site of the site collection, as in this example, and you are a site collection administrator, you see the Allow RSS Feeds In This Site Collection check box in the Site Collection RSS area. Clearing this check box dims the options in the Enable RSS area, and therefore no sites in this collection can allow RSS feeds. Leave this check box selected in this exercise.

All sites have the Allow RSS Feeds In This Site check box in the Enable RSS area. If this check box is cleared, no lists in this site are allowed to provide their data in the form of an RSS feed. As with the Allow RSS Feeds In This Site Collection check box, leave this check box selected in this exercise.

3. In the **Copyright** text box, enter **2011**.

4. In the **Managing Editor** text box, enter **Bill Malone**.

5. In the **Webmaster** text box, enter **Todd Rowe**.

6. Leave the **Time to Live** text box at **60** minutes. This instructs the aggregator to wait at least this long before checking for updates. A shorter period will increase the frequency that a site could receive requests from aggregators, while a longer duration can help to reduce the number of aggregator requests.

7. Click **OK** to commit the changes.

 CLEAN UP Close the browser.

Deleting a Site

There will be times when you want to remove a site that you either created in error or no longer need. SharePoint Foundation automatically generates all the necessary user interface elements to create, review, update, manage, and delete your sites.

The creator of the Important Meeting child site at Wide World Importers had a change in priorities and no longer needs the site. In this exercise, you will delete the Important Meeting child site from the Buyers child site.

 **SET UP** Open the Buyers site from the address bar of your browser: *http:// wideworldimporters/buyers*. If prompted, type your user name and password, and click OK.

BE SURE TO verify that you have sufficient rights to delete a site. If in doubt, see the Appendix at the back of this book.

1. On the **Site Actions** menu, click **Site Settings**.

2. On the **Site Settings** page, in the **Site Administration** area, click **Sites and workspaces** to display the **Sites and Workspaces** page.

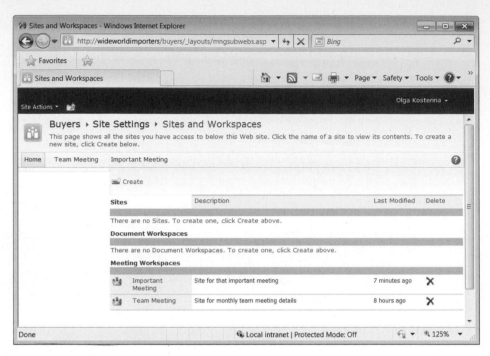

3. To the far right of the **Important Meeting** line, in the **Delete** column, click the cross icon to begin the site deletion process.

4. On the **Delete Web Site** page, click **Delete** to confirm the deletion request.

5. Click **OK** in the message box that appears to confirm the site removal. The site has been deleted.

    Important SharePoint Foundation will prevent you from deleting a parent site that still contains child sites.

6. On the **Sites and Workspaces** page, verify that the Important Meeting site is no longer displayed.

Tip It is also possible to delete the site that you are in by clicking Delete This Site in the Site Actions section of the site's Site Settings page. This is the only way to delete a top-level site without removing the entire site collection.

 CLEAN UP Close the browser.

Key Points

- Sites are containers for lists, document libraries, and web pages prepopulated with Web Parts.

- The top-level site is the initial site created in a SharePoint Foundation site collection.

- To create a child site, you must navigate to the Create dialog.

- Don't use spaces in site names, and keep them short and intuitive.

- Sites are easy to create and secure.

- Only after a site is using unique permissions can you manage its users and SharePoint groups.

- Permission levels are named collections of permissions.

- All associated permissions are aggregated, and the cumulative list of unique permissions applies.

- Each site can have its own theme.

- Sites can be saved as custom templates and used immediately to create other clone sites in a site collection.

- Features combine custom functionality and can be installed and activated at farm, Web application, site collection, or site level, depending on their scope.

- Sites can allow or disallow RSS feeds on the lists and libraries contained within them.

- SharePoint Foundation will prevent you from deleting a site that contains subsites.

Chapter at a Glance

Create a new list, page 89

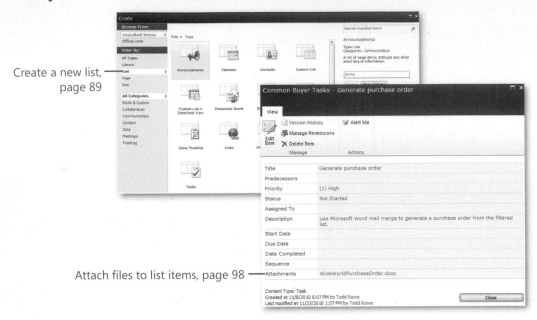

Attach files to list items, page 98

Sort and filter a list, page 111

Set up alerts, page 113

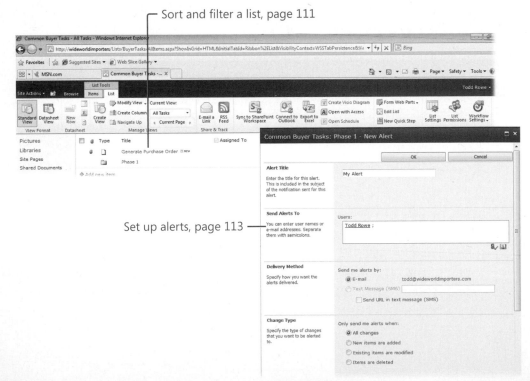

4 Working with Lists

In this chapter, you will learn how to

- ✔ Discover default lists in a site.
- ✔ Create a new list.
- ✔ Add and edit list items.
- ✔ Delete and restore a list item.
- ✔ Attach files to list items.
- ✔ Add, edit, and delete list columns.
- ✔ Add summary tasks to a Task list.
- ✔ Sort and filter a list.
- ✔ Set up alerts.

You can think of the *lists* found in Microsoft SharePoint Foundation 2010 as spreadsheets that you and your coworkers can use simultaneously on the Internet. SharePoint lists represent editable, web-based tables that facilitate concurrent, multi-user interactions against a common, centralized, extensible set of columns and rows. They empower you to provision your own repositories of structured information in which *list items* behave like rows consisting of self-labeled *columns*. All the web pages needed to create, review, update, delete, and manage a list and its data are generated automatically and dynamically by SharePoint Foundation.

Tip Unstructured information is typically stored as a document with associated columns in a document library. The document library can be thought of as a list of documents. Document libraries are discussed at length in Chapter 5, "Working with Libraries," and Chapter 8, "Working with Library Settings."

In this chapter, you will discover the default lists that already exist on your site, create new lists, and alter existing lists. Depending on the site that you initially create, some lists (such as Announcements, Events, and Links) may be provisioned when the site is created, and you need only begin using them. Yet, there will come a time when the lists that are provided automatically do not quite meet your needs. Therefore, this chapter explores web pages that allow you to not only alter existing lists, but also create your own custom lists.

See Also For more information on how to manage the SharePoint lists, refer to Chapter 7, "Working with List Settings."

Practice Files You don't need any practice files to complete the exercises in this chapter.

Important Remember to use your SharePoint site location in place of *http://wideworldimporters* in the following exercises.

Discovering Default Lists in a Site

Many default lists are included with SharePoint Foundation. When you need to create a list, you can use the default *list templates* to generate a new list with a static set of predefined columns by using More Options from the Site Actions menu. Later in this chapter, we'll explore how additional columns can be added and how most default columns can be altered or deleted, even after data have been entered into a list. There are many list and library templates built into SharePoint Foundation, which are described in the following table.

Icon	List Template	Site Type	Description
	Agenda	Meeting Workspace	Create an Agenda list when you want to outline the meeting topics, who will cover them, and how much time each presenter is allotted.
	Announcements	All	Create an Announcements list when you want a place to share news, status, and other short pieces of information.
	Attendees	Meeting Workspace	Create an Attendees list to track who will be attending the meeting.
	Calendar	All	Create a Calendar list when you want a calendar-based view of upcoming meetings, deadlines, and other events. You can share information between your Calendar list and Microsoft Outlook.
	Categories	Blog Site	Create a Categories list to categorize blog posts.
	Circulations	Group Work Site	Create a Circulations list when you want publication and receipt publication to be sent to specific recipients. These lists contain many unique capabilities for distributing information to selected users.

Icon	List Template	Site Type	Description
	Comments	Blog Site	Create a Comments list to capture comments on blog posts.
	Contacts	All	Create a Contacts list when you want to manage information about people with whom your team works, such as customers and partners. You can share information between your Contacts list and Outlook.
	Custom List	All	Create a Custom list when you want to specify your own columns. This list opens as a web page and allows you to add or edit items one at a time.
	Custom List in Datasheet view	All	This is similar to a Custom list, but this list opens in a spreadsheet-like environment. It requires Microsoft Access on the client and ActiveX control support.
	Decisions	Meeting Workspace	Create a Decisions list when you want to keep track of decisions made at the meeting. Attendees and others can then review the results of the meeting.
	Directions	Social Meeting Workspace	Create a Directions list to capture directions to various locations for Social Meeting Workspace sites.
	Discussion Board	All	Create a discussion board when you want to provide a place for newsgroup-style discussion. Discussion boards have features for managing discussion threads and ensuring that only approved posts appear.
	Document Library	All	Create a document library when you have a collection of documents or other files that you want to share. Document libraries support features such as folders, versioning, and checkout.
	External Data	All	Create an External Data list to connect with external content types.
	Form Library	All	Create a form library when you have Extensible Markup Language (XML)–based business forms, such as status reports or purchase orders, that you want to manage. These libraries require an XML editor, such as InfoPath.

Icon	List Template	Site Type	Description
	Group Calendar	Group Work Site	Create a group calendar when you want to keep a group informed of upcoming meetings, deadlines, and other important events.
	Import Spreadsheet	All	Import a spreadsheet when you want to create a list that has the same columns and contents as an existing spreadsheet. Importing a spreadsheet requires Microsoft Excel.
	Issue Tracking	All	Create an Issue Tracking list when you want to manage a set of issues or problems. You can assign, prioritize, and follow the progress of issues from start to finish.
	Links	All	Create a Links list when you have links to web pages or other resources that you want to share.
	Objectives	Meeting Workspace	Create an Objectives list when you want to let your attendees know your goals for the meeting.
	Phone Call Memo	Group Work Site	Create a Phone Call Memo list to capture and store phone messages.
	Picture Library	All	Create a picture library when you have pictures you want to share. Picture libraries provide special features for managing and displaying pictures such as thumbnails, download options, and a slide show.
	Posts	Blog Site	Create a Posts list for a blog site to store all blog posts.
	Project Tasks	All	Create a Project Tasks list when you want a graphical view (such as a Gantt chart) of a group of work items that you or your team needs to complete. You can share information between your Project Tasks list and Outlook.
	Resources	Group Work Site	Create a Resources list to document shared assets. Users can reserve and track listed resources in the group calendar.
	Survey	All	Create a survey when you want to poll other website users. Surveys provide features that allow you to quickly create questions and define how users provide their answers.

Icon	List Template	Site Type	Description
	Tasks	All	Create a Task list when you want to track a group of work items that you or your team must complete.
	Text Box	Meeting Workspace	Create a text box when you want to insert custom text into the Meeting Workspace, such as instructions or motivational quotes.
	Things To Bring	Meeting Workspace	Create a list of things that attendees should bring to be prepared for the meeting, such as notebooks or handouts.
	Whereabouts	Group Work Site	Create a Whereabouts list to track the location of individuals throughout the day quickly and easily.
	Wiki Page Library	All	Create a wiki page library when you want to have an interconnected collection of wiki pages. Wiki page libraries support pictures, tables, hyperlinks, and wiki links.

As discussed in Chapter 3, "Creating and Managing Sites," SharePoint Foundation will provision some of these lists and libraries for you when you create a new site, depending on which site template you use. The SharePoint site templates provision lists as follows:

- The *Blank Site* template has no lists or document libraries.

- Both the *Team Site* template and *Document Workspace* template provision a Shared Documents library and four lists (Announcements, Calendar, Links, Tasks), as well as a Team Discussion board. We will discuss Document Workspaces in detail in Chapter 12, "Working with Workspaces and Blogs."

- The *Group Work Site* template provisions a Shared Documents library and eight lists (Announcements, Circulations, Group Calendar, Links, Phone Call Memo, Resources, Tasks, and Whereabouts), as well as a Team Discussion board.

- The *Blog Site* template provisions a picture library called Photos and five lists: Categories (Custom list), Comments (Custom list), Links, Other Blogs (Links list), and Posts (Custom list).

- The *Meeting Workspace* templates provision unique lists, such as Agenda, Attendees, Decisions, Objectives, and Things To Bring. We will discuss Meeting Workspaces in Chapter 12.

In the following exercise, you will first browse to the lists created for the top-level site. Subsequently, you will navigate to the Create page to see the list templates available when you create a new Team site.

 SET UP   Open a top-level SharePoint site. The exercise will use the *http://wideworldimporters* site, but you can use whatever site you wish. If prompted, type your user name and password, and click OK.

BE SURE TO verify that you have sufficient rights to create a list. If in doubt, see the Appendix at the back of this book.

1. On the Quick Launch, click **Lists** to display the **All Site Content** page in the **Lists** view.

This team site has four default lists (Announcements, Calendar, Links, and Tasks) and a discussion board called Team Discussion.

2. On the top of the page, click **Create**. On the **Create** page, under **Filter By**, click **List** to display list templates.

Tip Don't be confused by the naming convention here. The names of list templates are identical to the names of the default lists generated by SharePoint Foundation; however, they are radically different. Each list template shown on the Create page could be used to create one or more uniquely named instances in the All Site Content page. For example, the Announcements list template was used to create the Announcements list, but the resulting list could have been called something entirely different, such as Sales Notices. The names do not have to be identical.

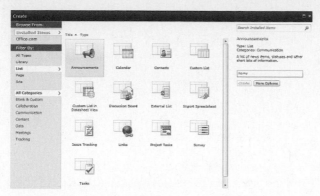

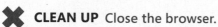

CLEAN UP Close the browser.

Tip Because the SharePoint Foundation pages are security-trimmed, you would see only the items on the Create page that you have permission to create.

Creating a New List

The first step in creating a new list is to ask yourself, "What kind of information do I want to gather/display?" The answer to this question will help you determine which list template to choose. Perhaps you want to start with a list that is close to your goal and then add, delete, and alter the default columns to provide the solution that you are trying to achieve. For example, if you are planning to collect information such as names and addresses, you can choose to use the Contacts list template to create your initial list and then modify it. Perhaps you want to start with a bare-bones list and build it entirely from scratch. In that case, you would likely choose to use the Custom List template to create your initial list.

Tip If the list items in the list that you want to create always begin with a document, consider using a document library instead of a list. Document libraries are discussed at length in Chapters 5 and 8.

In the following exercise, you will create a list for the buyers at Wide World Importers to track the status of tasks involved in the buying process. This Task list will be based on the Tasks list template. Once the list is created, you will alter the display name so that it displays "Common Buyer Tasks."

SET UP Open the SharePoint site where you would like to create the new list. The exercise will use the *http://wideworldimporters* site, but you can use whatever site you want. If prompted, type your user name and password, and click OK.

BE SURE TO verify that you have sufficient rights to create lists in this site. If in doubt, see the Appendix at the back of this book.

1. On the **Site Actions** menu at the top left of the page, click **More Options** to display the **Create** page.

2. On the **Create** page, under **Filter By**, click **List**, and then, in the middle pane, click **Tasks**.

3. Click **More Options** on the far-right side. The Create dialog changes to display information to create the Task list.

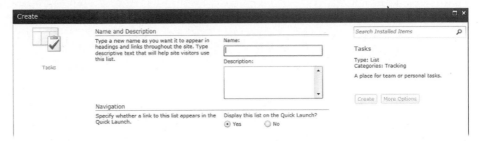

You will use this page to create a Task list based on the Tasks list template. You can name your new Task list anything you want.

Tip There is no restriction on the number of copies of any list that you can create in a site. You can create as many Task lists as you like.

4. In the **Name** text box, type **BuyerTasks** to establish a display name for the new list.

Because there is no text box with which to provide the Uniform Resource Locator (URL) name, this text box also supplies the value that SharePoint Foundation uses for the internal names.

Important When you initially create a list in SharePoint Foundation, you are establishing two name values: the display name, usually labeled Name or Title, and the URL name, also known as the internal name. However, only the display name can be changed after the list is created. When the URL name cannot be set on a SharePoint Foundation Create page, the display name (usually labeled Title) is used to populate both names.

Tip Best practices to follow when initially naming a list in SharePoint Foundation include the following: The initial name should be descriptive, intuitive, and easy to remember. The initial name should be concise. The initial name should not contain spaces. The initial name should be consistently used throughout the site. Your organization may also have specific naming conventions that you will want to follow

See Also More details about these naming recommendations and the reasons they are needed can be found in the sidebar entitled "Naming a URL," in Chapter 3.

5. In the **Description** text box, type the description **List for tracking buyer process** to help users understand the purpose for the new list.

6. Check that the option indicating whether you want to see this new list on the Quick Launch is selected. This is a default setting.

Tip Meeting Workspaces are different. Because there isn't a Quick Launch on the home page, the Quick Launch option is not presented. Instead, there is an option to Share List Items Across All Meetings (Series Items)

7. Click **Create** to complete the list creation. The BuyerTasks default list view page (AllItems.aspx) is displayed.

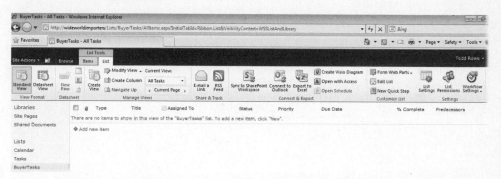

8. Go to the home page of the site by clicking **Navigate Up** and selecting your Team site. In our scenario, it is **Wide World Importers.**

The new BuyerTasks list is now showing in the Quick Launch.

Lists
Calendar
Tasks
BuyerTasks

Because this list was named without a space between Buyer and Tasks, it would be useful to change the display name so that it has a space in it. The remainder of this exercise demonstrates that revisions to the list name affect only the display name, not the URL name.

See Also For more information on configuring the lists, refer to Chapter 7.

9. On the Quick Launch, click **BuyerTasks** to redisplay the BuyerTasks default list view page.

List
Settings

10. On the **List Tools** group on the Ribbon, click the **List** tab, and then click **List Settings** in the **Settings** group.

11. In the **General Settings** area, click **Title, description and navigation** to display the **General Settings** page.

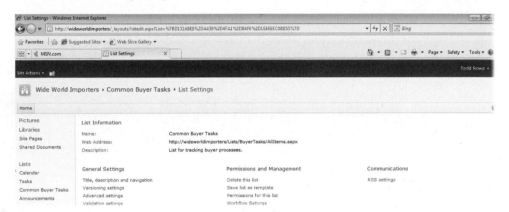

12. In the **Name and Description** area, in the **Name** box, replace the **BuyerTasks** name by typing **Common Buyer Tasks** (with spaces).

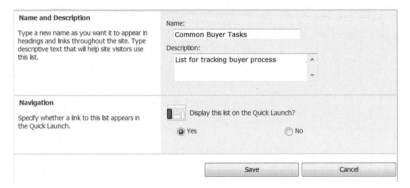

13. Click **Save** to save the change and display the **List Settings** page.

14. On the breadcrumb, click **Common Buyer Tasks** to navigate to the **Common Buyer Tasks** default list view page. The Quick Launch shows the new display name.

    The title on the tab on the top of this page and all other pages associated with this list now reflects the modified display name. However, you can see that the browser's address bar still reflects the initial name (internal name) given to this list.

    Tip Changing the name in the address bar requires Microsoft SharePoint Designer 2010 or Microsoft SharePoint Server 2010.

 CLEAN UP Leave the browser open if you are continuing to the next exercise.

Adding and Editing List Items

Creating a SharePoint list automatically generates the pages needed to view the list as a whole, view a list item, add a new list item, and edit an existing list item. The interface also provides options to delete a list item and subscribe to an *alert* for the list or list item, as well as other options, such as importing and exporting list items.

See Also Subscribing to an alert is covered later in this chapter, while importing and exporting of list items is covered in Chapter 14, "Using SharePoint Foundation with Excel 2010 and Access 2010."

While some lists have only a single view when initially created, multiple *list views* are generated when a new Task list is created. The Common Buyer Tasks list was created using the Tasks list template that has the following list views: All Tasks (default), Active Tasks, By Assigned To, By My Groups, Due Today, and My Tasks. All views are public, which means that they are available to anyone who looks at the list.

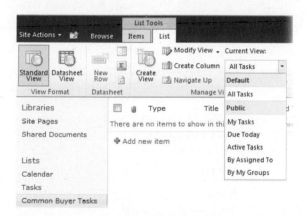

You can navigate to a list's default list view page by clicking the list's name in the Quick Launch or clicking the link at the top of any List View Web Part for that list.

In this exercise, you will add several Task list items for the buyers at Wide World Importers to use in their buying process and then edit one of the items.

SET UP Open the SharePoint site where you would like to modify the list, if it is not already open. The exercise will use the *http://wideworldimporters* site, but you can use whatever site you want. If prompted, type your user name and password, and click OK.

BE SURE TO verify that you have sufficient rights to modify this list. If in doubt, see the Appendix at the back of this book.

1. On the Quick Launch, click the **Common Buyer Tasks** list that you created in the last exercise to display the **Common Buyer Tasks** default list view page, if it is not already displayed.

2. Click **Add new item**. The **Common Buyer Tasks: New Item** dialog is displayed.

   Tip To add a new item to a list, you can also click the Items tab on the Ribbon, and then click New Item.

3. In the **Title** text box, type **Create vendor SharePoint list**.

4. Leave the default values for the **Priority**, **Status**, and **% Complete** fields.

5. In the **Description** text box, type **List for vendors to submit products offered this year**.

6. From the **Start Date** text box, delete today's date.

7. Leave the **Due Date** text box empty.

8. Click **Save** to save the list item and redisplay the **Common Buyer Tasks** default list view page.

The newly created list item shows in the body of the page. The green icon NEW displays to the right of the Title text, indicating that this list item was created recently.

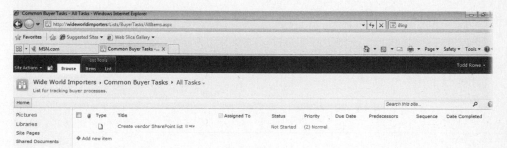

9. Using steps 2–8 as a guide, create four new list items using the values in the following table.

Title	Description
Ensure vendor access	Ensure vendor has access to add a list item for each product line offered
Identify products to purchase	Identify which vendor products to purchase
Generate purchase order	Use Microsoft Word mail merge to generate a purchase order from the filtered list
Notify Receiving about purchase	Notify Receiving about the anticipated arrival of vendor products

Tip When you need to create several items for a list, creating one item at a time can become tedious. It is possible to create multiple list items using a Datasheet view. This option is covered in detail in Chapter 9, "Working with List and Library Views."

Todd suggests that generating the purchase order should be changed to a high-priority task. You will now edit the Generate Purchase Order list item to implement this suggestion.

Edit
Item

10. Select the **Generate purchase order** list item by hovering your mouse over its title and then clicking the check box to the left of it. Then click the **Edit Item** button on the Ribbon.

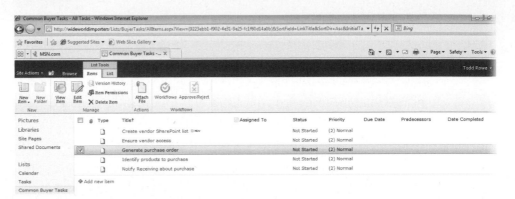

11. The **Common Buyer Tasks – Generate purchase order** page is displayed. Change the **Priority** field from **(2)Normal** to **(1)High**, and then click **Save** to save the change and redisplay the default list view page.

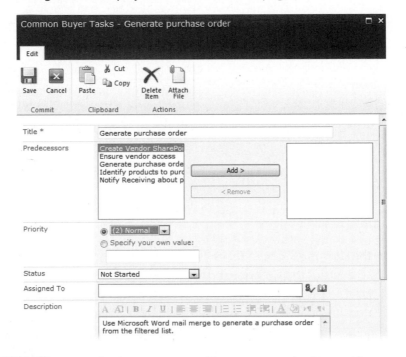

CLEAN UP Leave the browser open if you are continuing to the next exercise.

Deleting and Restoring a List Item

When documents, list items, folders, or even entire lists are deleted, they are simply flagged as removed so that they no longer appear in the site from which they were deleted. By default, sites in a SharePoint web application are configured to display the deleted item in the site's Recycle Bin for 30 days. If the user hasn't restored the deleted item in that time period, it is then permanently expunged from the database. If the user empties the Recycle Bin before the 30 days have elapsed, the deleted item is still available to a site collection administrator from the site collection's Recycle Bin. However, the total size of the deleted items must remain below a given percentage (50% by default) of the total size that a site is allowed to consume, which is called the *site quota*.

If a deleted item exceeds the configured size allowed by the SharePoint central administrator for sites in the web application, the items deleted first are purged, even if 30 days have not elapsed, to make room for the newly deleted item. In this way, SharePoint central administrators can make disaster recovery plans based on the Recycle Bin's allowable total maximum size. Of course, SharePoint central administrators can set the number of days that Recycle Bins retain deleted items, ranging from the default 30 days to some other specific number of days; they can also select to never retain deleted items or to never remove deleted items.

Todd suggests that creating the vendor SharePoint list is done only when a new vendor is established, rather than at each buying cycle. He therefore wants the task removed. In the next part of the exercise, you will delete the **Create vendor SharePoint list** task from the list.

 SET UP Open the SharePoint site where you would like to delete an item from the list. The exercise will use the *http://wideworldimporters* site, but you can use whatever site you want. If prompted, type your user name and password, and click OK.

BE SURE TO verify that you have sufficient rights to delete list items. If in doubt, see the Appendix at the back of this book.

 1. Open the **Common Buyer Tasks** list, if it is not already displayed. Click the check box to the left of the **Create vendor SharePoint list** list item to select it, and then click the **Delete Item** button on the **Items** tab on the Ribbon. You will be prompted to confirm the deletion.

   Once a list item is deleted, it is moved into the site's Recycle Bin.

   Todd realizes that the deletion of the **Create vendor SharePoint list** task that he just performed was a mistake. He visits the Recycle Bin and restores the data.

2. In the left navigation area, click **Recycle Bin** to display the site **Recycle Bin** page.

	Type	Name	Original Location	Created By	Deleted↓	Size
☐		Create vendor SharePoint list	/Lists/BuyerTasks	Todd Rowe	11/14/2010 9:06 PM	< 1 KB

3. Click the check box to the left of the **Create vendor SharePoint list** to select it.

4. Click **Restore Selection** to restore the list item.

5. Click **OK** to confirm the restoration.

6. Go to the **Home** page of the site by clicking a link to it on the breadcrumb or top-link bar.

7. On the Quick Launch, click **Common Buyer Tasks** to display the **Common Buyer Tasks** default list view page.

The **Create vendor SharePoint list** item is once again visible in the list view.

 CLEAN UP Close the browser.

Attaching Files to List Items

Occasionally, you might want to attach one or more documents to a list item. By default, all lists in SharePoint Foundation allow attachments. However, if every list item always has one and only one document, reconsider the use of a list and opt for using a document library instead.

Tip It is possible to disable attachments to list items. To do this, choose List Settings from the Settings menu, click Advanced Settings, and finally select the Disabled option in the Attachments area. Refer to Chapter 8 for more information on how to configure list attachments.

In the following exercise, you will create a simple Word document to simulate a purchase order and attach it to an existing list item in the Common Buyer Tasks list.

SET UP Open the SharePoint site where you would like to attach a file to a list item. The exercise will use the *http://wideworldimporters* site, but you can use whatever site you want. If prompted, type your user name and password, and click OK.

BE SURE TO verify that you have sufficient rights to attach a file to a list item. If in doubt, see the Appendix at the back of this book.

1. Open **Microsoft Word**.

2. In the new document, type **Purchase Order**.

3. On the **File** tab, select the **Save As** option. Save the document to the **Documents** folder on your hard disk as **WideWorldPurchaseOrder.docx**.

   Tip You can save documents directly to a document library by specifying the HTTP location in place of the hard disk, such as *http://wideworldimporters/Shared Documents/.* Only saved documents can be attached to list items as attachments.

4. Close **Microsoft Word**.

5. In the browser, on the Quick Launch, click **Common Buyer Tasks**. The Common Buyer Tasks default list view page is displayed.

6. Select the **Generate purchase order** list item by clicking the check box to the left of it.

Attach
File

7. On the **Items** tab on the Ribbon, click **Attach File.**

8. Click **Browse. . .** and navigate to the **Documents** folder on your computer to locate the **WideWorldPurchaseOrder.docx** file that you created in steps 1–3.

9. Click **WideWorldPurchaseOrder.docx** and then click **Open**, or double-click the document to open it.

   Once chosen, the location of the selected document is displayed in the Name text box on the Attach File page.

   Important At this point, the document is associated with the list item only in memory. Closing the browser, for example, abandons the attachment. You must click OK to save the attachment's association with this task.

10. Click **OK** to attach the document to the list item. The default list view page is displayed. Each list item in the list that has one or more attachments will display with an attachment icon in the leftmost column.

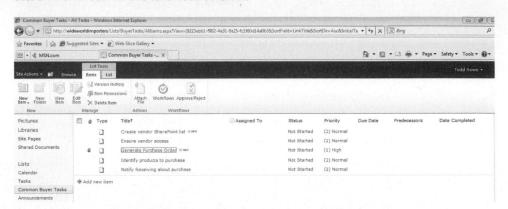

11. You will now verify that the document has been attached to the list item. Click the **Generate purchase order** list item. The **Common Buyer Tasks – Generate purchase order** page is displayed, and the attachment is listed at the bottom of the page.

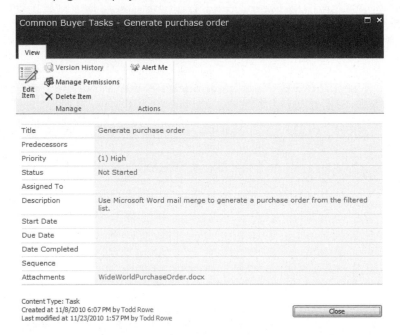

> **Tip** Multiple attachments are supported on each list item. You can click Attach File repeatedly and attach as many documents as you want. However, the interface supports attaching only a single document at a time.

12. Click **Close** to close the list item. The default list view page is displayed once again.

 CLEAN UP Leave the browser open if you are continuing to the next exercise.

Adding, Editing, and Deleting List Columns

The list templates provided by SharePoint Foundation provide an easy way to generate a list with very little effort. However, should you need to customize the templates, SharePoint Foundation allows you to add, edit, and delete columns.

There are many column types available when you want to extend a list with an additional column. Once you name your new column, you need to select one of the column types displayed in the following table.

> **Tip** Most, but not all, column types have both Required and Default value options. If Required is set to *true*, the user must enter a value into the column when creating or editing a list item. If the user doesn't enter a value, the Default value is used.

Because every column type has a Description option and an Add To Default View option, these options are not listed explicitly in the table.

Column Type	Used to	Options	Edit Using
Single Line Of Text	Enter a word or free-form phrase up to 255 characters.	• Required • Maximum Number Of Characters • Default Value	Single-line text box
Multiple Lines Of Text	Optionally, enter free-form prose, including formatted text.	• Required • Number Of Lines To Display (default 6) • Type Of Text • Allow Changes Or Append • Default Value	Multiple-line text box with toolbar to edit text
Choice	Select one or more options from the static list.	• Required • List Of Choices • Display Choices • Allow 'Fill-In' Choices • Default Value	Drop-down list, option buttons, or group of check boxes

Column Type	Used to	Options	Edit Using
Number	Enter a number.	<ul><li>Required</li><li>Minimum And Maximum Values</li><li>Number Of Decimals</li><li>Default Value</li><li>Show As Percentage</li></ul>	Single-line text box
Currency	Enter a monetary value.	<ul><li>Required</li><li>Minimum And Maximum Values</li><li>Number Of Decimals</li><li>Default Value</li><li>Currency Format</li></ul>	Single-line text box
Date And Time	Enter date, time of day, or both.	<ul><li>Required</li><li>Date Format</li><li>Default Value</li><li>Calculated Value</li></ul>	Date text box with pop-up calendar and drop-down lists for hours and minutes
Lookup	Select one list item from a list in the site.	<ul><li>Required</li><li>Get Information From</li><li>In This Column</li></ul>	Drop-down list
Yes/No	Enter **true** or **false.**	<ul><li>Default Value</li></ul>	Single check box
Person Or Group	Select one or more users.	<ul><li>Required</li><li>Allow Multiple Selections</li><li>Allow Selection Of People/Groups</li><li>Choose From All Users/SharePoint Group</li><li>Show Field</li></ul>	Text box with Check Names icon
Hyperlink Or Picture	Enter a link to a page or picture.	<ul><li>Required</li><li>Format URL As</li></ul>	Single-line text box
Calculated	Calculate information from columns on this list, columns on another list, dates, or numbers using standard mathematical operators.	<ul><li>Formula</li><li>The Data Type Returned From This Formula Is</li></ul>	Single-line text box
External Data	Pull data from an external content type.	<ul><li>Required</li><li>External Content Type</li><li>Field to be Shown in Column</li></ul>	Actions menu

After a column has been added, it is possible to make changes to it. You can change the display name, but the internal name cannot be changed easily. Most other column options can be changed even after data has already been entered into the list. If changing an option will potentially result in the loss of information, SharePoint Foundation prompts you to confirm the change before proceeding.

Tip You can also change a field from "not required" to "required" after data has already been entered into the list. The underlying data is not affected unless someone attempts to edit an existing record. The new Required rule is enforced, and the list item cannot be saved without providing a value in the Required column.

Most columns in the list can be deleted. However, all lists have at least one column that cannot be removed. For instance, the Title column can be renamed but not deleted. Certain lists also prevent the deletion of columns so that the list can display properly or integrate with the Microsoft Office suite properly. For example, the Assigned To, Status, and Category columns of any list based on the Issues list template cannot be deleted, and no default columns in any list based on the Calendar list template can be deleted.

Other columns that are created and populated automatically for each list item and cannot be changed include the following: ID, Created, Created By, Modified, and Modified By. The ID column ensures that the list item is unique in the list. It contains a sequential number beginning with 1 and increments by 1 for each new list item. SharePoint Foundation automatically captures when the list item was created, by whom it was created, when it was last modified, and by whom it was last modified. Initially, the Created and Modified columns are equal, as are the Created By and Modified By columns.

SharePoint Foundation allows for a special type of column to be added to the list called a *site column*. These columns are typically defined once by an administrator and represent a common set of data used across multiple lists. They are stored at the site level in a *site column gallery*, but the collective site columns in all the galleries in the current site's parentage can be used on a list or *content type* in this site. Thus, an administrator could define a site column in the top-level site for users in all sites in the site collection to use. Site columns provide several very valuable enhancements over regular list columns:

- Administrators can change site columns at any time, and the change can be pushed down to all content types and lists that have used that site column within a given site collection. If the site column changes, the changes will be pushed down and will override any changes that were made to the column at the site level.

- Because site columns define a common set of data, lists that contain multiple content types can sort, filter, and group the disparate list items using their common site columns.

In the following exercise, you will enhance the Common Buyer Tasks list by adding a Sequence column, adding a Date Completed site column, editing the Priority column to include an additional option, and deleting the % Complete column. Finally, you will change the order of the columns on the New, Display, and Edit pages to show the Description column immediately after the Title column.

 SET UP Open the SharePoint site where you would like to modify a list, if it is not already open. The exercise will use the *http://wideworldimporters* site, but you can use whatever site you want. If prompted, type your user name and password, and click OK.

BE SURE TO verify that you have sufficient rights to modify columns in this list. If in doubt, see the Appendix at the back of this book.

1. On the Quick Launch, click **Common Buyer Tasks** to display the **Common Buyer Tasks** list.

2. In the **List Tools** group on the Ribbon, click the **List** tab, and then click **List Settings**.

3. On the **List Settings** page, in the **Columns** section, scroll down and click **Create column** to display the **Create Column** page.

Columns

A column stores information about each item in the list. Because this list allows multiple content types, some column settings, such as whether information is required or optional for a column are now specified by the content type of the item. The following columns are currently available in this list:

Column (click to edit)	Type	Used in
% Complete	Number	Task, Summary Task
Assigned To	Person or Group	Task, Summary Task
Description	Multiple lines of text	Task, Summary Task
Due Date	Date and Time	Task, Summary Task
Predecessors	Lookup	Task, Summary Task
Priority	Choice	Task, Summary Task
Sequence	Number	Task, Summary Task
Start Date	Date and Time	Task, Summary Task
Status	Choice	Task, Summary Task
Task Group	Person or Group	
Title	Single line of text	Task, Summary Task
Created By	Person or Group	
Modified By	Person or Group	

Create column
Add from existing site columns
Indexed columns

4. On the **Create Column** page, in the **Name and Type** section, in the **Column name** box, type **Sequence**.

5. In the list of column types, click **Number**.

6. In the **Additional Column Settings** section, in the **Description** text box, type **Used to order tasks**.

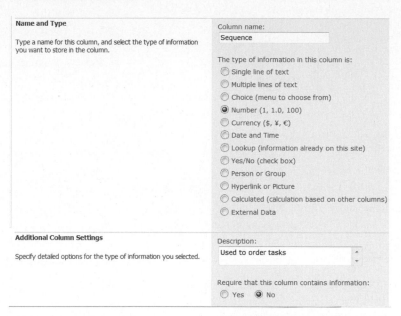

7. Leave the default values for the rest of the column's settings, and click **OK** to finish adding the **Sequence** column to the list. The **List Settings** page is displayed.

Todd Rowe would like to see a column added to track the date that each task is completed. You will now add the Date Completed column to the list.

8. On the **List Settings** page, in the **Columns** section, scroll down and click **Add from existing site columns**. The Add Columns from Site Columns page is displayed.

9. On the **Add Columns from Site Columns** page, open the **Select site columns from** drop-down list and click **Core Task and Issue Columns**, so that the list of available site columns shows only the task-oriented site columns.

10. Click **Date Completed** and then click **Add**, or simply double-click **Date Completed** to move it to the **Columns to add** list.

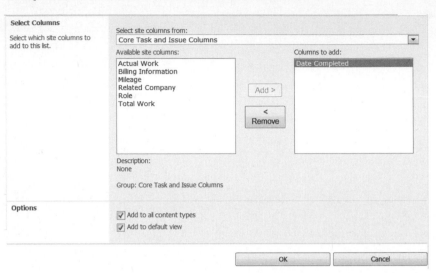

11. Click **OK** to add the column to the list. The **List Settings** page is displayed.

Some tasks are commonly very low on the Task list, and the buyers want to add an option to the Priority column to reflect this. They typically use Medium rather than Normal to rank their tasks, and they would like to allow people to type in priorities other than High, Medium, Low, or Very Low. You will now edit the setting for the existing Priority column.

12. On the **List Settings** page, in the **Columns** section, under **Column (click to edit)**, click **Priority** to edit the settings for the existing column. The **Change Column** page is displayed.

13. On the **Change Column** page, in the **Additional Column Settings** area, in the **Type each choice on a separate line** text box, type **(4) Very Low** as the last line to add another option to the drop-down list.

14. In the **Type each choice on a separate line** text box, type **(2) Medium** in the second line to replace the *(2) Normal* text. This will alter the options available in the Priority drop-down list during data entry.

Tip Any list items that previously had the (2) Normal option chosen need to be changed manually to the new option, (2) Medium. Also, when leaving the Choice text box, the Default value changes to the first choice—(1) High, in this case. If you want the Default value to remain the second option, you must type **(2) Medium** into the Default value text box. For this exercise, you can use the default, (1) High.

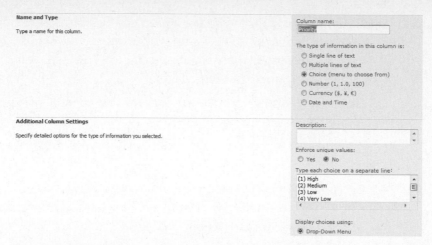

15. For the **Allow 'Fill-in' choices** option, select **Yes** to allow values that are not included in the column's list of choices to be entered.

    Tip If you want, you can choose to display the choices using Radio Buttons or Checkboxes. Choosing Checkboxes will allow multiple values to be selected.

16. Click **OK** to save changes to the **Priority** column. The **List Settings** page is displayed.

    The buyers don't plan to use the % Complete column, and it can therefore be deleted. In the next part of the exercise, you will delete this column from the list.

17. On the **List Settings** page, in the **Columns** section, click **% Complete**. The **Change Column** page is displayed.

18. At the bottom of the **Change Column** page, click **Delete** to initiate deletion of the **% Complete** column from the list. The deletion confirmation message box is displayed.

19. Click **OK** to finish deleting the **% Complete** column. The **List Settings** page is displayed.

    When creating or editing list items, the buyers would like to show the Description column immediately after the Title column. In the next part of the exercise, you will change the order of the columns in the list.

20. In the **Content Types** area, click the **Task** content type. On the **Task** list content type page, in the **Columns** area, scroll down and click **Column order**. The **Column Ordering** page is displayed.

21. In the **Column Order** section, to the right of the **Description** column, on the **Position from Top** drop-down list, select **2** to change the sequence of the fields displayed on the **New, Display,** and **Edit** pages so that the **Description** column comes immediately after the **Title** column.

22. Click **OK** to save the sequence change. The **Task** list content type page is displayed. The column has moved to the second position.

23. In the breadcrumb at the top of the page, click **Common Buyer Tasks** to navigate to the list.

24. Click the **Items** tab on the Ribbon, and then, in the **New** section, click the down arrow on the **New Item** button. Select **Task** from the drop-down menu to display the **Common Buyer Tasks – New Item** page.

25. On the **Common Buyer Tasks – New Item** page, verify that the order of the fields has changed so that the **Description** field comes second, immediately after the **Title** field.

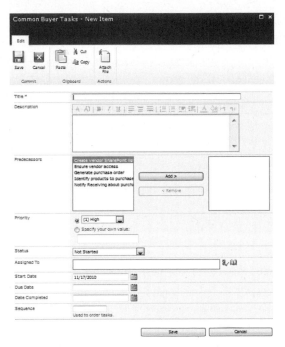

26. Click **Cancel** on the **Common Buyer Tasks – New Item** page to close it and return to the list.

CLEAN UP Leave the browser open if you are continuing to the next exercise.

Adding Summary Tasks to a Task List

When creating tasks in a Project Tasks list, it's important to plan which tasks might fall under larger tasks. For example, your project might be completed in phases, with several tasks occurring within each phase. Having the phases represented in your Project Tasks list provides a useful, high-level look at what's going on in your project.

In this exercise, you will create a summary task for Phase 1 of the project.

SET UP Open the SharePoint site where you would like to create the summary task, if it is not already open. The exercise will use the *http://wideworldimporters* site, but you can use whatever site you want. If prompted, type your user name and password, and click OK.

BE SURE TO verify that you have sufficient rights to create list items. If in doubt, see the Appendix at the back of this book.

1. On the Quick Launch, click **Common Buyer Tasks** to display the **Common Buyer Tasks** list, if it is not already displayed.

2. On the **Items** tab, in the **New** group, click the down arrow on the **New Item** button, and then click **Summary Task**.

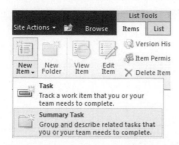

You will now complete the form to create the new summary task.

3. On the **New Item** page, type **Phase 1** as the name of the summary task.

4. Do not select any **Predecessors** for this summary task.

    Tip If you're unsure of your understanding of predecessors, or if you aren't far enough along in your planning to have all the summary task's predecessors added to your Project Tasks list, you can leave this blank for now and add predecessor relationships later.

5. Select the priority of **(1) High**.

6. Choose the descriptor that most accurately reflects the status of the set of tasks that fall within this summary task. If you are just planning a project and none of the tasks in this summary task have begun, choose **Not Started**.

7. Type a percentage that best represents how much work is completed on the set of tasks that fall within the summary task. If you are just planning a project and none of the tasks in this summary task have begun, leave this field blank or type **0%**. Do not assign anyone to this summary task.

8. Type a brief description of this summary task, such as **The following tasks will be associated with Phase 1 of this project**.

9. Enter the date when the first subtask within this summary task should begin. For example, enter today's date.

10. Enter the date by when the last subtask in this summary task should be completed. Do not enter a due date for the summary task.

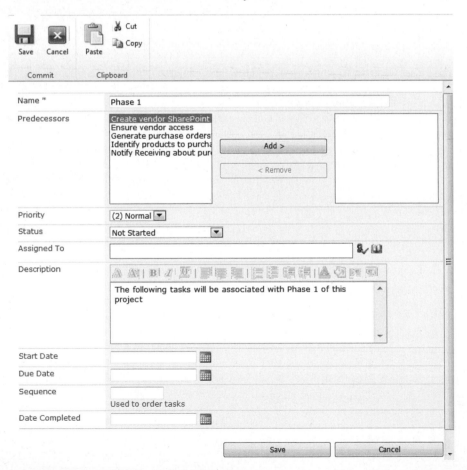

11. Click **Save** to create the summary task.

Once the summary task is created, you can click the title of the summary task in the list page to open the summary task page. On that page, you can add the tasks that fall within that summary task. To get back to the page that lists your summary task, on the List tab, in the Manage Views group on the Ribbon, click Navigate Up.

 CLEAN UP Leave the browser open if you are continuing to the next exercise.

Sorting and Filtering a List

As the list grows, it eventually becomes difficult to see the entire list on a single page. To this end, SharePoint Foundation provides built-in sorting and filtering capabilities. On any standard list view page, individual column headers can be used to sort the entire list alphabetically, by ascending or descending order.

Filtering on the list page works similarly to the way that an AutoFilter works in Excel. Filtering is enabled on the upper-right corner of every column, and a unique list of the values for each column is generated and presented as a drop-down list above that column. Filters are cumulative but temporal; the next time a list view is chosen, its settings, including filters, will be applied to the list, regardless of what was previously chosen for a given column.

Tip In Datasheet view, sorting and filtering are available from the drop-down arrow, which is also located on the upper-right corner of every column.

In this exercise, you will sort and filter the Common Buyer Tasks list.

 SET UP Open the SharePoint site where you would like to filter the list, if it is not already open. The exercise will use the *http://wideworldimporters* site, but you can use whatever site you want. If prompted, type your user name and password, and click OK.

BE SURE TO verify that you have sufficient rights to sort and filter lists. If in doubt, see the Appendix at the back of this book.

1. On the Quick Launch, click **Common Buyer Tasks** to display the **Common Buyer Tasks** page, if it is not already displayed.

2. You will now assign a sequence number to a list item. Select the **Ensure vendor access** list item by hovering your mouse over its title and clicking the check box that appears on the left.

Edit
Item

3. On the **Items** tab of the Ribbon, in the **Manage** group, click **Edit Item**.

4. At the bottom of the dialog, in the **Sequence** box, type **1**, and click **Save**.

5. Using steps 2–4 as a guide, edit other list items to add sequence numbers, as indicated in the following table.

Title	Sequence
Ensure vendor access	1
Notify Receiving about purchase	2
Identify products to purchase	3
Generate purchase order	4

6. In the list page, hover your mouse over the **Sequence** column heading. When the column heading is underlined, click the **Sequence** column heading. The list items are displayed in ascending numerical order sorted by this column, and a thin down-arrow icon displays to the right of the column name, indicating that the list is sorted by this column in ascending order.

7. Click the **Sequence** column heading again. The list items are displayed in descending order, and a thin up-arrow icon displays to the right of the column name.

Tip Clicking another column will abandon the sort on the current column. You must use a list view to sort more than one column.

8. Next, hover your mouse over the **Priority** column and click the down arrow that appears on the right to show the sorting and filtering options for this column.

9. On the menu, click **(1) High** for **Priority**, and the page redisplays the filtered list with only those list items that are set to High priority.

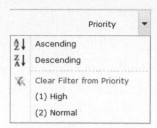

The Filtered icon displays to the right of each column that has an applied AutoFilter, such as Priority.

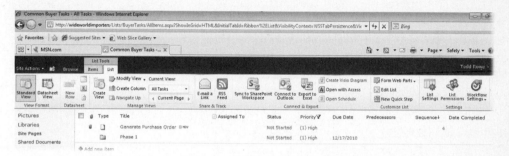

10. To display a full list, hover your mouse over the **Priority** column, click the down arrow to display a menu, and then click the **Clear Filter from Priority** option.

CLEAN UP Leave the browser open if you are continuing to the next exercise.

Setting up Alerts

SharePoint Foundation includes a handy feature that sends an email notification or a text message whenever changes are made to content in a site, including changes made to items in a list. The setup for this notification is called an *alert*. No alerts are set up automatically, so you must sign up for the alerts that you want.

Alerts are quite easy to set up. Every list in a SharePoint Foundation site displays an Alert Me option on the Ribbon. Clicking this option allows you to subscribe to a list-level alert. You also find a similar Alert Me option on the Ribbon when viewing any list item, as well as on the menu for each list item. This option allows you to subscribe to a list item–level alert.

Alerts specify to whom the alert will be sent and the kind of changes and frequency for which the alert will be sent. By default, the alert is sent to the email address of the user setting up the alert. If no email address has been established for the authenticated user, an email prompt is generated in the Send Alerts To area. Once provided, the address will be remembered for subsequent subscriptions.

When setting up alerts, you have a choice as to the type of change for which you want an alert to be initiated. List-level alerts allow subscriptions for All Changes To Any List Item, New Items Are Added Only, Existing Items Are Modified Only, or Items Are Deleted Only. If you want to see added and changed items but not deleted items, you need to set up two alerts. List item–level alerts, on the other hand, are fired only when that item changes because you can set up this alert only when the list item already exists, and a deletion is considered a change to the list item.

Tip Administrators of the SharePoint Foundation environment can establish quotas for the total number of alerts to which any user can subscribe. By default, this quota is set to 50. This number can be changed or even set to unlimited. Alerts can also be turned off entirely.

You must specify a filter concerning when to send alerts; the default is when anything in a list changes. Different lists have different filters. For example, the Task list that you are working with has the following filters:

- Anything changes
- A task is assigned to me
- A task becomes complete
- A high-priority task changes
- Someone else changes a task assigned to me
- Someone else changes a task
- Someone else changes a task created by me
- Someone else changes a task last modified by me
- Someone changes an item that appears in the following view (choose a list view)

You must also specify the alert frequency. Three choices exist for any type of alert:

- Send email immediately
- Send a daily summary
- Send a weekly summary

Choosing to receive an alert immediately actually queues the notice to be sent with the running of the next job after the alert is triggered. By default, the alert job runs every 5 minutes, but it could be configured by your administrator to wait as long as 59 minutes. The daily and weekly summaries store all changes made to the list or list item and send a summary at the end of the period chosen. By default, daily summary alerts are generated at midnight each night, and weekly summary alerts are generated at midnight every Sunday night.

Important Alerts must be deleted manually when users are removed from a site; otherwise, their alerts will be orphaned. Also, when users set up alerts for themselves, they will continue to receive them even when they are removed from access to the list. It is important to delete these alerts to prevent unauthorized users from accessing site and user information.

In this exercise, you will set up an alert for the list item in the Common Buyer Tasks list.

SET UP Open the SharePoint site where you would like to set up an alert, if it is not already open. The exercise will use the *http://wideworldimporters* site, but you can use whatever site you want. If prompted, type your user name and password, and click OK.

BE SURE TO verify that you have sufficient rights to set up alerts. If in doubt, see the Appendix at the back of this book.

1. On the Quick Launch, click **Common Buyer Tasks** to display the **Common Buyer Tasks** page, if it is not already displayed.

2. Select the **Phase 1** summary task by hovering your mouse over its title and clicking the check box that appears on the left.

Alert
Me ▾

3. On the **Items** tab of the Ribbon, in the **Share & Track** group, click **Alert Me**, and then select **Set alert on this item** from the drop-down menu.

   Tip For email alerts to be available, the SharePoint Farm administrator must configure the outgoing email settings for your server. Similarly, for the text alerts to be available, the SharePoint Farm administrator must configure the SMS/MMS service settings. Both settings can be configured using the E-mail and Text Messages settings in System Settings in SharePoint Central Administration. If these settings are not configured, the Alert Me button will not be available, and you will not be able to complete the exercise.

4. On the **New Alert** page, in the **Alert Title** section, type **My Alert**. Leave the other options unchanged and click **OK**.

The email alert has been set. You will now modify the list item to trigger an alert.

5. Using step 2 as a guide, select the **Phase 1** list item. On the **Items** tab of the Ribbon, click **Edit Item**.

6. On the **Phase 1** page, in the **Priority** field, select **3 (Low)**, and then click Save.

7. Open Outlook and verify that you have received two email messages. The first message indicates that an alert was created successfully. The second message is an email alert notifying you of a change in priority in this list item.

 **CLEAN UP** Close Outlook 2010 and then close the browser.

Key Points

- Lists are like editable, web-based tables.

- List templates can be used to generate a new list with a static set of default columns. SharePoint Foundation provides many prebuilt list templates

- Create lists in SharePoint Foundation by using descriptive, memorable, and consistent names.

- Deleted list items can be restored from the site Recycle Bin.

- One or more documents can be attached to a list item if you want.

- SharePoint Foundation allows you to add, edit, and delete the columns in any list.

- Summary tasks can be created in SharePoint Foundation Task lists.

- Lists can be sorted and filtered using the column headings.

- You can set up alerts to be notified about changes to the list and list items.

Chapter at a Glance

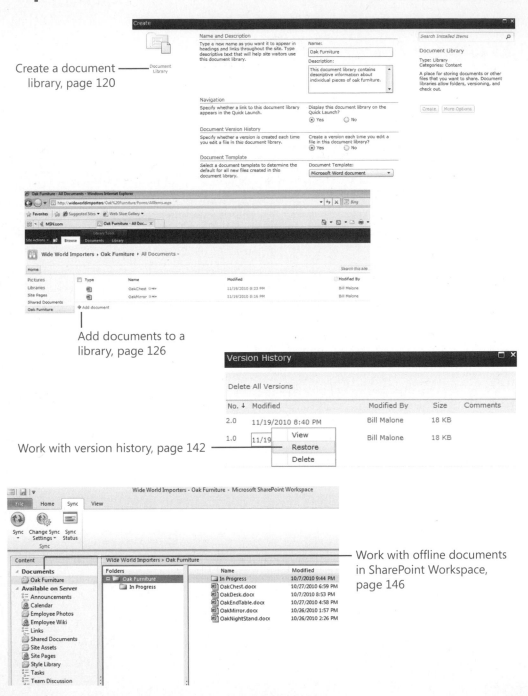

Create a document library, page 120

Add documents to a library, page 126

Work with version history, page 142

Work with offline documents in SharePoint Workspace, page 146

5 Working with Libraries

In this chapter, you will learn how to
- ✔ Create a document library.
- ✔ Create a new document.
- ✔ Edit documents.
- ✔ Add documents.
- ✔ Create a picture library and add pictures.
- ✔ Create a form library.
- ✔ Create a wiki page library.
- ✔ Create a new folder in a library.
- ✔ Check documents in and out.
- ✔ Work with version history.
- ✔ Use alerts.
- ✔ Delete and restore documents.
- ✔ Work offline with SharePoint Workspace.
- ✔ Work offline with Outlook.

One of the most useful features that Microsoft SharePoint Foundation 2010 provides is libraries. Libraries are a great place to store documents, pictures, forms, or web pages. In the business world, being able to work with documents quickly and effectively is of paramount importance. In the previous chapter, you learned that lists provide an effective way to work with all types of data. SharePoint libraries function similarly for documents and forms, such as Microsoft Word documents. Using Microsoft SharePoint document libraries, you can filter and group documents, as well as view metadata for documents stored in the library.

In this chapter, you will learn how to work with libraries and their documents in SharePoint Foundation 2010. This chapter focuses on creating libraries, adding documents and pictures, and working with documents in document libraries. In Chapter 8,

"Working with Library Settings," we will focus on modifying and configuring document libraries.

> **Practice Files** Before you can complete the exercises in this chapter, you need to download the Chapter 5 practice files from the book's catalog page to the following folder on your computer: Documents\Microsoft Press\SBS_SPF\Chapter05. See "Using the Practice Files" at the beginning of this book for more information.

Important Remember to use your SharePoint site location in place of *http://wideworldimporters* in the following exercises.

Creating a Document Library

A *library* is a location on a site where you can create, collect, update, and manage files with other team members. Each library displays a list of files and key information about the files, which helps people to use the files to work together. SharePoint's information managing capabilities come through the document libraries and lists.

You can use *document libraries* to store your documents on a SharePoint site rather than on your local computer's hard disk so that other employees can find and work with them more easily. Libraries are used to store files, whereas lists are used to store other types of content. Like lists, libraries contain metadata that allow you to filter, sort, and group items in the libraries easily.

When you create a new SharePoint site, a generic document library called Shared Documents is created. Because this library lacks a descriptive name, you should create new libraries for a particular business category or subject instead. In the examples used in this book, Bill Malone of Wide World Importers could create a document library for documents describing different types of art that the company carries, or one for company newsletters. You want to make sure that the name of a document library is descriptive and that each library has a specific topic to make it easier to find documents. Storing all documents together in the Shared Documents—or any other—document library defeats the purpose of using SharePoint sites to make information easier to locate.

In the following exercise, you will open your SharePoint site and create a new document library called Oak Furniture.

 SET UP Open the SharePoint site in which you would like to create your document library. The exercise will use the *http://wideworldimporters* site, but you can use whatever site you want. If prompted, type your user name and password, and click OK.

BE SURE TO verify that you have sufficient rights to create a library in this site. If in doubt, see the Appendix at the back of this book.

1. From the **Site Actions** menu, select **New Document Library**.

   Tip Alternatively, you can select More Options from the Site Actions menu. Then, in the left pane of the Create dialog, under Filter By, click Library. Make sure the Document Library is selected, and then click More Options.

2. The **Create** dialog opens and displays the options for your new library. In the **Name** box, type the name that you want to give to the new document library, such as **Oak Furniture**.

3. In the **Description** box, type the description of the document library, such as **This document library contains descriptive information about individual pieces of oak furniture.**

4. In the **Document Version History** area, under **Create a version each time you edit a file in this document library?**, click **Yes**.

   Leave all other options on the page at their default settings. You have entered all the necessary information to create a document library.

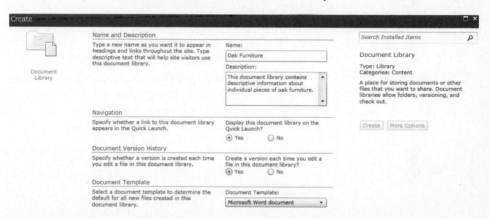

5. Click **Create**. The new Oak Furniture document library has been created and is displayed in the browser. The link to this library is shown on the Quick Launch.

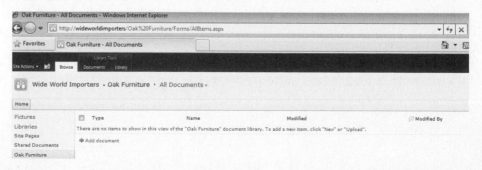

 CLEAN UP Leave the browser open if you are continuing to the next exercise.

Creating a New Document

After a library has been created, you can populate it with documents. In this section, you will create a new document from the SharePoint document library. The new document will use the default template for the library.

See Also For more information about templates in document libraries, refer to Chapter 8.

The new document can be created in the Word 2010 client application that is installed on your computer, or in the online Word Web App using the browser.

Tip Microsoft Office Web Apps should be installed and configured on your SharePoint Foundation server to enable creating and editing documents in online Microsoft Word, Excel, or PowerPoint Web Apps. These Office Web Apps can be used from any device where a browser is available, but they have less functionality in comparison with associated client applications.

In the following exercise, you will create a new document from the SharePoint document library.

 SET UP Open the SharePoint site where you want to create a new document. If prompted, type your user name and password, and then click OK.

BE SURE TO verify that you have sufficient rights to create a document in this library. If in doubt, see the Appendix at the back of this book.

1. On the Quick Launch, click the **Oak Furniture** document library.

New
Document ▾

2. Click the **Documents** tab on the Ribbon, and then click **New Document**.

   Depending on your server settings, a new document will open either in the browser or in Word. If a new document opens in the browser, skip to step 7. Otherwise, continue to the next step.

3. A new document opens in Word. It is based on the default template for this SharePoint library called template.dotx. If a warning about this template appears in the Open Document message box, click OK to confirm that you want to proceed with opening a new file based on this template.

4. If prompted, provide your user name and password. Word opens. In the new document, type some text, such as **Oak Mirror**.

5. Click the File tab and then click Save to save the document to the Oak Furniture document library.

6. The Save As dialog box opens. Note that Location points to the Oak Furniture document library. Enter OakMirror as the name of your new document, and then click Save.

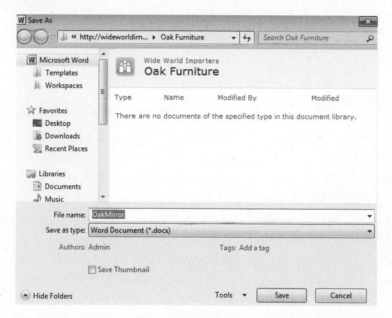

Go back to the browser where the Oak Furniture library is displayed, and then skip to step 9.

7. The browser opens an empty document based on the library's default template in the Word Web App. If prompted, provide your user name and password. The Word Web App interface is similar to Word's interface, and you can perform many light editing tasks in the Word Web App. In the new document, type some text, such as **Oak Mirror**.

8. Click the **File** tab and then click **Save** to save the document to the **Oak Furniture** document library. The Oak Furniture library is displayed.

9. Validate that OakMirror.docx is listed in the Oak Furniture library. There is a **New** flag next to the document, indicating that this document is a new addition to this library.

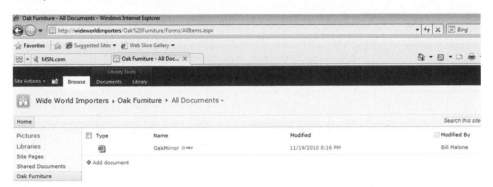

CLEAN UP Close the browser and then close Word.

Editing Documents

Once documents are placed in the library, you can search and filter them to make it easier to find what you are looking for, as well as collaborate with others to help develop the final version of the document. You will find at times that you have a need to edit a document in a SharePoint document library.

SharePoint allows you to edit documents in Office client applications, such as Word and Excel, or in the browser using Office Web Apps that provide online companions to Office client applications, such as Word Web App or Excel Web App. For in-browser editing to be available, Office Web Apps must be installed and configured on the SharePoint Foundation server.

In the following exercise, you will edit in Word the document called OakMirror.docx that was created in the previous exercise in the Oak Furniture library.

SET UP Open the SharePoint site where you'd like to edit a file in a document library. If prompted, type your user name and password, and then click OK.

BE SURE TO verify that you have sufficient rights to edit a document in this library. If in doubt, see the Appendix at the back of this book.

1. On the Quick Launch, click the **Oak Furniture** document library.

2. Hover your mouse over a document that you would like to edit, such as **OakMirror.docx**. An arrow appears to the right of the document name. Click the arrow to open a drop-down menu and select **Edit in Microsoft Word**.

3. The document opens in Word. If a warning about the template appears in the Open Document message box, click **OK** to confirm that you want to proceed.

4. In Word, make some changes to the document. For example, select the text "Oak Mirror" and make it bold and centered.

5. Click **File, Save** to save the document back to the **Oak Furniture** document library, and then click **Save** to confirm the file name.

6. Go back to the browser and validate that the document has been saved to the document library.

 CLEAN UP Close Word. Leave the browser open if you are continuing to the next exercise.

When you're on the move, it is often very useful to be able to edit your document within the browser, without needing the client application to be installed on the device that you're using. In the following exercise, you will modify the OakMirror.docx document using in-browser editing in the Word Web App.

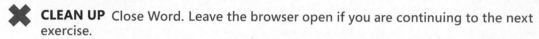 **SET UP** Open the SharePoint site where you'd like to edit a file in a document library, if it is not already open. If prompted, type your user name and password, and then click OK.

BE SURE TO verify that you have sufficient rights to edit a document in this library. If in doubt, see the Appendix at the back of this book.

1. On the Quick Launch, click the **Oak Furniture** document library.

2. Hover your mouse over a document that you would like to edit, such as **OakMirror.docx**. An arrow appears to the right of the document name. Click the arrow to open a drop-down menu and select **Edit in Browser**.

    Troubleshooting Office Web Apps must be installed and configured on your SharePoint Foundation server to enable in-browser editing. If the Edit In Browser option is not shown on the drop-down menu, it means that Office Web Apps have not been installed and activated in your environment. You will not be able to complete this exercise.

3. The document opens in the Word Web App in the browser. Make some changes to the document. For example, select the text "Oak Mirror" and make it italicized.

4. Click the **File** tab and then click **Save** to save the document back to the **Oak Furniture** document library.

5. Validate that the newly edited document has been saved to the document library by checking its time stamp.

 **CLEAN UP** Close the browser.

Adding Documents

Document libraries give you the ability to keep track of new versions of a document as it is modified and revert to older versions if necessary. First, you need to ensure that your documents are uploaded to and available in the SharePoint library.

There are several ways to add documents to a document library, including the following:

- Use the browser to upload documents to the library via the SharePoint interface.
- Use Windows Explorer to copy or move documents into the library.
- Use a SharePoint Workspace to upload the documents stored offline.

You can also add a document to an email-enabled document library by sending it as an attachment to an email.

In this section, you will practice the first two methods: using the browser and using Windows Explorer. Later in this chapter, you will use the SharePoint Workspace to add a document to the library as well. We will cover email-enabling a library in Chapter 8.

You will now add documents to the library using a browser. In the following exercise, you will upload two new furniture descriptions to the Oak Furniture library.

> **Practice Files** You will use the practice files OakDesk.docx and OakChest.docx, located in the Documents\Microsoft Press\SBS_SPF\Chapter05 folder.

 SET UP Open the SharePoint site where you'd like to upload a file to a document library. If prompted, type your user name and password, and then click OK.

BE SURE TO verify that you have sufficient rights to add a document in this library. If in doubt, see the Appendix at the back of this book.

1. On the Quick Launch, click the Oak Furniture document library.
2. In the Oak Furniture document library, click the Add document link. The Oak Furniture - Upload Document dialog appears.

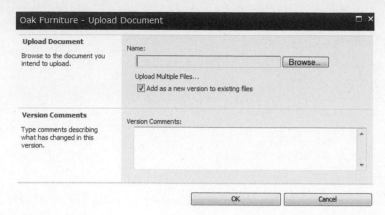

3. Click **Browse**.

   Tip To upload multiple documents from the same location at the same time, click Upload Multiple Files. In this exercise, you'll upload a single document.

4. In the **Choose File to Upload** dialog, browse to the file that you would like to upload, such as **OakChest.docx**, select it, and then click **Open**.

5. In the **Upload Document** dialog, type a comment in the **Version Comments** text box stating that this is a new document for this library, such as **Initial upload of new document**.

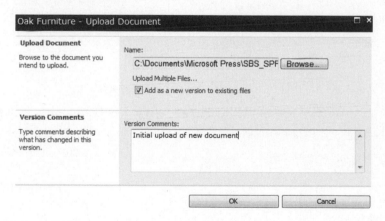

6. Click **OK** to confirm the upload and return to the **Oak Furniture** library.

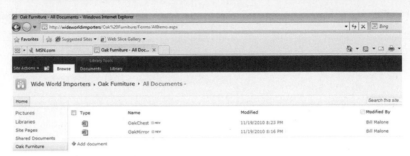

7. Repeat steps 2–6 for the **OakDesk.docx** file. You have added two documents to the library using the browser.

Another way to add a document to the library is via Windows Explorer. In the following exercise, you will copy a document to the SharePoint library by using the Explorer view of the Oak Furniture document library.

> **Practice Files** You will use the practice files OakEndTable.docx and OakNightStand.docx, located in the Documents\Microsoft Press\SBS_SPF\Chapter05 folder.

 SET UP Open the SharePoint site where you'd like to add files to a document library. If prompted, type your user name and password, and then click OK.

BE SURE TO verify that you have sufficient rights to add a document in this library. If in doubt, see the Appendix at the back of this book.

1. On the Quick Launch, click the **Oak Furniture** document library.

 2. Click the **Library** tab on the Ribbon and then click **Open with Explorer**. The library content is displayed in Explorer view.

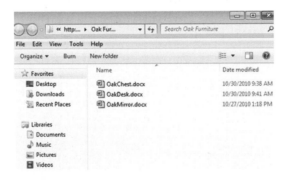

3. Open a new **Windows Explorer** window and navigate to the folder on the file system where the documents are stored that you want to copy to the library, such as Documents\Microsoft Press\SBS_SPF\Chapter05.

4. Select the files titled **OakNightStand.docx** and **OakEndTable.docx** by clicking the first file and then holding down the **CTRL** key and clicking the second file.

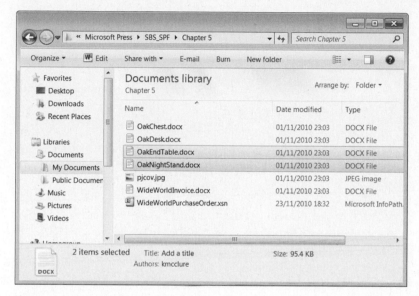

5. Right-click in **Windows Explorer** and select **Copy**, or press **CTRL+C** on the keyboard.

Tip You can also drag files between Windows Explorer and SharePoint library in Explorer view to copy them.

6. Go back to the **Explorer** view of the **Oak Furniture** library. In the **Explorer** window that shows files in the **Oak Furniture** library, right-click and select **Paste**, or press **CTRL+V** on the keyboard, to add the files to the library.

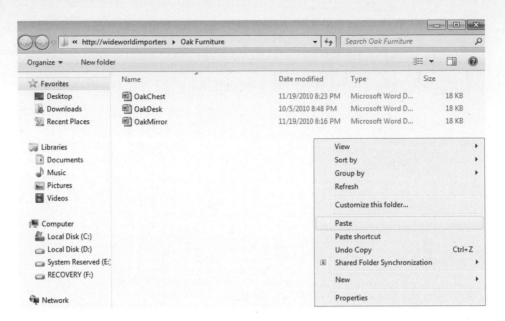

7. Go back to the browser where the **Oak Furniture** library is displayed and verify that **OakNightStand.docx** and **OakEndTable.docx** are shown. You might need to refresh the page to see the new files.

 CLEAN UP Close the browser and then close the two Windows Explorer windows.

Creating a Picture Library and Adding Pictures

A *picture library* is used to share a collection of pictures. Although picture files can be stored in other types of SharePoint libraries (such as document libraries), picture libraries are designed especially for storing image file types and therefore have several advantages. For example, from a picture library, you can view pictures in a slideshow, download pictures to your computer, and edit pictures with graphics programs that are compatible with SharePoint.

Picture libraries work in the same way as document libraries, except that they are geared to storing the image file types. The picture library provides special views for looking at all the pictures in the library as a slideshow. It also provides enhanced features for editing and downloading pictures by integrating with Microsoft Picture Manager.

In this exercise, you will create a picture library for storing photographs of employees.

SET UP Open the SharePoint site where you'd like to create a picture library. If prompted, type your user name and password, and then click OK.

BE SURE TO verify that you have sufficient rights to create a library in this site. If in doubt, see the Appendix at the back of this book.

1. On the **Site Actions** menu, click **More Options**.

2. In the **Create** dialog, in the left pane, under **Filter By**, click **Library**.

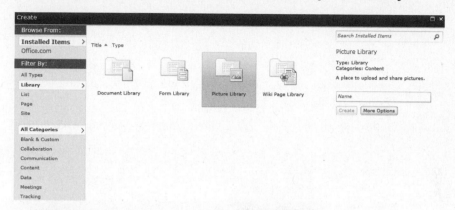

3. Select **Picture Library**, and then click **More Options**.

4. In the **Create** dialog, in the **Name** box, type **Employee Photos**.

5. In the **Description** box, type **Contains photographs of each employee**.

Leave all other options on the page at their default settings. You have entered all the necessary information to create a picture library.

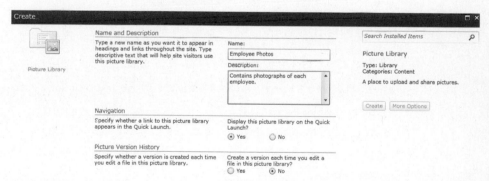

6. Click **Create**.

The picture library is created, and a new Employee Photos picture library is displayed in the browser.

After the new library has been created, you can add pictures to it. Adding pictures to a picture library is like adding documents to a document library. In the following exercise, you will add an employee picture to the Employee Photos document library using the browser.

> **Practice Files** You will use the practice file pjcov.jpg, located in the Documents\
> Microsoft Press\SBS_SPF\Chapter05 folder.

 SET UP Open the SharePoint site where you'd like to upload a picture to a picture library. If prompted, type your user name and password, and then click OK.

BE SURE TO verify that you have sufficient rights to add a picture to this library. If in doubt, see the Appendix at the back of this book.

1. On the Quick Launch, click the **Employees Photos** picture library. The Employee Photos picture library is displayed.

2. On the menu bar, click **Upload**, and then select **Upload Picture**.

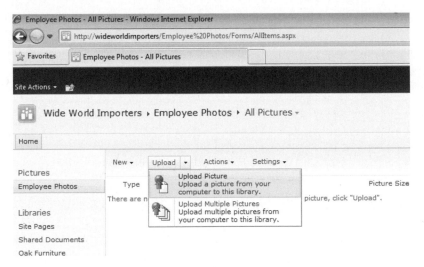

3. The **Employee Photos - Select Pictures:** dialog appears. Click **Browse**.

4. In the **Choose File to Upload** dialog, browse to the file that you would like to upload, such as **pjcov.jpg**, and then click **Open**.

5. Click **OK** to confirm the selection and upload of the picture. The Employee Photos: pjcov dialog appears.

   This page is used to provide metadata for the picture, including Name, Title, Date Picture Taken, Description, and Keywords.

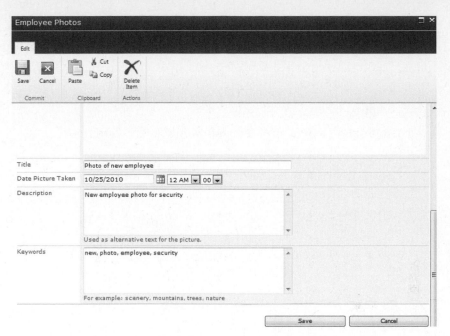

6. Fill in the metadata if needed (Title, Date Picture Taken, Description, and Keywords), and then click **Save**.

The picture has been uploaded, and you are taken back to the Employee Photos picture library.

 CLEAN UP Close the browser.

Creating a Form Library

Form libraries function similarly to document libraries, but they store specific types of documents—forms—and have enhanced integration with Microsoft InfoPath, such as allowing you to create form libraries from InfoPath. Chapter 15, "Using SharePoint Foundation with InfoPath 2010," discusses in detail how SharePoint Foundation and InfoPath work together.

Forms are a more structured type of information than documents. They contain a set of fields that are filled out in a uniform manner. Form libraries are excellent repositories for structured documents, such as purchase orders or vacation requests. To obtain the full benefit of form libraries, you must use InfoPath for designing and filling out forms.

The following exercise walks you through creating a new form library by using SharePoint Foundation. You will open the SharePoint site and create a new form library called Purchase Orders. You will then associate a Purchase Order form template with that library so that when someone fills out the form, they are presented with the standard Purchase Order form.

Note that this is a long series of steps to perform, so keep in mind that you will be accomplishing the following tasks:

● Creating a new form library

● Associating a new form template with the form library

● Setting this form template as the primary form that is invoked when the New Document command is invoked

> **Practice Files** You will use the practice file WideWorldPurchaseOrder.xsn, located in the Documents\Microsoft Press\SBS_SPF\Chapter05 folder.

  SET UP Open the SharePoint site where you'd like to create a form library. If prompted, type your user name and password, and then click OK.

BE SURE TO verify that you have sufficient rights to create a form library and modify a content type on this site. If in doubt, see the Appendix at the back of this book.

1. On the **Site Actions** menu, click **More Options** to display the list and library templates in the **Create** dialog.

2. In the left pane, under **Filter By**, click **Library**. Select **Form Library** and then click **More Options**.

3. In the **Name** box, type **Purchase Orders**.

4. In the **Description** box, type **Contains purchase orders**.

   You have now entered all the necessary information to create a form library.

5. Click **Create**.

   The form library is created, and you are taken to the new Purchase Orders form library page. At this point, if you click New Document on the Document tab on the Ribbon, you will be presented with a blank form. You still need to associate a necessary form template with the newly created library. To associate a form template with a form library, it is necessary to create a new content type as the default selection when the New Document button is clicked.

6. On the **Site Actions** menu, click **Site Settings**.

7. Under **Galleries**, click the **Site Content Types** link. The Site Content Types page appears.

8. On the top of the page, click **Create**.

9. On the **New Site Content Type** page, in the **Name** box, type **Purchase Order**.

10. From the **Select Parent Content Type From:** drop-down list, select **Document Content Types**.

11. From the **Parent Content Type:** drop-down list, select **Form**. Leave the rest of the page at the default settings.

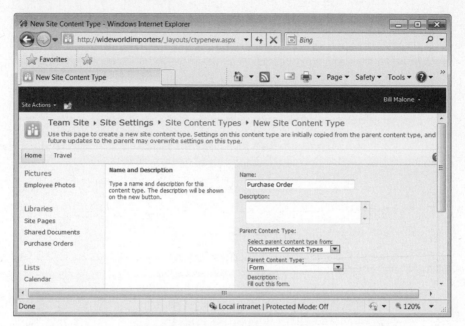

12. Click **OK**. The **Site Content Types-Purchase Orders** page appears.

13. Under **Settings**, click **Advanced Settings**.

14. Select the **Upload a New Document Template** option.

15. Click **Browse** and navigate to the new form template, such as **WideWorldPurchaseOrder.xsn**.

16. Click **Open** to upload the template.

17. On the **Site Content Types-Purchase Orders-Advanced Settings** page, click **OK**. You are taken to the **Site Content Type-Purchase Orders** page.

18. On the Quick Launch, click the **Purchase Orders** form library.

19. On the **Purchase Orders** library page, under **Library Tools,** click the **Library** tab on the Ribbon.

Library Settings

20. Click the **Library Settings** button on the Ribbon. The Purchase Orders-Form Library Settings page appears.

21. Under **General Settings**, click **Advanced Settings**. The Advanced Settings page appears.

22. In the **Content Types** area, under **Allow management of content types?**, select **Yes**.

23. Leave the rest of the page at the default settings, and then click **OK**.

24. On the **Purchase Orders-Form Library Settings** page, scroll down to the **Content Types** section. One content type, called Form, is associated with this form library.

25. Click **Add from existing site content types**. The Add Content Types page appears.

26. From the **Available Site Content Types** list, select the **Purchase Order** content type.

27. Click **Add**, and then click **OK**.

28. On the **Purchase Orders-Form Library Settings** page, in the **Content Types** section, click the **Change new button order and default content type** link.

29. On the **Position from Top** drop-down list, ensure that the **Purchase Order** content type is assigned the number one **(1)**, and then click **OK**.

30. On the Quick Launch, click **Purchase Orders**. On the **Purchase Orders** library page, click the **Documents** tab, and then click the **New Document** button on the Ribbon.

    This action invokes InfoPath 2010 (if it is installed on your computer), and the default Wide World Importers Purchase Order form appears.

✖ **CLEAN UP** Close the browser and InfoPath 2010.

Creating a Wiki Page Library

A *wiki* is a website containing wiki web pages that enable users to collect team knowledge, plan events, or work on projects together. Wikis are a way for many members of the community to come together and edit content collaboratively.

The very first wiki (pronounced *wee-kee*) site, WikiWikiWeb, was created for the Portland Pattern Repository in 1995 by Ward Cunningham, who devised a system that created web pages quickly and allowed users to create and edit web page content freely by using a web browser, as well as allowing users to create an interconnected collection of wiki pages. *Wiki* is the Hawaiian word for quick, and as Hawaiian words are doubled for emphasis, *wikiwiki* means very quick. WikiWikiWeb is the proper name of the concept, of which *wiki* and *wikis* are abbreviations.

Tip One wiki implementation is Wikipedia, from Wikimedia Foundation Inc. (*http://www.wikipedia.org*), which is an encyclopedia-like website that has inherited many of the nonencyclopedic properties of a wiki site.

Wiki page libraries can be created and used on any site in SharePoint Foundation 2010. We will look at creating wiki pages in detail in Chapter 6, "Working with Web Pages."

In the following exercise, you will create a wiki page library where employees can create and modify their own wiki pages.

 SET UP Open the SharePoint site where you'd like to create a wiki page library. If prompted, type your user name and password, and then click OK.

BE SURE TO verify that you have sufficient permissions to create a library on this site. If in doubt, see the Appendix at the back of this book.

1. On the **Site Actions** menu, click **More Options** to display the list and library templates in the **Create** dialog.

2. In the left pane, under **Filter By**, click **Library**.

3. Select **Wiki Page Library** and then click **More Options**. The Create dialog appears.

   Tip There is no restriction on the number of copies of any library type that you can create in a site. You can create as many wiki page libraries as you like.

4. In the **Name** box, type **Employee Wiki**.

5. In the **Description** box, type **Contains wiki pages created by company employees**.

   You have entered all the necessary information to create a wiki page library.

6. Click **Create**. Your new wiki page library has been created and is displayed in the browser.

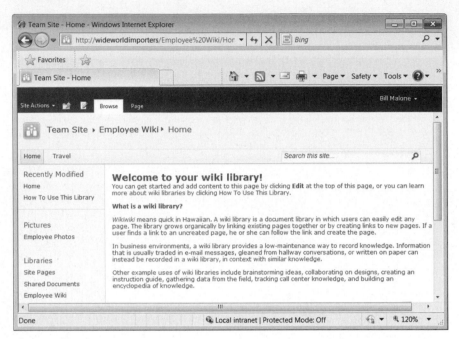

 CLEAN UP Close the browser.

Creating a New Folder in a Library

Using folders provides a common way to organize documents in an efficient way. SharePoint 2010 allows you to create folders in a library.

Tip SharePoint Foundation 2010 provides other mechanisms for organizing your documents, such as views and filters. However, people often are most familiar with folders, and thus they may find it easier to create a folder structure.

In this exercise, you will create a folder for documents classified as In Progress so that they can be differentiated from completed documents.

SET UP Open the SharePoint site where you'd like to add a folder to a document library. If prompted, type your user name and password, and then click OK.

BE SURE TO verify that you have sufficient permissions to create a folder in the document library. If in doubt, see the Appendix at the back of this book.

1. On the Quick Launch, click **Oak Furniture**. The Oak Furniture document library appears.

New
Folder

2. Click the **Document** tab on the Ribbon, and then click **New Folder**. The **New Folder** dialog appears.

3. In the **Name** box, type the name of the folder that you would like to create, such as **In Progress**.

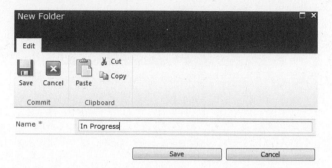

4. Click **Save**.

The updated Oak Furniture page appears, with the In Progress folder added to the page.

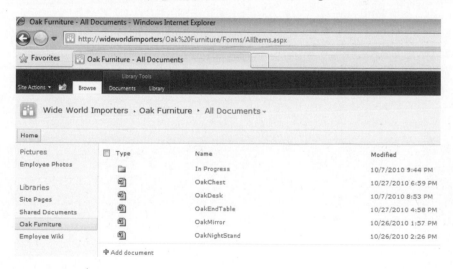

 CLEAN UP Close the browser.

Checking Documents In and Out

One of the features provided by SharePoint Foundation 2010 is basic document management. *Checking out* and *checking in* a document allows you to work on a document exclusively, while letting others know that you are editing this document so that they don't try to change it at the same time. When a document is checked out, other users will not be able to open this document for editing, so your changes will not get overwritten. When you are checking in a document, you can also enter comments about what you've changed that others can then view.

When you check out a file, you lock the file for editing to prevent other users from editing the file at the same time. When you have finished editing the file, you check the file back in, allowing other users to edit the file.

In the following exercise, you will check out a document from a document library, and then check it back in and change the comments to reflect that this is the final version of the document.

 SET UP Open the SharePoint site where you'd like to check in or check out a document. If prompted, type your user name and password, and then click OK.

BE SURE TO verify that you have sufficient permissions to the document library to check out and check in documents. If in doubt, see the Appendix at the back of this book.

1. On the Quick Launch, click **Oak Furniture**. The Oak Furniture document library appears.

2. Hover your mouse over a document that you would like to check out, such as **OakChest.docx**. A check box appears to the left of the document name. Click the check box to select the document.

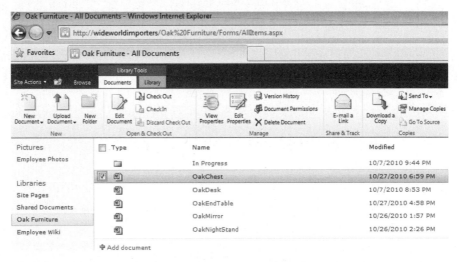

Check Out   3. Click **Check Out** on the **Documents** tab on the Ribbon.

4. Click **OK** in the confirmation message box that appears.

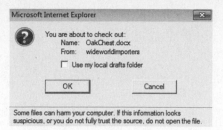

The document now has been checked out. The file icon in the Type column has changed and shows a green, downward-pointing arrow, indicating that the document is checked out.

Hover the mouse over this icon. A tooltip is displayed, showing who has checked out the document (you, in this case). This is useful to know when you want to edit a document that is checked out to another user. For example, you can contact that person and ask him or her to check the document back in.

See Also With appropriate permissions, it is possible to enforce the check-in of a document that has been checked out by another user. For more information, refer to Chapter 8.

When you have a document checked out, no one else can change it, and no one else can see the changes you've made while you have it checked out.

You will now check the document back in.

5. In the browser window, select the document **OakChest.docx** (see step 2 for instructions on doing that, if necessary).

Check In 6. Click **Check in** on the **Documents** tab on the Ribbon. The Check In dialog appears.

7. In the **Check In** dialog, in the **Comments** box, type **This is the final version of this document**.

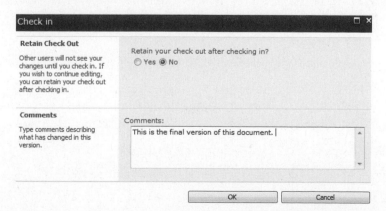

8. Click **OK** to check the document in and return to the **Oak Furniture** document library. The document now has been checked in, and its icon no longer shows a green arrow.

 **CLEAN UP** Close the browser.

Working with Version History

When *versioning* is enabled, SharePoint Foundation 2010 creates a separate copy of the document each time that it is edited. Although this takes up extra space on the server, it also makes it easy to revert to an older version of the document if necessary.

You can keep major versions only, or major and minor versions. Major versions have whole numbers such as 1, 2, 3, and so on. Minor versions have decimal numbers such as 1.1, 1.2, 1.3, and so on. A major version number is associated with a version that has been published (in other words, with the version that is available in the library). A minor version number is associated with a version that is in progress but is not yet published.

See Also A more in-depth discussion of versioning will be covered in Chapter 8.

When you view a document's version history, you see a list of the occasions when this document was edited and saved, as well as the author's comments on those changes.

In the following exercise, you will see what changes have been made to the OakChest.docx document and then revert to the final copy of the document.

 SET UP Open the SharePoint site where you'd like to see the version history for a document. If prompted, type your user name and password, and then click OK.

BE SURE TO verify that you have sufficient permissions to the document library to check out, modify, and check in documents. If in doubt, see the Appendix at the back of this book.

1. On the Quick Launch, click **Oak Furniture**. The Oak Furniture document library appears.

2. Hover your mouse over a document that you would like to check out, such as **OakChest.docx**. A check box appears to the left of the document name. Click the check box to select the document.

3. On the **Documents** tab on the Ribbon, click **Version History**.

You are taken to the Version History dialog, which shows the versions saved for the OakChest.docx page. Each version of the saved document, the date and time that version was created, and any comments for the version appear.

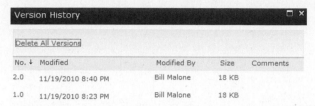

4. Hover the mouse over the time stamp in the **Modified** column that identifies an earlier version of the document, and then click the arrow that appears on the right of the time stamp.

5. On the drop-down menu, click **Restore**.

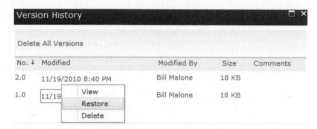

6. A message box appears, indicating that you are about to replace the current version with the selected version. Click **OK**.

Tip If minor versioning is enabled, then there is now an additional, unpublished version. SharePoint Foundation 2010 actually copies the version that you want to restore and makes it the newest minor version. If you want to publish this version, you need to do so manually, using the Publish button on the Ribbon.

 CLEAN UP Close the browser.

Using Alerts

One of the most difficult obstacles encountered in the business world is knowing when information changes. SharePoint Foundation 2010 can help address this problem by allowing you to subscribe to an *alert*. When a document to which you subscribe changes, you receive a message stating that the document has changed.

Alerts are a great way for users to be notified when a document is changed or deleted. Users can specify if they want to receive the alert notification via email or as a text message (SMS). Users can also specify if they want to be notified immediately or receive a summary alert on either a weekly or monthly basis.

For example, you (Bill Malone, in this example) may want to know when the OakChest.docx document is updated. In the following exercise, you will set up an alert for this document and then receive an alert via email that it has been changed.

 SET UP Your server has to be configured to send email messages. Otherwise, you will not be able to complete the steps in this exercise.

 SET UP Open the SharePoint site where you'd like to set up an alert on a document. If prompted, type your user name and password, and then click OK.

BE SURE TO verify that you have sufficient permissions to create alerts. If in doubt, see the Appendix at the back of this book.

1. On the Quick Launch, click **Oak Furniture**. The Oak Furniture document library appears.

View Properties

2. Select the document for which you would like an alert, such as **OakChest.docx**, by hovering the mouse over it and clicking the check box that appears to the left of the document. Click **View Properties** on the **Documents** tab on the Ribbon. The Oak Furniture - OakChest.docx dialog appears.

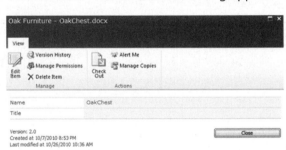

3. Click **Alert Me** in the **Actions** section.

4. The Oak Furniture: OakChest.docx - New Alert dialog appears. You are given several options about the frequency of alerts, as well as when you want to be alerted. Retain the default values for this exercise and click **OK**.

   Important If your server is not configured to send outgoing email, an error message will appear and you will be unable to complete step 4 of this exercise.

   You are returned to the Oak Furniture document library.

5. You will now modify the document, and then you will receive an alert that this document has been modified. Click the check box to the left of the **OakChest.docx** document to select it, and then, on the **Documents** tab on the Ribbon, click

Check Out, and then click **OK** in the message box that appears. Click the arrow to the right of the document name, and then select **Edit in Microsoft Word** from the drop-down menu.

6. The document opens in Word. If a warning about the template appears in the **Open Document** message box, click **OK** to confirm that you want to proceed.

7. Make some changes to the document. For example, make some text bold.

8. On the **File** tab, click **Save** to save the document back to the document library, and then click **Exit** to close Word.

9. Word prompts you to check in your document. Click **OK**.

10. Open Outlook. You should receive two email messages. The first message indicates that an alert was created successfully. The second message indicates that OakChest.docx has been modified.

 CLEAN UP Close the browser, and then close Outlook.

Deleting and Restoring Documents

Documents accumulate over time, and you eventually need to delete the ones that are no longer needed. In this exercise, you will delete a document that is no longer in use.

The *Recycle Bin* provides a safety net when deleting documents, document sets, list items, lists, folders, and files. When you or other site members delete any of these items, the items are placed in the Recycle Bin instead of immediately being deleted permanently. Items remain in the Recycle Bin until you decide to delete them permanently from your site or until the items are deleted permanently after a set number of days, which is based on a schedule defined in SharePoint Central Administration. The default is 30 days.

If you click Recycle Bin in the left navigation pane, you can see all the items that you have deleted from your site. You can either restore or delete each item from the Recycle Bin. When you delete an item from the site Recycle Bin, the item is sent to the Site Collection Recycle Bin. Note that to retrieve items from the Site Collection Recycle Bin, you must contact the Site Collection Administrator.

In the following exercise, you will delete a document from the Oak Furniture library and then restore it from the site Recycle Bin.

 SET UP Open the SharePoint site where you'd like to delete a document. If prompted, type your user name and password, and then click OK.

BE SURE TO verify that you have sufficient permissions to delete a document in the document library. If in doubt, see the Appendix at the back of this book.

1. On the Quick Launch, click **Oak Furniture**. The Oak Furniture document library appears.

2. Select the document that you would like to delete, such as **OakChest.docx**, by clicking the check box to the left of the document.

✕ Delete Document   3. On the **Documents** tab on the Ribbon, click **Delete Document**.

4. In the message box that asks whether you are sure that you want to delete the document, click **OK**. The document is deleted from the library and placed into the site Recycle Bin.

 Recycle Bin   5. To recover your document, click **Recycle Bin** in the left navigation pane.

6. In the Recycle Bin, select the **OakChest.docx** document by clicking the check box next to it, and then click the **Restore Selection** link. Click **OK** in the message box to confirm that you want to restore the document.

7. Go back to the **Oak Furniture** library and verify that the **OakChest.docx** document has been restored and is listed on the library page.

✖ **CLEAN UP** Close the browser.

Working Offline with SharePoint Workspace

For mobile users, it's not always possible or convenient to connect to SharePoint every time they want to read or modify a document. SharePoint Foundation 2010 provides the ability to work with documents offline. We will look into two ways of taking your documents offline. The first way is to synchronize your documents with a SharePoint Workspace. The second way is to copy the documents to your Outlook client.

SharePoint Workspace allows mobile users to download SharePoint content to their local machine to work offline. This can be either an entire SharePoint site or a subset of a site defined by the user. You can synchronize various lists and libraries from different sites to the same Workspace.

When working offline, you can view and modify the content in the same way that you can when working in SharePoint. When connected back to the network, you can synchronize your changes back to SharePoint, either automatically or manually.

SharePoint Workspace also includes additional functionality to help you keep track of documents, such as notification icons to show which documents you have read and which ones have been modified recently.

Tip There are limits on the number of files and the size of each SharePoint Workspace. Each Workspace is limited to approximately 500 files and a maximum size of 2 gigabytes (GB). You cannot store more than 1,800 files in all your SharePoint Workspaces.

In this exercise, you will create an account and then synchronize documents to a SharePoint Workspace. You need to create an account only once on the first use of the SharePoint Workspace with the server.

SET UP Open the SharePoint site that you want to synchronize to SharePoint Workspace. If prompted, type your user name and password, and then click OK.

BE SURE TO verify that you have sufficient permissions to synchronize to SharePoint Workspace. If in doubt, see the Appendix at the back of this book.

Sync to SharePoint Workspace

1. On the Quick Launch, click the **Oak Furniture** library. On the **Library** tab on the Ribbon, in the **Connect & Export** section, click **Sync to SharePoint Workspace**.

2. The Account Configuration Wizard is displayed.

   Tip If the Account Configuration Wizard does not open, an indicator will be flashing on the taskbar.

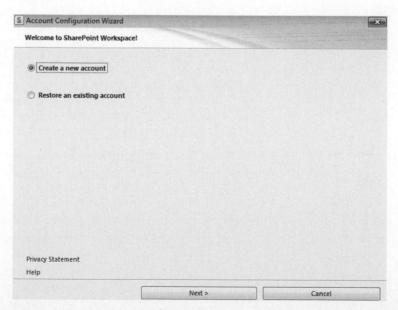

3. Leave the default option, **Create a new account**, selected and click **Next**.

4. Enter the appropriate information in the **Name** and **E-mail Address** boxes.

5. Click **Finish**. If prompted, provide your user name and password and then click **OK**. You will see the following dialog, indicating that the account is being created.

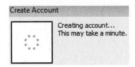

6. In the **Sync to SharePoint Workspace** message box that appears, click **OK**.

7. A dialog appears, indicating that the Workspace is ready. Steps that have been completed are shown with a green check mark. Items that are not supported for offline editing are shown with an exclamation mark. Items that are available but have not been selected for download do not show any mark next to them. Click **Open Workspace**.

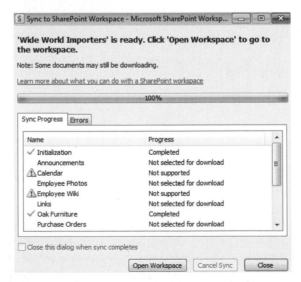

8. The Wide World Importers – Oak Furniture – Microsoft SharePoint Workspace window opens. You now have the Oak Furniture library and its contents available offline while you are not connected to the network. Click the **Oak Furniture** document library to see its contents.

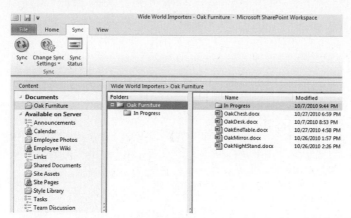

9. Note that all files and folders from the Oak Furniture library are synchronized to the SharePoint Workspace client, which holds copies of its documents on your local hard disk. You can repeat these steps to connect to other SharePoint sites and synchronize their libraries and lists into a common Workspace.

 CLEAN UP Close the browser, and then close SharePoint Workspace.

After documents have been modified offline, they need to be synchronized with the server. In this exercise, you will upload an offline document to the Oak Furniture document library using SharePoint Workspace. First, you will add the document to the library in the SharePoint Workspace, and then you will synchronize the library with the server.

> **Practice Files** You will use the practice file WideWorldInvoice.docx, located in the Documents\Microsoft Press\SBS_SPF\Chapter05 folder.

 SET UP Open the SharePoint site that you want to synchronize to SharePoint Workspace. If prompted, type your user name and password, and then click OK.

BE SURE TO verify that you have sufficient permissions to add a document to a library. If in doubt, see the Appendix at the back of this book

1. Open SharePoint Workspace by clicking the **Start** button on your computer, and then selecting **All Programs\Microsoft Office\Microsoft SharePoint Workspace 2010**.

2. The **Wide World Importers** site that you synchronized in the previous exercise is shown under **Read**.

3. Double-click **Wide World Importers** to open the content from this site that has been taken offline. The Oak Furniture library opens. Oak Furniture is currently the only library on the Wide World Importers site that you have synchronized to SharePoint Workplace, so it is the only library shown.

Add
Documents

4. Click the **Home** tab, and then click **Add Documents** on the Ribbon to add a new document to the Oak Furniture library in the SharePoint Workspace.

5. In the **Add Files** dialog, navigate to the location **C:\Documents\Microsoft_Press \SBS_SPF\Chapter05**.

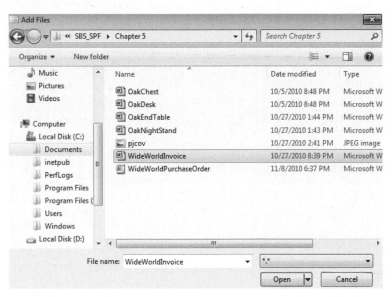

6. Select the document titled **WideWorldInvoice.docx**, and click **Open**. The document has been added to the Oak Furniture library in the SharePoint Workspace.

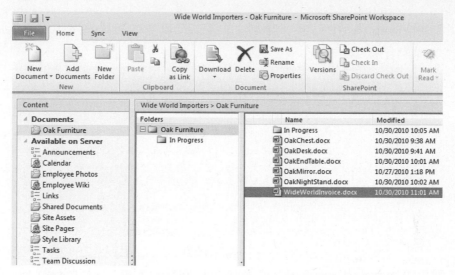

7. You will now synchronize the SharePoint Workspace with the SharePoint site. In the SharePoint Workspace, click the **Sync** tab on the Ribbon and then click **Sync Workspace**. The offline changes you made in the Oak Furniture library are synchronized with the live site.

8. In the browser, navigate to the **Oak Furniture** library and verify that the new file, **WideWorldInvoice.docx**, has been uploaded to the library on the SharePoint server.

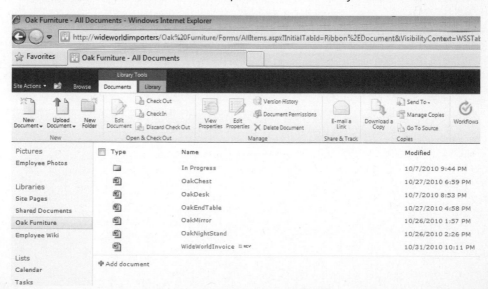

 CLEAN UP Close the browser, and then close SharePoint Workspace.

Working Offline with Outlook

Another method of taking your documents offline is by using an Outlook client. The documents are emailed to you as attachments and placed into the SharePoint list in Outlook.

 SET UP Open the SharePoint site where you'd like to copy documents offline. If prompted, type your user name and password, and then click OK.

BE SURE TO verify that you have sufficient permissions to the document library to check out, modify, and check in documents. If in doubt, see the Appendix at the back of this book.

In the following exercise, you will take documents offline by using Outlook.

1. On the Quick Launch, click the **Oak Furniture** library.

2. On the **Library** tab on the Ribbon, click **Connect to Outlook**.

3. A message box appears, asking whether you want to allow this website to open a program on your computer (Microsoft Outlook). Click **Allow**.

4. Outlook opens, and a SharePoint list is created in Outlook. The documents in the library are downloaded automatically into this new list as attachments to emails.

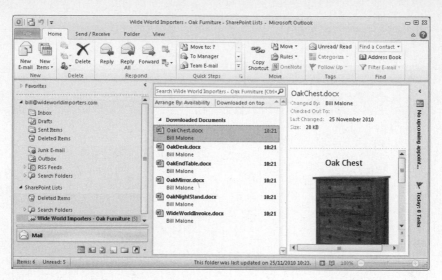

See Also For more information on SharePoint Foundation integration with Outlook, refer to Chapter 13, "Using SharePoint Foundation with Outlook 2010."

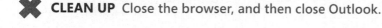 **CLEAN UP** Close the browser, and then close Outlook.

Key Points

- Libraries provide a central location to store documents, forms, and pictures so that they can be shared easily.

- You can create document libraries for specific topics and give them descriptive names.

- You can add existing documents to a document library in many ways, including by using the browser, using Windows Explorer, and using SharePoint Workspace.

- Remember to check out a document before you edit it.

- You can check in and check out documents by using Office suite applications.

- You can use versioning to manage the history of your documents in SharePoint.

- Set up alerts on documents when you want to know that a document has been changed or deleted.

- Deleted documents can be restored from the site Recycle Bin.

- You can take the documents in the SharePoint library offline in several ways, including using SharePoint Workspace and also Outlook.

Chapter at a Glance

Edit a page, page 156

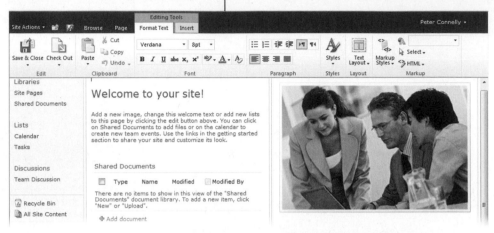

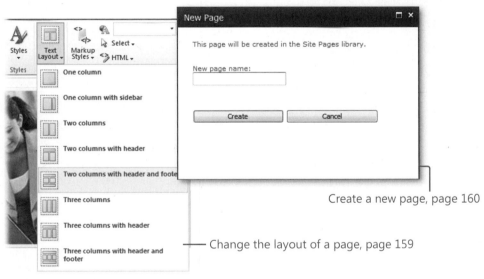

Create a new page, page 160

Change the layout of a page, page 159

Add a Web Part from the Web Part pane, page 168

6 Working with Web Pages

In Microsoft SharePoint Foundation 2010, a website is a collection of web pages. You will find this approach more natural than in Microsoft Windows SharePoint Services 3.0, where a site was seen as a container for list and library data and web pages were used to display data held in the lists and libraries. In Windows SharePoint Services 3.0, the addition of static text and images was possible only by adding the Content Editor Web Part.

In SharePoint Foundation, when you create a Team site, SharePoint creates a wiki page library, named Site Pages, where the web pages are stored and where the new pages can be created from the Site Actions menu. There are two types of web pages—wiki pages and Web Part pages. Wiki pages are the default pages at sites created from the Team, Blank, or Document Workspace site template. Both *wiki pages* and *Web Part pages* can contain Web Parts. *Web Parts* are reusable components that can contain any type of web-based information, including analytical, collaborative, and database information. Wiki pages consist of a mix of free-format static text and images in addition to Web Parts, whereas Web Part pages can contain only Web Parts. To include free-format static text or images on a Web Part page, you must use the Content Editor Web Part or the Image Web Part.

Both types of pages are flexible and highly customizable using three types of tools:

- A browser
- A SharePoint Foundation–compatible web page editing tool, such as Microsoft SharePoint Designer 2010
- A professional development tool such as Microsoft Visual Studio 2010

No one tool can do everything, and therefore it is likely that in any deployment of SharePoint Foundation, all three tools will be used at some point.

This chapter introduces the basic concepts of wiki pages, Web Part pages, and Web Parts. Using the browser, you will learn how to view wiki pages and Web Part pages in different ways, as well as how to change the appearance of these pages by adding and removing static text and images and adding and removing Web Parts.

> **Practice Files** Before you can complete the exercises in this chapter, you need to download the Chapter 6 practice files from the book's catalog page to the following folder on your computer: Documents\Microsoft Press\SBS_SPF\Chapter06. See "Using the Practice Files" at the beginning of this book for more information.

Important Remember to use your SharePoint site location in place of *http:// wideworldimporters* in the following exercises.

Editing a Page

On a Team site, blank site, or Document Workspace, the default web pages are wiki pages. They are stored in a SharePoint Foundation–based wiki library, named Site Pages.

The wiki library, Site Pages, inherits its permissions from the site. Therefore, anyone who is mapped to the Contribute permission level at the site level—that is, anyone who is a member of the site's Members SharePoint group—is allowed to change any wiki page or create new pages, which is known as "open editing." If a page is found to be incomplete or poorly organized, any member of the site can edit it as he or she sees fit. Therefore, as users share their information, knowledge, experience, ideas, and views, the content evolves. Site members can work together to change or update information without the need to send emails or attend meetings or conference calls. All users are allowed to control and check the content, because open editing relies on the assumption that most members of a collaboration site have good intentions.

When you edit a page, you should always check it out before you modify the content. This is to prevent other users in your team from editing the page at the same time.

Tip Wiki pages stored in a SharePoint Foundation–based wiki library can include static text, images, and Web Parts, without the need for Web Part zones.

In this exercise, you will edit the home page of a site.

> **Practice Files** You will use the practice file pjcov.jpg, located in the Documents\Microsoft Press\SBS_SPF\Chapter06 folder.

SET UP Open the SharePoint Team site where you would like to edit the home page. The exercise will use the *http://wideworldimporters* site, but you can use whatever site you want. If prompted, type your user name and password, and then click OK.

BE SURE TO verify that you have sufficient rights to edit the home page of this site. If in doubt, see the Appendix at the back of this book.

Edit

1. Click the **Edit** icon that is displayed to the left of the **Browse** tab.

   The Editing Tools ribbon tabs—Format Text and Insert—are displayed on the right side of the Page tab, and the Ribbon is displayed above the two wiki page content areas. The Edit icon that was displayed to the left of the Browse tab is replaced with the Save & Close icon.

 Check Out

2. On the **Format Text** tab, click **Check Out** in the **Edit** group.

   A notification message briefly appears below the Ribbon and to the right, displaying the text "Page Checked Out," and a yellow status bar appears below the Ribbon stating that the page is checked out and editable. On the Format Text tab, the Check Out command in the Edit group is replaced with the Check In command.

Status: Checked out and editable. | Page checked out

Tip The Status bar and notification area are new to SharePoint 2010. Both give you contextual information. The Status bar displays persistent information and uses four predefined background colors to identify the level of importance of the information. Very important information has a red background, important information has a yellow background, success information has a green background, and all other information has a blue background.

3. Place the cursor to the left of the **Welcome** title. Press **CTRL+A** to select all the content in the left content area of the page, and then press **DELETE**.

   The contents in the left area of the wiki page are deleted.

   Tip Other keyboard shortcuts can be found by placing the cursor above the commands on the Ribbon.

4. In the left content area, type **Welcome to the Financial team site**, and then press **ENTER** to move the cursor to a new line.

5. On the **Format Text** tab, click **Styles**, and then click **Normal**.

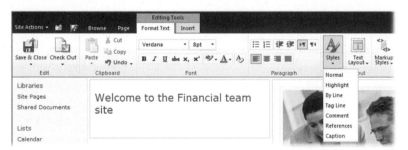

6. Type **This web site is used by members of the Wide World Importers Financial team and allows us to share content** and then press **ENTER**.

   Tip Start the home page of a Team site with an introduction that states its purpose. The first page in the Site Pages wiki library is labeled Home and should contain the context or any assumptions that will apply to all pages, as well as list or library content that is stored in the site. If you edit an existing wiki page, you should not place new content before the introduction, nor should the content necessarily be added to the bottom of the page. You should emphasize the flow of ideas, be concise, write factual information, and stay on topic for the page. Check for spelling and grammatical errors that can detract from the content. You might consider entering the text in Microsoft Word first, check it for spelling and grammar using the Spelling & Grammar feature of Word, and then paste it into the wiki content area.

Picture

7. Click the **Insert** tab, and then click **Picture** in the **Media** group.

   The Select Picture dialog opens.

8. Click **Browse**, and then navigate to the **Chapter06** practice file folder. Click **pjcov.jpg** and then click **Open**.

9. Leave the default library where the image will be uploaded to **Site Assets**, and then click **OK**.

   The Site Assets – pjcov.jpg dialog opens.

10. Click **Save** to upload the image and display the image on the page. The Design tab is displayed.

 11. On the **Format Text** tab, click **Check In** in the **Edit** group.

   The Check In dialog is displayed.

12. In the **Comments** box, type **Welcome message added to the page**, and then click **Continue**.

   The page is saved, the Editing Tools ribbon tabs disappear, and the Save & Close icon to the left of the Browse tab is replaced with the Edit icon. The Browse tab becomes the active tab.

✖ **CLEAN UP** Leave the browser open if you are continuing to the next exercise.

Changing the Layout of a Page

The home page of a Team site contains two content areas. You can change the number of content areas that a wiki page contains using the Format Text contextual ribbon and clicking the Text Layout command in the Layout group.

In this exercise, you will change the layout of your page.

➡ **SET UP** Open the SharePoint site that you used in the previous exercise, if it is not already open.

BE SURE TO verify that you have sufficient rights to edit the home page of this site. If in doubt, see the Appendix at the back of this book.

1. Click **Site Actions**, and then click **Edit Page**.

2. On the **Format Text** tab, click **Text Layout** in the **Layout** group, and then click **Two columns with header and footer**.

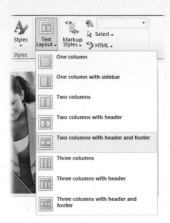

The page redisplays and now contains four content areas.

Cut

3. Select **Welcome to the Financial team site**, and then, on the **Format Text** tab, click **Cut**.

4. Place the cursor in the top content area, and then, on the **Format Text** tab, click the down arrow on the **Paste** command and click **Paste plaintext**.

Paste

5. On the **Format Text** tab, click **Save & Close** in the **Edit** group.

Save & Close

 CLEAN UP Leave the browser open if you are continuing to the next exercise.

Creating a New Page

Typically, pages are limited to no more than two or three screens of information. This enables the information on the page to be in an easily accessible and modifiable format. There are four methods that you can use to create a new page in a wiki page library:

- Create a forward link and then click it to create a page. This is the recommended method, because it is easier for people to find a page when another page is linked to it.

- The New Page command on the Site Actions menu.

- The All Pages view of the Site Pages library.

- The More Options command on the Site Actions menu.

In this exercise, you will create a wiki page by using these four methods.

SET UP Open the SharePoint site that you used in the previous exercise, if it is not already open.

BE SURE TO verify that you have sufficient rights to create a page in this site. If in doubt, see the Appendix at the back of this book.

Edit

1. Click the **Edit** icon that is displayed to the left of the **Browse** tab.

2. In the top content area, place the cursor on a new line under **Welcome** and type **WideWorldImporters are specialist importers of unique furniture ([[**

   A list of pages that exist in the Site Pages wiki library is displayed.

3. Type **B**.

   A message appears that the Item does not exist—that is, there is no page in the Site Pages library with a name starting with the letter *B*.

4. Type **edRoom]], [[OfficeFurniture]] and [[GardenFurniture]])** and then press **ENTER**.

5. Click **Save & Close**.

   The home page is displayed with the words "BedRoom," "OfficeFurniture," and "GardenFurniture" shown as hyperlinks and underlined with a dotted line. By using double brackets on the edit form, you have created three linked pages. Linked pages do not have to exist, and such nonexistent pages are denoted by a dotted underline, as is the case with "BedRoom," "OfficeFurniture," and "GardenFurniture."

Tip The naming convention for wiki pages, known as *WikiWords* or *WikiNames*, is to concatenate two or more words. Each word is composed of two or more letters, with no spaces between words. The first letter of each word is capitalized, and the remaining letters are lowercase. This formatting is known as *Camel case*. The wiki page name is used to form part of the Uniform Resource Locator (URL).

6. Click **BedRoom**. The New Page dialog is displayed.

7. Click **Create**.

The BedRoom page is displayed, and BedRoom appears in the list of Recently Modified pages in the left navigation pane.

8. Click **Site Actions**, and then click **New Page**.

The New Page dialog is displayed.

9. In the **New page name** box, type **KitchenFurniture** and then click **Create**.

The KitchenFurniture page is displayed, and KitchenFurniture appears in the list of Recently Modified pages in the left navigation pane.

View All
Pages

10. Click the **Page** tab, and then click **View All Pages** in the **Page Library** group. The Site Pages library is displayed in the All Pages view.

11. Click **Add new page**. The New Page dialog is displayed.

12. In the **New page name** box, type **Seating**, and then click **Create**.

The Seating page is displayed, and Seating appears under Recently Modified in the left navigation pane.

13. Click **Site Actions**, and then click **More Options**.

The Create dialog is displayed.

14. Under **Filter By**, click **Page**.

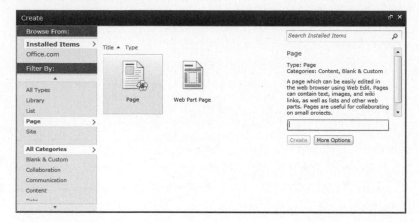

In the middle pane, the types of pages are shown—Page and Web Part Page, with Page selected.

15. Under **Page** in the right pane, type **FloorCoverings**, and then click **Create**.

The FloorCovering page is displayed, and FloorCoverings appears under Recently Modified in the left navigation pane.

✖ CLEAN UP Leave the browser open if you are continuing to the next exercise.

Adding Links

In the previous section, you created a forward link to a page yet to be created by enclosing the name of the page in double square brackets on the edit form. In the following exercise, you will create a link to a page and have the link display text that is different from the page name. You will then use the Incoming Links feature to identify those pages that link to a wiki page before you delete the page.

Tip When you add content to a wiki page and suggest a topic that other contributors to the Team site may know the answer to, try to enter text on the page in the form of a forward link; that is, place text between double square brackets. Other contributors to the page can enter information by clicking the forward link and creating new pages.

In this exercise, you will add a forward link.

SET UP Open the SharePoint site that you used in the previous exercise, if it is not already open. Be sure to complete the previous exercises in this chapter before beginning this exercise.

BE SURE TO verify that you have sufficient rights to edit the home page in this site. If in doubt, see the Appendix at the back of this book.

1. On the Quick Launch, under **Libraries**, click **Site Page**, and then, in the **Name** column, click **Home**. The home page of the Team site appears.

Edit

2. Click the **Edit** icon that is displayed to the left of the **Browse** tab.

3. Place the cursor on a new line below **WideWorldImporters**. Type **[[s**, and then press **TAB** to select **Seating**, and then type **| Seating Furniture]]**.

   Tip To display double open or closed square brackets without making a link, type a backslash before the two brackets, such as *[[* or *]]*.

4. Click **Close & Save**.

   The words "Seating Furniture" are not underlined with dashes; therefore, this forward link points to the existing Seating page that you created in the previous exercise.

5. Click **Seating Furniture**. The Seating page is displayed.

6. Click the **Page** tab, and then click **Incoming Links** in the **Page Actions** group. The pages that link to the Seating page are listed; the home page is the only one listed here.

7. Click **Home**, and then click the **Edit** icon that is displayed to the left of the **Browse** tab.

8. In the content area, select **[[Seating|Seating Furniture]]**, press **DELETE**, and then click **Save & Close**.

9. On the Quick Launch, under **Libraries**, click **Site Pages**, and then click **Seating**.

Delete Page

10. Click the **Page** tab, and then click **Delete Page** in the **Manage** group.

11. Click **OK** to send the page to the Recycle Bin.

> **Important** If you do not delete the forward links to a page before you delete the page, the forward links are displayed with a dashed underline, identifying them as forward links to a nonexistent page—that is, a page that has yet to be created.

 CLEAN UP Leave the browser open if you are continuing to the next exercise.

Working with Page History and Versions

A SharePoint Foundation–based wiki library has all the features of a document library, such as history and version management. Therefore, no amendments are lost. Major versioning is turned on by default when you create a wiki page library. You can also use content approval and workflow, as well as restrict the rights as to who can publish and edit pages.

In the following exercise, you will view the history of a page, observe the changes to the page, and then revert to the previous copy of the page.

SET UP Open the SharePoint site that you used in the previous exercise, if it is not already open. Be sure to complete the previous exercises in this chapter before beginning this exercise.

BE SURE TO verify that you have sufficient rights to manage pages in this site. If in doubt, see the Appendix at the back of this book.

Page
History

1. Click the **Page** tab, and then click **Page History** in the **Manage** group.

You are taken to the History page of the home page. In the content area, deletions have a strikethrough red font, and additions have a green background color. In the left navigation pane, each version of the page is listed with the date and time that the version was created.

2. In the left navigation pane, in the **Compare with version** list, select **4.0**.

   The current version of the page is compared with version 4.0 of the page.

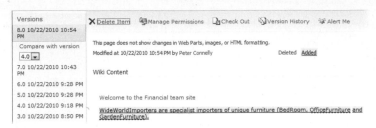

3. In the left navigation pane, under **Versions**, click **4.0**. The fourth version of the page is displayed.

4. Click **Restore this version**. A Message From Webpage dialog box appears.

5. Click **OK** to replace the current version of the wiki page with the selected version. The home page is displayed. A yellow status bar appears, stating that the current page has been customized from its template. This can occur when you restore a previous version of a page using the browser or when using a program such as SharePoint Designer 2010.

   See Also To learn more about customized pages, see Chapter 1, "Exploring SharePoint Designer 2010" in *Microsoft SharePoint Designer 2010 Step by Step* by Penelope Coventry (Microsoft Press, 2010).

6. On the status bar, click **Revert to template**. A Message From Webpage dialog box opens.

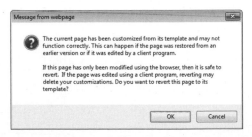

7. Click **OK** to revert the page to its template.

✖ **CLEAN UP** Leave the browser open if you are continuing to the next exercise.

Using Alerts

One of the most difficult obstacles encountered in the business world is knowing when information changes. SharePoint Foundation can help with this problem by enabling you to subscribe to an alert. When a web page to which you subscribe undergoes changes, you will receive an email message stating that the page has changed.

In the following exercise, you will set up an alert for a page and then receive an alert that it has been changed. You will then remove the alert.

➡ **SET UP** Open the SharePoint site you used in the previous exercise, if it is not already open.

BE SURE TO verify that you have sufficient rights to create alerts and edit the home page in this site. If in doubt, see the Appendix at the back of this book.

Alert
Me ▾

1. Click the **Page** tab. Click **Alert Me** in the **Share & Track** group, and then, from the drop-down list, click **Set an alert on this page**.

The Site Pages: Home.aspx – New Alert dialog appears. You are given several options on the frequency of alerts, as well as when to be alerted.

2. Retain the default values for this exercise and click **OK**.

Troubleshooting If your server is not configured to send an email message, an Error page will appear. If this page appears, you cannot complete the rest of the steps in this section. Check with your server administrator before you proceed.

You are returned to the home page of your Team site.

Edit

3. Click the **Edit** icon that is displayed to the left of the **Browse** tab.

4. Place the cursor in the content area to the left of the **Welcome** pane, press **CTRL+A** to select all the content in the top area, and then press **DELETE**.

The contents of the header area are deleted.

Tip Other keyboard shortcuts can be found by placing the cursor over the Ribbon commands on the Format Text tab.

5. Click **Save & Close**.

After a few minutes, you should receive two email messages. The first message indicates that an alert was successfully created. The second message indicates that home.aspx has been modified.

6. Click the **Page** tab. Click **Alert Me** in the **Share & Track** group, and then, from the drop-down list, click **Manage My Alerts**.

The My Alerts On This Site page is displayed.

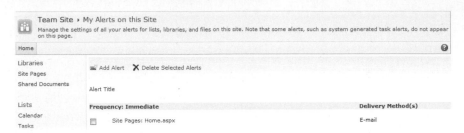

7. Click the check box to the left of **Site Pages: Home.aspx**, and then click **Delete Selected Alerts**.

8. Click **OK** to confirm the deletion of the selected alerts.

✖ CLEAN UP Leave the browser open if you are continuing to the next exercise.

Adding a Web Part from the Web Part Pane

As you customize your site, you might decide to add information other than static text and images. This information may be stored in lists or libraries or in some other data source. You can do this by adding Web Parts. You can insert Web Parts on multiple pages and also insert a Web Part multiple times on the same web page. SharePoint Foundation provides built-in Web Parts for each website created. Two types of Web Parts are most commonly used via the browser:

● **XSLT List View (XLV) Web Parts** Web Parts that display the contents of lists and libraries. These Web Parts are displayed in the Lists and Libraries category. Each time that data in the list or library changes, the changes are reflected in the XLV Web Part. SharePoint Foundation introduced this new version of the List View Web Part (LVWP), which uses Extensible Stylesheet Language Transformation (XSLT) to define how to display the data from lists or libraries.

● **Built-in Web Parts** Web Parts that display other content. There are 13 built-in Web Parts displayed in five categories.

The 13 built-in Web Parts available on websites created from the Team site, Blank site, or Document Workspace template are summarized in the following table.

Category	Web Part	Description
Content Rollup	Relevant Documents	Use this Web Part to display documents that are relevant to the current user. This Web Part generates a personalized view of documents checked out by, created by, or last modified by the current user. You can configure the Web Part to use more than one criterion. To improve the performance of the Relevant Documents Web Part in a large-scale document management environment, use Column indexing on the Modified By, Created By, or Checked Out By columns. Make sure that the Show Items From The Entire Site Collection check box is not selected when configuring the Web Part.
	XML Viewer	Use this Web Part for Extensible Markup Language (XML) with Extensible Stylesheet Language (XSL) to define how the XML is displayed. You might use the XML Web Part to display structured data from database tables or queries as well as XML-based documents.
Forms	HTML Form Web Part	Use this Web Part if you want to send data to another Web Part via a Web Part connection. The content displayed in the other Web Part depends on the data that it receives.
Media and Content	Content Editor	Use this Web Part to add content to a Web Part page such as formatted text, tables, and images. This Web Part allows you to add content by using a Rich Text Editor or HyperText Markup Language (HTML) source editor. The HTML *<FORM>* element is not allowed in the Content Editor Web Part. If you need to add a Web Part that uses the *<FORM>* element, consider using the Page Viewer or Form Web Part.
	Image Viewer	Use this Web Part to display pictures and photos. This Web Part is included by default on the home Web Part page of many sites to display a logo.
	Page Viewer	Use this Web Part to display the content of a linked resource such as a website, web pages, files, or folders. In this way, you can display an entire web page within a Web Part. The linked content is isolated from other content on the web page, and hence the content is displayed asynchronously from the rest of the page. This means that you can view and use other content in other Web Parts on the page even if the link in this Web Part happens to take a long time to return its content. Also use this Web Part if you want to retrieve data from a server that requires authentication.

Category	Web Part	Description
	Picture Library Slideshow Web Part	Use this Web Part to display a slideshow of images and photos from a picture library. The images can be displayed in a random or sequential order, which you can configure using the Web Part tool pane.
	Silverlight Web Part	Use this Web Part to display a Silverlight application. Silverlight applications can be created using Visual Studio 2010 or Microsoft Expression Blend.
Social Collaboration	Site Users	Use this Web Part to view a list of the site users and their online status.
	User Tasks	Use this Web Part to display tasks that are assigned to the current user.
	What's New	Available on sites created from the Group Work Site template. Use this Web Part to show new information from specified lists and libraries, where the [Modified] column is configured as an Indexed column.
	Whereabouts	Available on sites created from the Group Work Site template. Use this Web Part to display Whereabouts information.
SQL Server Reporting	SQL Server Reporting Services Report Viewer	Use this Web Part to view Microsoft SQL Server Reporting Services reports.

Tip In addition to built-in Web Parts, you can create your own Web Parts by using tools, such as SharePoint Designer and Visual Studio 2010. You can also import custom Web Parts.

SharePoint Designer allows you to add a Data Form Web Part (DFWP), also known as the Data View Web Part (DVWP). The DFWP is very similar to the XLV Web Part. Not only does it allow you to view data, but it can provide you with a form to enter data using XSLT. The DFWP can be used with a variety of data sources such as SQL Server databases, XML files, web and Representational State Transfer (REST) services, as well as data held in SharePoint lists and libraries. SharePoint Designer provides a "What You See Is What You Get" (WYSIWYG) XSLT editor to format the DFWP and XLV Web Parts. For example, you can create a DFWP or XLV Web Part that applies a style to a selected HTML tag or data values when the data meet specified criteria. If you use SharePoint Designer with the Furniture Sales list, you could highlight items when there are no units in stock.

In this exercise, you will customize the home page of a SharePoint site. You will add an XLV Web Part and restore a Web Part from the Web Part Page Gallery.

 SET UP Open a SharePoint site that contains a list with data, for example, the Furniture Price list that is created in Chapter 14, "Using SharePoint Foundation with Excel 2010 and Access 2010." Alternatively, you can create a practice site for this chapter based on the Chapter06_Starter.wsp site template located in the Documents \Microsoft Press\SBS_SPF\Chapter06 folder. See "Using the Practice Files" at the beginning of this book for more information.

BE SURE TO verify that you have sufficient rights to edit the home page in this site. If in doubt, see the Appendix at the back of this book.

Edit

1. Click the **Edit** icon that is displayed to the left of the **Browse** tab.

2. Place the cursor in the top content area, if it is not already there, and then click the **Insert** tab.

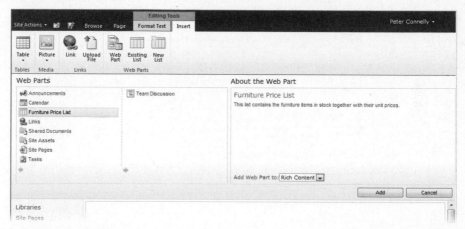

Existing
List

3. Click **Existing List** in the **Web Parts** group.

The Web Parts pane is displayed at the top of the page below the Ribbon. A Web Part for each list or library created for this site is displayed.

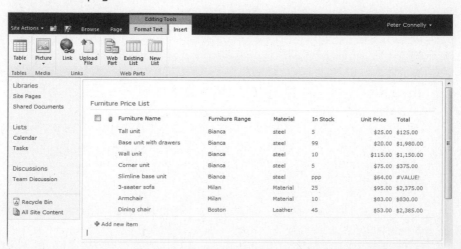

4. In the **Web Parts** pane, click the list that contains data, such as **Furniture Price List**, and then click **Add**.

A Loading dialog briefly appears, and then the Furniture Price List Web Part is added to the page.

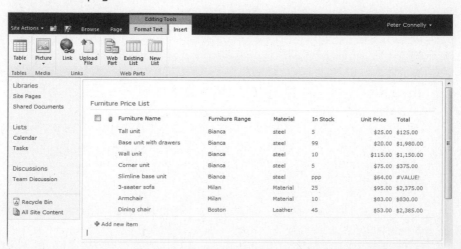

New List

5. Place the cursor in the top content area in front of the **Furniture Price List** Web Part, if it is not already there, and then, on the **Insert** tab, click **New List**.

   The Create List dialog appears.

6. In the **List Title** box, type **Financial Links**. Under **Tracking**, click **Links**, and then click **OK**.

   The Financial Links list is created, and a Financial Links Web Part is displayed on the page.

Web Part

7. Place the cursor in the top content area, if it is not already there, and then, on the **Insert** tab, click **Web Part**.

   The Web Parts pane is displayed at the top of the page below the Ribbon.

8. Under **Categories**, click **Media and Content**, and then, under **Web Parts**, click **Picture Library Slideshow Web Part**.

9. Click **Add**.

   The Picture Library Slideshow Web Part is placed above the Furniture Price List Web Part.

10. On the **Page** tab, click **Save & Close**.

✖ CLEAN UP Leave the browser open if you are continuing to the next exercise.

Removing a Web Part

When created, SharePoint sites can contain a number of libraries, lists, and one or more web pages that can contain one or more Web Parts. As you customize your site, you might decide that you do not need all the Web Parts on your pages and might want to remove them.

In this exercise, you will delete and close Web Parts to remove them from a website's home page. You will then restore a closed Web Part.

SET UP Open a SharePoint Team site.

BE SURE TO verify that you have sufficient rights to edit the home page in this site. If in doubt, see the Appendix at the back of this book.

Edit

1. Click the **Edit** icon that is displayed to the left of the **Browse** tab.

2. In the top content area, hover the mouse over the title of the **Financial Links** Web Part and select the check box that appears.

   The List Tools and Web Part Tools contextual tab sets appear in the Ribbon.

Delete

3. Click the **Options** tab in the **Web Part Tools** contextual tab set, and then click the **Delete** command in the **State** group.

4. Click **OK** to confirm that you wish to delete the Web Part permanently.

5. In the top content area, hover the mouse over the title of the **Furniture Price List** Web Part, click the down arrow that appears, and then click **Close**, which temporarily removes the Web Part from the page.

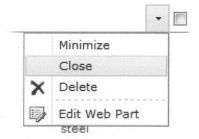

   The browser redisplays the page with only one Web Part—the Picture Library Slideshow Web Part.

6. Click the **Insert** tab, and then click **Web Part** in the **Web Parts** group.

   The Web Parts pane now includes a category Closed Web Parts, which holds Web Parts that are temporarily removed from a web page by using the Close option. Currently, the Closed Web Parts category contains only one Web Part—the Furniture Price XLV Web Part that you removed in step 5.

7. Under **Categories**, click **Closed Web Parts**, and then, under **Web Parts**, click **Furniture Price List**.

   The Furniture Price List Web Part is displayed on the page.

8. Click the **Insert** tab, and then click **Web Part** in the **Web Parts** group.

   Note that the Closed Web Parts category is not displayed now. This category is displayed only when your page contains closed Web Parts.

Note You can liken the Closed Web Parts category to the Recycle Bin; however, Web Parts are placed here only when the Close option is used. When the Delete option is used, the Web Part is permanently deleted from the page. Web Parts placed in other categories act like templates. Web Parts from the other categories can be placed on a web page multiple times. Once a Web Part is placed on a page, it can be uniquely customized, but the template from which the Web Part is created remains in the category displayed in the Web Part pane.

9. Click **Save & Close**.

 CLEAN UP Leave the browser open if you are continuing to the next exercise.

Tip Web Parts can be badly written. If they are not tested thoroughly, you might find that a web page does not display when you add a Web Part to it. In such situations, append *?Contents=1* to the URL of the Web Part page, such as *http://wideworldimporters/SitePages/ home.aspx?contents=1*. The Web Part Page Maintenance page is displayed, which can be used to delete the offending Web Part. The Web Part Page Maintenance page can be very useful in determining if a page has any closed Web Parts and can be used to delete any closed Web Parts quickly. Having closed Web Parts on a page can cause the browser to take some time to display the page, which can be very annoying to users who frequently visit the page.

Customizing a Web Part by Using the Web Part Tool Pane

Once you add a Web Part to a web page, you might find that you have to customize it to display the content that you want visitors to your website to see. You might also have to tailor the Web Part's properties for it to take on the look and feel that you want.

In the following exercise, you will customize the Picture Library Slideshow Web Part and a SharePoint XLV Web Part.

 SET UP Open the SharePoint site that you used in the previous exercise, if it is not already open. Be sure to complete the previous exercise in this chapter before beginning this exercise.

BE SURE TO verify that you have sufficient rights to edit the home page in this site. If in doubt, see the Appendix at the back of this book.

1. Hover the mouse over the title bar of the **Picture Library Slideshow Web Part**, click the down arrow that appears, and then click **Edit Web Part**.

The Picture Library Slideshow Web Part tool pane is displayed to the right of the page.

2. From the **Picture Library** list, select the picture library whose images you wish to display in the Web Part, such as **Site_Pictures**, and then, under **Appearance** in the **Title** box, delete **Picture Library Slideshow Web Part** and type **Logos**.

3. In the **Chrome Type** drop-down list, click **None**, and then scroll to the bottom of the Web Part tool pane and click **OK**.

Images from the chosen picture library are displayed at the top of the page, and the tool pane disappears. The title of the Web Part is not displayed.

Tip When a Web Part title is not displayed, to customize the properties of a Web Part, display the page in Edit mode. The Web Part title is then visible. You can either use the Web Part menu to edit the Web Part or select the check box on the Web Part title and, on the Options tab in the contextual Web Part Tools tab set, use the Web Part Properties command in the Properties group to open the Web Part tool pane.

4. Place the cursor over the title bar of the **Furniture Price List** Web Part, click the down arrow that appears, and click **Edit Web Part**.

The Furniture Price List Web Part tool pane is displayed.

5. In the **Furniture Price List** tool pane, below the **Selected View** list, click the **Edit the current view** link. The Edit View of the Furniture Price List page is displayed.

6. In the **Columns** area, clear the **Attachments**, **In Stock**, **Unit Price**, and **Total** check boxes.

> **Tip** In this exercise, you will display only Bianca furniture; therefore, you will use the Furniture Range column to filter data. When the filter is applied, in the XLV Web Part, the Furniture Range column always contains the text "Bianca." Hence, you could choose not to display the Furniture Type column. However, when you first customize a view, it is good practice to leave the filter column, such as the Furniture Type column, in place so you can check that the filter is configured correctly.

7. Scroll down the page until the **Filter** area is visible. Select the **Show items only when the following is true** option.

8. On the **Show the items when column** list, click **Furniture Range**. In the **Value** box, type **Bianca**.

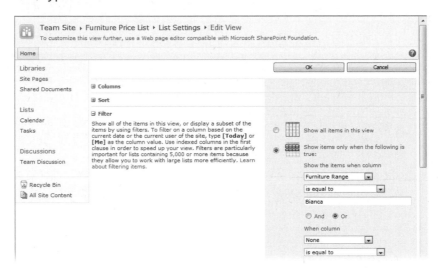

9. At the bottom of the page, click **OK**.

    Your web page is displayed. The Furniture Price List tool pane is no longer visible.

10. Place the cursor over the title bar of the **Furniture Price List** Web Part, click the down arrow that appears, and click **Edit Web Part**. The Furniture Price List tool pane is displayed.

11. Click the expand (+) icon to the left of **Appearance**, and then, in the **Title** text box, type **Sale – Bianca Furniture at half price**.

12. Click the expand (+) icon to the left of **Advanced** and clear the **Allow Minimize** check box.

13. At the bottom of the **Furniture Price List** tool pane, click **OK**.

14. Place the cursor over the title bar of the Sale – Bianca Furniture at half price Web Part, click the down arrow that appears, and notice that the **Minimize** option is no longer available.

✖ **CLEAN UP** Leave the browser open if you are continuing to the next exercise.

Editing Web Part Pages

Web Part pages are the default type of page on sites such as group work sites, Meeting Workspaces, and blog sites. In addition, they are the type of pages used by lists and libraries to display their contents. Web Part pages consist only of Web Part zones. They do not contain wiki page content areas and, therefore, can contain only Web Parts. To add static text or images to a Web Part page, you must first add either the Content Editor Web Part or the Image Web Part, and then use the Web Part tool pane properties to add text or images.

Tip Using a tool such as SharePoint Designer, you can add Web Parts outside of Web Part zones on a Web Part page.

There are two versions of a Web Part page:

- **Shared Version** This version is the Web Part page that every user with the appropriate permissions on a site can view. To edit the Shared version of a Web Part page, place the page in Edit mode by using the Site Actions, Edit Page command.

- **Personal Version** This version of a Web Part page is available only to you and not to others. To edit the Personal version of a Web Part page, click the down arrow to the right of your name in the top corner of the page, and then click Personalize This Page. When you have a Personal view of a Web Part page, then it will be displayed by default when you first visit the page.

To customize the Shared version of any Web Part page for a list or library, you must have the following rights, all of which are included in the Design and Full Control permission levels by default:

- Manage Lists
- Add and Customize Pages
- Apply Themes and Borders
- Apply Style Sheets

A member of a website's Site Owners group has Full Control permissions and, therefore, is able to customize the Shared version of Web Part pages.

To customize the Personal view of any Web Part page, the Web Part page must be designed to be personalized. You must have the following rights, all of which are included in the Contribute, Design, and Full Control permission levels by default:

- Manage Personal Views
- Add/Remove Personal Web Parts
- Update Personal Web Parts

A member of a website's Members group has Contribute permissions and, therefore, is able to customize the Personal version of Web Part pages if they are designed to be personalized.

Tip When a Web Part page is designed to be personalized, editors of the page can disable the personalization of Web Parts on an individual basis by configuring the Web Part properties by using the Web Part tool pane.

Web Parts within Web Part zones can be connected to one another to provide interactive dashboards displaying related data from a number of data sources. A Ribbon command in SharePoint Foundation makes it easy to create a Web Part connection when two lists have a related column. For example, on a blog site, the Posts list has a lookup column to the Comments list. On a page where you are displaying the Posts XLV Web Part, on the Options tab in the Web Part Tools contextual tool set, you can click the Insert Related List command. This will add the Comments XLV Web Part to the page and connect the two Web Parts. Then, when users click a blog post in the Posts Web Part, the comments related to that post will be shown in the Comments Web Part. Using a tool such as SharePoint Designer, you can also connect Web Parts on one page with Web Parts on another page.

See Also For more information on connecting Web Parts, see Chapter 6, "Working with Data Sources," in *Microsoft SharePoint Designer 2010 Step by Step* by Penelope Coventry (Microsoft Press, 2010).

In the following exercise, you will familiarize yourself with editing a Web Part page.

 SET UP Open the SharePoint site that you used in the previous exercise, if it is not already open.

BE SURE TO verify that you have sufficient rights to edit views in the Shared Documents library. If in doubt, see the Appendix at the back of this book.

1. On the Quick Launch, under **Libraries**, click **Shared Documents**. The All Documents view of the library, Shared Documents, is displayed.

2. Click **Site Actions**, and then click **Edit Page**.

Tip Web Part pages do not display the Edit icon or the Save & Close icon to the left of the Browse tab.

The browser redisplays the Web Part page in Edit mode. The Web Part page displays one Web Part zone denoted by a blue border labeled Main. At the top of each Web Part page zone is a white rectangle surrounded by a blue line containing the text "Add a Web Part".

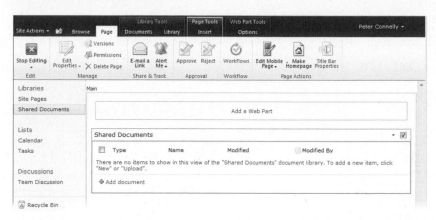

Tip Other Web Part pages might be comprised of more than one Web Part zone, depending on the Web Part page template used when creating the page. You can also add or remove zones from a Web Part page by using a tool such as SharePoint Designer.

Stop
Editing

3. On the **Page** tab, click **Stop Editing**.

4. In the top right corner of the page, click the arrow next to **<your name>** and click **Personalize this Page**.

The browser redisplays the Web Part page in Edit mode. A yellow status bar states that this is the Personal version of the page. Any changes that you make to the Web Part page affect only your view of this web page.

Tip When a Web Part page is not in Edit mode, there is no visible indication as to whether the page shows the Shared version or the Personal version. If the Show Personal View option is displayed on the *<your name>* drop-down menu, you are viewing the Shared version of the page. If the Show Shared View option appears, you are viewing the Personal version of the page. You can remove the Personal version of the page by clicking Reset Page Content on the *<your name>* drop-down menu. The Shared version of the page, then, is your default version. As an Administrator or web designer, you cannot customize the Personal views of specific users; you can customize only the Shared view and your own Personal view.

5. On the **Page** tab, click **Stop Editing**.

 CLEAN UP Close the browser.

Moving Web Parts

As you customize your web page by adding and removing Web Parts, you might find that the Web Parts are not located where you would like them to be. In this situation, you can move the Web Parts around on the page to obtain the layout that you want.

In this exercise, you will move Web Parts on the home page of a SharePoint site.

 SET UP Open the SharePoint site that you used in the previous exercise, if it is not already open.

BE SURE TO verify that you have sufficient rights to edit the home page of this site. If in doubt, see the Appendix at the back of this book.

1. Click **Site Actions**, and then click **Edit Page**.

The browser displays the home page of your site in Edit mode.

2. Move the mouse over the title bar of the Sale – Bianca Furniture at half price Web Part so that the pointer changes to a hand. While holding down the mouse button, drag the Web Part to the content area to the left of **Getting Started**.

3. Click **Save & Close**.

 **CLEAN UP** Close the browser.

Key Points

- In SharePoint Foundation 2010, a website is a collection of web pages.

- There are two types of web pages—wiki pages and Web Part pages. On a Team site, blank site, or Document Workspace, the default web pages are wiki pages that are stored in a SharePoint Foundation–based wiki library named Site Pages.

- Both wiki pages and Web Part pages can contain Web Parts.

- A page can contain static and dynamic content, which is typically limited to no more than two or three screens of information.

- Create forward links to pages by using double square brackets around a WikiWord. For example, type **[[BedRoom]]** to create a link to the page named BedRoom. The page does not have to exist when the forward link is created.

- The easiest way to create a new wiki page is to create a forward link to a nonexistent page.

- Major versioning is enabled on wiki page libraries, and therefore no amendments are lost.

- Web Parts are reusable components that can contain any type of web-based content. They can display the contents of lists and libraries, as well as other content, such as the results of database queries, websites, web pages, files, and folders.

- Web Parts are organized by categories.

- The Lists and Libraries category contains an XLV Web Part for each list or library created in the site.

- The Closed Web Parts category is a temporary storage space for Web Parts that have been removed from a web page by using the Close button.

- A Web Part page can have two versions: a Shared version and a Personal version. All users can see changes made to the Shared version. Changes made to the Personal version are visible only to the user who altered his or her Personal version of the Web Part page. A user can reset the Personal view to the Shared view setting if desired.

Chapter at a Glance

Configure a SharePoint list, page 185

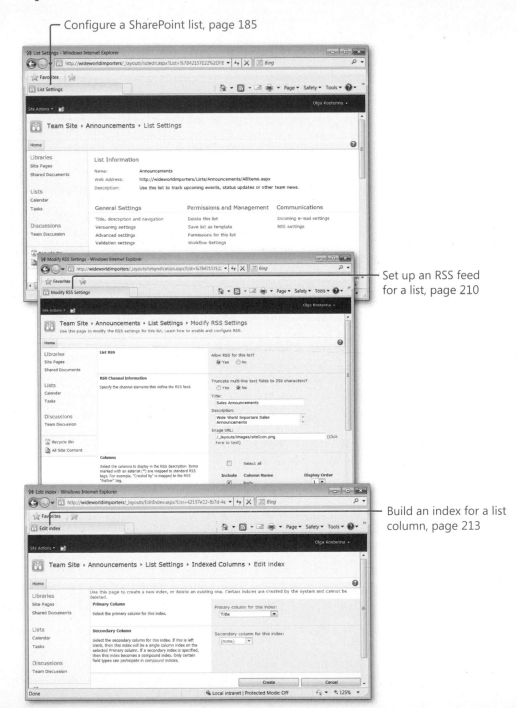

Set up an RSS feed for a list, page 210

Build an index for a list column, page 213

7 Working with List Settings

In this chapter, you will learn how to

✔ Set the list title, description, and navigation.

✔ Configure content approval and versioning.

✔ Work with advanced list settings.

✔ Create a content type.

✔ Associate a content type with a list.

✔ Use list validation.

✔ Delete and restore a list.

✔ Manage users and permissions.

✔ Grant list item permissions.

✔ Configure incoming email settings.

✔ Configure RSS feeds for a list or library.

✔ Create indexed columns.

✔ Prevent duplicate list items.

In this chapter, we focus on list settings. In Chapter 4, "Working with Lists," we discuss how to create and use Microsoft SharePoint lists, how to add and remove content, and how to sort and filter them. Now that we have a good grasp of SharePoint lists, this chapter will explore the list settings available to manage and configure the lists.

List settings allow us to configure the options for the list, including name, navigation, content types, versioning, validation, email settings, Really Simple Syndication (RSS) feeds, and indexing options, as well as permissions for the users who may require access to the list. You can also delete lists that are no longer needed.

The options for a list are configured using the List Settings page. You can navigate to this page by clicking the List tab from the List Tools tab set on the Ribbon that appears when you open a list, and then clicking the List Settings button in the Settings group on the right side of the Ribbon.

The List Settings page groups configuration settings in six sections, as follows: General Settings, Permissions and Management, Communications, Content Types, Columns, and Views.

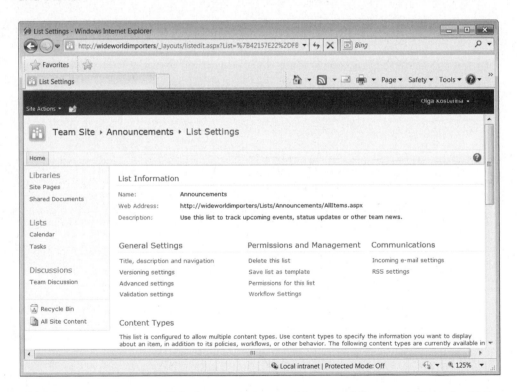

The General Settings section, for example, provides the ability to change the Title, description and navigation, Versioning settings, Advanced settings, and Validation settings.

In this chapter, we will discuss configuration options, available on the List Settings page, that allow you to manage the lists on your site.

> **Practice Files** You don't need any practice files to complete the exercises in this chapter.

Important Remember to use your SharePoint site location in place of *http://wideworldimporters* in the following exercises.

Setting the List Title, Description, and Navigation

As discussed in Chapter 4, it is important to give the Name and Description And Navigation settings some thought when you create a list. The default names for lists are descriptive, but they could be made more descriptive within an organization. For example, if a Contacts list contains only employees, then Employees or Staff may be a better name for it. Concerning the list navigation, some list types, such as Contacts, do not display on the Quick Launch by default, while you may need to display your new list on the Quick Launch. However, if you have added a list as a List View Web Part on the page of your site, you may find it unnecessary to have a link to it on the Quick Launch as well. With the Title and Description And Navigation options, you can turn the Quick Launch link on or off for the list in question.

See Also To make navigation to a list easier, avoid using spaces within the list name when the list is created. A space in the name shows as *%20* within the Uniform Resource Locator (URL). For more information, refer to the sidebar entitled "Naming a URL," in Chapter 3, "Creating and Managing Sites." You can also rename the list after setting up its URL when it is created. For more information, refer to the exercise in the section entitled "Creating a New List," in Chapter 4.

In this exercise, you will modify the Name and Description of a Links list, allowing the name to be more descriptive of the contents.

 SET UP Open the SharePoint site in which you would like to rename a Links list. The exercise will use the *http://wideworldimporters* site, but you can use whatever site you want. If prompted, type your user name and password, and click OK

BE SURE TO verify that you have sufficient rights to manage a list. If in doubt, see the Appendix at the back of this book.

1. On the Quick Launch, click the **Lists** hyperlink.

   The All Site Content page is displayed in the Lists view.

2. Under the **Lists** section, click **Links**.

   The Links list is displayed.

List
Settings

3. On the Ribbon, from **List Tools**, select the **List** tab, and then, in the **Settings** group, click the **List Settings** button to display the **List Settings** page.

4. Click **Title, description and navigation** from the **General Settings** section.

5. In the **Name and Description** section, replace the text "Links" with **Useful Web Sites** in the **Name** field. Remove the default text from the **Description** field.

6. In the **Navigation** section, click **Yes** to **Display this list on the Quick Launch?**

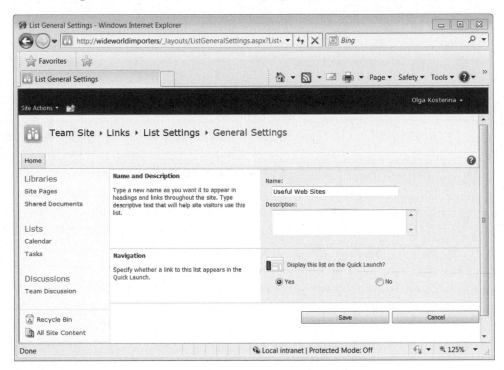

7. Click **Save**.

8. Navigate to the home page and verify that the **Useful Web Sites** list is displayed on the Quick Launch under **Lists**.

9. On the Quick Launch, click the **Useful Web Sites** list. Using steps 3–7 as a guide, remove the link to this list from the Quick Launch.

10. On the Quick Launch, click **Lists** and verify that the **Useful Web Sites** list is displayed under **Lists** on the **All Site Content** page.

✖ **CLEAN UP** Leave the browser open if you are continuing to the next exercise.

Configuring Content Approval and Versioning

The Versioning settings option under General Settings provides Content Approval, Item Version History, and Draft Item Security options. Turning on Content Approval allows list items to be created as draft items that are not displayed to other users unless the item has been approved. This means that you can work on the item in draft mode and then submit the item for approval when you are ready to do so. An approver (that is, a user with Approve permission) can then approve the item, which allows the list item to show for all users with Read permission.

Tip When a list item is submitted for approval, a notification email is not sent automatically to the approver. The approver should visit the list periodically to see if list items are waiting for approval. Alternatively, you could use an Approval Workflow or consider configuring alerts for this list. For more information, refer to Chapter 11 "Working with Workflows."

Draft Item Security is an option that is specific to draft items. It provides additional user permissions to the Permission settings on list items. Using the Draft Item Security settings, you can choose who is allowed to view the item in draft form. The default setting is Any User Who Can Read Items, but you can also choose Only Users Who Can Edit Items or Only Users Who Can Approve Items. Users with Contribute permissions or higher will see the draft version, while users with less than Contribute permissions will see the last approved item and not the more recent draft item. Therefore, users with different permissions are likely to see different list items and different versions of those list items.

The Item Version History provides you with the benefit of being able to track the editing history of a list item. If enabled, a new version of the list item will be stored upon each edited version of the list item. This allows you to view the history, as well as restore a previous version so that it becomes the latest version of the list item. You may specify how many versions to keep in the history. The Item Version History is available only if versioning is enabled.

See Also SharePoint lists allow you to use Major versions only, whereas libraries allow you to use Major and Minor versions. More information on major and minor versioning can be found in Chapter 8, "Working with Library Settings."

In this exercise, you will configure the Versioning settings and set up the content approval for an Announcements list.

 SET UP Open the SharePoint site in which you would like to configure an Announcements list, if not already open. The exercise will use the *http:// wideworldimporters* site, but you can use whatever site you wish. If prompted, type your user name and password, and click OK.

BE SURE TO verify that you have sufficient rights to manage a list. If in doubt, see the Appendix at the back of this book.

1. On the Quick Launch, click **Lists**.

2. Under **Lists**, click **Announcements**.

3. On the Ribbon, under **List Tools**, click the **List** tab, and then click **List Settings** in the **Settings** group.

4. Under **General Settings**, click **Versioning Settings**.

The Versioning Settings page is displayed.

5. You will now set up content approval. In the **Content Approval** section, under **Require content approval for submitted items?**, click **Yes**.

Notice that in the **Draft Item Security** section, under **Who should see draft items in this list?**, the selected option is **Only users who can approve items (and the author of the item)**.

6. You will now configure versioning. In the **Item Version History** section, click **Yes** to **Create a version each time you edit an item in this list?**

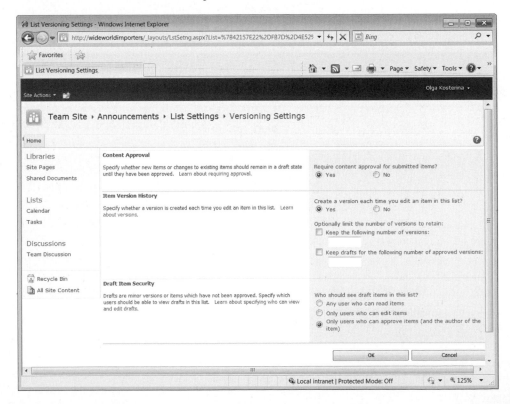

7. Click **OK** to save the changes.

The List Settings page is displayed.

8. Click **Announcements** in the breadcrumb trail. The All Items view of the Announcements list is displayed.

The Approval Status column has been created within the list, and any existing announcement items are set to Approved.

9. Click **Add new announcement**.

10. In the **Title** field, type **New Product Announcement**. Notice the warning that the items on this list require approval. Click **Save** to save the announcement.

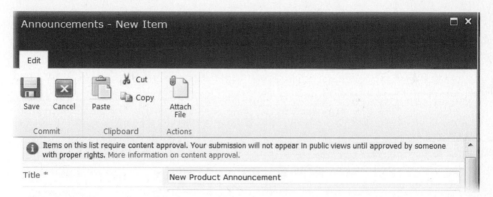

11. A new item has been created. It has an Approval Status of Pending. Hover the mouse over the title of the new announcement, click the down arrow that appears to the right of the title, and then click **Approve/Reject** from the drop-down menu. The Approve/Reject dialog appears.

Tip You can also use the Approve/Reject button on the Item tab on the Ribbon to approve or reject list items.

12. In the **Approval Status** section, select **Approved**. In the **Comment** section, type a comment, such as **Product details correct,** and then click **OK**.

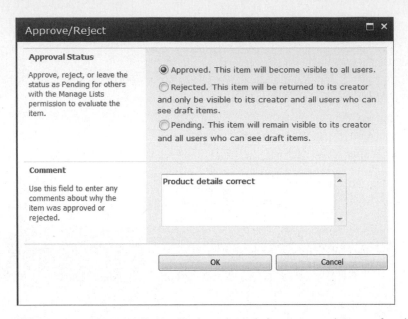

The Announcements list is displayed, and the Approval Status for this list item is now Approved.

13. Hover the mouse over the title of the new item, click the down arrow that appears, and then click **Version History** to see the current version number of the list item in the **Version History** dialog.

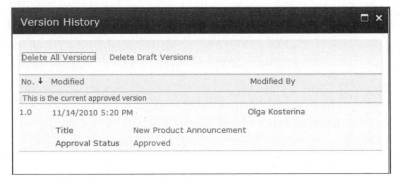

14. Close the **Version History** dialog to display the **Announcements** list page.

15. Using steps 3–5 as a guide, disable the requirement for content approval for the **Announcements** list.

CLEAN UP Leave the browser open if you are continuing to the next exercise.

Working with Advanced List Settings

In this section, we will look into configuration options that are available on the Advanced Settings page, with the exception of content type settings, which we will cover in the next section in this chapter, "Creating a Content Type."

On the Advanced Settings page, you will find the following settings:

- **Item Level Permissions** This option allows you to refine the default permissions levels, such as Read, Contribute, Design, and Full Control, for a list item. For example, you can use this option to set up what the creator of the list item is allowed to do. This option allows you to set whether people with Read access may read all items or only those that they created. You may also set whether users with Create and Edit access can edit all items or just those that they created, or they can be prevented from creating and editing any list item by selecting the None option. By selecting the None option, you are effectively making users with Contribute permissions readers for this list. However, users with rights to manage this list are able to read and edit all items.

> **Item-level Permissions**
>
> Specify which items users can read and edit.
>
> **Note:** Users with the Manage Lists permission can read and edit all items. Learn about managing permission settings.
>
> **Read access:** Specify which items users are allowed to read
> - ⦿ Read all items
> - ○ Read items that were created by the user
>
> **Create and Edit access:** Specify which items users are allowed to create and edit
> - ⦿ Create and edit all items
> - ○ Create items and edit items that were created by the user
> - ○ None

- **Attachments** Using this option, you can allow or disallow attachments to list items. By default, the attachments to list items are enabled.

    See Also Refer to the section entitled "Attaching Files to List Items," in Chapter 4, for an exercise on attaching documents to list items.

> **Attachments**
>
> Specify whether users can attach files to items in this list.
>
> Attachments to list items are:
> - ⦿ Enabled
> - ○ Disabled

    Tip You may wish to disable attachments if you would prefer users to store documents within document libraries.

- **Folders** This option provides the ability for you to disable the New Folder command in the list. This command is enabled by default.

An alternative to using folders is using the custom columns. Since the introduction of SharePoint, users have been taking advantage of custom columns to organize their content. This means that through the use of custom columns, you can organize content into views using filters rather than folders. If you prefer this method to using folders within lists, you can turn off the use of folders so that users do not become confused as to which they should use. If you do use folders, you should consider carefully training your users on how to use them effectively.

Folders	Make "New Folder" command available?
Specify whether the "New Folder" command is available. Changing this setting does not affect existing folders.	○ Yes ◉ No

See Also For a debate on when to use columns or folders to organize your content, refer to *http://www.endusersharepoint.com/2010/01/29/sharepoint-folders-vs-metadata/*.

Tip In SharePoint 2010, the recommended number of items within a view or folder is limited to 5,000. This limitation is related to the time that it takes to display the number of items in a view or folder. Therefore, if you have 6,000 list items in a list, it would be better to create views or folders to display 5,000 or fewer list items.

See Also More information on recommended limits with lists and libraries can be found at *http://technet.microsoft.com/en-us/library/cc262787.aspx#ListLibrary*.

- **Search** Searching content in SharePoint Foundation will return search results from any list or library by default. All the items that the current user has permission to view will display within the results, and no users will see content that they do not have permission to view. You may exclude an entire list from displaying within search results by setting the Allow Items From This List To Appear In Search Results option to No.

Search	Allow items from this list to appear in search results?
Specify whether this list should be visible in search results. Users who do not have permission to see these items will not see them in search results, no matter what this setting is.	◉ Yes ○ No

See Also For more information on searching, refer to Chapter 16, "Finding Information on the SharePoint Site."

- **Offline Client Availability** This setting defines if the list is available for offline viewing in client applications, such as SharePoint Workspace 2010, that allow you to synchronize data for offline use so that you have access to the SharePoint content while in a disconnected environment. Microsoft Outlook 2010 also can be used for offline access to list and library content. The default setting is to allow items to be downloaded to offline clients. If the list contains sensitive information, you can ensure that it is available only in an online environment and switch off the offline availability.

Offline Client Availability	Allow items from this list to be downloaded to offline clients?
Specify whether this list should be available for offline clients.	◉ Yes ○ No

See Also For more information on taking lists offline, see Chapter 13, "Using SharePoint Foundation with Outlook 2010."

- **Datasheet** This setting defines whether editing of the list using the datasheet is allowed. It is enabled by default. The Datasheet view of a list provides a spreadsheet-type view of the list content, allowing you to enter data more quickly and use operations such as Fill Down. The updates are provided in bulk, all at once, which is convenient for making modifications quickly. However, using such operations can result in accidentally overwriting content, and the disadvantage is that it is difficult to undo a mistake that has been made in bulk. Therefore, you can decide not to allow the editing of the list using the datasheet, and then the Datasheet View button on the Ribbon in the List tab will be disabled.

Datasheet	Allow items in this list to be edited using the datasheet?
Specify whether the datasheet can be used to bulk edit data on this list.	⊙ Yes ◉ No

Note Some lists or libraries, such as external lists and picture libraries, do not allow the use of Datasheet views.

See Also For more information on the Datasheet view, see Chapter 9, "Working with List and Library Views."

- **Dialogs** SharePoint Foundation 2010 in conjunction with Microsoft Silverlight, provides the New, View, and Edit forms within the Silverlight dialog when accessing an item. The Silverlight dialog is displayed within the web page, and the rest of the web page is dimmed. This is a much better way of manipulating list items than in the previous version of SharePoint because it does not require reloading of the page. If your work environment has desktops that do not have Silverlight installed, you may consider either installing Silverlight or disabling this option.

Dialogs	Launch forms in a dialog?
If dialogs are available, specify whether to launch the new, edit, and display forms in a dialog. Selecting "No" will cause these actions to navigate to the full page. Note: Dialogs may not be available on all forms.	◉ Yes ⊙ No

In this exercise, you will disable the Datasheet and Attachments options for an Announcements list. Because this list contains only two columns besides the Body column, using the Datasheet view is not of much benefit. Formatted content can appear within the Body field, and therefore it would be better to type the content than link to an attachment.

SET UP Open the SharePoint site you used in the previous exercise if it is not already open.

BE SURE TO verify that you have sufficient rights to manage a list. If in doubt, see the Appendix at the back of this book.

1. On the Quick Launch, click **Lists**.

2. Under **Lists**, click **Announcements**.

3. On the Ribbon, under **List Tools**, click the **List** tab and then click the **List Settings** button in the **Settings** group.

4. On the **List Settings** page, in the **General Settings** section, click **Advanced Settings**.

5. In the **Attachments** section, set **Attachments to this list are** to **Disabled.**

6. In the **Datasheet** section, set the **Allow items in this list to be edited using the datasheet?** option to **No**.

7. Click **OK**. If the confirmation message appears that notifies you that disabling attachments will remove all existing attachments within the list, click OK.

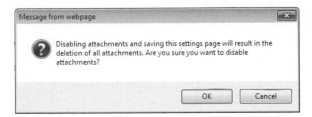

You have disabled attachments in the Announcements list and also disabled editing the Announcements list using the datasheet.

 CLEAN UP Close the browser.

Creating a Content Type

Often, we need to redesign a list and add a new column. For example, in Chapter 4, you added new columns to a list. You would add a new column to a list if you needed to collect more information from the user than what is there by default within the list template. Consider the Announcements list, for example. It has three visible columns; Title, Body, and Expires. You may want to create a new column to store the type of announcement, providing choices, such as Sales, Product, Employee, and General. Collecting the type of announcement would be useful when creating a view and filtering by type, and also if you decide to roll up the announcements using an aggregation Web Part. You would then want to ensure that all Announcements lists have the option of using this new column, but it would be tedious adding that new column to every Announcements list. You could get around the tediousness of creating the list with the additional column by using a custom list template. However, what would happen if the choices for the type of announcement changed? You may want to add another choice to the type of announcement column, such as Internal and External announcement. That is where site columns and content types are useful. A site column could also be described as a shared column. You create a site column once, and it resides in a gallery at Site or Site Collection level. It is inherited by the all sites in the collection that are beneath the site in which it was created. A content type is made up of site columns as well as other configurations such as workflows. This enables you to reuse a group of site columns and perhaps have a workflow associated with the content type, which you would then add to an existing list. Lists can use more than one content type.

In this exercise, you will create a custom content type.

SET UP Open the SharePoint site in which you would like to create a custom content type. The exercise will use the *http://wideworldimporters* site, but you can use whatever site you wish. If prompted, type your user name and password, and click OK.

BE SURE TO verify that you have sufficient rights to create a content type. If in doubt, see the Appendix at the back of this book.

1. Click **Site Actions**, and then click **Site Settings**.

2. On the **Site Settings** page, under **Galleries,** click **Site content types**. The Site Content Types page is displayed, showing a list of existing content types for this site.

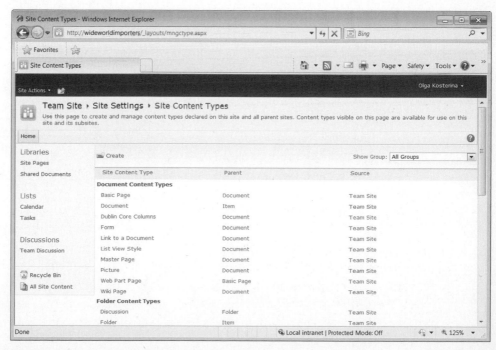

3. At the top of the page, click **Create**.
   The New Site Content Type page is displayed.

4. In the **Name** box, type a name for the content type, such as **Wide World Announcements**.

5. From the **Select parent content type from** list, choose **List Content Types**. From the second drop-down list, select **Announcement**, if not already selected.

6. In the **Group** section, leave the **Existing Group** setting as **Custom Content Types**, and then click **OK**.

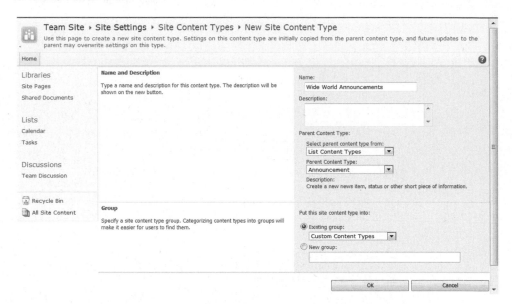

The Site Content Types – Wide World Announcements page is displayed.

7. In the **Columns** section, click **Add from new site column**. The New Site Column page is displayed.

8. In the **Name and Type** section, in the **Column name** box, type **Type of Announcement**.

9. Set **The type of information in this column is** to **Choice (menu to choose from)**.

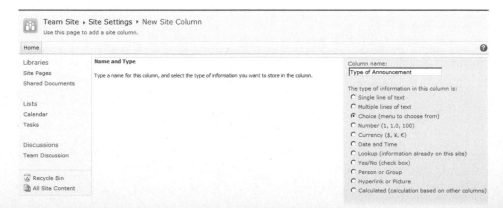

10. In the **Additional Column Settings** section, in the **Type each choice on a separate line** box, delete the existing text and type **Products** on the first line, **Sales** on the second line, **General** on the third line, and **Other** on the fourth line,

11. Leave the other options as the defaults and click **OK**.

    The Wide World Announcements content type page is displayed. The new site column that you have just created, Type of Announcement, has been added to the content type and is listed under the Columns section.

12. Navigate back to your **Team Site** home page, using the breadcrumb on top of the page.

 CLEAN UP Leave the browser open if you are continuing to the next exercise.

Associating a Content Type with a List

Now that you have created a custom content type, you can add that content type to any list or library within the current site or any site within the hierarchy of the site collection below where the content type is stored.

In this exercise, you will add a content type to the Announcements list.

SET UP Open the SharePoint site that you used in the previous exercise, if it is not already open.

BE SURE TO verify that you have sufficient rights to associate a content type with a list. If in doubt, see the Appendix at the back of this book.

1. On the Quick Launch, click **Lists**, and then under **Lists**, click **Announcements**.

2. On the Ribbon, in the **List Tools,** click the **List** tab, and then click **List Settings**.

3. On the **List Settings** page, in the **General Settings** section, click **Advanced Settings**.

4. On the **Advanced Settings** page, make sure that in the **Content Types** section, **Allow Management of Content Types** is set to **Yes**. Click **OK**. The List Settings page is displayed.

5. In the **Content Types** section, click **Add from existing site content types**. The Add Content Types page is displayed.

6. In the **Select Content Types** section, from the **Select site content types from** drop-down list, choose **Custom Content Types**.

7. In **Available Site Content Types**, scroll down to see the **Wide World Announcements** content type. Click this content type to select it, and then click **Add**.

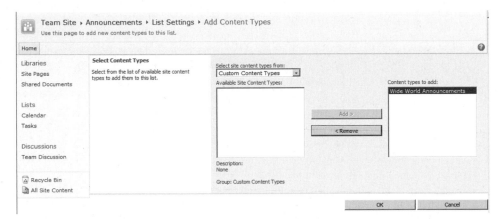

8. The Wide World Announcements content type is now displayed under Content types to add. Click **OK**.

   The List Settings page is displayed. The Wide World Announcements content type has been added and is listed in the Content Types section.

9. In the **Content Types** section, click **Change new button order and default content type**. The Change New Button Order and Default Content Type page is displayed.

10. Clear the **Visible** check box for the **Announcement** content type, and click **OK**.

The List Settings page is displayed.

11. Click **Announcements** on the breadcrumb to navigate to the **Announcements** list.

12. Click **Add new announcement**.

13. The **Announcements – New Item** dialog opens. The new Type of Announcement field has been added, with selections of Products, Sales, General, and Other in the drop-down list. Type a title for a new announcement, such as **My Announcement**, select **General** in the **Type of Announcement** field, and then click **Save**. The new item has been created based on the Wide World Announcements content type.

Note You can now add this new content type to any Announcements list within this site or any child of this site. Modifying the choices in the site column will also populate all lists that use this content type with the new choice. Before creating a custom content type, you may want to explore the existing content types available, such as Timecard and Resources, to see if they offer similar functionality to what you want to create.

 CLEAN UP Leave the browser open if you are continuing to the next exercise.

Using List Validation

The list validation options provide you with the ability to validate user entries into each column in a list. When a user enters a value that does not meet the requirements that you have defined, a custom message is displayed, allowing the user to correct the value.

Note Validation Settings is a new option in SharePoint Foundation. Previously, SharePoint 2007 allowed only basic validation criteria such as Age Is Required, but not Age Must Be Between 18 and 50.

Tip Validation of user entry can be configured in two places. You can configure validation using validation settings for a list, and you can also do it at column level when creating or modifying the column properties. The difference between the two methods is that using the column properties does not provide ability to compare two columns in the same list, whereas the List Settings validation option does. The column properties validation settings are useful when comparing a column value with a static value.

In this exercise, you will add validation to an Announcements list to ensure that only future dates are added to the Announcement Expires column.

 SET UP Open the SharePoint site that you used in the previous exercise and navigate to the Announcements list, if it is not already open.

BE SURE TO verify that you have sufficient rights to manage a list. If in doubt, see the Appendix at the back of this book.

1. Click **Add new announcement** to create a new list item.

2. Type **Past Announcement** in the **Title** field. In the **Expires** field, click the calendar icon to open a calendar, and then choose a date before today's date.

3. Click **Save**.

4. You have created an announcement with an expiration date set in the past. You will now create a validation rule to check that the expiration date of a new announcement is in the future. On the **List Tools,** click the **List** tab, and then click the **List Settings** item in the **Settings** group.

   The List Settings page is displayed.

5. Under **General Settings**, click **Validation Settings**.

   The Validation Settings page is displayed.

6. In the **Formula** section, in the **Formula** box, type =[**Expires**]>=[**Created**].

7. In the **User Message** section, in the **User Message** box, type an error message, such as **Expiration date must be in the future**.

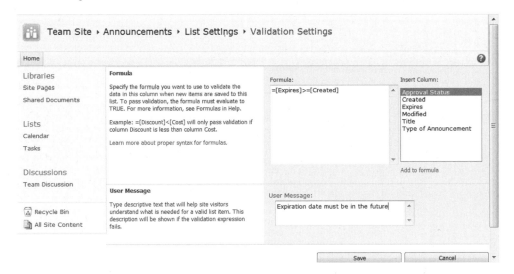

8. Click **Save**. The List Settings page is displayed.

   You will now verify the validation rule. On the breadcrumb, click **Announcements** to navigate to the list.

9. Using steps 1–3 as a guide, add a new announcement with the title **Validated Announcement**, and then select a past date using the calendar in the **Expires** field.

10. Click **Save**. The error message that you have set up is displayed, indicating the date is invalid.

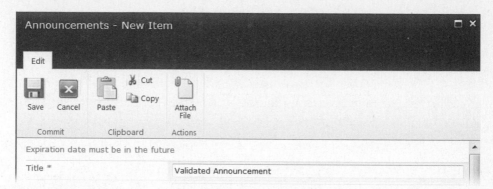

11. In the **Expires** field, set the date in the future. Click **Save**. The new Validated Announcement item has been created and is shown in the Announcements list.

12. Using steps 4–7 as a guide, remove the validation settings by deleting the formula for validating the **Expires** date that you have created.

 CLEAN UP Leave the browser open if you are continuing to the next exercise.

Deleting and Restoring a List

When a SharePoint list is no longer required or was perhaps created by mistake, you may want to delete the list. Deleting the list will also delete all the list items (content) within that list, so this should be used with caution. For reassurance, note that sufficient permissions are required to delete the list. For example, a user with the Contribute permission level for a site or a list will not be able to delete the list. If a list is deleted accidentally, it will be placed within the site Recycle Bin for 30 days and can be restored, just like the list items.

In this exercise, you will delete and restore a SharePoint List.

Important Do not use a list for this exercise that contains data that you wish to keep. If you get through half the exercise and come back to it after 30 days, your list will not be available for restoring.

SET UP Open the SharePoint site in which you would like to delete the list, and navigate to this list, if it is not already open. The exercise will use the *http:// wideworldimporters* site, but you can use whatever site you want. If prompted, type your user name and password, and click OK.

BE SURE TO verify that you have sufficient rights to delete and restore this list. If in doubt, see the Appendix at the back of this book.

1. If it is not already open, navigate to the **Announcements** list by choosing **Lists** on the Quick Launch, and then clicking **Announcements**.

2. On the Ribbon, in the **List Tools**, click the **List** tab, and then click **List Settings**.

3. On the **List Settings** page, in the **Permissions and Management** section, click **Delete this list**.

4. Click **OK** in the message that appears, confirming that you want to send the list to the Recycle Bin. You have now moved the Announcements list into the site's Recycle Bin.

5. On the Quick Launch, click **Lists**. Verify that the Announcements list no longer appears under **Lists**.

6. You will now restore the list. In the left navigation area, click **Recycle Bin**.

7. Select the **Announcements** list by selecting the check box to the left of its name, and then click **Restore Selection**.

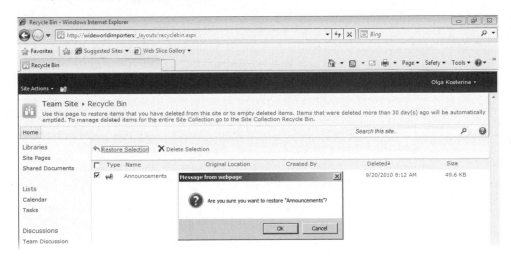

8. Click **OK** to restore the **Announcements** list.

9. On the Quick Launch, click **Lists**. Verify that the **Announcements** list is now displayed under **Lists**. Navigate to the **Announcements** list to verify that it has been restored successfully.

✖ CLEAN UP Leave the browser open if you are continuing to the next exercise.

Managing Users and Permissions

Within an organization, you are going to find that there are many different roles, and therefore, different levels of permissions are going to be required on sites, lists, and list items. Consider a Team site for a sales team, for example. There may be a sales manager and sales executives who use the site. The sales manager is likely to have different permissions from the sales executives.

There are multiple permissions that can be granted to users and groups in SharePoint Foundation. To make life simpler, these permissions are grouped into permission levels such as Full Control, Design, Contribute, and Read. Each user or group of users is then assigned a permission level, which in turn provides all the included permissions.

As we discussed in Chapter 3, when you first create a site, you have the choice of setting unique permissions on the newly created site or inheriting the permissions from the parent site. When you inherit the permissions from the parent site, you have to manage the permissions at the parent site. Lists automatically inherit their permissions from the site in which they reside. This means, for example, that users who are assigned Contribute permissions to the site will also have Contribute permissions to the list.

Users within an organization may play different roles within a site. For example, Olga is responsible for making announcements in the Announcements list, whereas Todd is responsible for assigning tasks. Therefore, the permission inheritance of those two lists must be stopped, and unique permissions assigned.

See Also You can find more information on permission levels at *http://technet.microsoft.com /en-us/library/cc721640.aspx*.

In this exercise, you will open a SharePoint site, navigate to the Tasks list, and stop permission inheritance for this list. You will then configure unique permissions for a group. We will use a group called Sales, but you can use any group or user from your environment.

SET UP Open the SharePoint site in which you would like to assign permissions, if not already open. The exercise will use the *http://wideworldimporters* site, but you can use whatever site you wish. If prompted, type your user name and password, and click OK.

BE SURE TO verify that you have sufficient rights to manage permissions. If in doubt, see the Appendix at the back of this book.

1. On the Quick Launch, under **Lists**, click **Tasks**.

   The Tasks list appears.

2. On the Ribbon, in the **List Tools**, click the **List** tab, and then, in the **Settings** group, click **List Permissions**.

   Tip Alternatively, you can click List Settings, and then, on the List Settings page, in the Permissions and Management section, click Permissions For This List.

   The Permissions page is displayed, showing a yellow bar across the top that states that the permissions for this list are inherited from its parent.

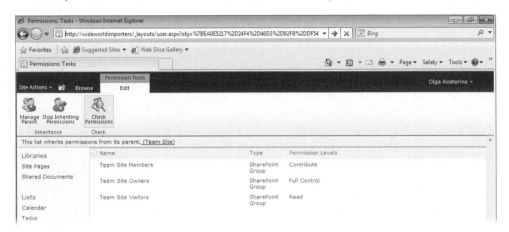

Stop Inheriting Permissions

3. On the **Edit** tab, in the **Inheritance** group, click **Stop Inheriting Permissions**.

4. Click **OK** to confirm that you are about to create unique permissions for this list.

   Notice that the yellow bar now contains the text "This list has unique permissions."

Grant Permissions

5. On the **Edit** tab, click **Grant Permissions** to display the **Grant Permissions** dialog.

6. In the **Grant Permissions** dialog, in the **Select Users** section, click the address book icon below the **Users/Groups** box.

   The Select People and Groups dialog opens.

7. Select the group or user to which you would like to grant permissions, such as **Sales**, and then click **Add**. Click **OK**.

   Tip You can type the first few characters of a group name in the Find box, and then click the magnifying glass icon to search for the group.

   The Select People and Groups dialog closes, and the selected name appears in the Users/Groups box.

8. In the **Grant Permissions** section, click **Grant users permission directly**, and then select **Contribute**.

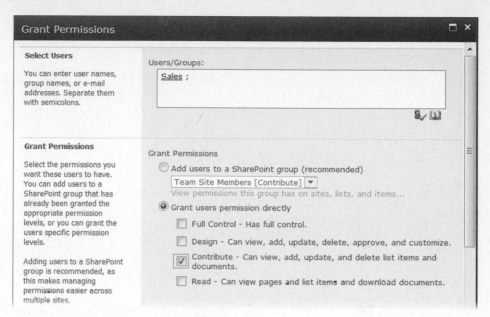

9. Click **OK**. The Grant Permissions dialog closes.

    You will now verify that the Contribute permissions have been granted.

10. On the **Permissions** page, on the **Edit** tab, in the **Check** group, click **Check Permissions** to ensure that the group has been granted **Contribute** permissions to the list.

    The Tasks: Check Permissions dialog is displayed.

11. Type the group or user name, such as **Sales**, and then click **Check Now**.

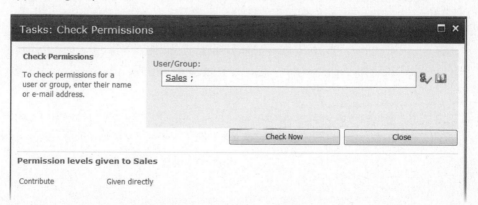

    The permission level granted to this user or group account is displayed.

12. Click **Close** in the **Tasks: Check Permissions** dialog.

 CLEAN UP Leave the browser open if you are continuing to the next exercise.

Granting List Item Permissions

Permissions may be granted to a list item or a folder contained within a list. List items and folders in the root of the list inherit permissions from the list itself. In other words, the same inheritance rules that apply to lists also apply to the list items. A list item or a subfolder that is stored within a folder inherits permissions from the parent folder. Permission inheritance can be stopped for any list item or folder at any level.

In this exercise, you will modify the permissions of a list item within the Tasks list.

 SET UP Open the SharePoint site in which you would like to assign list item permissions, if not already open. This exercise will use the *http://wideworldimporters* site, but you can use whatever site you wish. If prompted, type your user name and password, and click OK.

BE SURE TO verify that you have sufficient rights to manage permissions for the list. If in doubt, see the Appendix at the back of this book.

1. On the Quick Launch, click the **Tasks** list.

2. You will now create a new list item. Click **Add new item**.

3. In the **New Item** dialog, in the **Title** box, type **My Task**, and then click **Save**. The new item has been created.

4. Hover the mouse over the title **My Task** in the **Tasks** list, click the drop-down arrow that appears to the right of the title, and then select **Manage Permissions**.

   Tip Alternatively, select the list item by hovering the mouse over it, clicking its check box on the left, and then clicking the Item Permissions button on the Ribbon.

   The Permissions page for this list item is now displayed, with a yellow bar stating that this list item inherits permissions from its parent. You will now create unique permissions for this list item and remove all permissions to it from the Sales group.

5. On the **Edit** tab, click the **Stop Inheriting Permissions** button in the **Inheritance** group. Click **OK** in the warning message box that appears.

6. Select the user or group that you assigned list permissions to in the previous exercise, such as **Sales**, by clicking the check box at the left of its name.

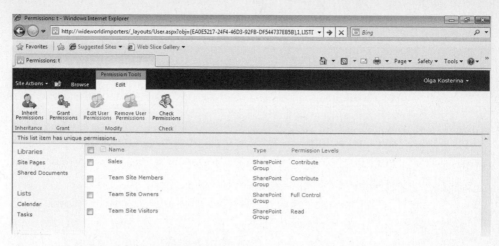

Remove User Permissions

7. Click the **Remove User Permissions** button on the Ribbon, and then click **OK** to confirm removal of all permissions from this group.

The Sales group now has Contribute permissions to the Tasks list but does not have Contribute permissions to the My Task list item that you created in this list.

Tip It is possible that within your environment, you also see custom permission levels that have been created by your server administrator.

 CLEAN UP Close the browser.

Configuring Incoming Email Settings

SharePoint Foundation allows list managers to assign an email address to several of the built-in lists. Once configured, you can send an email to the list. At first, emailing a SharePoint Foundation list seems like an odd thing to do; yet, consider the following ways that this capability could be used:

● You have an announcement to make to the entire company. Emailing a distribution list in Outlook creates a lot of email traffic. So rather than sending everyone within your company an email, you can simply email one message to the Announcement list instead.

● You are on an airplane working with a Microsoft Word document. When you are finished, you email the document to a specific list or a document library. This email sits in your outbox until the next time you connect to the Internet, at which time it is sent to the list or document library automatically. When SharePoint Foundation receives the document, it is inserted into the list or the document library for you.

● An email distribution group is set up that includes all the members of your team. The email address of a discussion board is also included in the distribution group. Every message sent to the group is also inserted into the list. When team members visit the SharePoint Foundation site that contains the list, they see the entire conversation that took place via email. They can even use the list to reply to the messages posted to the list.

See Also Enabling a discussion board for email is covered in Chapter 10, "Working with Surveys and Discussion Boards."

The following table differentiates between those lists that can and cannot be email-enabled in SharePoint Foundation (lists are in alphabetical order).

Email-Enabled Lists	Lists That Are Not Email-Enabled	
Announcements	Agenda	Phone Call Memo
Blog Posts	Attendees	Project Tasks
Calendar	Circulations	Resources
Discussion Board	Contacts	Survey
Document Library	Custom List	Tasks
Form Library	Decisions	Text Box
Picture Library	Issue Tracking	Things To Bring
Group Calendar	Links	Wiki Page Library
	Objectives	Whereabouts

Tip Before a list can be configured to get the incoming email, the SharePoint Foundation farm administrator must configure the Web application to enable incoming email. This can be done in SharePoint 2010 Central Administration using the System Settings, Configure Incoming E-Mail Settings, and selecting the Yes option in the Enable Incoming E-mail section.

See Also For more information on how to configure the email settings in SharePoint Central Administration, refer to *http://technet.microsoft.com/en-us/library/cc262947.aspx*.

In this exercise, you will configure the Announcements list to accept incoming emailed announcements.

SET UP Open the SharePoint site in which you would like to email-enable a list. The exercise will use the *http://wideworldimporters* site, but you can use whatever site you wish. If prompted, type your user name and password, and click OK.

BE SURE TO verify that you have sufficient rights to manage lists. If in doubt, see the Appendix at the back of this book.

1. Navigate to the **Announcements** list by choosing **Lists** on the Quick Launch, and then clicking the **Announcements** list.

2. On the Ribbon, on the **List Tools**, click the **List** tab, and then click **List Settings**.

3. On the **List Settings** page, in the **Communications** section, click **Incoming e-mail settings**.

4. In the **Incoming E-Mail** section, click **Yes** to allow this list to receive email.

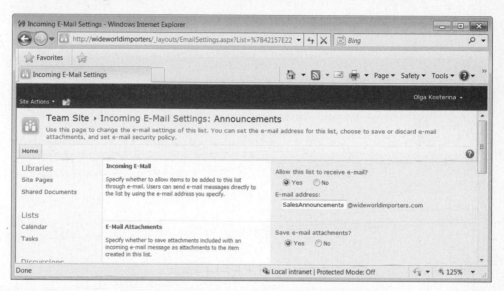

5. In the **Incoming E-Mail** section, in the **E-mail address** box, type a unique email address for this list, such as **SalesAnnouncements**.

   The email address for this list will now be SalesAnnouncements@wideworldimporters.com.

6. Leave the other options unchanged and click **OK**.

7. Open Outlook 2010 and send an email to salesannouncements@wideworldimporters.com or to an email address that you've just configured.

8. Set the Subject in your email message to **My Announcement**, and, in the body of the message, type **Wide World Importers hits the sales target**. Send the email.

9. In the browser, navigate to the **Announcements** list to see a newly created **My Announcement** list item. You might need to wait a minute for the mail to arrive and the item to be created.

 CLEAN UP Close Outlook and then close the browser.

Configuring RSS Feeds for a List or Library

Each list and library within SharePoint Foundation has the option of displaying its content in an RSS feed. RSS feeds are enabled by default for a site collection and all sites within it, but they can be disabled by a site collection administrator.

In this exercise, you will verify that the RSS settings for the site and the site collection are enabled.

SET UP Open the top-level SharePoint site in which you would like to verify that the RSS feeds are enabled. The exercise will use the *http://wideworldimporters* site, but you can use whatever site you want. If prompted, type your user name and password, and click OK.

BE SURE TO verify that you have sufficient rights to manage site collection. If in doubt, see the Appendix at the back of this book.

1. On the **Site Actions** menu, click **Site Settings**.

2. On the **Site Settings** page, in the **Site Administration** section, choose **RSS**.

   The RSS settings page is displayed.

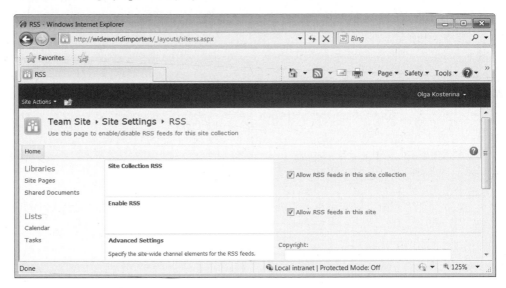

3. In the **Site Collection RSS** section, make sure that the **Allow RSS feeds in this site collection** check box is selected.

4. In the **Enable RSS** section, make sure that the **Allow RSS feeds in this site** check box is selected.

   You have now verified that RSS feeds are enabled for the site collection.

5. Using the breadcrumb, navigate back to the home page of your site.

 CLEAN UP Leave the browser open if you are continuing to the next exercise

Now that you have ensured that RSS feeds are available for your site and the site collection, you can enable RSS feeds for a list or a library. Within SharePoint, RSS feeds are especially useful within the Announcements list. Using RSS feeds, users can read announcements using an RSS viewer such as Outlook 2010 or the browser.

Tip The Data View Web Part in SharePoint Designer 2010 can be used as a good RSS reader Web Part in SharePoint Foundation.

In this exercise, you will configure the RSS feed for an Announcements list and then subscribe to this RSS feed using the browser.

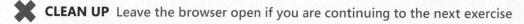 **SET UP** Open the SharePoint site that you used in the previous exercise, if it is not already open.

BE SURE TO verify that you have sufficient rights to manage lists. If in doubt, see the Appendix at the back of this book.

1. Navigate to the **Announcements** list by choosing **Lists** on the Quick Launch, and then clicking the **Announcements** list.

2. On the Ribbon, on the **List Tools**, click the **List** tab, and then click **List Settings**.

3. In the **Communications** section, click **RSS settings**.

4. In the **List RSS** section, make sure that **Allow RSS for this list?** is set to **Yes**.

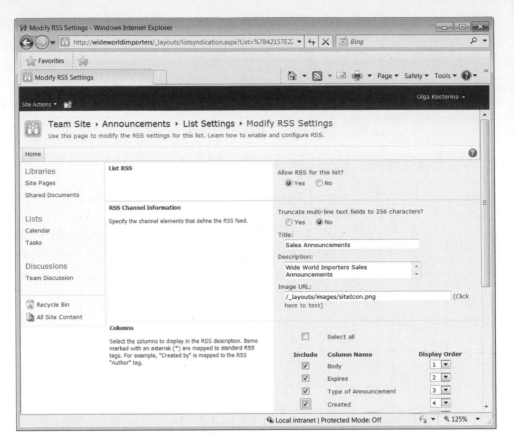

5. In the **RSS Channel Information** section, leave the **Truncate multi-line text fields to 256 characters?** option set to **No**, so all text is sent to everyone that subscribes to the feed. If you anticipate a great deal of data in the feed, but the first few sentences are all that most people need to read, you want to change this option to **Yes**. Anyone viewing the feed item has the option to browse the entire contents.

6. The Title, Description, and Image URL settings are used as part of the feed details. Change **Title** to **Sales Announcements**.

7. Change **Description** to **Wide World Importers Sales Announcements**.

8. In the **Columns** section, check the **Created By** column to make sure it is included in the feed.

9. Leave the **Item Limit** as the default, and click **OK**.

Tip The Item Limit area helps control the cost to your site's bandwidth and your farm's network when thousands of people subscribe to hundreds of lists and come to the site every hour to check for updates. (60 minutes is the default Time To Live setting in the RSS settings on the Site Settings page for each site.) The Maximum Items to Include field indicates how many list items to include in the feed, and the Maximum Days to Include field indicates how long a list item should be included. This example includes up to 25 items for any items modified in the last week (7 days). The default value for Maximum Items to Include is 25, and the default value for Maximum Days to Include is 7.

10. The RSS feed has been configured. You will now subscribe to this RSS feed using the browser. Using the breadcrumb, navigate to the **Announcements** list.

RSS
Feed

11. On the Ribbon, in the **List Tools,** click the **List** tab, and then click the **RSS Feed** button in the **Share & Track** group.

12. The Announcements RSS feed page is displayed. It isn't much to look at or interact with, but viewing it in the browser is not the intent of the page. Click **Subscribe to this feed** on the top of the page, and then, in the **Subscribe to this Feed** message that appears, click **Subscribe**.

Tip The web address shown in the browser can be used in your RSS aggregator to view the contents of this list offline.

13. The confirmation is displayed that you've successfully subscribed to this feed. Verify that you've subscribed to this feed through your browser by choosing **Favorites**, clicking the **Feeds** tab, and selecting the **Sales Announcements** RSS feed that you have just configured.

 CLEAN UP Close the browser.

Creating Indexed Columns

We tend not to use a telephone directory much these days unless we are using it to raise the height of something, such as a computer monitor. However, everyone is familiar with the concept of a telephone directory. Imagine trying to find someone's phone number in a telephone directory for Wide World Importers if the names in the directory were not stored in alphabetical order. You would eventually find what you were looking for, but it would take a very long time. Therefore, an organization's telephone directory is organized by the column in which it is most likely to be searched, such as the last name. Indexing on one column isn't always enough, since there could be thousands of people with the same last name, so there is a secondary index on the first name column. Organizing the telephone directory by these two columns makes it much faster to find the telephone number that you are looking for.

All content in a site collection is stored within a SQL database that could contain thousands of items. When you create a view with a filter for a list, SharePoint needs to organize the content by finding all the list items for that list in the content database and then finding all the list items that match the filter and sort options. To improve performance, you can create indexed columns. You may think that creating an index on every column would be wise; however, these indexes also require resources and you would never search a telephone directory to find the person by looking up his or her telephone number. Therefore, you should use indexing wisely. For example, within an Announcements list, you can create an index on the Title column but not on the Body column. Once you have created an indexed column, you will see a performance gain when viewing information within a list with a large number of items.

In this exercise, you will create an indexed column within an Announcements list.

 SET UP Open the SharePoint site in which you would like to configure an indexed column. The exercise will use the *http://wideworldimporters* site, but you can use whatever site you wish. If prompted, type your user name and password, and click OK.

BE SURE TO verify that you have sufficient rights to manage lists. If in doubt, see the Appendix at the back of this book.

1. Navigate to the **Announcements** list by choosing **Lists** on the Quick Launch, and then clicking the **Announcements** list.

2. On the Ribbon, in the **List Tools**, click the **List** tab, and then click **List Settings**.

3. On the **List Settings** page, scroll to the bottom of the **Columns** section and click **Indexed Columns**.

4. On the **Indexed Columns** page, click **Create a new Index**.

5. In the **Primary Column** section, select **Title** from the drop-down list of available columns. The Title column is likely to be the most commonly sorted and searched column.

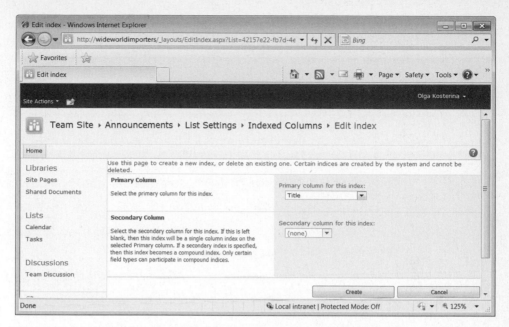

The Secondary column is dimmed because it wouldn't make sense to index Body or Expires—they are Rich Text and Date type columns, respectively.

6. Click **Create**. After some processing identified by a processing page, a confirmation page is displayed, saying that the index is now created. You can create multiple indexes for a list if required.

7. Using the breadcrumb, navigate to the **Announcements** list.

✖ CLEAN UP Leave the browser open if you are continuing to the next exercise.

Preventing Duplicate List Items

SharePoint list items could be duplicated quite easily by human error, by an error in a workflow, or by copying and pasting using Windows Explorer (if you are using a library). It is possible to stop the duplication of list items within a list and a library by setting a column's property to Enforce Unique Values. Enforce Unique Values should be set to Yes only on columns where duplicate values would clearly indicate that an item is duplicated. For example, you would not set the Status column of a Tasks list to enforce unique values; otherwise, that would mean that you could only ever have one completed task at a time. However, it would also mean that you could have only one task that was not started, which could be seen as a benefit.

Tip You can enforce unique values only for the indexed columns.

In this exercise, you will enforce unique values for items in the Announcements list.

SET UP Open the SharePoint site in which you would like to enforce unique values for a list column. The exercise will use the *http://wideworldimporters* site, but you can use whatever site you wish. If prompted, type your user name and password, and click OK.

BE SURE TO verify that you have sufficient rights to manage lists. If in doubt, see the Appendix at the back of this book.

1. Navigate to the **Announcements** list by choosing **Lists** on the Quick Launch**,** and then clicking the **Announcements** list.

2. On the Ribbon, in the **List Tools**, click the **List** tab, and then click **List Settings**.

3. On the **List Settings** page, in the **Columns** section, click the **Title** column link.

4. On the **Change Column** page, in the **Additional Column Settings** section, click **Yes** in the **Enforce unique values** option.

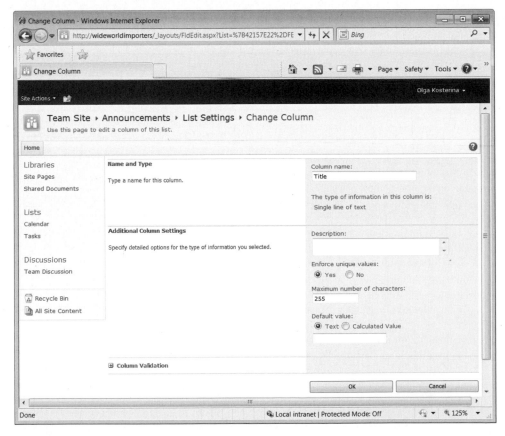

5. Click **OK**.

   You have now enabled the Enforce Unique Values option for the Title column in the Announcements list.

6. You will now verify that duplicate items are prevented. Using the breadcrumb, navigate to the **Announcements** list. Click **Add new announcement** and, in the **Title** box, type the title of an existing list item, such as **My Announcement**. An error message appears, saying that this title already exists in the list.

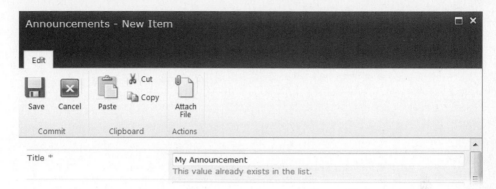

7. Change the title to a unique value, such as **My New Announcement**, and click **Save**. The new announcement with the unique title is created and displayed in the list.

CLEAN UP Close the browser.

Key Points

- List configuration settings are accessed via the List Settings page. There are six groups of settings: General Settings, Permissions and Management, Communications, Content Types, Columns, and Views.

- Versioning enables you to view the history of a list item and restore previous versions of it if required.

- Adding validation to list columns helps to create more consistent and accurate content.

- Content types give you the ability to group custom columns and other configurations together and make these combinations available to any list within the current site or child site.

- Lists inherit permissions from the site that contains them. However, you can stop that inheritance and configure unique permissions for lists and list items by granting access to individual users or groups.

- Setting an RSS feed provides an easy way to view list content outside SharePoint in the browser or any other RSS reader.

- You can email-enable SharePoint lists.

- Indexed columns improve the performance of SharePoint lists.

- If a list is deleted by accident, you can restore the list from the site's Recycle Bin.

Chapter at a Glance

Configure library settings, page 220

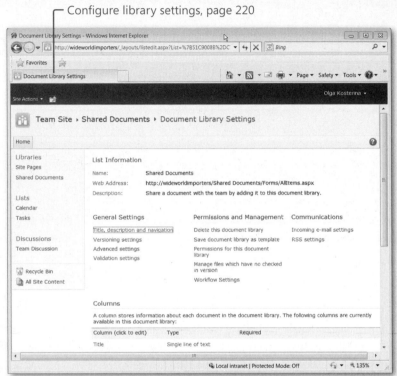

Open documents in the client or browser, page 221

Opening Documents in the Browser

Specify whether browser-enabled documents should be opened in the client or browser by default when a user clicks on them. If the client application is unavailable, the document will always be opened in the browser.

Default open behavior for browser-enabled documents:
- ○ Open in the client application
- ○ Open in the browser
- ○ Use the server default (Open in the browser)

Require Check Out

Specify whether users must check out documents before making changes in this document library.   Learn about requiring check out.

Require documents to be checked out before they can be edited?
- ◉ Yes   ○ No

Configure required checkout, page 224

Document Version History

Specify whether a version is created each time you edit a file in this document library.   Learn about versions.

Create a version each time you edit a file in this document library?
- ○ No versioning
- ○ Create major versions
  Example: 1, 2, 3, 4
- ◉ Create major and minor (draft) versions
  Example: 1.0, 1.1, 1.2, 2.0

Optionally limit the number of versions to retain:
- ☐ Keep the following number of major versions:

- ☑ Keep drafts for the following number of major versions:
  10

Enable versioning, page 226

8 Working with Library Settings

In this chapter, you will learn how to

- ✔ Open documents in the client or the browser.
- ✔ Modify a library template.
- ✔ Configure required checkout.
- ✔ Enable versioning.
- ✔ Manage checked-out files.
- ✔ Configure the Sites Assets library.
- ✔ Create a custom Send To destination.
- ✔ Manage users and permissions.
- ✔ Create content types.
- ✔ Create a Standard view.
- ✔ Delete and restore a library.
- ✔ Configure other library types.

In Chapter 5, "Working with Libraries," we discussed how to create SharePoint libraries and how to work with the documents that are stored in these libraries. In this chapter, we will look at managing library settings and how to configure a library's functionality by modifying its settings in Microsoft SharePoint Foundation. You can access the settings for a library using the Library Settings button in the Settings group on the Ribbon located on the Library tab on the Library Tools tab set.

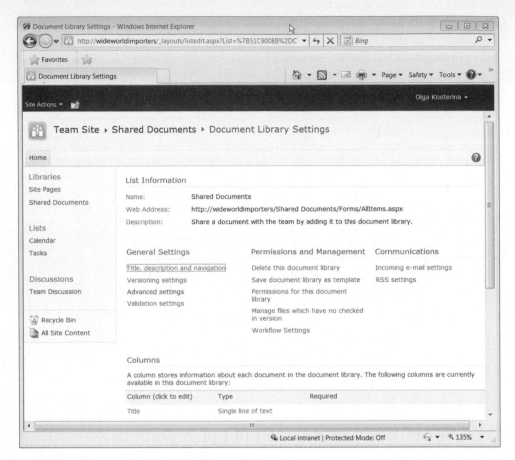

Because a library is a list of files, list settings and library settings are very similar. The list settings that we discussed in Chapter 7, "Working with List Settings," such as naming and navigation, are applicable to libraries as well. For example, you can set up a document library on the Quick Launch to make it easier to find, the same way as you do for a list.

In addition, in this chapter, we will explore configuration settings that are specific to libraries, including configuring default behavior for opening documents, managing library templates, setting up required checkout and versioning, permission management, and the deletion and restoration of a library.

> **Practice Files** Before you can complete the exercises in this chapter, you need to download the Chapter 8 practice files from the book's catalog page to the following folder on your computer: Documents\Microsoft Press\SBS_SPF\Chapter08. See "Using the Practice Files" at the beginning of this book for more information.

Important Remember to use your SharePoint site location in place of *http://wideworldimporters* in the following exercises.

Opening Documents in the Client or the Browser

SharePoint document libraries have the ability to open a document within the browser, as opposed to having them display in their native Microsoft Office client application, such as Microsoft Word or Microsoft Excel. The default option is to open in a browser using Office Web Apps, such as Word Web App or Excel Web App, so that users can use their browser to enter information online. This feature, however, does depend on Office Web Apps being installed and activated on the SharePoint Foundation server. The benefit of opening Microsoft Word, Excel, PowerPoint, and One Note documents in the browser is that you can edit them using Office Web Apps from any computer or other device that has a browser. While the online functionality of Word Web App, for example, is lighter than a Word client application, there are many everyday editing tasks that Word Web App supports, and this is very handy for making changes to the documents when you are traveling and only have access to your SharePoint site via a browser. You can configure the default behavior for a document to always open documents in the client application, to always open documents in the browser, or to go by the server default, which is to open in the browser. Regardless of the default opening behavior configured for a library, it is always possible to select another opening option from the document drop-down context menu. For example, if the library is configured to always open documents in a client application but you would like to edit a particular document in the browser, you can select the Edit In Browser option for this document using the document's drop-down context menu.

In this exercise, you will configure the library so that its documents always open in the Office client applications.

 SET UP Open the SharePoint site that contains the library that you want to configure. The exercise will use the *http://wideworldimporters* site, but you can use whatever site you want. If prompted, type your user name and password, and click OK.

BE SURE TO verify that you have sufficient rights to manage this library. If in doubt, see the Appendix at the back of this book.

1. On the Quick Launch, click **Shared Documents**.

2. In the **Library Tools**, click the **Library** tab.

Library Settings

3. In the **Settings** group on the Ribbon, click the **Library Settings** button to display the **Document Library Settings** page.

4. Click **Advanced Settings** from the **General Settings** section. The Advanced Settings page is displayed.

5. In the **Opening Documents in the Browser** section, select the **Open in the client application** option, scroll to the bottom of the page, and then click **OK**.

Opening Documents in the Browser	Default open behavior for browser-enabled documents:
Specify whether browser-enabled documents should be opened in the client or browser by default when a user clicks on them. If the client application is unavailable, the document will always be opened in the browser.	⦿ Open in the client application ◯ Open in the browser ◯ Use the server default (Open in the browser)

From now on, documents from this document library always open in the client application.

✖ **CLEAN UP** Leave the browser open if you are continuing to the next exercise.

Modifying a Library Template

When a document library is created, you can choose the document template for this library. Then, when you click the New Document command on the Documents ribbon tab, the document template determines which Office client program or which Office Web App is opened. The document template is then used as a basis for the new document. For example, the Shared Documents library on a Team site uses a blank Word document as its document template by default.

You can change the template for a library. For example, you may prefer to use a blank Excel workbook or a Word template that contains a header such as your corporate logo. The template document resides in a hidden folder called Forms within the library. You can upload an alternative document template file for the library, or you can edit the existing template.

In this exercise, you will modify the default template for the Shared Documents document library and then create a new document based on the modified template.

 SET UP Open the SharePoint site that you used in the previous exercise, if it is not already open, and navigate to the Shared Documents library.

BE SURE TO verify that you have sufficient rights to manage this library. If in doubt, see the Appendix at the back of this book.

1. In the **Library Tools**, click the **Library** tab, and then click the **Library Settings** button in the **Settings** group on the Ribbon to display the **Document Library Settings** page, if it is not already displayed.

2. Under **General Settings**, click **Advanced Settings**. The Advanced Settings page is displayed.

3. In the **Content Types** section, confirm that the **Allow management of content types?** option is set to **No** so that the **Template URL** field in the **Document Template** section is enabled.

4. Click **Edit Template** below the **Template URL** box in the **Document Template** section.

5. The Open Document message box appears. Click **OK** to open the template.dotx file in Word.

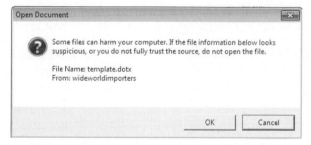

6. Double-click the top of the blank Word document to enter the **Header** section.

7. Type **Wide World Importers**, set the text to bold, and increase the point size as desired.

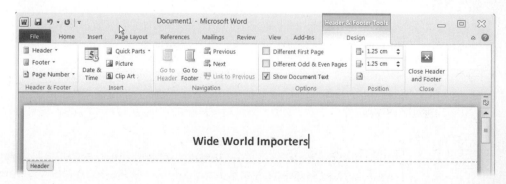

8. Click **File**, **Close** to close the document. When the **Microsoft Word** message box opens, click **Save**.

9. The modified template has been saved to the library. You will now create a new document based on this template. In the browser, navigate back to the document library by clicking **Shared Documents** on the breadcrumb.

New
Document ▾

10. Click the **Documents** tab on the Ribbon, and then click **New Document**.

11. If a warning message appears, click **OK**.

12. Word opens a new document that is based on the template that you've just created. In the document, type **Proposal**.

13. Click **File, Save As**, type **Proposal** in the **Name** box, and then click **Save**. The new document, called Proposal.docx, is saved back to the library.

✖ **CLEAN UP** Close Word. Leave the browser open if you are continuing to the next exercise.

Configuring Required Checkout

Checking documents out of the library is invaluable when several people could be making changes to the same document at the same time. In Chapter 5, you learned how to check out a document and then check it back in the library. You can also enforce the checkout of a document before a user can edit it by configuring the Require Check Out option. The default for this option is set to No, meaning that users are not required to check out a document before it can be edited. Many organizations, however, have a policy requiring that all documents are always checked out for editing. To meet this requirement, a SharePoint library can be configured to require checkout before a document can be edited.

In this exercise, you will configure a Shared Documents library to require checkout of all documents, and then explore how this setting is working.

➡ **SET UP** Open the SharePoint site that you used in the previous exercise, if it is not already open, and navigate to the Shared Document library.

BE SURE TO verify that you have sufficient rights to manage this library. If in doubt, see the Appendix at the back of this book.

1. In the **Library Tools**, click the **Library** tab, and then click the **Library Settings** button in the **Settings** group to display the **Document Library Settings** page, if not already displayed.

2. Click **Versioning settings** under **General Settings**.

3. On the **Versioning Settings** page, in the **Require Check Out** section, select **Yes**. Click **OK** at the bottom of the page.

4. The Document Library Settings page is displayed. You will now edit a document in the Shared Documents library to validate the required checkout setting. On the breadcrumb at the top of the page, click **Shared Documents**.

5. The Shared Documents library is displayed in the **All Documents** view. Click the **Proposal** document.

6. An **Open Document** message box appears. You can either open the document as read-only or check it out for editing. Make sure that the default option, **Read Only**, is selected and then click **OK**.

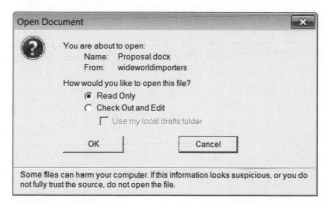

Tip If you intend to edit the document, you need to click Check Out And Edit, and the document will open in Word. For this exercise, we will keep the Read Only default to explore the behavior of the required checkout setting.

7. Word 2010 opens and displays the information bar, requiring that you check out the document. To edit a document, click **Check Out** on the information bar.

8. The information bar disappears, and the Word ribbon is displayed. Type some text in the document, and then, on the Quick Access Toolbar, click the **Save** icon.

9. Close Word by clicking the cross in the upper-right corner of the window.

10. A Word message box opens, stating that other users cannot see your changes until you check in the document and asking whether you want to check in the document. Click **Yes**.

11. The Check In dialog opens. Click **OK**. The document is saved and checked back in the library so that other users can edit it.

✖ **CLEAN UP** Leave the browser open if you are continuing to the next exercise.

Enabling Versioning

You can turn on or turn off the versioning of documents stored in the library via Versioning settings. Each time a document is changed when versioning is turned on, SharePoint Foundation saves a copy of the edited version of the document. This provides you with multiple versions of the same document so that you can easily see what the document contained before the modifications and revert to a previous version if necessary.

When versioning is turned on, you can select between two types of versioning: major versions only, or major and minor versions. Major versions store a full-text copy of each document version. The latest version is always published, meaning that those with access to the document library can view the most recent version of the document.

Major and minor versioning allows you to publish major versions of a document while creating modified, minor versions of the same document that only a subset of users with access to the library can view and edit. You can control who views a minor version by using the Draft Item Security configuration setting. Using major and minor versions is useful when performing multiple modifications of a document prior to submitting it for approval. When major and minor versioning is selected, you can control how many versions of each document are retained in the document library.

Tip Only SharePoint libraries provide the ability to use both major and minor document versions. SharePoint lists also have versioning settings, but you cannot use major and minor versions as you can with libraries.

In this exercise, you will configure a document library to use both major and minor versions, and then explore a major and a minor version of a document.

 SET UP Open the SharePoint site that you used in the previous exercise, if it is not already open, and navigate to the Shared Document library.

BE SURE TO verify that you have sufficient rights to manage this library. If in doubt, see the Appendix at the back of this book.

1. In the **Library Tools**, click the **Library** tab, and then click the **Library Settings** button in the **Settings** group to display the **Document Library Settings** page.

2. Click **Versioning Settings** under **General Settings**.

3. In the **Document Version History** section, select **Create major and minor (draft) versions**.

4. Select the **Keep drafts for the following number of major versions** check box, and then type **10** in the text box.

5. Scroll to the bottom of the page and click **OK** to enable versioning.

6. You will now create a version of a document in this library. Using the breadcrumb at the top of the page, navigate to the **Shared Documents** library.

7. Click **Proposal**, and then, in the **Open Document** message box, click **Check Out and Edit**.

   Word 2010 opens and displays the contents of the document.

8. Make any changes to the document. For example, you might decide to type **=rand()** followed by **ENTER** to insert some text. On the Quick Access Toolbar in Word, click the **Save** icon. Close the document by clicking the cross in the upper-right corner of the Word window.

9. A Word message box opens, stating that other users cannot see your changes until you check in the document. Click **Yes** to check in the document now.

10. The Check In dialog opens. Leave the default option, **1.1 Minor version (draft)**, selected. In the **Version Comments** box, type **WideWorldChanges**, and then click **OK**.

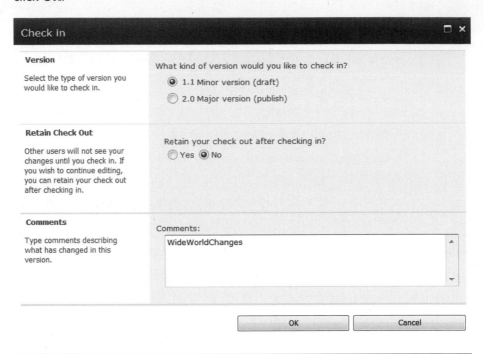

11. Word closes, and the library page displays in the browser. In the **Shared Documents** library, hover the mouse over the name of the document and click the arrow that appears on the right. Click **Version History** from the drop-down context menu.

Notice that the latest version is 1.1.

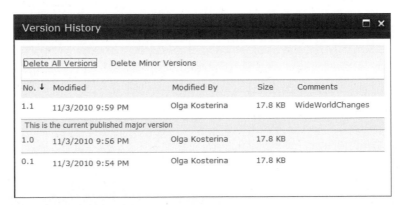

12. Close the **Version History** dialog.

13. Hover the mouse over the name of the document again, click the down arrow, and choose **Publish a Major Version**.

14. In the **Publish Major Version** dialog, in the **Comments** field, delete the existing text. Type **Ready to send to the customer**, and click **OK**.

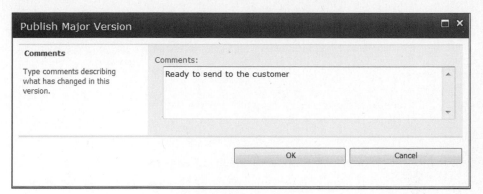

15. The Shared Documents library is displayed. You will now restore the previous version of the document. Hover the mouse over the name of the document, click the down arrow, and select **Check Out**. Click **OK** to confirm the checkout.

16. Hover the mouse over the name of the document, click the down arrow, and then click **Version History**. Note that version 2.0 is now the latest version.

17. In the **Version History** dialog, hover the mouse over the **Modified date** for version 1.0, and click the down arrow.

18. Select **Restore** from the menu to restore version 1.0 as the latest version.

19. Click **OK** in the warning message box that appears.

Note that the latest version is now version 2.1, which is the same as 1.0 and does not have the version comments that you set for version 2.0.

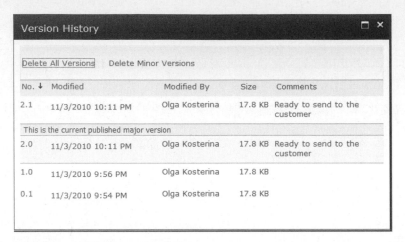

Close the Version History dialog.

20. On the library page, hover the mouse over the document, click the down arrow, and select **Check In**. In the **Check In** dialog, in the **Version** section, select **2.1 Minor version (draft)** and click **OK**.

21. Hover the mouse over the **name** of the document again, click the down arrow, and choose **Publish a Major Version**. Click **OK** in the Publish Major Version dialog. The restored version is now published.

❌ **CLEAN UP** Leave the browser open if you are continuing to the next exercise.

Managing Checked-Out Files

Imagine how many times during the day you are interrupted by telephone calls or last-minute meetings that divert your attention from an open document you are working with. As a result, you may inadvertently leave a document checked out of a SharePoint library. Many people work collaboratively in different time zones nowadays, and it is possible that somebody will need to see and edit a document that you have left checked out while you are offline. To address this problem, SharePoint Foundation allows users with permission to override the check out in this library to check a document back in a library even if the document has been checked out by another user. If the document has a checked-in version that is displayed on the library page, then a user with appropriate permissions can override the checkout by another user and check the document in using the Check In command on the context menu or on the Ribbon. However, if the checked-out document is new and does not have a checked-in version displayed on the library page, an additional step is required to take ownership of this document using the Library Settings.

In this exercise, you will check in a new document that has been left checked out by another user.

> **Practice Files** You will use the practice file Contoso Proposal.docx, located in the Documents\Microsoft Press\SBS_SPF\Chapter08 folder.

SET UP For this exercise, you need to have two sets of user credentials. The first user should have sufficient permissions to check out and edit documents in a library. The second user should have sufficient permissions to override the checkout in the library. For more information about permissions, see the Appendix at the back of this book.

BE SURE TO open the SharePoint site that you used in the previous exercise, log in as the first user, and navigate to the Shared Document library.

Check Out

1. You will first add a new document to the library, which then will be checked out to you. In the **Shared Documents** library that you have been working with, click **Add Document**, and then, in the **Upload Document** dialog, browse to the practice files folder **Documents\Microsoft Press\SBS_SPF\Chapter08**, select **Contoso Proposal.docx**, and click **Open**.

   Tip Remember that in the exercise earlier in this chapter, this library was configured to require checkout when opening documents.

2. In the **Upload** dialog, click **OK**.

   In the Shared Documents-Contoso Proposal.docx dialog that appears, notice the confirmation that the document has been uploaded and is currently checked out to you, and then close the dialog.

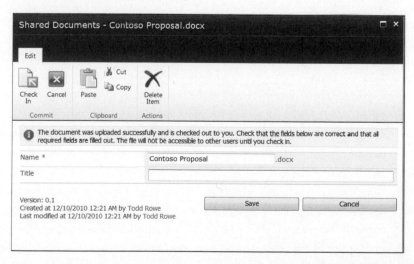

3. You will now sign in as a different user. Click the down arrow to the right of your name in the right corner of the page and click **Sign in as a Different User**.

Enter the **Username** and **Password** for a second user who has permissions to manage this library.

4. The library page is displayed. Notice that you cannot see the new document, My Proposal.docx, any longer because it does not have the checked-in version that is available to the users other than its owner, whom the new document is checked out to.

You will now take ownership of the document, so that you can check it back in.

5. In the **Library Tools**, click the **Library** tab, and then click the **Library Settings** button in the **Settings** group on the Ribbon.

6. In the **Document Library Settings** page, in the **Permissions and Management** section, select **Manage files which have no checked in version**.

The Checked Out Files page is displayed.

7. Select the document that you added to the library in step 1.

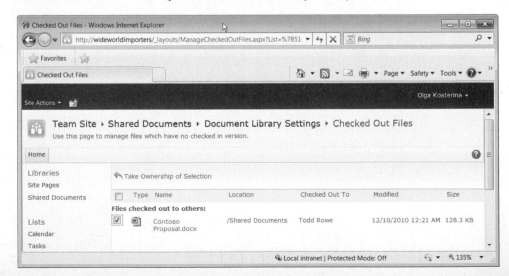

8. Click **Take Ownership of Selection**, and then click **OK** in the confirmation message box that appears.

    You now have taken ownership of the document and can check it back in so that other users can have access to it. Notice that the check box has disappeared because you are the document's owner.

9. You will now check the document back in so that it is available to other users. On the breadcrumb, click **Shared Documents** to go back to the library.

10. Notice that you can see the document on the library page because you are now its owner. Hover the mouse over the document, click the down arrow, and then click **Check In** from the context menu.

11. In the **Check In** dialog that appears, click **OK** to check the document in the library.

    You have now checked in a new document that has been checked out to another user.

✖ **CLEAN UP** Click the arrow next to the user name in the upper-right corner of the browser window and choose Sign Out from the drop-down menu, and then close the browser.

Configuring the Sites Assets Library

The Sites Assets library is a library that is created by default by SharePoint Foundation when a new Team site is created. It is especially useful when you work with wiki web pages. Site assets are usually images that are uploaded to this library for use within a wiki web page. When you upload a file to a site via the Ribbon commands on the Insert tab while editing a wiki web page, the Site Assets library can be used as the default location instead of you being prompted to choose a location. This makes it easier to find site assets for wiki web pages. You can set up any document library as the default location for your site's assets.

See Also For more information on editing wiki web pages, refer to Chapter 6, "Working with Web Pages."

In this exercise, you will set the Shared Documents library as the default location for storing images or other files in wiki web pages.

> **Practice Files** You will use the practice file WideWorldImportersLogo.png, located in the Documents\Microsoft Press\SBS_SPF\Chapter08 folder.

 SET UP Open the SharePoint site that you used in the previous exercise, if it is not already open, and navigate to the document library that you want to make the default location, such as Shared Documents Library.

BE SURE TO verify that you have sufficient rights to manage this library. If in doubt, see the Appendix at the back of this book.

1. In the **Library Tools**, click the **Library** tab, and then click the **Library Settings** button in the **Settings** group on the Ribbon to display the **Document Library Settings** page.

2. Click **Advanced Settings** from the **General Settings** section. The Advanced Settings page is displayed.

3. In the **Site Assets Library** section, click **Yes** to confirm that this library should be a site assets library and should store images and other files that users upload to their wiki pages.

Site Assets Library

Specify whether this library should be presented as the default location for storing images or other files that users upload to their wiki pages.

Should this document library be a site assets library?

⦿ Yes   ◯ No

4. Click **OK**. The **Document Library Settings** page is displayed.

5. You will now validate that this library has become the site assets library by editing a wiki web page. Click the **Home** link on the top link bar to display the home page of your Team site.

6. On the **Site Actions** menu, click **Edit Page** to put the page into Edit mode.

7. In the **Editing Tools**, click the **Insert** tab, and then click the **Upload File** button in the **Links** group on the Ribbon.

Upload
File

The Upload Document dialog appears, with the name of the document library that you have chosen as the default site assets library listed in the Upload to text box.

Upload Document

Name: [   ] [Browse...]

Upload to: [Shared Documents   ▼]

☑ Overwrite existing files

[OK]   [Cancel]

8. Click **Browse** and, in the **Choose File to Upload** dialog, navigate to the practice files folder **Documents\Microsoft Press\SBS_SPF\Chapter08**.

9. Select the **WideWorldImportersLogo.png** image and click **Open**.

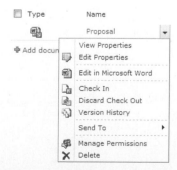

10. In the **Upload Document** dialog, click **OK**. The Shared Documents-WideWorldImportersLogo.png dialog opens.

11. Type a name for your image, such as **Logo**, and then click **Save**.

    The image is uploaded to the document library that you have configured to be the site assets library, and a link to that file is used on the wiki page.

✖ **CLEAN UP** Leave the browser open if you are continuing to the next exercise.

Creating a Custom Send To Destination

The Custom Send To Destination feature allows you to enter a Uniform Resource Locator (URL) for a document library other than the repository that your SharePoint administrators might have set at the SharePoint Foundation 2010 farm level, where users can send their documents automatically once they are finished and ready for a wider audience's consumption. This is handy if you want to ensure that all documents under development are written in one document library, while those available for public consumption are hosted in a different document library with different permissions in the same site.

Tip You can also ensure that the contents in this library are not included in the search results by removing them from the indexing feature in SharePoint Server 2010.

Each document within a document library contains a drop-down context menu known as the Edit Control Block (ECB).

You can add to the ECB a menu item that allows you to send a document from this library to another location, such as a document archive. To set up the Send To destination menu item, you simply enter the URL of the destination location to which you want to send documents.

In this exercise, you will configure a custom Send To destination setting to allow users to move documents easily from Shared Documents to a new library called Accepted Proposals.

 SET UP Open the SharePoint site that you used in the previous exercise, if it is not already open.

BE SURE TO verify that you have sufficient rights to manage this library and create libraries on this site. If in doubt, see the Appendix at the back of this book.

1. You will first create a new library that will serve as the destination. On the **Site Actions** menu, click **New Document Library**. The Create dialog opens.

2. In the **Name** text box, type **Accepted Proposals**, and then, at the bottom of the dialog, click **Create** to accept all the default options.

3. You will now configure the Custom Send To Destination setting in the Shared Documents library. On the Quick Launch, under **Libraries**, click **Shared Documents,** and then, in the **Library Tools**, click the **Library** tab.

4. Click the **Library Settings** button in the **Settings** group on the Ribbon to display the **Document Library Settings** page, and then click **Advanced Settings** from the **General Settings** section. The Advanced Settings page is displayed.

5. In the **Custom Send To Destination** section, in the **Destination** text box, type **Accepted Proposals**.

6. In the **URL** text box, type **http://wideworldimporters/Accepted%20Proposals** (where %20 in the URL represents a space in the library name). Click **OK**.

7. You will now explore how the setting works. Navigate back to the **Shared Documents** library using the breadcrumb.

8. Hover the mouse over a document, such as **Proposal**, click the down arrow, and then click **Send To**. Click **Accepted Proposals** from the drop-down menu.

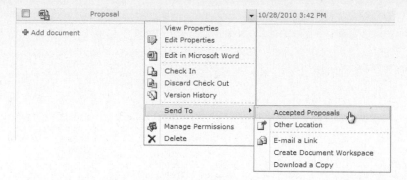

9. The Copy page is displayed. In the **Update** section, click **Yes** to prompt the author to send out updates when the document is checked in, and then click **OK**.

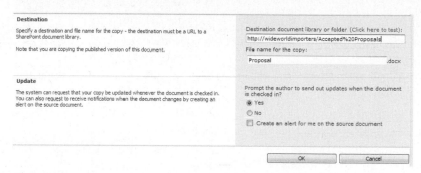

10. The Copy Progress message box opens. Click **OK**.

11. The Copy Progress message box states that the copy operation was successful. Click **Done**.

12. Using the Quick Launch, navigate to the **Accepted Proposals** library to confirm that the document has been copied.

CLEAN UP Leave the browser open if you are continuing to the next exercise.

Managing Users and Permissions

A document library can inherit its permissions from the site where the library is located, or it can have its own unique permissions. If the permissions are inherited, they are managed either on the site in which the library resides or on a parent site, depending on where the inheritance starts. A folder or a document within a library can inherit their permissions from the library, or unique permissions can be granted for a folder or a document within the library.

SharePoint Foundation includes 12 library permissions that determine the specific actions that users can perform in the library. They are listed in the following table.

Library Permissions	Description
Manage Lists	Allows the user to create and delete lists and libraries, add or remove columns in a list or a library, and add or remove public views of a list or a library
Override Check Out	Allows the user to discard or check in a document that is checked out to another user
Add Items	Allows the user to add items to lists and add documents to document libraries
Edit Items	Allows the user to edit items in lists, edit documents in document libraries, and customize Web Part Pages in document libraries
Delete Items	Allows the user to delete items from a list and documents from a document library
View Items	Allows the user to view items in lists and documents in document libraries
Approve Items	Allows the user to approve a minor version of a list item or document
Open Items	Allows the user to view the source of documents with server-side file handlers
View Versions	Allows the user to view past versions of a list item or document
Delete Versions	Allows the user to delete past versions of a list item or document
Create Alerts	Allows the user to create alerts
View Application Pages	Allows the user to view forms, views, and application pages, and enumerate lists

The library permissions can be assigned to permission levels. Each permission level is a named collection of permissions that can be assigned to SharePoint users and groups. There are five default permission levels: Read, Contribute, Design, Full Control, and Limited Access. You can use the default permission levels or create your own.

See Also For more information about permissions, see the Appendix at the back of this book.

After creating a library, you might want to grant more privileges to certain people, or restrict their privileges. More often than not, you might want to give some people more access rights to a particular library. For example, Olga Kosterina might have given Read permission for the overall site to Todd Rowe when it was created. However, she might decide later that she wants him to manage the Accepted Proposals library. Todd currently has only Read access to this library because that is his overall permissions level on the site, but Olga can assign Todd a permission level of Full Control for the Accepted Proposals library so that Todd can manage it.

In this exercise, you will configure the permissions for the Accepted Proposals document library so that a user such as Todd has a permission level of Full Control in this document library. You will then remove the Full Control permission level from the site owners so that only Todd has the Full Control permission level in this library.

SET UP Open the SharePoint site that you used in the previous exercise, if it is not already open.

BE SURE TO verify that you have sufficient rights to manage permissions for this library. If in doubt, see the Appendix at the back of this book.

1. On the Quick Launch, click **Accepted Proposals**.

2. On the **Library** tab, click the **Library Settings** button in the **Settings** group on the Ribbon to display the **Document Library Settings** page.

3. In the **Permissions and Management** section, click **Permissions for this document library**. The Permissions page appears.

   Notice that the yellow status bar below the Ribbon states that this library inherits permissions from its parent.

Stop Inheriting Permissions

4. On the **Edit** tab, click **Stop Inheriting Permissions**.

   A message box opens, warning you that you are about to create unique permissions for this document library and that changes made to the parent site permissions will no longer affect this document library.

5. Click **OK**.

   Notice that the yellow status bar below the Ribbon now states that this library has unique permissions.

Grant Permissions

6. On the **Edit** tab, click **Grant Permissions**. The Grant Permissions dialog appears.

7. In the **User/Groups** box, type the user name or email address of the user to whom you would like to grant permissions, such as **Todd,** and then click the **Check Names** icon.

8. In the **Grant Permissions** section, under **Grant users permission directly**, select the **Full Control** check box and click **OK**.

   Todd is now added to the list of users and groups who have access to the document library. Todd is mapped to the Full Control permission level.

9. You will now remove the Full Control permission level for this library from the site owners group. Click the check box to the left of **<*site name*> Owners** group to select it (your site name will be shown in the name of the group).

10. On the **Edit** tab, click **Remove User Permissions**, and then click **OK** to confirm removal of all permissions for the Owners SharePoint group. Todd is now the only user who has Full Control over the Accepted Proposals library.

Remove
Permissions

Tip You can check the permissions for any specific user within the document library. An exercise in the section entitled "Managing Users and Permissions," in Chapter 7, describes the process for a list, and the same process can be used for a library.

✖ CLEAN UP Close the browser.

Creating Content Types

Content types are very useful within document libraries. Document Content Types allow you to specify a template document for each content type that is used within a library. For example, consider a Sales Team site that allows salespeople to create quotations, proposals, and invoices. These three document types could be created within the same document library, each one using its own template and metadata.

In this exercise, you will create a content type for proposal documents and then create a new document based on this content type. The new content type will consist of a new document template, along with custom metadata that will capture the Customer and the Proposal Value properties.

> **Practice Files** You will use the practice file ProposalsTemplate.docx, located in the Documents\Microsoft Press\SBS_SPF\Chapter08 folder.

 SET UP Open the SharePoint site in which you would like to create a content type.

BE SURE TO verify that you have sufficient rights to create content types. If in doubt, see the Appendix at the back of this book.

1. Click **Site Actions**, and then click **Site Settings**.

2. In the **Site Settings** page, under **Galleries**, click **Site content types**. The Site Content Types page is displayed.

3. Click **Create**.

4. On the **New Site Content Type** page, in the **Name** box, type **Proposals**, and in the **Description** box, type **Wide World Importers Customer Proposals**.

5. Make sure that the **Select parent content type from** option is set to **Document Content Types**, and then, in the **Parent Content Type** list, select **Document**.

6. Leave the other options at the default settings and click **OK**.

    The Proposals content type page is displayed.

7. Under **Settings**, click **Advanced settings**. The Advanced Settings page is displayed.

8. In the **Document Template** section, click **Upload a new document template**, and then click **Browse**.

9. In the **Choose File to Upload** dialog box, navigate to the **Documents\Microsoft Press\SBS_SPF\Chapter08** folder and click **ProposalsTemplate.docx**. Click **Open**.

10. On the **Advanced Settings** page, accept the defaults and click **OK**.

    The Proposals content type page is displayed.

11. In the **Columns** section, click **Add from new site column** to create the first custom column for this content type. The New Site Column page is displayed.

12. In the **Column name** box, type the name of your column, such as **Customer Name**, and ensure that **Single Line of Text** is selected. Accept the defaults and click **OK**.

    The Proposals content type page is displayed.

13. In the **Columns** section, click **Add from new site column** again to create another custom column with the name **Proposal Value**, column type **Currency**, **minimum** value of **50**, and **maximum** value of **10000**. Click **OK**.

    The Proposals content type page is displayed.

    You have created a new content type and have added two custom columns. You will now add this content type to the Shared Documents library.

14. On the Quick Launch, click **Shared Documents**. Click the **Library** tab, and then click **Library Settings** in the **Settings** group on the Ribbon to display the **Document Library Settings** page.

15. In the **General Settings** section, click **Advanced settings**, and in the **Content Types** section, under **Allow management of content types**, select **Yes**. Scroll down the page and click **OK**.

    The Document Library Settings page is displayed.

16. In the **Content Types** section, click **Add from existing site content types**. The Add Content Types page is displayed.

17. From the **Available Site Content Types** list, select **Proposals**, and then click **Add**. Click **OK** to confirm the addition of the content type.

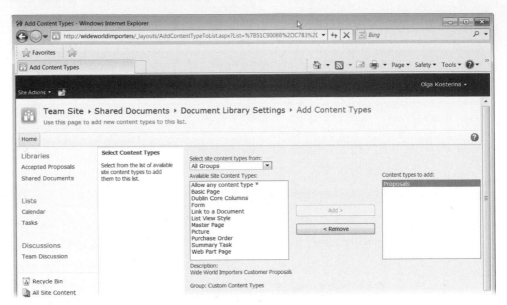

18. You will now create a new document that is based on this content type. Using the breadcrumb, navigate back to the **Shared Documents** library.

19. Click the **Documents** tab, and then click the down arrow on the **New Document** button.

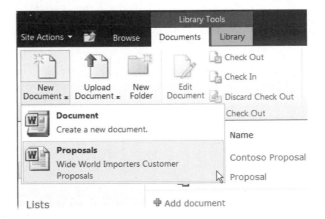

20. Select **Proposals**, and then click **OK** in the **Open Document** message box (if it appears) to confirm the opening of the file.

> **Troubleshooting** If you see an error that states that the Office application or the browser is incompatible, it may be because you are using a 64-bit browser. Switch to a 32-bit browser. More information on this error can be found at *http://technet.microsoft.com/en-us/library/cc288142.aspx.*

21. Word opens. In the document information panel displayed on the top of the **Word** window, set the **Title** to **My Company Proposal**, **Customer Name** to **My Company**, and **Value** to **$1000**.

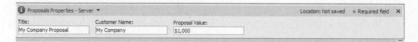

22. In Word, click **File**, **Save As**, type **My Company Proposal** in the **File name box**, and then click **Save** to save the new document to the library. Click **OK** in the **Check In** dialog if it appears.

23. In the browser, hover the mouse over the name of the document that you have just created and click the down arrow that appears on the right to display the context menu.

24. Click **View Properties**. In the **Shared Documents – My Company Proposal** dialog that appears, notice the values that you set for the **Title**, **Customer Name**, and **Proposal Value** properties.

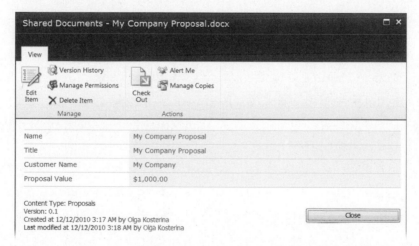

25. Close the **Shared Documents – My Company Proposal** dialog.

Note The properties that you set will not display in the default view because you have used a content type. If you had created custom columns directly in the library, the option to display them in the default view would be available. In the next exercise, you will create a view to display these columns.

 CLEAN UP Close Word. Leave the browser open if you are continuing to the next exercise.

Creating a View

Creating a view in a library is a beneficial way of organizing content within a library. A view can be created with filters based on the columns, allowing for an easy way to find documents. If a library contains custom metadata, you may want your view to be created with a filter on that custom column. Custom views work very well with the content types that were described in the previous exercise. For example, if you would like to display all proposal documents in a separate view to set documents apart from invoices, you could create a filter on each view based upon the content type column.

See Also We will look into views in more detail in Chapter 9, "Working with List and Library Views."

In this exercise, you will create a new view within a document library to display all the proposal documents that are created with the new proposal template. The custom columns of Customer Name and Proposal Value will become the columns within the view.

SET UP Open the SharePoint site and display the document library where you would like to create a new view.

BE SURE TO verify that you have sufficient rights to create views in this library. If in doubt, see the Appendix at the back of this book.

Create
View

1. On the **Library** tab, click the **Create View** button in the **Manage Views** group on the Ribbon. The Create View page is displayed.

2. Under **Choose a view format**, click **Standard View**.

3. In the **View name** box, type a view name, such as **Proposals**.

4. In the **Columns** section, click the **Customer Name** and **Proposal Value** columns to add them to the selection of columns for the new view.

5. In the **Sort** section, set the **First sort by the column** field to **Customer Name**.

6. In the **Filter** section, set **Show items only when the following is true**, and set the filter to **Content Type is equal to Proposals**.

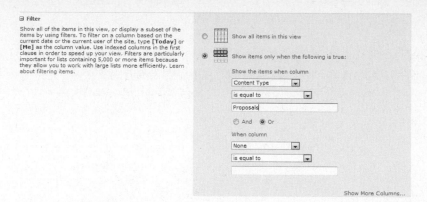

7. Expand the **Totals** section, and for the **Proposal Value** column, from the **Total** drop-down list, select **Average**.

8. Click **OK**.

The library page displays in the Proposals view and shows only proposals created using the Proposals content type. Two custom columns that you created are displayed, along with an average value in the Proposal Value column.

Tip You can select the library view in the Manage Views section on the Ribbon. To display all documents in the library, select the default All Documents view.

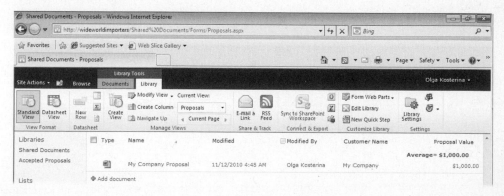

 CLEAN UP Leave the browser open if you are continuing to the next exercise.

Deleting and Restoring a Library

Libraries can be deleted if they are no longer required within a Team site. Note that deleting a library will delete the content within the library as well. If a library is deleted accidentally, it can be restored from the Recycle Bin at the site level.

In the exercise, you will delete the Shared Documents document library and then restore it from the site Recycle Bin.

 SET UP Open the SharePoint site and navigate to the library you would like to delete, if not already open. The exercise will use the Shared Documents library on *http:// wideworldimporters* site, but you can use whatever site you want. If prompted, type your user name and password, and click OK.

BE SURE TO verify that you have sufficient rights to delete and restore this library. If in doubt, see the Appendix at the back of this book.

1. Within the library that you would like to delete, in the **Library Tools**, click the **Library** tab, and then click the **Library Settings** button in the **Settings** group on the Ribbon.

2. Click **Delete this document library** from the **Permissions and Management** section.

3. Click **OK** to the warning message that appears.

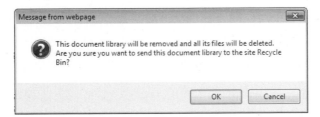

The document library is now deleted.

4. You will now restore the deleted library. In the left navigation area, click the **Recycle Bin**.

5. On the **Recycle Bin** page, select the deleted library by clicking the check box to the left of its name.

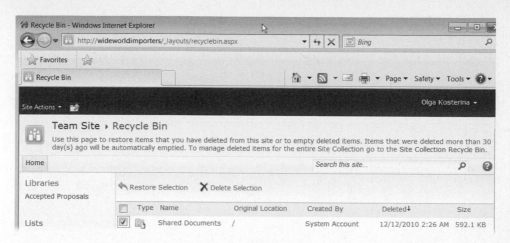

6. Click **Restore Selection**, and then click **OK** in the confirmation message box that appears. The document library has been restored.

7. Navigate to the library and verify that it has been restored.

CLEAN UP Close the browser.

Configuring Other Library Types

So far in this chapter, we've been focusing on configuring the document libraries. You may also need to configure other library types, such as form libraries, picture libraries, and wiki page libraries. While there are no unique configuration settings for each of these library types, the navigation to the library settings is different for wiki page libraries and picture libraries.

Wiki libraries do not have a Library Tools tab or a Library ribbon. Instead, there is a Page tab that displays a ribbon. The Library Settings button is located in the Page Library section of the Ribbon.

Picture libraries do not use the Ribbon interface in SharePoint Foundation. The Picture Library Settings are accessible from the Settings menu in the Library page.

In this exercise, you will explore the Picture Library Settings.

SET UP Open the SharePoint site in which you would like to explore picture library settings. The exercise will use the *http://wideworldimporters* site, but you can use whatever site you want. If prompted, type your user name and password and click OK.

BE SURE TO verify that you have sufficient rights to create libraries on this site. If in doubt, see the Appendix at the back of this book.

1. Click **Site Actions**, and then click **More Options**. The Create page is displayed.

2. Under **Filter by**, click **Library**, select **Picture Library**, and then, in the **Name** field, type **Wide World Importers Images**, and click **Create**.

   The picture library has been created and is displayed in the browser.

3. On the picture library page, click the **Settings** menu on the toolbar at the top of the page, and choose **Picture Library Settings**.

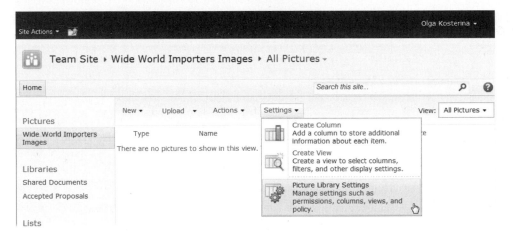

The Picture Library Settings page is displayed. Explore the page, and notice that the settings for the picture library are very similar to the ones for a document library.

 CLEAN UP Close the browser.

Key Points

- You can think about libraries as lists of files, and many library settings are similar to list settings.

- There are specific settings for libraries, including default open behavior, library templates, required checkout, and major and minor versioning.

- You can configure the default open behavior for a library by setting up whether documents from this library will open by default in the client application or in the browser.

- You can set up Required Check Out for the library to make sure that users do not make changes to a document at the same time.

- Custom Send To locations can be configured when documents need to be copied to other locations.

- Configuring a Site Assets library is useful to store resources for wiki pages.

- Content types are used to enable custom metadata, as well as multiple document templates within a document library.

- Custom views can be created to display the custom column values.

- If a library is deleted by accident, it can be restored from the site's Recycle Bin within 30 days.

Chapter at a Glance

Create a list or library view, page 252

Work with a Datasheet view, page 256

Work with a Gantt view, page 263

Create a Calendar view, page 270

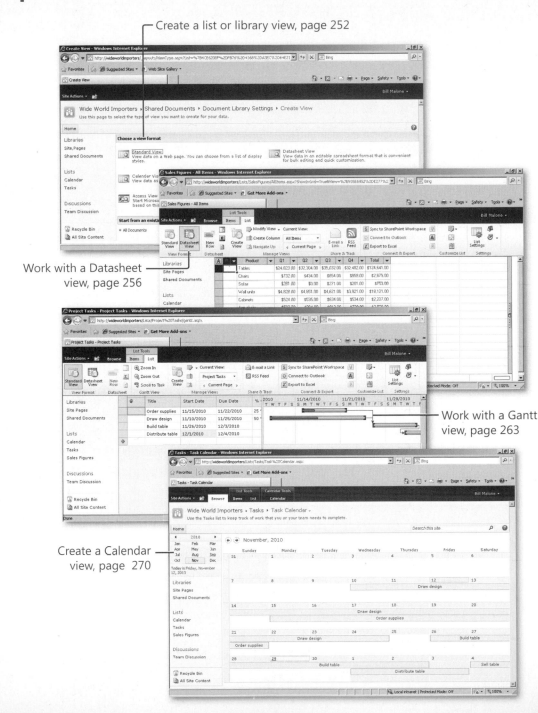

9 Working with List and Library Views

In this chapter, you will learn how to

- ✔ Work with a Standard view.
- ✔ Work with a Datasheet view.
- ✔ Work with a Gantt view.
- ✔ Work with an Access view.
- ✔ Work with a Calendar view.
- ✔ Create and use a list template.
- ✔ Create a lookup column.
- ✔ Create Web Part connections.

List and library *views* allow you to set up what information—and how—is displayed in a list or a library, thus making it easier for users of your site to find and work with the information. At least one default view is created for each list and library in Microsoft SharePoint Foundation. In some cases, the default view might not display the information that you think is most valuable to your users. By modifying a view or creating your own view, you can determine how the contents of a list or library are presented to the users. A view defines how the information in a list or library is displayed, including, for example, what columns are displayed and in what order. It also defines how to sort or group the contents of the list or library and what the contents should be filtered on.

Tip Because a library can be thought of as a list of files, working with views for libraries is very similar to working with views for lists.

In the previous chapters of this book, we've been using lists and libraries in the default Standard view. However, there are different types of built-in views provided by SharePoint Foundation 2010 that you can use to display your data to provide the most value to the users of your site, including Standard view, Datasheet view, Calendar view, Gantt view, and Access view.

Tip You can also create a custom view using SharePoint Designer.

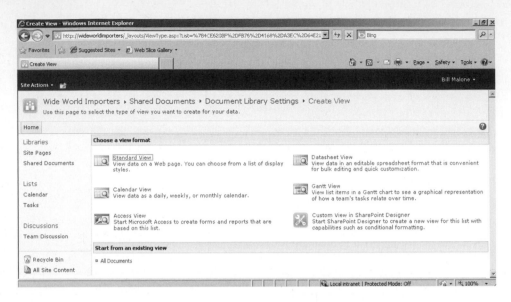

In this chapter, you will learn how to work with the different types of views in SharePoint Foundation.

> **Practice Files** Before you can complete the exercises in this chapter, you need to (1) download the Chapter 9 practice files from the book's catalog page to the following folder on your computer: Documents\Microsoft Press\SBS_SPF\Chapter09 and (2) install the Chapter 9 practice site using the Chapter09_Starter.wsp file. See "Using the Practice Files" at the beginning of this book for more information.

Important Remember to use your SharePoint site location in place of *http://wideworldimporters* in the following exercises.

Working with a Standard View

A Standard view of a SharePoint Foundation 2010 list or library displays the contents of the container as a list on a web page. The Standard view is available for lists and libraries, but not for surveys and discussions.

In Chapter 8, "Working with Library Settings," we created a Standard view within a document library using the columns of a content type. In this chapter, we will look at more options that are available to you when creating a Standard view.

When creating a new view, you can choose whether you want to create a personal or a shared view. A personal view will be visible only to you, while a shared view will be visible to other users of the site as well. You can also decide to enable inline editing in a list or a library. This means that you will not have to go into the edit page of an item to change its properties, but instead you can simply click the Edit button in the view and edit the item.

In the following exercise, you will create two new library views based on a Standard view. The first view will group and sort the documents and also provide the inline editing capabilities. The second view will enable the preview pane to be displayed within the page.

SET UP Open the SharePoint site that contains the library that you want to configure. The exercise will use the Shared Documents library on *http://wideworldimporters* site, but you can use whatever library you want. If prompted, type your user name and password, and click OK.

BE SURE TO verify that you have sufficient rights to manage this library. If in doubt, see the Appendix at the back of this book.

1. On the Quick Launch, click **Shared Documents**.

2. In the **Library Tools**, click the **Library** tab.

3. Click **Create View** in the **Manage Views** group on the Ribbon. The **Create View** page is displayed.

Create
View

4. Under **Choose a view format**, click **Standard View**.

5. In the **View name** box, type a view name, such as **Products**.

6. In the **Columns** section, clear the check box in front of the **Type (icon linked to document)** column to remove the selection.

7. In the **Sort** section, set the **First sort by the column field** option to **Modified**, and select **show items in descending order**.

8. Expand the **Inline Editing** section and select **Allow inline editing**.

9. Expand the **Group By** section and set **First group by the column** to **Type (icon linked to document)**. Set **By default, show groupings** to **Expanded**.

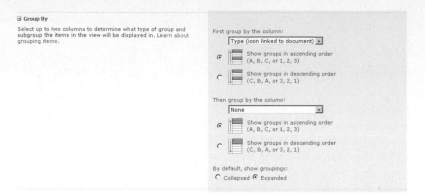

10. Click **OK**. The view has been created.

    The library page displays in the new view and shows the documents grouped by document type and sorted on the date the documents were modified. Within the grouped documents, it will display the newest document first.

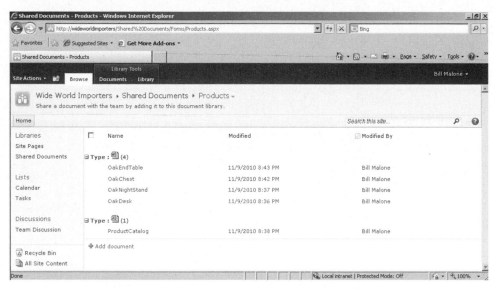

Edit inline

11. You will now verify that the inline editing is enabled. Hover the mouse over the white space to the left of an item's name, such as **OakNightStand**, and then click the **Edit inline** icon that appears.

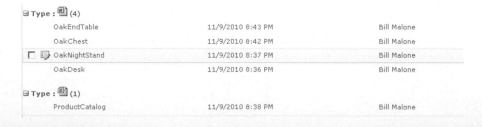

12. Change the name of the document to **OakBedTable**.

13. Click the **Save** icon that is displayed to the left of the item.

Save

The name of the document has been changed.

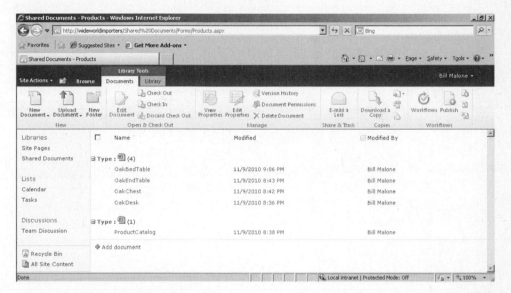

So far, you have been working with the default style of the Standard view. You will now use an alternative style that allows you to change the way the list items or documents are displayed.

14. In the **Library Tools**, click the **Library** tab.

15. Click **Create View** in the **Manage Views** group on the Ribbon. The **Create View** page is displayed.

16. Under **Choose a view format**, click **Standard View**.

17. In the **View name** box, type a view name, such as **Document Preview**.

18. Expand the **Style** section and select **Preview Pane**.

19. Click **OK**. The new view has been created.

20. You will now verify that the preview pane is enabled. Hover your mouse over a document name and note that the properties of the document are displayed in the preview pane on the right side of the screen.

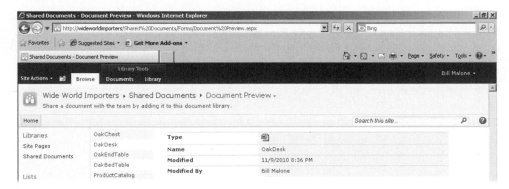

Tip There are two ways to select a view: by selecting it from the drop-down list in the Manage Views section on the Ribbon, and by clicking the down arrow next to the view name on the right of the breadcrumb and then selecting the view of your choice from the list of available views.

CLEAN UP Close the browser.

Working with a Datasheet View

If you have installed the Microsoft Office 2010 Tools on your computer and your browser supports ActiveX controls, you can use the Datasheet view of a list. You can install the Office 2010 Tools with any Office 2010 application like Microsoft Word, Microsoft Excel, or Microsoft Access. Datasheet view presents all the list items in a grid, which facilitates easy editing across the entire table. Drop-down lists, check boxes, and column edits are all maintained. You can use the keyboard or your mouse to move from cell to cell to make changes to any row in the list. When you move off a row, the changes are saved automatically. In a library, you can only edit and delete items using the Datasheet view, while in a list, you can also add items using the Datasheet view. Even though Datasheet view is a lot more useful for some list types than others, you can use Datasheet view with almost any list or library type except for the Picture Library, External List, and Survey types.

When a list is displaying in Datasheet view, it is doing so in an Access Web Datasheet. Using the Access Web Datasheet is like editing a table in Excel 2010 or Access 2010. The datasheet consists of rows, and each row corresponds to a list item. A column corresponds to a list field. The down arrow in the column headings is used to filter and sort data.

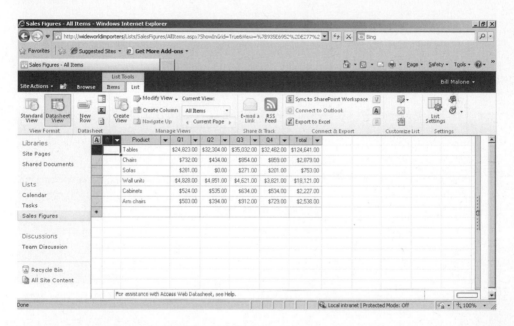

The Access Web Datasheet in SharePoint Foundation 2010 works in a very similar way to the Datasheet view in the Access 2010 client application. An Access icon appears in the upper-left corner of the Access Web Datasheet, and the words "Access Web Datasheet" are displayed at the bottom of the page in what can be thought of as the status bar of the Datasheet view.

Note If you are using an older version of Access, the icon displayed will be that of the Access version that you are using.

You can use the keyboard or mouse to move from cell to cell to make changes to any row in the list. The last row of a list in the Access Web Datasheet is always empty, and there is an asterisk (*) displayed in the left column. This empty row can be used to add list items to the list.

Tip There is no empty row in a Datasheet view of a document library.

When you type a value in a cell or choose a value from a drop-down list, an Edit icon displays at the far left, indicating that changes have been made to the row. When you leave a row that has been modified or navigate away from the web page, a Saving icon flashes, indicating that SharePoint is updating the database with your changes. You can continue making changes to different rows, and SharePoint saves your changes in the background. If your changes result in a conflict or error, the datasheet will be updated with the necessary information to resolve it.

Tip All items in the list are displayed on one web page in the Access Web Datasheet, regardless of the size of the list. Therefore, it isn't practical to edit very large lists (more than 5,000 items) by using the Access Web Datasheet. If the SharePoint administrator has enabled the list throttling feature, then only the newest items up to the throttle limit will be returned; but using the Access Web Datasheet, there is no way for your user to retrieve the rest of the items from the list. To improve the performance of an Access Web Datasheet, or to improve the usability for the users of your site if you are using a throttle, create a view that hides unnecessary columns. Apply one or more filters to hide rows that are not relevant to the view, but do not hide the columns that are marked as Required because that will prevent users from adding list items using the Access Web Datasheet.

You can switch easily between Standard view and Datasheet view by clicking the Datasheet View button on the Library tab of an existing library or on the List tab of an existing list. If you don't want to switch between Standard and Datasheet view but want to view your data in Datasheet view by default instead, you can create a Datasheet view from the Create View page.

Tip Alternatively, you can create a Custom List in Datasheet view from the Create page that uses Datasheet view as the default view.

In the following exercise, you will work with the Datasheet view of a list. You will first display the items in a list in the Datasheet view, then create a new Datasheet view, set this view as the default view of the list, add, edit, and delete items using the Datasheet view, delete and add columns, and finally briefly explore the Task pane.

 SET UP Open the SharePoint site that contains the list that you want to configure. The exercise will use the *http://wideworldimporters* site, but you can use whatever site you want. If prompted, type your user name and password, and click OK.

BE SURE TO verify that you have sufficient rights to manage the list. If in doubt, see the Appendix at the back of this book.

1. On the Quick Launch, click **Sales Figures**.

2. In the **List Tools,** click the **List** tab.

Datasheet View

3. Click the **Datasheet View** button in the **View Format** group on the Ribbon. The list is now displayed in Datasheet view instead of Standard view.

4. In the first row of the list, in the **Product** column, type **Dinner tables**.

5. Press **ENTER**. The new product name for the top item has now been saved to the database.

   If you click the Sales Figures link on the Quick Launch again, it will take you back to Standard view because that is how the current default view was created. You will now create a new Datasheet view for the list and make it a default view.

6. In the **List Tools,** click the **List** tab, and then, in the **Manage Views** group on the Ribbon, click **Create View**. The Create View page is displayed.

7. Under **Choose a view format**, click **Datasheet View**.

8. In the **View name** box, type a view name, such as **Grid View**.

9. Click **Make this the default view** check box.

10. Click **OK**. The new default Datasheet view has been created.

    Clicking the Sales Figures list link will now open the list in Datasheet view.

11. You will now create a new list item. In the last row of the list in the **Product** column, type **Bench**, and then press the right arrow key on the keyboard. Type **0**, and press the right arrow five times. Press **ENTER**.

Edit item

    The new row changes to become the currently edited row, and the Edit icon displays on the left, indicating that the row is being edited. Another new row is added at the bottom of the list.

    Tip As in other Office applications, you can use the keyboard keys: for example, **CTRL+X** to cut, **CTRL+C** to copy, **CTRL+V** to paste, **CTRL+Z** to undo last changes, and **ESC** to cancel an edit on the current list item.

12. Position the mouse cursor on the boundary between the **Product** and the **Q1** columns, and then drag the column boundary to reduce the size of the **Product** column.

    Tip Rows can be resized in much the same way. However, dragging one row's boundary will resize all rows in the list. Both columns and rows can be resized based on their contents by double-clicking the boundary. You can also re-order columns by selecting them and simply dragging them to the desired location.

13. Click the far-left cell to highlight the entire **Bench** list item.

14. Click your right mouse button and click **Delete Rows** to remove the item from the list permanently.

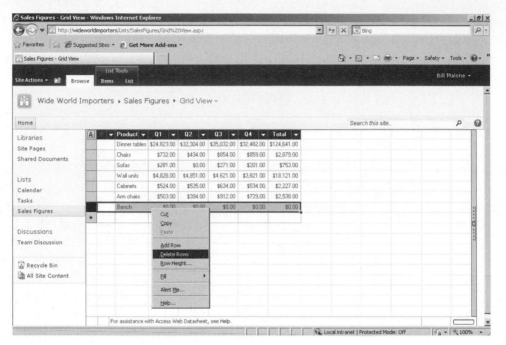

15. In the message box that appears, click **Yes** to confirm deleting the list item and redisplay the Datasheet view of the list.

> **Tip** You can select and then delete multiple list items. Alternatively, you can copy and paste the highlighted list items into Office applications. You can select the entire list with a single click in the upper-left logo cell, where the list select icon appears.

> **Tip** By holding down the Shift key while selecting the far-left cell so that the row select pointer appears, and then clicking the far-left cell of another row, you can select all rows between the first row clicked and the second row clicked. Similarly, holding down the Shift key while selecting the top row of a column so that the column select pointer appears, and then clicking the top row of another column, will select all columns between the two clicks. However, holding down the **CTRL** key while selecting does not select or clear list items regardless of whether they are adjacent, as you might expect. Instead, it exclusively selects the clicked row and abandons all other selections, just as if you had clicked the items without holding down the **CTRL** key.

16. In the **List Tools,** click the **List** tab.

Show Totals

17. Click the **Show Totals** button in the **Datasheet** group on the Ribbon.

18. Click in the bottom cell in the **Q1** column.

19. Open the drop-down list and select **Sum**.

20. Double-click the boundary between the **Q1** and the **Q2** column.

21. Repeat steps 18, 19, and 20 for the **Q2**, **Q3**, **Q4**, and **Total** columns.

22. Replace the **$0.00** in the **Q2** figures for **Sofas** with **10**.

A	▼	Product ▼	Q1 ▼	Q2 ▼	Q3 ▼	Q4 ▼	Total ▼
		Dinner tables	$24,823.00	$32,304.00	$35,032.00	$32,482.00	$124,641.00
		Chairs	$732.00	$434.00	$854.00	$859.00	$2,879.00
		Sofas	$281.00	$10.00	$271.00	$201.00	$753.00
		Wall units	$4,828.00	$4,851.00	$4,621.00	$3,821.00	$18,121.00
		Cabinets	$524.00	$535.00	$634.00	$534.00	$2,227.00
		Arm chairs	$503.00	$394.00	$912.00	$729.00	$2,538.00
*							
		Total	$31,691.00	$38,528.00	$42,324.00	$38,626.00	$151,159.00

The view now displays the totals for the Q1, Q2, Q3, Q4, and Total columns. Changing a value in one of these columns will update the value in the Total row at the bottom of the view. Because the Total column on the right of the list is a Currency column, the values of this column are not updated automatically when the figures for one of the quarters change. To make the Total column update automatically, it must be of the Calculated data type. The data type of an existing column cannot be changed to a Calculated data type. Instead, you must delete the existing Total currency column and re-create it as a new column using the Calculated data type. You will do this next.

23. Right-click the **Total** column and select **Edit/Delete Column**.

24. Scroll to the bottom of the page and click the **Delete** button.

25. In the confirmation message box that appears, click **OK** to confirm the deletion of the list column and redisplay the **Datasheet** view of the list.

26. Right-click the **Q4** column and click **Add Column**.

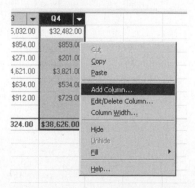

27. In the **Name and Type** area, in the **Column Name** text box, type **Total Sales**, and then select the **Calculated (calculation based on other columns)** option.

28. In the **Additional Column Settings** area, under **Insert Column**, double-click **Q1**, **Q2**, **Q3**, and **Q4**, and then add a plus sign (+) between each of the fields.

29. Make sure the formula in the **Formula** area reads **[Q1]+[Q2]+[Q3]+[Q4]**.

30. Under **The data type returned from this formula is**, select **Currency**. Click **OK**.

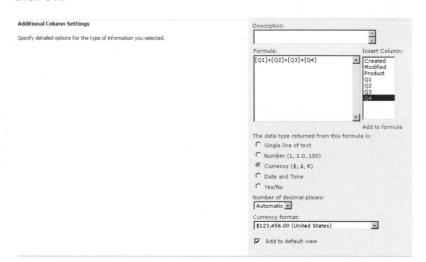

31. To display the total sales for all products, click in the bottom cell of the Total Sales column, open the drop-down menu, and select **Sum**.

    The Total Sales column will now add up the sales figures automatically for all quarters for each product

32. You will now explore the Task pane. In the **List Tools**, click the **List** tab.

Show Task Pane

33. Click the **Show Task Pane** button in the **Datasheet** group on the Ribbon to display the Task pane, which allows you to integrate quickly with Excel 2010 and Access 2010.

Note that at the top of the Task pane, there is a series of buttons for common commands, such as Cut, Copy, Paste, Undo, Custom Sort, and Remove Filter/Sort.

There is also a Help icon that provides access to the help topics for the Access Web Datasheet.

Tip In addition to clicking the Help icon in the Task pane, you can get to the relevant help topics by clicking the Help link in the status bar of the Access Web Datasheet, or clicking a cell in the Access Web Datasheet and pressing F1, or right-clicking a cell inside the Access Web Datasheet and then clicking Help.

 CLEAN UP Close the browser.

Working with a Gantt View

A Gantt chart is a horizontal bar chart that is used to provide a graphical illustration of a project timeline. The Gantt chart has a horizontal axis that represents the time span of the project, broken down into increments such as days, weeks, or months. The vertical axis represents the project tasks. The Gantt chart shows the start and finish dates of different tasks and can also show the dependencies between the tasks.

In SharePoint Foundation 2010, you can create a Gantt view for most SharePoint list and library types, although it would make the most sense to use the Gantt view for a Tasks or a Project Tasks list. When you create a Project Tasks list, the Gantt view is automatically created as the default view of that list. Several lists and libraries do not provide a Gantt view: Picture Library, External List, Discussion Board, and Survey.

For a Gantt view to be created successfully, the following columns need to be defined in a list or library:

- **Title** A required text field that contains a description of the task.

- **Start Date** A required date field that contains the date on which the task is supposed to start.

- **Due Date** A required date field that contains the date on which the task is supposed to be completed.

- **Percent Complete** An optional number field, the value of which indicates what percentage of a task is already completed. If you don't want to define a Percent Complete column in your Gantt view, you can select Optional for this column, which means the Gantt chart won't use it.

- **Predecessors** An optional lookup field that does a look up to the Title field of the same list. This column is used to show dependencies between tasks. The Predecessors column is optional; if you want to leave it out, you can select Optional for this column and the Gantt chart won't show dependencies between tasks.

Tip The data types of the columns are required and cannot be modified, while the names can be changed.

A Gantt view in SharePoint 2010 is split into two parts. The left side of the view shows a spreadsheet-like view of the data in the list. It is possible to add or hide columns in this view and to change the order in which the columns are displayed. In most cases, all columns will not fit on the screen, and you can use the arrow keys to move through the columns. The right side of the view shows the actual Gantt chart. It displays a timeline with tasks plotted against it. It may also display the percentage of completeness for each task by using a different color. In addition, it can display the dependencies between tasks by using arrows to connect the tasks. If the Gantt chart doesn't fit on the screen, you cannot use your mouse or arrow keys to scroll through it. Instead, you can use the Zoom In, Zoom Out, and Scroll to Task buttons in the Gantt View group on the List tab.

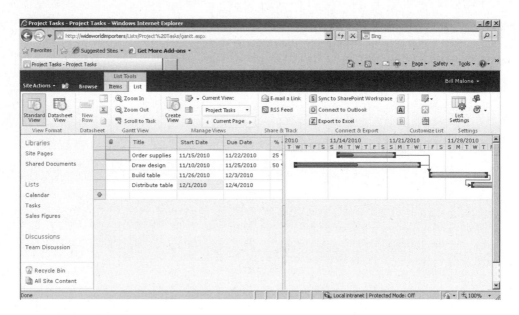

In the following exercise, you will create a Gantt view for a Tasks list, hide columns, add and edit items in the Gantt view, and navigate through a Gantt chart.

SET UP Open the SharePoint site that contains the list that you want to configure. The exercise will use the *http://wideworldimporters* site, but you can use whatever site you want. If prompted, type your user name and password, and click OK.

BE SURE TO verify that you have sufficient rights to manage the list. If in doubt, see the Appendix at the back of this book.

1. On the Quick Launch, click **Tasks**.

2. In the **List Tools**, click the **List** tab.

3. Click **Create View** in the **Manage Views** group. The Create View page is displayed.

4. Under **Choose a view format**, click **Gantt View**.

5. In the **View name** box, type a view name, such as **Project Tasks**.

6. Select **Make this the default view**.

7. In the **Gantt Columns** area, select **Title** from the **Title** drop-down list, select **Start Date** from the **Start Date** drop-down list, select **Due Date** from the **Due Date** drop-down list, select **Optional** from the **Percent Complete** drop-down list, and select **Predecessors** from the **Predecessors** drop-down list.

8. Click **OK**.

   The Gantt view for the Tasks list is displayed. On the left side of the screen, there is a spreadsheet-like view of the list contents. On the right side of the screen, there is a Gantt chart. There is quite a lot of white space in the left section because not all columns in the list are being used.

9. Hover the mouse over the left column heading displaying the paperclip symbol and click the arrow next to it on the right. Select **Hide Column**. Repeat this step for the **Type** and **Assigned To** columns.

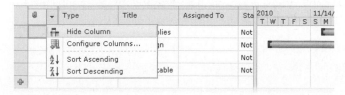

10. Hover the mouse over the **Title** column heading and click the arrow next to it on the right. Select **Configure Columns...**.

11. Select the **Priority** entry and click **Move Down** three times to move the Priority column to the bottom of the list.

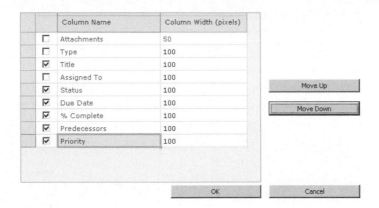

	Column Name	Column Width (pixels)
☐	Attachments	50
☐	Type	100
☑	Title	100
☐	Assigned To	100
☑	Status	100
☑	Due Date	100
☑	% Complete	100
☑	Predecessors	100
☑	Priority	100

Move Up

Move Down

OK   Cancel

12. Click **OK**. The **Priority** column now has been moved to the far right of the screen.

Note that the changes made directly to the spreadsheet won't be saved to the view. The next time you or another user browses to the view, the hidden columns will be back and the Priority column won't be the far-right column anymore. To make lasting changes, you need to make changes to the view.

13. In the **Draw Design** row, click in the **% Complete** cell and type **50**.

14. Press **ENTER**.

SharePoint Foundation automatically changes the 50 you just filled in to 50%. However, the Gantt chart won't reflect the fact that the Draw Design task is 50% done because in step 7, the Percent Complete Gantt column was set to Optional. You will now modify the view to change this and a few other settings.

15. In the **List Tools**, click the **List** tab.

Modify View

16. Click the **Modify View** button in the **Manage Views** group on the Ribbon. The Edit View page is displayed.

17. In the **Columns** area, clear the **Attachments**, **Type (icon linked to document)**, and **Assigned To** check boxes. Change the value of **Priority** to **10** using the drop-down list. Click the check box next to **Start Date** and change the value to **3** using the drop-down list.

18. In the **Gantt Columns** area, from the **Percent Complete** drop-down list, select **% Complete**.

19. Click **OK**.

    The Gantt chart now reflects the fact that the Draw Design task is 50% completed, and the changes to the columns are now persistent when you navigate away from the view.

20. Click in the **Title** cell in the bottom row of the spreadsheet and type **Sell table**. Press **TAB** and select **Not Started** in the **Status** row. Press **TAB** and select **12/4/2010** in the **Start Date** row. Press **TAB** and select **12/8/2010** in the **Due Date** row. Press **TAB** twice and select the **Distribute table** in the **Predecessors** row. Press **ENTER**.

    The row has been added to the **Tasks** list, but depending on your screen resolution, you might not be able to see the horizontal bar for this task in the Gantt chart. You will now use the Gantt view tools to zoom in and out and scroll through the chart.

21. In the **List Tools,** click the **List** tab.

22. Click the **Zoom Out** button in the **Gantt View** group on the Ribbon. The complete Gantt chart for the list is now visible.

Title	Status	Start Date	Due Date
Order supplies	Not Started	11/15/2010	11/22/2010
Draw design	Not Started	11/10/2010	11/25/2010
Build table	Not Started	11/26/2010	12/3/2010
Distribute table	Not Started	12/1/2010	12/4/2010
Sell table	Not Started	12/4/2010	12/8/2010

23. Click the **Zoom In** button in the **Gantt View** group to go back to the previous view.

24. Select the **Distribute table** row and click the **Scroll to Task** button in the **Gantt View** group. The Gantt chart will now scroll to the right so that the complete bar for the Distribute table task is visible.

✖ CLEAN UP Leave the browser open if you are continuing to the next exercise.

Working with an Access View

In SharePoint Foundation 2010, you can use Access 2007 or 2010 to create a view of a list or library. Using Access, it is easy to create advanced views and reports based on the columns and data in the list or library. When editing the list data in Access view, the values will be updated in the SharePoint list automatically. The Access view is available for all list types except the External List and Survey.

Important The option to create an Access view is available only if the Access client is installed on your computer.

See Also For more information about using Access with SharePoint Foundation, see Chapter 14, "Using SharePoint Foundation with Excel 2010 and Access 2010."

When creating an Access view, the list will be opened in the Access client application, and you can then choose what view you want to use to display the list data. When you are satisfied with the view, you need to save the file to a document library in the SharePoint environment.

Tip In SharePoint Foundation 2010, Access view won't appear in the existing views of the list for which the view was originally created. To use this view, a user would have to go to the document library where the Access file was saved and open it from there.

In the following exercise, you will create an Access view for a Tasks list and save it to a document library.

 SET UP Open the SharePoint site that contains the list that you want to configure. The exercise will use the *http://wideworldimporters* site, but you can use whatever site you want. If prompted, type your user name and password, and click OK.

BE SURE TO verify that you have sufficient rights to manage the list. If in doubt, see the Appendix at the back of this book.

1. On the Quick Launch, click **Tasks**.

2. In the **List Tools,** click the **List** tab.

3. Click **Create View** in the **Manage Views** group on the Ribbon. The Create View page is displayed.

4. Under **Choose a view format**, click **Access View**. The Access client application opens.

Tip If Access is not installed on your computer, you will not be able to select the Access view, nor will you be able to complete this exercise.

5. Save the file on your local machine. You can change the file name if you want.

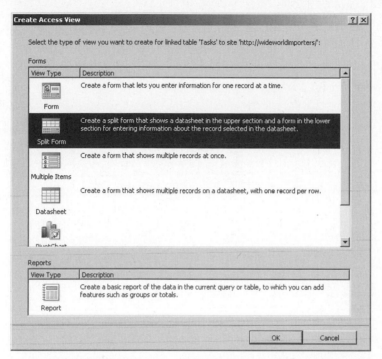

6. Select the **Split Form** view and click **OK**. The Layout view for the form opens.

The Access form can be adjusted by using Layout or Design view. To switch between views, you can use the View button on the upper left of the screen. The Form view can be used to view and edit the data in the list.

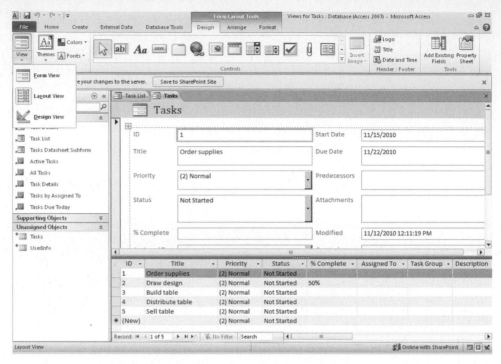

7. Click the **Save to SharePoint Site** button on the yellow bar below the Ribbon.

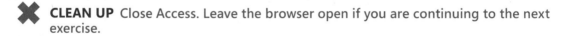

8. Leave the file name unchanged. To save the file to the **Shared Documents** library, click **Yes**, and then click **OK**.

   The Access database that contains the new view is now saved to the Shared Documents library. You can open it again by browsing to the library and clicking the file name.

   CLEAN UP Close Access. Leave the browser open if you are continuing to the next exercise.

Working with a Calendar View

SharePoint Foundation 2010 allows you to create a Calendar view for the data in your lists and libraries. You can use Calendar view in most lists and libraries, but the list will need to have at least one date field for the Calendar view to work properly. A Calendar view cannot be created for the following list types: External List, Discussion Board, and Survey.

When you create a Calendar list, the Calendar view is the default. The Calendar view can be very useful for actions such as plotting tasks on or entering announcements into a calendar.

In the following exercise, you will create a Calendar view for a Tasks list, and you will then modify the scope of the calendar.

 SET UP Open the SharePoint site that contains the list that you want to configure. The exercise will use the *http://wideworldimporters* site, but you can use whatever site you wish. If prompted, type your user name and password, and click OK.

BE SURE TO verify that you have sufficient rights to manage the list. If in doubt, see the Appendix at the back of this book.

1. On the Quick Launch, click **Tasks**.

2. In the **List Tools,** click the **List** tab.

3. Click **Create View** in the **Manage Views** group on the Ribbon. The Create View page is displayed.

4. Under **Choose a view format**, click **Calendar View**.

5. In the **View name** box, type a view name, such as **Task Calendar**.

6. In the **Time Interval** area, select **Start Date** from the **Begin** drop-down list and select **Due Date** from the **End** drop-down list.

7. In the **Calendar Columns** area, select **Title** from the **Month View Title**, the **Week View Title**, and the **Day View Title** drop-down lists. Leave the **Week View Sub Heading** and the **Day View Sub Heading** set to **Optional**.

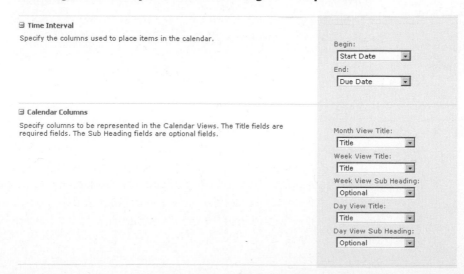

8. Click **OK**.

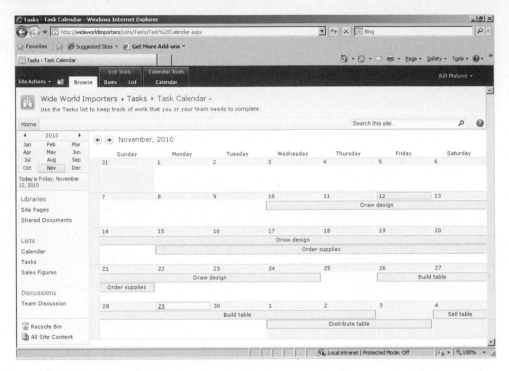

The page displays the items from the Tasks list plotted onto a calendar. By default, the current month is displayed in Calendar view, and the current day is highlighted in blue. On the left side of the screen, the current day is also displayed. Above the current day, the months for this year are listed. Clicking one of the months will show the calendar for that month. You can navigate to different years by using the arrows to the left and right of the year at the top of the panel.

9. In the **Calendar Tools,** click the **Calendar** tab.

Week

10. Click **Week** in the **Scope** group on the Ribbon. The calendar will now display the current week.

The calendar panel on the left of the screen now displays all dates in the current month. You can scroll through months by using the arrows next to the month at the top of the panel.

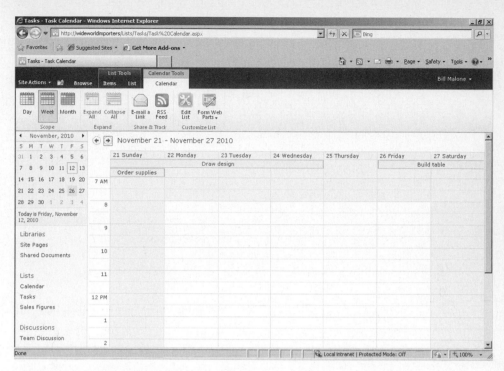

The Expand All and Collapse All buttons can be used when the Month scope is used if certain days have too many items in them to show them all at once. Expand All will show all items for all days, and Collapse all will go back to showing only three items per day.

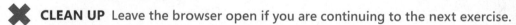 **CLEAN UP** Leave the browser open if you are continuing to the next exercise.

Creating and Using a List Template

If you have done a lot of work on creating views for a certain list, as you have on the Tasks list in this chapter, you might want to reuse those views. By saving an existing list or library as a template, you can create new lists or libraries based on the template that contains the same columns and views. The template can be used not only in the site in which the template was created, but also in other sites within the same site collection. By saving a list template to the file system and uploading it again into another site collection, it is even possible to use the template in other site collections, web applications, or SharePoint farms.

To create a list template, you just save an existing list as a template. When saving the list, you can choose whether you want to include the contents of the list. If you include the contents, the list template will include the rows that are in the list at the time that you are saving this list as a template. If you just want to create a template that contains the columns and views of the list, you do not need to save the contents of the list to the template. However, if you want to use the template to copy or move the list to other sites, you can save the contents to the list template and use the template to create a list with the same structure and content on another site.

Tip A list template is saved automatically to the List Templates gallery at the site collection level. You browse to the List Templates gallery by going to the Site Settings page and clicking List Templates under the Galleries heading. The List Templates gallery is a special kind of document library. A lot of what you can do on a document library is also available in the List Templates gallery; for instance, you can create your own views for the gallery. Two things that are different from a document library are that you can't create your own List Templates gallery and that you can't delete the existing List Templates gallery, even if you are an administrator on the site.

In the following exercise, you will save an existing Tasks list as a template, and then you will create a new list based on that template. You will then save the template file to your computer for reuse in another site collection, web application, or SharePoint farm.

 SET UP Open the SharePoint site that contains the list that you want to save as a template. The exercise will use the *http://wideworldimporters* site, but you can use whatever site you wish. If prompted, type your user name and password, and click OK.

BE SURE TO verify that you have sufficient rights to manage the list and the list templates in the site collection, and to create lists. If in doubt, see the Appendix at the back of this book.

1. On the Quick Launch, click **Tasks**.

2. In the **List Tools,** click the **List** tab.

List
Settings

3. Click **List Settings** in the **Settings** group on the Ribbon. The List Settings page is displayed.

4. Under **Permissions and Management**, choose **Save list as template**.

5. In the **File name** box, type a file name, such as **ExtendedTasks**.

6. In the **Template name** box, type a template name, such as **Extended Tasks**. This is the name that is displayed on the Create page, so make sure that the name accurately describes the template.

7. In the **Template Description name** box, type a description for the template, such as **A Tasks list that can be used for team or personal tasks, that contains a Gantt view for task planning and a calendar to provide an overview of tasks for a selected period of time.**

File Name	
Enter the name for this template file.	File name: `ExtendedTasks`
Name and Description	

The name and description of this template will be displayed on the Create page.	Template name:
	`Extended Tasks`
	Template description:
	`A Tasks list that can be used for team or`
	`personal tasks, that contains a Gantt`
	`view for task planning and a calendar to`

Include Content	
Include content in your template if you want new lists created from this template to include the items in this list. Including content can increase the size of your template.	☐ Include Content
Caution: Item security is not maintained in a template. If you have private content in this list, enabling this option is not recommended.	

8. Leave the **Include Content** check box cleared. Click **OK**.

9. A message box appears, telling you that the template has been saved successfully in the List Templates gallery. Click **OK**.

Important Saving a list as a template does not save the permissions for the list. This means that if you save a list as a template and you include the content, then any user that has sufficient permissions to create a list can create a list based on this template and view the data that you saved in it. If you are including sensitive content in your list template, make sure that only authorized users can get to it.

Tip By default, the size of a list template is limited to 50 megabytes (MB). A SharePoint farm administrator can increase this size limit to a maximum of 2 gigabytes (GB) if necessary.

10. You will now create a new list based on the template that you've just saved. Click the **All Site Content** link in the left navigation area.

11. Click the **Create** link at the top. The Create dialog opens.

12. Under **Filter By,** click **List**.

13. Click the **Extended Tasks** template.

14. Type **More Tasks** in the **Name** box on the right of the page.

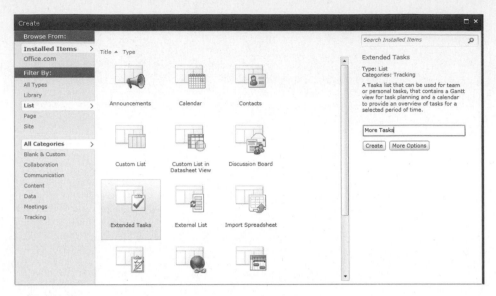

15. Click **Create**.

    A new list is created that is based on the Tasks list you saved as a template. You can see that the default view is the Gantt view, and if you check out the other views, you will find that the Task Calendar view is also present. The list is empty and doesn't contain any data because you did not include the content when saving the list as a template.

16. You will now save the list template file on your computer. Using the **Navigate Up** button in the upper-left corner of the screen, go to the top-level site in the site collection. In the top-level site, click **Site Actions**, and then click **Site Settings**.

17. In the **Galleries** section, click **List templates**.

    The List Templates gallery is displayed. The template that you have just saved is displayed in the gallery. Notice the Documents and Library tabs on the Ribbon, which show that the List Templates gallery is in fact a document library.

18. Click the **Extended Tasks** template. A message box is displayed, asking if you want to save the ExtendedTasks.stp file to your computer.

19. Click **Save**.

20. Browse to a location on your computer where you want to store the file and click **Save**. Do not change the extension of the file.

21. You will now delete the template from the gallery. In the browser, select **ExtendedTasks** by clicking the check box to the left of its name

✕ Delete Document 22. The **Documents** tab opens and displays the Ribbon. Click the **Delete Document** button, and then click **OK** in the confirmation message box that appears.

The list template has been deleted from the List Templates gallery. You or other users of your site are no longer able to create lists based on it. You will now upload the template to the gallery from your computer.

23. Click **Upload Document**.

24. Browse to the location on your computer where you saved the list template. Select the list template file and click **Open**.

25. In the **Upload Document** dialog, click **OK**.

26. In the **List Templates Gallery – ExtendedTasks** dialog, click **Save**.

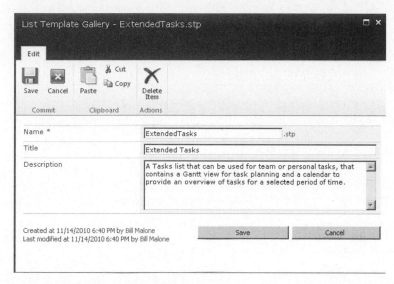

The list template is now available within your site, and it once again can be used to create lists based on it. Even though it was uploaded back to the same site where it was originally created, you could have uploaded it to another site to make the template available to users of that site as well.

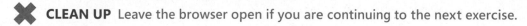 **CLEAN UP** Leave the browser open if you are continuing to the next exercise.

Relating List and Item Views

There are a couple of ways in which you can connect data in two different lists in SharePoint Foundation. One way to create a relationship between data in different lists is by creating lookup columns. A *lookup column* can be used to prevent the deletion of data from a list that still has items in another list that depend on it. You can also customize the display form of a list and show related items on it that are determined based on lookup columns.

Another way to display a relationship between data in two different lists is by using connected Web Parts. The list view Web Part in SharePoint Foundation 2010 is called the XSLT List View (XLV) Web Part. You can use lookup columns to create a connection between two list Web Parts, but you can also use columns based on other data types to create a connection so long as the contents of the columns in the two lists match. A Web Part connection allows one Web Part to pass data to another Web Part. The data doesn't have to be limited to a cell. It can also be a complete row, or even an entire list. If you are configuring a Web Part connection using your browser, the Web Parts have to be on the same page. If you are using SharePoint Designer 2010, you can also connect Web Parts on different pages within the same site collection.

In the following exercise, you will create a lookup column, customize the display form of a list, add a list view Web Part to a page, and connect two list view Web Parts.

SET UP Open the SharePoint site that contains the library that you want to configure, if it is not already open. The exercise will use the *http://wideworldimporters* site, but you can use whatever site you want. If prompted, type your user name and password, and click OK.

BE SURE TO verify that you have sufficient rights to manage libraries. If in doubt, see the Appendix at the back of this book.

1. On the Quick Launch, click **Shared Documents**.

2. In the **Library Tools,** click the **Library** tab.

Library
Settings

3. Click **Library Settings** in the **Settings** group on the Ribbon. The Library Settings page is displayed.

4. You will now create a lookup column. In the **Columns** section, click **Create Column**.

5. In the **Create Column** page, in the **Column name** box, type a column name, such as **Product Category**. Set **Lookup (information already on this site)** to the **Type of information in this column**.

6. In the **Additional Column Settings** section, from the **Get information from** drop-down list, select **Product Categories**. From the **In this column** drop-down list, select **Title**.

Note The Product Categories list is a simple custom list that has been set up for this exercise. It uses the standard Title column that contains a product category.

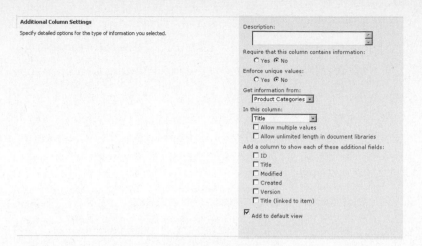

7. Leave other settings unchanged and click **OK**.

8. Navigate to the **Shared Documents** library using the Quick Launch. On the right side of the screen, there is a new Product Category column, but it is empty.

9. Hover your mouse over the **OakBedTable** document and click the check box on the left to select it. The **Documents** tab opens, and the Ribbon is displayed.

10. In the **Manage** group on the Ribbon, click the **Edit Properties** button.

11. In the **Shared Document - OakBedTable** dialog, select **Tables** from the **Product Category** drop-down list and click **Save**.

12. Repeat steps 9–11 for the **OakChest**, **OakDesk**, and **OakEndTable** documents, setting **Product Category** to **Chests**, **Desks**, and **Tables**, respectively.

	Type	Name	Modified	Modified By	Product Category
		OakBedTable	11/15/2010 8:46 PM	Bill Malone	Tables
		OakChest	11/15/2010 8:48 PM	Bill Malone	Chests
		OakDesk	11/15/2010 8:48 PM	Bill Malone	Desks
		OakEndTable	11/15/2010 8:48 PM	Bill Malone	Tables

13. You will now look into the display form of a list. Click **Product Categories** on the Quick Launch.

14. In the **List Tools,** click the **List** tab.

Modify Form
Web Parts

15. Click the **Modify Form Web Parts** button in the **Customize List** group on the Ribbon, and select **Default Display Form**. The display form is displayed in Edit mode.

Related List

16. In the **Page Tools,** click the **Insert** tab.

17. Click the **Related List** button and choose **Shared Documents**.

18. Click the **Page** tab and then click the **Stop Editing** button on the Ribbon.

19. Click the **Tables** link.

> The display form of the Tables product category is displayed. The page shows what documents are related to this product category. If you go to the display form of a different product category, like Desks, the documents that are related to that category will be displayed.

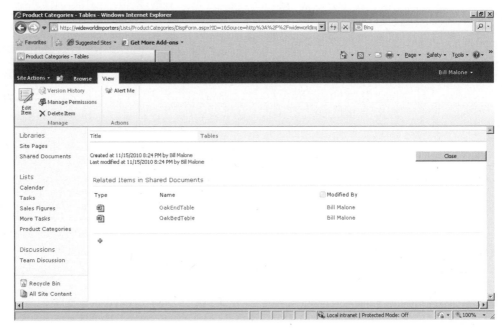

20. You will now add a list view Web Part to a page and then connect two list view Web Parts. Click the **Browse** tab, and then navigate to the home page of the site using the breadcrumb.

21. On the home page, click the **Page** tab. The Ribbon is displayed.

22. In the **Edit** group, click the **Edit** button. The page is displayed in Edit mode.

Edit

23. Scroll to the bottom of the page and position your cursor below the **Shared Documents** Web Part.

24. In the **Editing Tools,** click the **Insert** tab.

25. In the **Web Parts** group on the Ribbon, click the **Existing List** button.

Existing List

26. In the Web Parts pane that appears, select **Deadlines**.

27. Click **Add**. The Deadlines list will now be displayed in its own Web Part below the Shared Documents Web Part.

The Deadlines list is a custom list that has been created for this exercise. It has a Title column that contains a product name and a Deadline column that contains a date.

28. Click the down arrow on the upper-right section of the **Deadlines** Web Part and select **Edit Web Part**.

29. Click the down arrow on the upper-right section of the **Deadlines Web Part** once again, hover the mouse over **Connections**, hover it over **Get Filter Values From**, and finally click **Shared Documents**.

30. In the **Configure Connection** dialog that appears, from the **Provider Field Name** drop-down list, select **Title**. From the **Consumer Field Name** drop-down list, select **Title**.

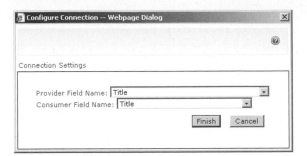

31. Click **Finish**. You now have connected the Web Parts.

32. **Click** the **Page** tab, and then click the **Save & Close** button in the **Edit** group on the Ribbon.

Save & Close

33. You will now verify the connection between two lists. In the **Shared Documents** Web Part, click the double arrow in the **Select** column for the **OakDesk** document. The corresponding deadline is displayed in the Deadlines Web Part.

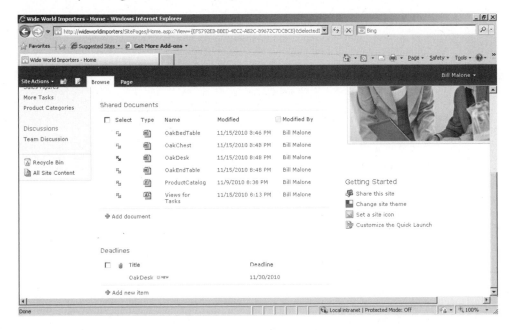

CLEAN UP Close the browser.

Key Points

- List and library views enable you to sort, filter, and group data, as well as to display data in different styles.

- SharePoint Foundation provides several view types for lists and libraries, including Standard view, Datasheet view, Calendar view, Gantt view, and Access view.

- You can create your own views to display data in a list or library in a way that makes the most sense to you.

- A Datasheet view is very useful for bulk editing.

- A Gantt view is used to display a work breakdown structure of a project and can best be used on a Tasks or a Project Tasks list.

- A Calendar view has different scopes that allow you to choose whether you want to look at a day, a week, or a month at a time.

- To reuse list views, you can create a list template.

- Relationships between SharePoint lists in different views can be created by using lookup columns and Web Part connections.

Chapter at a Glance

Create a survey, page 286

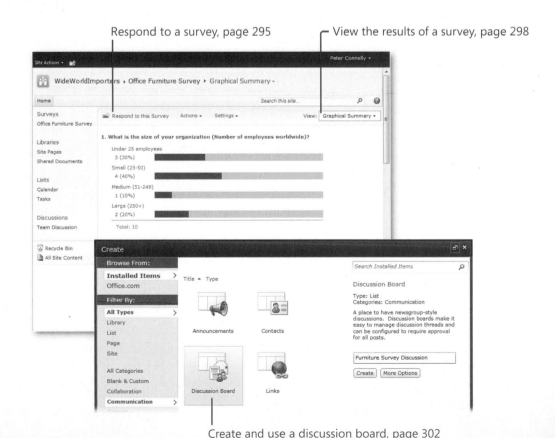

Respond to a survey, page 295

View the results of a survey, page 298

Create and use a discussion board, page 302

10 Working with Surveys and Discussion Boards

In this chapter, you will learn how to

✔ Create a survey.

✔ Respond to a survey.

✔ View the results of a survey.

✔ Create and use a discussion board.

✔ Enable a discussion board for email.

✔ View a discussion board in Microsoft Outlook.

Chapter 4, "Working with Lists," introduced you to lists in Microsoft SharePoint Foundation 2010. By using two specialized SharePoint list templates—Surveys and Discussion Boards—you can gather feedback and information from users of your site.

By creating a *survey*, you can determine the format of the user's feedback and configure whether respondents' names appear in the survey results. If names are configured to appear, you can see how each user responded; if names are configured not to appear, the survey is anonymous. SharePoint Foundation tallies the results and compiles a graphical summary of the responses.

By creating a *discussion board*, you can allow users to determine the type of response that they give. A discussion board invites users to discuss issues with one another by initiating topics and posting replies.

Tip Discussion boards are also known as *message boards* or, on the Internet, as *Internet forums*.

In this chapter, you will learn how to create and respond to a survey and then view the survey results. You will also learn how to create and use a discussion board, including viewing a discussion board from within Outlook 2010.

> **Practice Files** You don't need any practice files to complete the exercises in this chapter.

Important Remember to use your SharePoint site location in place of *http://wideworldimporters* in the following exercises.

Creating a Survey

Surveys are created for a number of reasons. For example, you might need to create a survey to ask for a user's opinions or to collect factual information for marketing purposes. No matter what their purpose, all surveys involve the creation of a survey "container," followed by the creation and administration of questions.

These questions can be formatted as one of two basic types:

- **Open** These questions have no definite answer. Open-ended questions give users the opportunity to answer in their own words, rather than by simply checking one of a limited list of alternatives. An example of an open-ended question is "Are there any other comments you would like to add about the services or products supplied by Wide World Importers?" The advantage of open-ended questions is that responses can be very useful, often yielding quotable material and an insight into the issues that are of most concern to the respondents of the survey. The disadvantage is that the responses are more difficult to catalog and interpret.

- **Closed** These questions have a finite set of answers from which the user must choose. One of the choices may be "Other" or "N/A" to allow users to specify that their answer is not one of those supplied or that the question is not applicable to them. The advantages of closed-ended questions are that data can be gathered from them easily and that they lend themselves to statistical analysis. The disadvantage is that they are more difficult to write than open-ended questions, because the choices must include all the possible answers that a user could offer for each question.

Users can respond to a survey in a number of ways, such as by typing text, selecting items from a menu, clicking yes or no, or entering a numeric or currency value. When you use SharePoint Foundation to create a question, you can specify the type of answer, as summarized in the following table.

Answer Type	Question Type	Description
Single Line Of Text	Open	Use this answer type when you want users to enter only a few words. You can specify the maximum number of characters that a user can type.
Multiple Lines Of Text	Open	Use this answer type when you want users to type one or more sentences. You can specify the maximum number of lines that a user can type and the type of text in which a user can format responses. The three formatting options are: ● Plain text ● Rich text, whereby users can change font or text color and alignment ● Enhanced text, whereby users can add pictures, tables, and hyperlinks
Choice	Open, Closed	Use this answer type when you want users to choose from a set of selections that you provide. You can create a multiple-choice question in which users pick the best answer or answers from among the possible choices, represented as a drop-down list, a set of option buttons, or a set of check boxes. You can make the question open-ended by allowing users to type their own answers.
Rating Scale	Closed	Use this answer type (often called a *Likert scale*) when you want users to choose their preference on a numeric scale. Questions with this type of answer are often used to obtain feedback on provided services. Users indicate how closely their feelings match the question or statement by using a rating scale. The number at one end of the scale represents the most agreement, or "Strongly Agree," and the number at the other end of the scale represents the least agreement, or "Strongly Disagree."
Number	Open	Use this answer type when you want users to enter a numeric value. You can specify a lower and upper limit for the value, as well as the number of decimal places that users can enter.
Currency	Open	Use this answer type when you want users to enter a monetary value. You can select the currency format based on a geographic region, a lower and upper limit for the value, and the number of decimal places that users can enter.
Date And Time	Open	Use this answer type when you want users to enter a date or a date and time.

Answer Type	Question Type	Description
Lookup	Closed	This answer type is very similar to the Choice answer type, in that responses are predetermined. Use this answer type to point users to an existing list on your site that contains the available choices. When you add this answer type to your survey, you can select to enforce relationship behavior and select to display multiple columns from the lookup list. You can then decide to display the lookup columns on the survey response form, on the Graphical Summary of Responses page, or on the All Responses page.
Yes/No	Closed	This answer type presents the user with a check box and can be used when you want users to respond with Yes or No (or True or False). Questions that require this answer type are sometimes known as *categorical* questions.
Person or Group	Closed	This answer type is very similar to the Choice answer type, in that responses are predetermined. Use this answer type to choose a user or SharePoint Group that has access to the SharePoint site. Multiple users or groups can be chosen.
Page Separator	Not applicable	Use this answer type when you want your survey to span multiple pages.
External Data	Closed	This answer type is very similar to the Choice answer type, in that responses are predetermined. Use this answer type to point users to external systems outside SharePoint Foundation that contain the available choices.
Managed Metadata	Closed	If your website is created on a Microsoft SharePoint Server 2010 installation, you are presented with this answer type. It is very similar to the Choice answer type, in that responses are predetermined. Use this answer type to point users to a Metadata term store that contains the available choices.

A survey is a type of list, and therefore survey answer types are comparable to column types, and survey questions are comparable to columns. You can specify whether an answer is required or optional and provide a default answer for each question. However, unlike other list data entry forms, surveys allow you to define a branch in the survey so that you can skip to a specific question based on the user response.

Important With surveys, as with columns, you can configure list-level validation, and when you use the answer types Single Line of Text, Choice, Number, Currency, and Date and Time, you can use column (survey answer) validation. However, on surveys, the user message that you provide is not displayed on the survey form. An error page is displayed with the generic text "List data validation failed" and a link to go back to the site. Therefore, you may not want to use list-level validation or column-level validation with surveys. A subsequent Microsoft hotfix or service may implement the same validation behavior on surveys that currently apply to other list types.

In the following exercise, you will create a survey on a SharePoint website.

 SET UP Open the SharePoint site in which you would like to create your survey. The exercise will use the *http://wideworldimporters* site, but you can use whatever site you want. If prompted, type your user name and password, and click OK.

BE SURE TO verify that you have sufficient rights to create a list. If in doubt, see the Appendix at the back of this book.

1. Click **Site Actions**, and then click **More Options**.

   The Create dialog is displayed.

2. In the left pane, under **Filter By** and then under **All Categories**, click **Data**, and then click **Survey**.

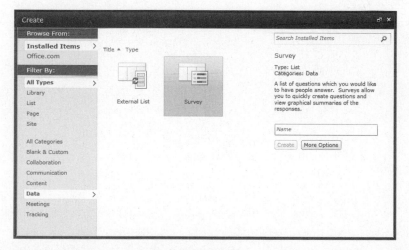

3. In the right pane, click **More Options**.

4. In the **Name** box, type **Office Furniture Survey**.

5. In the **Navigation** area, leave the **Yes** option selected.

6. In the **Survey Options** area, for the **Show user names in survey results?** and **Allow multiple responses?** options, select **Yes**.

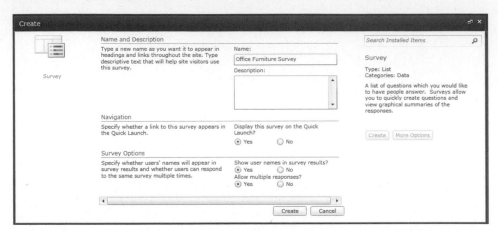

7. At the bottom of the page, click **Create**. The New Question page is displayed.

8. In the **Question and Type** area, in the **Question** box, type **What is the size of your organization (Number of employees worldwide)?**, and then select the **Choice (menu to choose from)** option.

9. In the **Additional Question Settings** area, for the **Require a response to this question** option, select **Yes**.

10. In the **Type each choice on a separate line** box, type the following four lines:

    Under 25 employees

    Small (25-50)

    Medium (51-249)

    Large (250+)

11. Under **Display choices using**, make sure that the **Radio Buttons** option is selected. This is the default setting.

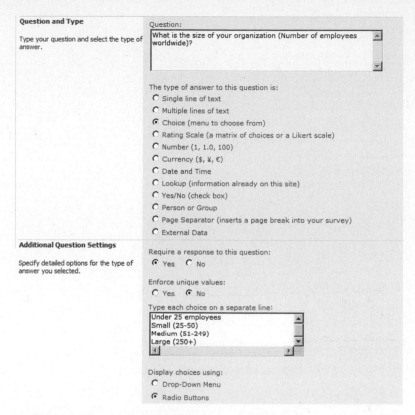

12. At the bottom of the page, click **Next Question**.

13. In the **Question and Type** area, in the **Question** box, type **To what extent do you agree or disagree with the following statements?**, and then select the **Rating Scale (a matrix of choices or a Likert scale)** option.

14. In the **Additional Question Settings** area, for the **Require a response to this question** option, select **Yes**.

15. In the **Type each sub-question on a separate line** box, replace the existing text with the following three lines:

    We try to buy furniture made from recycled material.

    We like unique furniture from around the world.

    We purchase the majority of our furniture at low prices from discount stores.

16. Click the down arrow to the right of the **Number Range** box, and then click **10**.

17. In the first **Range Text** box, type **Strongly Agree**. Delete the text in the middle box, and, in the last box, type **Strongly Disagree**.

Additional Question Settings

Specify detailed options for the type of answer you selected.

A rating scale question consists of a question and sub-questions that are rated on a scale such as 1 to 5. Type a question into the Question box, and then type sub-questions that support the main question. Select a Number Range to define the number of options that users can choose from. The Range Text appears above the option buttons to describe the meaning of the scale, such as Low, Average, and High or Strongly Disagree, Neutral, and Strongly Agree. Use the N/A option if you want users to select N/A or a similar response, if a question is not applicable.

Require a response to this question:
● Yes   ○ No

Type each sub-question on a separate line:

y furniture made from recycled material.
ue furniture from around the world.
e the majority of our furniture at low prices from discount stores.

Number Range:
10 ▾

Range Text:
ngly Agree | | y Disagree

Show N/A option:
☑

N/A option text: N/A

Branching Logic

Specify if branching is enabled for this question. Branching can be used to skip to a specific question based on the user response. A page break is

To define branching logic, add your questions and then, in the Survey Settings page, edit the questions to define the branching logic.

18. At the bottom of the web page, click **Next Question**.

19. In the **Question and Type** area, in the **Question** box, type **Would you like us to contact you?**, and then select the **Yes/No (check box)** option.

20. In the **Additional Question Settings** area, select **Yes**. This is the default setting.

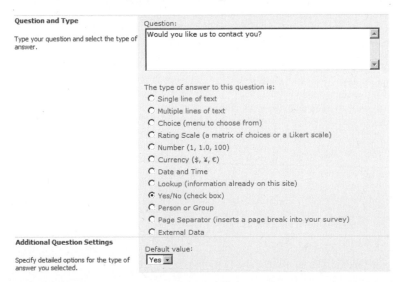

Question and Type

Type your question and select the type of answer.

Question:

Would you like us to contact you?

The type of answer to this question is:
○ Single line of text
○ Multiple lines of text
○ Choice (menu to choose from)
○ Rating Scale (a matrix of choices or a Likert scale)
○ Number (1, 1.0, 100)
○ Currency ($, ¥, €)
○ Date and Time
○ Lookup (information already on this site)
● Yes/No (check box)
○ Person or Group
○ Page Separator (inserts a page break into your survey)
○ External Data

Additional Question Settings

Specify detailed options for the type of answer you selected.

Default value:
Yes ▾

21. At the bottom of the web page, click **Next Question**.

22. In the **Question and Type** area, in the **Question** box, type **Please enter your name, address and any queries you may have:**, and then select the **Multiple lines of text** option.

23. In the **Additional Question Settings** area, for the **Require a response to this question** option, select **Yes**.

24. In the **Specify the type of text to allow** option, select **Enhanced rich text (Rich text with pictures, tables, and hyperlinks)**.

The type of answer to this question is:
- ○ Single line of text
- ● Multiple lines of text
- ○ Choice (menu to choose from)
- ○ Rating Scale (a matrix of choices or a Likert scale)
- ○ Number (1, 1.0, 100)
- ○ Currency ($, ¥, €)
- ○ Date and Time
- ○ Lookup (information already on this site)
- ○ Yes/No (check box)
- ○ Person or Group
- ○ Page Separator (inserts a page break into your survey)
- ○ External Data

Additional Question Settings

Specify detailed options for the type of answer you selected.

Require a response to this question:
● Yes   ○ No

Number of lines for editing:
6

Specify the type of text to allow:
- ○ Plain text
- ○ Rich text (Bold, italics, text alignment, hyperlinks)
- ● Enhanced rich text (Rich text with pictures, tables, and hyperlinks)

25. At the bottom of the web page, click **Next Question**.

26. In the **Question and Type** area, in the **Question** box, type **How much money, in total, did you spend on furniture over the last year?**, and then select the **Currency ($, ¥, £)** option.

27. In the **Additional Question Settings** area, for the **Require a response to this question** option, select **Yes**.

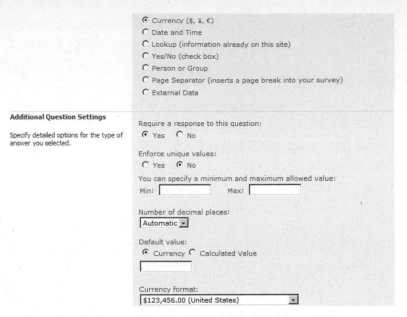

28. To the right of the **Number of decimal places** box, click the down arrow, and then click **2**.

29. At the bottom of the web page, click the **Finish** button. The Survey Settings page is displayed.

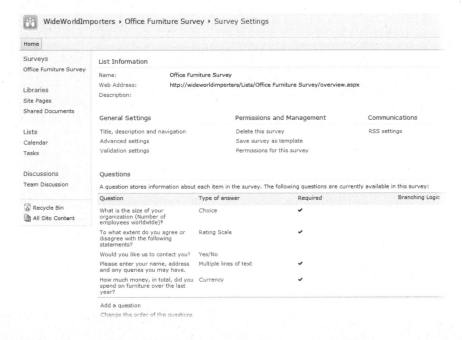

30. In the **Questions** area, under the **Question** column, click **Would you like us to contact you?** The Office Furniture Survey Survey Settings Edit Question page is displayed.

31. In the **Branching Logic** area, under **Possible Choices**, to the right of **Yes**, click the down arrow, and then click **Please enter your name, address and any queries you may have.**

32. To the right of **No**, click the down arrow, and then click **How much money, in total, did you spend on furniture over the last year?**

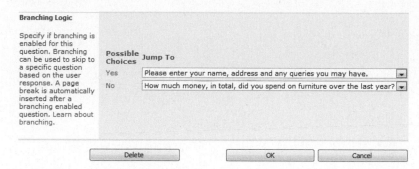

33. Click **OK**. The Survey Settings page is displayed.

Important You can use the Edit Question page to modify or delete an existing survey question. However, you must be careful not to change questions after you have allowed users access to the survey and received some responses. Changing a survey question might cause you to lose data that you have already collected.

 CLEAN UP Close the browser.

Responding to a Survey

As surveys are created on a SharePoint website, you might find that you need to take them yourself. Surveys are created to gather information, and users must respond to your survey so that you can analyze the information they give you. It is important that you know how people are interacting with the surveys that you create. Once you have created a survey, it is good practice to view the survey from a user's perspective by completing at least one test response.

In this exercise, you will respond to a survey.

SET UP Open the SharePoint site in which the survey is located. If prompted, type your user name and password, and click OK. The exercise uses the Office Furniture Survey created in the previous exercise, but you can use whatever survey you want.

BE SURE TO verify that you have sufficient rights to contribute to the list. If in doubt, see the Appendix at the back of this book.

1. On the Quick Launch, under **Surveys**, click **Office Furniture Survey**. The Office Furniture Survey Overview dialog is displayed.

Note Survey list pages do not use the Ribbon.

2. Click **Respond to this Survey**. The New Item dialog is displayed.

3. Select the **Under 25 employees** option. For the ranking question options, select **1**, **2**, and **8**, and leave the check box selected for the **Would you like us to contact you?** question.

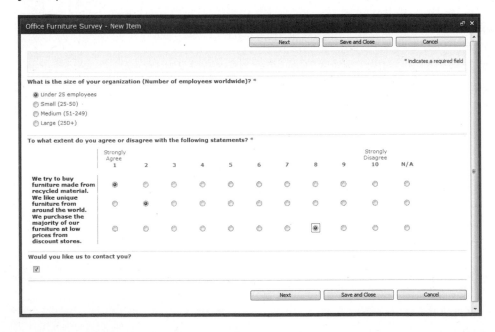

4. Click **Next**.

> **Important** When you add a page separator to a survey, a Save And Close button is added to all but the final page of the survey. You must answer all required responses on a survey page before you can successfully click Save And Close. If you click Save And Close, the survey responses are saved and categorized as not completed. You are not prompted for responses to questions on subsequent pages, even if the responses were set as required. For those questions in which you have enabled branching, survey questions automatically insert a page separator after the branch-enabled question.

5. Click under **Please enter your name, address and any queries you may have:** and type **Erin M. Hagens, erin@contoso.com**

6. Click in the money question box. The Ribbon tabs disappear, but the Ribbon remains visible. Type **200** in the money question box.

7. To display the **Editing Tools** ribbon tab to format the contents of the **Please enter your name, address and any queries you may have:** box, click **Erin**.

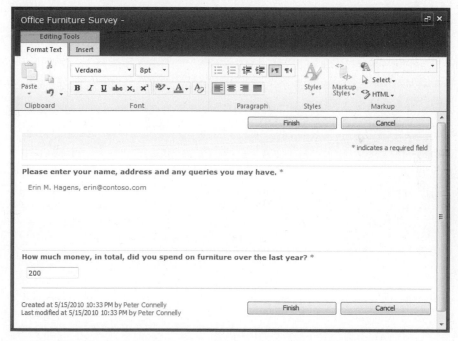

8. Click **Finish**. The Office Furniture Survey – Overview page is displayed.

9. Repeat Steps 2 through 7 several times, entering different responses each time.

> **Note** When you clear the check box for the Would You Like Us To Contact You? question, you are not presented with the Please Enter Your Name, Address And Any Queries You May Have: box.

 CLEAN UP Close the browser.

Troubleshooting If you do not allow multiple responses when you create a survey and you try to test the survey more than once, an Error page is displayed stating that you are not allowed to respond to the survey again. To correct this problem, display the Office Furniture Survey - Overview page, click Settings, and then click Survey Settings. On the Survey Settings page, under the General Settings area, click Title, Description And Navigation. On the Office Furniture Survey Survey Settings General Settings page, in the Survey Options area, select Yes for the Allow Multiple Responses option, and then click Save. In the Quick Launch, under Surveys, click Office Furniture Survey to enter additional responses.

Viewing the Results of a Survey

After users respond to your survey, you need to examine and analyze the results. SharePoint Foundation provides three ways to display a quick summary of the survey data:

- **Overview** This view displays the survey's name, description, date, and time of creation, as well as the number of responses.

- **Graphical Summary** This view displays the response data for each survey question in the form of a graph. The number of responses is displayed as a value and as a percentage of the total number of responses received.

- **All Responses** This view displays a list of each survey response, the date and time the response was last modified, whether the user completed the survey, and the name of the user who created it, if applicable. In this view, responses can be modified or deleted.

Important Surveys are created with item-level permissions so that all responses can be read by all users, but users can edit only their own responses. If you want to prevent users from changing their responses, display the survey, click Settings, and then click Survey Settings. On the Office Furniture Survey Survey Settings page, under the General Settings area, click Advanced Settings. On the Survey Settings Advanced Settings page, in the Item-Level Permissions area, under Create And Edit Access: Specify Which Responses Users Are Allowed To Create And Edit, click None.

Setting survey permissions is similar to setting document library permissions. On this page, you can also set whether the survey should be visible in the search results, whether the survey should be available for offline clients, and whether to launch forms as dialogs.

See Also For more information about setting document library permissions, see Chapter 5, "Working with Libraries."

You can also export survey result data to a spreadsheet, where you can use the data analysis features available in Microsoft Excel 2010.

In the following exercise, you will view the responses to your survey. After editing one of your responses to the survey, you will export the results of the survey to Excel and then find the average amount spent on office furniture by users who responded to your survey.

 SET UP Open the SharePoint site in which the survey is located. If prompted, type your user name and password, and click OK. The exercise will use the Office Furniture Survey used in the previous two exercises, but you can use whatever survey you want. You will need Excel 2007 or Excel 2010 to complete this exercise.

BE SURE TO verify that you have sufficient rights to edit the survey. If in doubt, see the Appendix at the back of this book.

1. On the Quick Launch, under **Surveys**, click **Office Furniture Survey**. The Office Furniture Survey Overview page is displayed.

2. To the right of the page, next to **View**, change the **Overview** setting to **Graphical Summary**. The Office Furniture Survey page is displayed in Graphical Summary view.

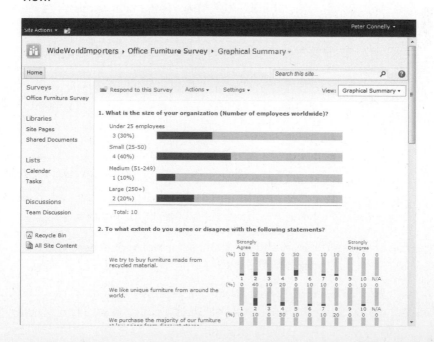

3. To the right of the page, next to **View**, click **Graphical Summary**, and then click **All Responses**. The Office Furniture Survey page is displayed in All Responses view.

4. Point to the **View Response #1** survey item, and click the down arrow. In the drop-down list, click **Edit Response**.

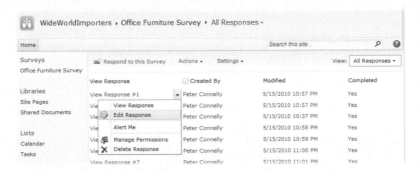

5. Select the **Medium (51-249)** option, and then click **Save and Close**.

6. Click **OK** in the information message dialog box that opens.

7. On the breadcrumb, click the down arrow to the right of **All Responses**, and then click **Overview**.

8. Click **Actions**, and then click **Export to Spreadsheet**.

   Tip The Export To Spreadsheet option is available only in the Overview view.

9. If the **File Download** dialog box appears with a warning that some files can harm your computer, click **Open**. In the **Microsoft Excel Security Notice** dialog box, click **Enable**.

The survey responses are displayed within Excel, with AutoFilter enabled in the header row of every column. The Excel workbook contains a column for each question and a column for Created By, Item Type, and Path To The List.

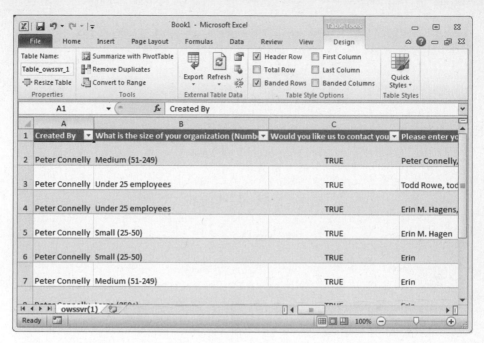

10. In column E, click the first blank cell outside the Excel list, and then click the **Formulas** tab.

11. Click the down arrow to the right of **AutoSum**, and click **Average**.

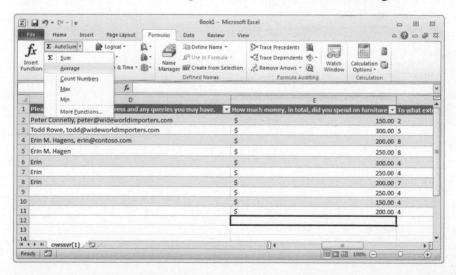

Excel displays the average amount that survey respondents spent on their office furniture in the last year.

12. On the **Quick Access Toolbar**, click **Save**. The Save As dialog box appears.

Save

13. In the **File name** box, type **OfficeFurnitureSurvey.xlsx**, and click **Save**.

 CLEAN UP Close Excel and the browser.

See Also For more information about how to use Excel with SharePoint Foundation, see Chapter 14, "Using SharePoint Foundation with Excel 2010 and Access 2010."

Creating and Using a Discussion Board

Discussion boards provide a forum on which visitors to your site can converse about topics of interest. SharePoint sites created with the Team, Document Workspace, or Social Meeting site templates include a discussion board. You can display the discussion board by using the Quick Launch.

You can use a discussion board to initiate new discussions, as well as sort and filter existing discussions. You can also change the design of the discussion board and create alerts that notify you of changes to the discussion board.

Discussion boards are usually displayed in one of three views:

- **Subject view** This view enables you to view a list of discussions.

- **Threaded view** This view enables you to view comments grouped by discussion or thread. All messages that are a part of the same thread appear together in the order in which they were created.

- **Flat view** This view lists replies in the order in which they were created.

You can post replies to the Team Discussion discussion board, or you can create new discussions. You can configure discussion board security settings so that users can participate in one discussion but not another.

Important Discussion boards are created with the same item-level permissions as surveys; that is, all discussions and replies can be read by all users, but users can edit only their own discussions and replies.

In this exercise, you will create a new discussion board, add a new topic, delete a topic, and then remove the discussion board.

 SET UP Open the SharePoint site in which you would like to create a discussion board. If prompted, type your user name and password, and click OK.

BE SURE TO verify that you have sufficient rights to create a list. If in doubt, see the Appendix at the back of this book.

1. On the Quick Launch, click **Discussions**. The All Site Content page is displayed.

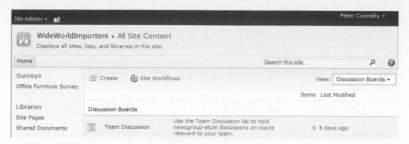

2. Click **Create**. The Create dialog is displayed.

3. In the left pane, under **Filter By** and then under **All Categories**, click **Communication**, and then click **Discussion Board**.

4. In the right pane under **Discussion Board**, type **Furniture Survey Discussion**.

   Tip The Name field is the Subject of the discussion, as well as part of the Uniform Resource Locator (URL) for the discussion board.

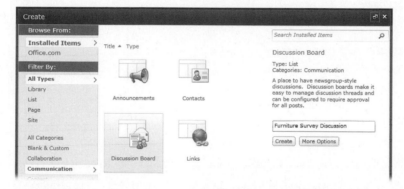

5. Click **Create**. The Furniture Survey Discussion page is displayed.

   Important Because surveys and discussion boards are both lists, the name of the list needs to be unique within the site. Therefore, you cannot call the discussion board in this exercise "Furniture Survey" because this name would conflict with the "Furniture Survey" survey that you created in the first exercise in this chapter.

6. Click **Add new discussion** to display the **New Item** dialog.

7. In the **Subject** box, type **Office Furniture Survey – overall comments**.

8. In the **Body** box, type **What did you think of the range of questions on the Office Furniture Survey?** and then click **Save**.

   The Subject view of the Furniture Survey Discussion list with the List Tools ribbon tab is displayed.

9. Click **Office Furniture Survey – overall comments**.

The Furniture Survey Discussion page is displayed in Flat view, where each reply has a title bar that displays the date and time the reply was created, a View Properties link, and Reply links.

10. Click **Reply** to display the **New Item** dialog.

11. In the **Body** box, type **We could add an additional question that asks users whether they subscribe to Wide World Importers' monthly newsletter. The answer type would be Yes/No**.

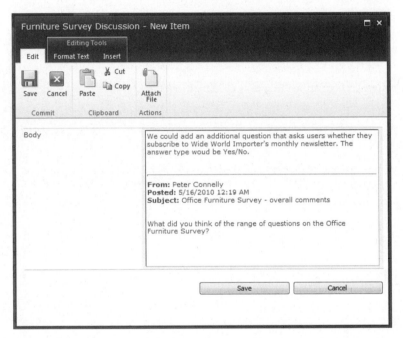

12. Click **Save**. The Discussion Board page is displayed in Flat view.

13. On the breadcrumb, click the down arrow to the right of **Flat**, and then click **Threaded**.

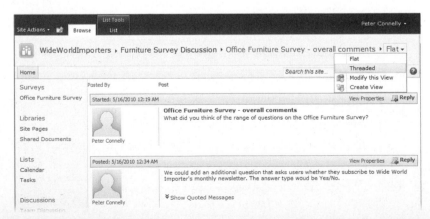

All replies to the Office Furniture Survey – Overall Comments discussion are displayed in Threaded view.

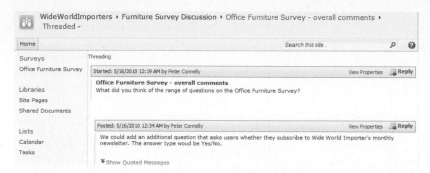

Tip To return to Subject view, click Furniture Survey Discussion on the breadcrumb or, in the Quick Launch, under Discussions, click Furniture Survey Discussion.

14. On the title bar for the reply **We could add an additional question . . .**, click **View Properties**. The Furniture Survey Discussion dialog is displayed.

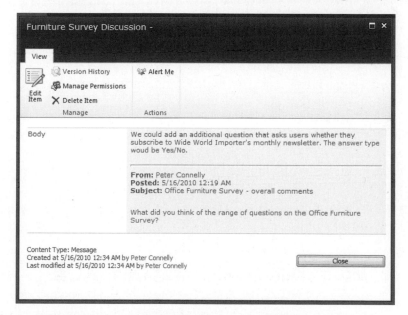

15. On the **View** tab, click **Delete Item** in the **Manage** group.

16. Click **OK** to send the item to the site's Recycle Bin.

The Office Furniture Survey – Overall Comments page is displayed.

17. On the Ribbon, under **List Tools**, click the **List** tab, and then click **List Settings** in the **Settings** group.

The Discussion Board Settings page is displayed.

18. In the **Permissions and Management** area, click **Delete this discussion board**.

19. In the browser's dialog box that asks whether you are sure you want to send this list to the site's Recycle Bin, click **OK**. The All Site Content page is displayed.

 CLEAN UP Close the browser.

Tip From the Discussion Board Settings page, you can enable content approval, create columns other than Subject and Body, and display views other than Threaded and Flat.

Enabling a Discussion Board for Email

As detailed in Chapter 4, SharePoint Foundation allows list managers to assign an email address to discussion boards. Before this email feature can be used, the SharePoint Foundation server administrator must configure the web application for outgoing email. You should contact this person in your organization if you want to use this email feature.

In the following exercise, you will configure a discussion board so that users can email their discussions.

 **SET UP** Open the SharePoint site in which the discussion board is located. If prompted, type your user name and password, and click OK. The exercise uses the Team Discussion created as part of a Team site, but you can use whatever discussion board you want.

BE SURE TO verify that you have sufficient rights to manage a list. If in doubt, see the Appendix at the back of this book.

1. On the Quick Launch, under **Discussions**, click **Furniture Survey Discussion**. The Furniture Survey Discussion Subject view is displayed.

2. On the **List** tab, click **List Settings** in the **Settings** group. The Discussion Board Settings page is displayed.

3. Under the **Communications** area, click **Incoming e-mail settings**.

Troubleshooting If this option is not available, a SharePoint Foundation farm administrator will need to configure the web application for incoming emails.

The Incoming E-Mail Settings: Furniture Survey Discussion page is displayed.

4. In the **Incoming E-Mail** area, for the **Allow this list to receive e-mail** option, select **Yes** and enter an email address, such as **SurveyDiscussion@ wideworldimporters.com**. You need to provide only the part of the email address that precedes the "at" sign (@).

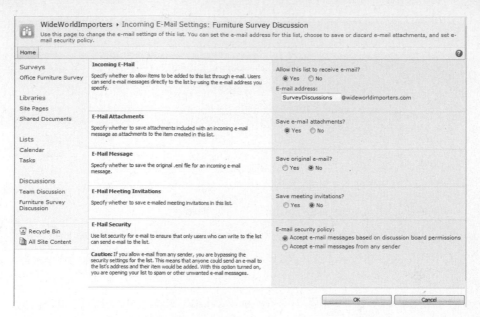

5. At the bottom of the page, click **OK**. The Discussion Board Settings page is displayed.

 CLEAN UP Close the browser.

See Also For more information about configuring email settings for a list, refer to Chapter 7, "Working with List Settings."

Viewing a Discussion Board in Outlook

SharePoint Foundation allows you to contribute and search discussion boards from within Outlook 2007 or Outlook 2010. Discussion questions and replies can be made available even when you are offline. Chapter 13, "Using SharePoint Foundation with Outlook 2010," provides more details on the integration of Outlook and SharePoint Foundation.

In the following exercise, you will view a discussion board from within Outlook.

 **SET UP** Open the SharePoint site in which the discussion board is located. If prompted, type your user name and password, and click OK. The exercise uses the Team Discussion created in a Team site, but you can use whatever discussion board you want.

BE SURE TO verify that you have sufficient rights to manage a list. If in doubt, see the Appendix at the back of this book.

1. On the Quick Launch, under **Discussions**, click **Furniture Survey Discussion**. The Furniture Survey Discussion Subject view is displayed.

2. On the Ribbon, under **List Tools**, click the **List** tab, and then select **Connect to Outlook** in the **Connect & Export** group.

3. If a dialog box appears, stating that a website wants to open web content using Outlook on your computer, click **Allow**.

   Outlook opens, and it might ask you to supply your user name and password.

   An Outlook dialog box appears, stating that you should connect lists only from sources you know and trust.

4. Click **Advanced**. The SharePoint List Options dialog box appears.

5. In the **Folder Name** box, type **WideWorldImporters – Furniture Survey Discussion**.

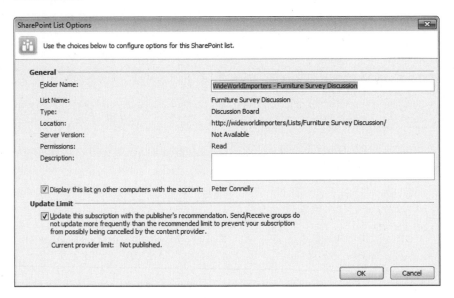

6. Click **OK**, and then, in the **Microsoft Outlook** dialog box, click **Yes**. Outlook displays the WideWorldImporters – Furniture Survey Discussion area under the Outlook SharePoint Lists folder.

 **CLEAN UP** Close Outlook and any browser windows that you might have open.

Key Points

- A survey allows you to create questions and control the format of responses.

- In a survey, you can create both open-ended and closed-ended questions.

- SharePoint Foundation provides three views in which to summarize survey responses: Overview, Graphical Summary, and All Responses. You can export survey responses to a spreadsheet to perform more complex data analysis.

- A discussion board allows users to create and reply to discussion subjects.

- You can view discussions in either Subject, Flat, or Threaded view.

- You can enable a discussion board to receive incoming emails.

- You can connect discussion boards to Outlook. These appear under the SharePoint Lists folder.

- Surveys and discussion boards are specialized lists. Their permissions can be controlled independently of both the site and of other lists. You can apply item-level permissions to prevent users from editing their survey responses or discussion messages.

Chapter at a Glance

Configure a workflow, page 315

Work with workflows, page 319

Manage workflows, page 323

Manage workflow tasks within Outlook 2010, page 326

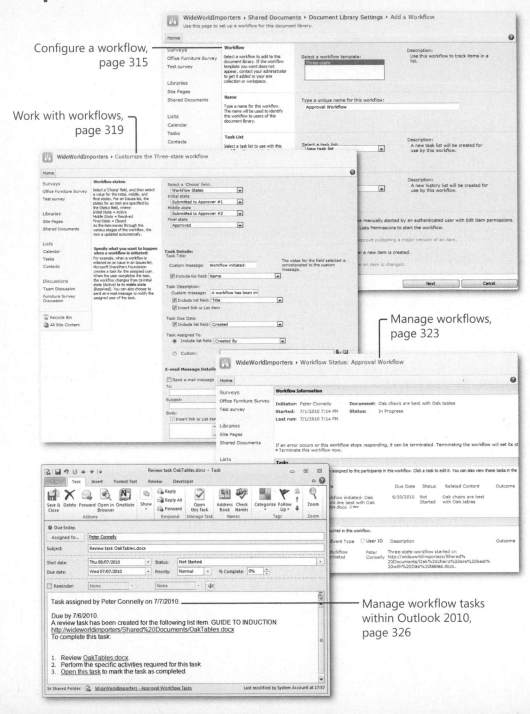

11 Working with Workflows

In this chapter, you will learn how to

- ✔ Automate business processes using SharePoint.
- ✔ Understand the built-in workflows of SharePoint.
- ✔ Configure a workflow.
- ✔ Work with workflows.
- ✔ Manage workflows.
- ✔ Manage workflow tasks within Outlook 2010.
- ✔ Terminate workflows.
- ✔ Remove workflows from lists and libraries.
- ✔ Associate workflows with content types.

The workflow technology included in Microsoft SharePoint Foundations 2010 and Microsoft SharePoint Server 2010 can help you automate new and existing business processes. In the past, creating a workflow was typically a task for developers. Most companies have many different types of workflows, and hiring a developer to create workflows can be time-consuming and expensive. SharePoint provides you with a number of built-in workflows that you can configure using the browser.

Traditionally, SharePoint workflows were attached to a list or library, and although SharePoint 2010 has introduced site workflows, attaching workflows to lists or libraries will probably still be the most popular type of SharePoint workflow.

In this chapter, you will learn the fundamentals of the workflow architecture and what workflows are provided by default when you install SharePoint Foundation. You will learn how to create, delete, and modify workflows, and how to track the status of workflows that are currently running using the browser and within Microsoft Outlook 2010. You will also learn how to associate workflows with content types.

Important Remember to use your SharePoint site location in place of *http://wideworldmporters* in the following exercises.

> **Practice Files** You don't need any practice files to complete the exercises in this chapter.

Automating Business Processes Using SharePoint

Automating frequently run or time-consuming business processes allows you to make efficient use of your time and the time of people on your team. Also, with the introduction of SharePoint in an organization, the initial productivity boom can be transformed into a management burden as more content is added to the SharePoint installation and the amount of work that users will need to do to maintain the content on a day-to-day basis increases. SharePoint can help you with your old and new business processes.

In previous chapters, you were introduced to how SharePoint can help you complete your work with the use of the following:

- RSS Feeds, for finding information from a variety of sources on an ad-hoc basis
- Alerts, for regular notifications of new, modified, or deleted content
- Content approval, which along with versioning allows you to manage content and who can see content that is classified as draft

However, none of these three methods allows you to automate business processes beyond a one-step process. You could combine these methods, such as using content approval with alerts to provide a lightweight workflow that sends you emails when your team members publish documents as a major version, so you can approve documents according to a specific timescale. However, such a solution can help solve only a small number of your business processes. You might want to route a document or a web page to a number of people before publishing it.

SharePoint provides two other methods to help automate processes:

- **Workflows** Used to automate and track processes that require human intervention, such as notifying users when their action is required to move the process forward. Such processes could take days, weeks, or months to complete and may need to wait for an event or another process to complete.

- **Event Receivers** Used to automate processes that require no human intervention, such as moving job applications from one document library to a series of other document libraries for some purpose.

Workflows and event receivers cannot automate a task unless time is taken to define exactly how the task should be automated, nor can they track the status of information stored on paper documents. They also cannot force users to perform a particular task. You must have a clear understanding of how the business process operates. If you do not understand how to complete a business process manually, you will not be able to describe the business process in sufficient detail to automate that process.

Therefore, some planning and startup tasks are needed to automate a process. You do not necessarily want to automate every little process in your organization. You want to automate processes that are predictable and those where the startup cost of creating a workflow and ensuring that your team is happy with the new process will be offset by the productivity improvement that the automated process will provide. You must also understand what SharePoint has to offer.

See Also Microsoft TechNet website contains articles on SharePoint Server 2010 workflows at *http://technet.microsoft.com/en-us/library/cc263134.aspx* and on content type and workflow planning at *http://technet.microsoft.com/en-us/library/cc262735.aspx*.

Understanding the Built-in Workflows of SharePoint

SharePoint provides a number of built-in workflows that you can configure using the browser. Additional workflows can be created using Microsoft SharePoint Designer 2010, Microsoft Visual Studio 2010, or Microsoft Visio 2010 in combination with SharePoint Designer 2010. Event receivers can be created only using Visual Studio 2010.

See Also SharePoint Designer is a free product, and information on downloading it can be found at: *http://office.microsoft.com/en-us/sharepoint-designer-help/*. More information on using SharePoint Designer to create workflows can be found in *Microsoft SharePoint Designer 2010 Step by Step*, by Penelope Coventry (Microsoft Press, 2010).

You can think of a workflow as a series of tasks that produce an outcome. In the same way that you base a new site, list, or library on a template, you can base a new workflow on a workflow template. These templates are implemented as features that can be activated or deactivated at the site or site collection level by using the browser or by using programs. A workflow template is available only when a workflow feature is activated.

In previous versions of SharePoint, you could create workflows only by associating a workflow template with a list, library, or content type. Therefore, most workflows were focused on documents. Not all workflows are like that, however, and to cater to other scenarios, SharePoint 2010 now supports the creation of site workflows by associating a workflow template at the site level.

Site workflows operate within the context of a SharePoint site instead of being attached to a specific list and operating on a specific list item. Site workflows are started manually or programmatically, but not automatically. SharePoint Foundation does not come with any workflow templates that you can associate at the site level; therefore, to create site workflows, you must use either Visual Studio 2010 or SharePoint Designer 2010.

SharePoint Foundation ships with only one generic workflow template, the three-state workflow template that can be used across multiple scenarios. On the other hand, SharePoint Server contains additional workflow templates, such as the following:

- **Approval** Provides an approval mechanism for documents.

- **Collect Feedback** Provides a feedback mechanism for documents.

- **Collect Signatures** Provides a mechanism for collecting digital signatures for completing a document.

- **Disposition Approval** Provides an expiration and retention mechanism that allows you to decide whether to retain or delete expired documents. This workflow can be started only by using the browser.

- **Group Approval** Similar to the Approval workflow; however, it is available only in East Asian versions of SharePoint Server.

- **Translation Management** Provides a mechanism for document translation by creating copies of documents to be translated and also assigns tasks to translators. This workflow is available only when you create the SharePoint Server Translation Management library. More information on the Translation Management library and the workflow can be found at: *office.microsoft.com/en-us/sharepoint-server-help /use-a-translation-management-workflow-HA010154430.aspx*.

You can use the Workflows page at the site collection level to see which workflow templates are available and active, the number of SharePoint objects (lists, libraries, content types, and sites) the workflow template is associated with, and the number of workflow instances that are running in those workflows. Unfortunately, this Workflows page does not provide any links that you can use to identify which SharePoint objects the workflow template is associated with or which sites, list items, or documents are progressing through the workflow.

SET UP Open the top level site of your site collection. This exercise will use the *http://wideworldmporters* site, but you can use whatever top level site you want. If prompted, type your user name and password, and then click OK.

BE SURE TO verify that you have sufficient rights to view the workflow page at the site collection level. If in doubt, see the Appendix at the back of this book.

1. Click **Site Actions**, and then click **Site Settings**.

2. Under **Site Administration**, click **Workflows**.

   Troubleshooting If you do not see the Workflows link under Site Administration, you are probably at a child site within the site collection. Under Site Collection Administration, click Go To Top Level Site Settings to navigate to the top of the site collections, and then repeat step 2.

   The Workflows page is displayed.

 CLEAN UP Close the browser.

Configuring a Workflow

Each of the built-in workflow templates can be customized in a limited fashion to define the exact process necessary to meet your business needs. An instance of a workflow uses the configured workflow template as a blueprint, which defines the conditions that should be tested to decide which tasks to complete to produce the outcome.

For example, you can configure the three-state workflow template to define an expense approval workflow process. Members of your team create an expense form, and when they upload it into a document library, you want the document to progress through the expense approval workflow process.

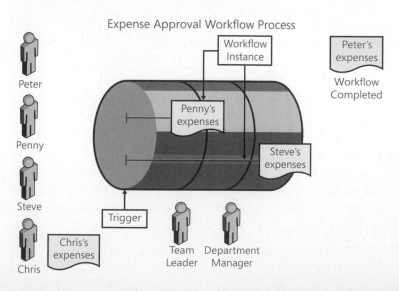

The workflow process always has a start and an end. The trigger for entering the process is uploading the document into the document library. An instance of workflow is created when a workflow event is triggered. Each expense form must be approved by Approver #1 (stage 1) and Approver #2 (stage 2), in sequence. Once the expense form has completed both stages, it is approved (stage 3). When the workflow instance reaches the end of the workflow process, it is set to Completed. The workflow process then does no other work until a new workflow instance is created.

To maintain the status of the document as it progresses through the workflow, you must create a Choice column that can store the three states of the workflow and allow you to track the progress of the document through the workflow.

The three-state workflow can be triggered in the following ways:

- Manually, using the browser or using SharePoint Server from a Microsoft Office 2010 application. You can restrict who can start workflow instances manually to those users who have the Manage Lists permissions.

- Automatically, when you create a list item or document.

Other SharePoint Server workflows can have other trigger events. For example, the Approval workflow template can be configured for any of the following:

- To start a workflow instance automatically when a list item or document is changed.

- To start a workflow instance automatically when a major version of a document is saved. If you choose this option, a workflow instance will not automatically start when a minor version of a document is saved. Therefore, to use this option, the library must be configured with major and minor versioning enabled. See Chapter 8, "Working with Library Settings" for more information on how to configure a library to use major and minor versions.

The three-state workflow uses both a Task and History list as the workflow process executes. The workflow adds task items to a Task list so that users can keep track of all the work that needs to be finished to complete the workflow process for a particular workflow instance. Users can be sent emails when a task item is assigned to them.

The History list keeps track of the workflow instances that are running or that have been completed for a given list item or document. This is a hidden document library and is not shown on the All Site Content web page. You can display this list in the browser by appending */lists/workflow history/* to your site's Uniform Resource Locator (URL); for example, *http://wideworldimporters/lists/workflow history/*.

Tip You could export the contents of the Workflow History list to Microsoft Excel and create reports to analyze the workflow process.

In the following exercise, you will add a site column to a document library that gives you a choice for each workflow state. You will then associate a workflow template with the document library.

SET UP Open a Team SharePoint site where you would like to associate a workflow template with a document library. This exercise will use the *http://wideworldmporters* site, but you can use whatever SharePoint Team site you want. If prompted, type your user name and password, and then click OK.

BE SURE TO verify that you have sufficient rights to manage the document library. If in doubt, see the Appendix at the back of this book.

1. On the Quick Launch, click the document library where you want to associate a workflow template.

Create
Column

2. On the **Library** tab, in the **Library Tools** tab set, click **Create Column** in the **Manage Views** group.

3. In the **Column name** box, type **Workflow States** and select the **Choice** option.

4. In the **Type each choice on a separate line** box, enter three choices: **Submitted to Approver #1**, **Submitted to Approver #2**, and **Approved**. Be sure to delete the three predefined generic choices first. Then click **OK**.

   Tip You can create more than one Choice list column, and a Choice list can have more than three choices. However, the three-state workflow can be configured to use only three values.

   Once the new column is created, you can create the new workflow.

Workflow
Settings

5. On the **Library** tab, in the **Library Tools** tab set, in the **Settings** group, click the arrow to the right of **Workflow Settings**, and then click **Add a Workflow**.

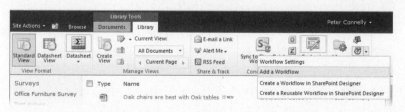

The Add a Workflow page is displayed. By default, when using SharePoint Foundation, one workflow appears named Three-State.

Troubleshooting If the Three-State workflow does not appear, then you may need to activate the Three-State Workflow feature at the site collection level. See Chapter 3, "Creating and Managing Sites," for more information on features.

6. Select **Three-state**, if it is not already selected, and then, in the **Name** section, type a new name for this workflow, such as **Approval Workflow**.

7. In the **Select a task list**, select **New Task List**.

    Note The name of the new Task list will take the format of *<workflow name>* Tasks, such as Approval Workflow Tasks. Create a new Task list if you will have many documents progressing through a workflow.

8. In the **Start Options** section, leave the selections at their default settings.

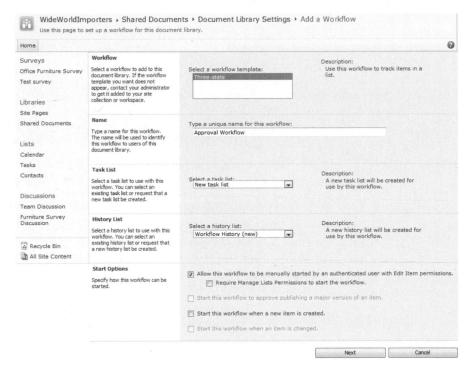

9. Click **Next** to display the second workflow settings page.

10. In the **Workflow states** section, the new column that you added to the document library automatically appears with the three choices that you entered for the three states of the workflow. If it does not appear, from the **Select a Choice field** list, click **Workflow States**, and enter the initial, middle, and final states in the three lists if needed.

11. In the **Specify what you want to happen when a workflow is initiated** section, in the **Tasks Details** area, leave the selections at their default settings and clear the **Send e-mail message** check box.

12. Repeat step 11 for the **Specify what you want to happen when a workflow changes to its middle state** section.

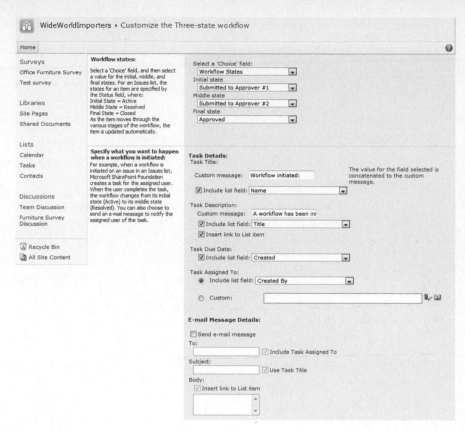

13. Click **OK**.

 CLEAN UP Leave the browser open if you are continuing to the next exercise.

Working with Workflows

Once a workflow template is associated with a list or library and customized to define the process as required to meet your business needs, a list item or document can be sent through the process. Depending on the configuration of your three-state workflow, you can start a workflow instance by either starting the workflow manually or by uploading or creating a new document.

In the following exercise, you manually start a workflow instance for a document and complete the tasks for the workflow process.

Important If the workflow is configured to allow only users with Manage Lists permissions to start workflows manually, and you do not have the Manage Lists permissions for the document library, you will not be able to complete this exercise.

SET UP Open the All Documents view of the document library where you associated the workflow template, if it is not already open. Make sure that you have at least one document in the library before you start this exercise.

BE SURE TO verify that you have sufficient rights to start a workflow for a document. If in doubt, see the Appendix at the back of this book.

1. Move your mouse over the document for which you want to start a workflow, and then select the check box that appears to the left of the document.

Workflows

2. On the **Documents** tab, in the **Library Tools** tab set, click **Workflows** in the **Workflows** group.

The *<document library name>* Workflows *<document name>* page is displayed.

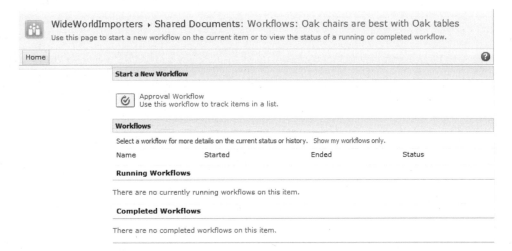

WideWorldImporters ▸ Shared Documents: Workflows: Oak chairs are best with Oak tables
Use this page to start a new workflow on the current item or to view the status of a running or completed workflow.

Home	

Start a New Workflow

Approval Workflow
Use this workflow to track items in a list.

Workflows

Select a workflow for more details on the current status or history. Show my workflows only.

Name	Started	Ended	Status

Running Workflows

There are no currently running workflows on this item.

Completed Workflows

There are no completed workflows on this item.

3. Under **Start a New Workflow**, click **Approval Workflow**.

The All Documents view is displayed. Two new columns appear: Workflow States and Approval Workflow. For the document you selected in step 1, the Workflow States column has a value of Submitted To Approver #1; the Approval Workflow column has a value of In Progress, which indicates that a workflow instance for this document is running in the Approval Workflow; and in the Modified By column, the user ID of the person who last updated the document or its properties is System Account.

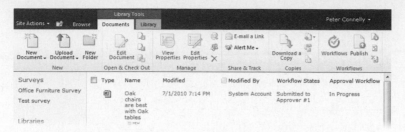

4. In the **Approval Workflow** column, click **In Progress**.

The Workflow Status: Approval Workflow page is displayed. This page is divided into three parts: Workflow Information, Tasks, and Workflow History. In the Tasks section, one task item is listed as being assigned to you, with a status of Not Started. In the Related Content column, there is a link to the document with which the workflow instance is associated. There is also a link to the document in the Workflow Information section. In the Workflow History section, there is one entry with an Event Type of Workflow Initiated.

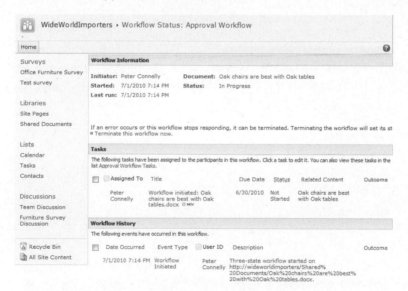

5. In the **Tasks** section, under **Title**, click **Workflow initiated**.

The Approval Workflow Tasks – Workflow Initiated dialog appears.

6. On the **View** tab, click **Edit Item**. The dialog displays the task input form.

7. From the **Status** list, select **Completed**, and then, on the **Edit** tab, click **Save** in the **Commit** group.

   The task input form closes, and the Workflow Status: Approval Workflow page is displayed again. The Tasks section contains two task items; the first is Completed, and the second is Not Started. The Workflow History section has two entries: Workflow Initiated and Task Completed.

   Troubleshooting If the two tasks do not appear in the Tasks section and in the Workflow Information section, a message in red text states that due to heavy loads, the latest workflow operation has been queued. Refresh the page and click OK in the message box that appears.

8. In the **Tasks** section, click **Approval Workflow Tasks**.

   The All Tasks view of the task list, Approval Workflow Tasks, is displayed where the two workflow tasks are listed.

9. Click the task item with a title of **Review task**, and repeat steps 6 and 7.

   The All Tasks page refreshes again, and the two task items related to the workflow have a status of Completed.

10. On the Quick Launch, click the document library with which you are working in this exercise.

The All Documents view is displayed. The Workflow States column has a value of Approved, and the Approval Workflow column has a value of Completed for the document for which you started a workflow instance in step 3.

11. In the **Approval Workflow** column, click **Completed**.

The Workflow Status: Approval Workflow page is displayed. In the Workflow Information section, the workflow instance has a status of Completed. In the Tasks section, the two tasks have a status of Completed, and in the Workflow History section, there are four events: a Workflow Initiated event, two Task Completed events, and a Workflow Completed event.

 CLEAN UP Leave the browser open if you are continuing to the next exercise.

Managing Workflows

As you use the workflow process, you may find that it does not match your business requirements. Therefore, you will need to modify the workflow as time progresses, perhaps to change the person who does the first stage or second stage of the process.

In the following exercise, you modify a workflow process for a document library, complete both of the tasks for the workflow process, and then terminate the workflow instance.

SET UP Open the All Documents view of the document library where you associated the workflow template.

BE SURE TO verify that you have sufficient rights to modify the workflow process for the document library. If in doubt, see the Appendix at the back of this book.

Workflow
Settings

1. On the **Library** tab, in the **Library Tools** tab set, click **Workflow Settings** in the **Settings** group.

The Workflow Settings page is displayed.

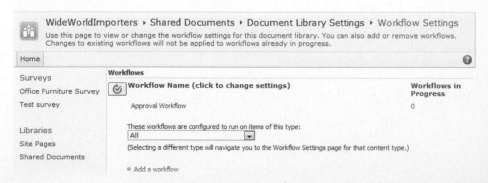

2. Under **Workflow Name**, click **Approval Workflow**.

   The Change a Workflow page is displayed.

3. In the **Start Options** section, select the **Start this workflow when a new item is created** check box, and then click **Next**.

   The Customize the Three-state Workflow page is displayed.

4. In the **Specify what you want to happen when a workflow is initiated** section, in the **Custom message** box, type **Review Stage 1**, and under **Task description**, in the **Include list field** list, select **Version**.

Check Name

5. Under **Task Assigned To**, select **Custom**, and then, in the **Custom** box, enter the user name of a person to approve the document, and click the **Check Name** icon to the right of the **Custom** box to verify that you have entered a valid user name.

   Note By specifying a person to assign a task to, you have not modified the permissions of the Task list. You have configured the workflow to store the user name in the Assign To column on the Task list. Any user who has Edit List Item permissions on the list can complete a task item.

6. Click **OK**.

   The All Documents view of the library is displayed.

Upload Document

7. On the **Documents** tab, in the **Library Tools** tab set, click **Upload Document** to display the **Upload Document** dialog, and then click **Browse**.

8. In the **Choose File to Upload** dialog box, browse to the file that you would like to upload, such as **OakTable.docx**. Click **Open** and then click **OK**.

   The CompanyInduction.docx dialog opens with a Workflow Status of Submitted to Approver #1.

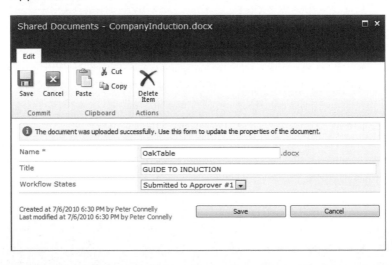

9. Click **Save**.

The All Documents view of the document library refreshes. The new document that you uploaded is listed on the page with an Approval Workflow status of In Progress.

10. Move your mouse over the document you uploaded in step 8, click the arrow that appears, and then click **Workflows**.

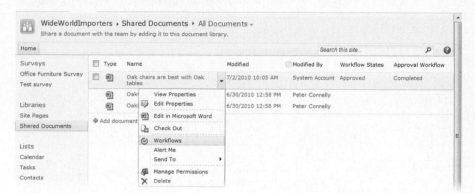

The Workflows: *<document name>* page is displayed. In the Workflows section, there is a running workflow for the Approval Workflow, with a status of In Progress. The Approval Workflow is not listed in the Start a New Workflow section.

Note If the Approval Workflow is not listed in the Start a New Workflow section, you cannot start another workflow instance for that workflow until the running workflow instance has completed.

11. Under **Running Workflows**, click **Approval Workflow**.

The Workflow Status page is displayed. In the Tasks section, there is a task assigned to the user you specified in step 5.

12. Click **Review Stage 1**.

The Approval Workflow Tasks dialog opens. In the Description field, the version number of the document is displayed along with a message box with the text, "A workflow has been initiated on the following list item," and a link to the document.

13. Click **Close** to return to the **Workflow Status** page.

 CLEAN UP Leave the browser open if you are continuing to the next exercise.

Managing Workflow Tasks within Outlook 2010

Workflow tasks are assigned to participants by using a Tasks list. You can use Outlook 2007 or Outlook 2010 as a place to receive workflow-related notifications and complete workflow tasks.

See Also More information on using Outlook 2010 with SharePoint can be found in Chapter 13, "Using SharePoint Foundation with Outlook 2010."

In the following exercise, you will manage workflow tasks in Outlook 2010.

 SET UP Open the Workflow Status page for the document you used in the previous exercise, if it is not already open.

BE SURE TO verify that you have sufficient rights to manage tasks in the Approval Workflow Tasks list. If in doubt, see the Appendix at the back of this book.

1. In the **Tasks** section, click **Approval Workflow Tasks**.

   The All Tasks page is displayed and contains a task named "Review Stage 1: <*document name*>" with a status of Not Started, which you created in the previous exercise.

Connect to Outlook

2. On the **List** tab, in the **Lists Tools** tab set, click **Connect to Outlook** in the **Connect & Export** group.

3. Click **Allow** twice to confirm that you want to open Outlook.

   Outlook opens.

4. Click **Yes** to connect the Task list to Outlook.

5. In the **Tasks** navigation pane, under **Other Tasks**, click the Tasks list that you associated with the workflow.

   In the detail pane, the Review Stage 1: <*document name*> task appears.

Mark Complete

6. Click the task, and, on the **Home** tab, click **Mark Complete**.

   The text of the task, Review Stage 1: <*document name*>, is struck through, denoting that the task is completed.

7. Press **F9**.

   In the detail pane, a second task, Review task <*document name*>, is added.

8. Double-click the task.

The Review task *<document name>* Task form opens. The task contains two links to the document: the task item in the Tasks list and a link to the Tasks list. By using these links, you can open, review, and modify the document's contents.

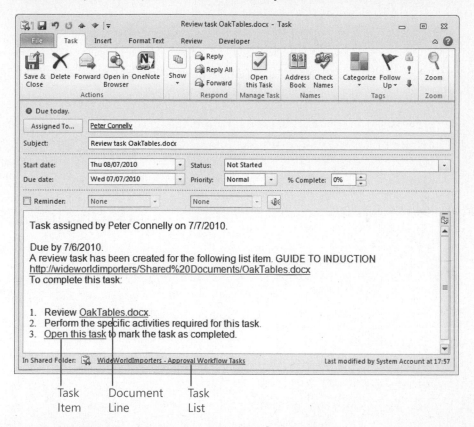

Task   Document   Task
Item   Line   List

9. From the **Status** drop-down list, select **Completed**, and then, on the **Task** tab, click **Save & Close**.

The text of the Review task: *<document name>* task is struck through.

Save & Close

10. In Outlook, in the **Tasks** navigation pane, under **Other Tasks**, click the **Tasks** list that you associated with the workflow and, on the **Folder** tab, click **Open in Web Browser** in the **Actions** group.

Open in
Web Browser

The browser opens, and the Tasks List page is displayed with the two completed tasks.

11. In the browser, on the Quick Launch, under **Documents**, click **Shared Documents**. The Shared Documents library is displayed.

The *<workflow name>* column for the document on which you started the workflow appears with a status of Completed.

 CLEAN UP Close Outlook. Leave the browser open if you are continuing to the next exercise.

Terminating Workflows

From time to time, you may need to terminate a workflow instance. For example, a person may have left your organization, and you have used a different business process to pay expenses to him or her. In the following exercise, you will start a workflow instance on a document; you will then terminate that workflow instance.

 SET UP Open the All Documents view of the document library where you associated the workflow template.

BE SURE TO verify that you have sufficient rights to create and delete workflow instances on a document. If in doubt, see the Appendix at the back of this book.

1. Move your mouse over the document where you want to start a workflow, select the arrow that appears to the right of the document, and then click **Workflows**.

2. Under **Start a New Workflow**, click **Approval Workflow**.

The All Documents page is displayed, with the Approval Workflow column for your document set to In Progress.

3. In the **Approval Workflow** column, click **In Progress**.

4. In the **Workflow Information** section, click **Terminate this workflow now**.

Workflow Information

Initiator:	Peter Connelly	Document:	OakChest
Started:	7/7/2010 7:38 PM	Status:	In Progress
Last run:	7/7/2010 7:38 PM		

If an error occurs or this workflow stops responding, it can be terminated. Terminatin
▫ Terminate this workflow now.

A Message From Webpage dialog box opens, asking if you are sure that you want to terminate this workflow.

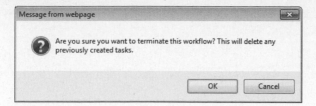

5. Click **OK**.

   The Workflow Status page refreshes. The Workflow Information section has a status of Canceled. There are no task items listed in the Tasks section, and in the Workflow History section, the last event in the list has an event type of Workflow Canceled.

6. On the Quick Launch, click the document library with which you are working.

   The All Document view is displayed, with the Approved Workflow column for your document set to Canceled.

 CLEAN UP Leave the browser open if you are continuing to the next exercise.

Removing Workflows from Lists and Libraries

When an automated business process is no longer needed, you should remove the workflow from the list or library. This will prevent confusion for users who use that list or library. In the following exercise, remove a workflow from a document library.

SET UP Open the All Documents view of the document library where you associated the workflow template.

BE SURE TO verify that you have sufficient rights to remove a workflow from the document library. If in doubt, see the Appendix at the back of this book.

1. On the Quick Launch, click the document library or list where you associated a workflow template.

Workflow
Settings

2. On the **Library** tab, in the **Library Tools** tab set, in the **Settings** group, click **Workflow Settings**.

   The Workflow Settings page is displayed.

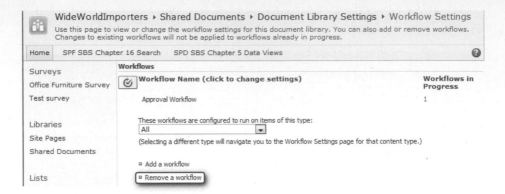

3. Click **Remove a workflow**.

The Remove Workflows page is displayed.

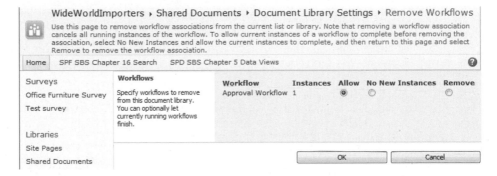

4. Select **Remove**.

Note When there are a number of instances in progress for the workflow, select No New Instances, and then return to this task in a day or two, allowing the people in your team to complete the outstanding tasks for these workflow instances.

The Workflow Settings page is displayed, showing that the workflow is no longer associated with the list or library.

✖ CLEAN UP Leave the browser open if you are continuing to the next exercise.

Associating Workflows with Content Types

Content types are designed to help users define a reusable collection of settings that can include columns, workflows, and other attributes. They can be associated with their own document template and with their own workflow and retention policies. Content types and site columns can be defined at the site or site collection level. When created at the site collection level, they can be used by lists and libraries or by any site within the site collection hierarchy. When created at the site level, they can be used only by lists and libraries within that site and any child sites.

If you need to use the same workflow process with a particular type of list or library or a specific document type, then you should consider associating a workflow template with a content type and customizing it to define the process necessary to meet your business needs. This will reduce the amount of rework you would otherwise need to complete to achieve this consistency.

You may want the same approval process on every document library in a site or site collection, so users can send a document through the approval process manually when needed. To create this solution, you would amend the document content type at the top of the site collection and select the Update All Content Types That Inherit From This Type With These Workflow Settings option.

Tip When a site collection contains many sites, it may take some time for the content type configuration to be applied to all child sites. If you are creating a new site hierarchy, then create all your content types and site columns first before creating any child sites.

Another example could be the need to have two types of announcements—team announcements that must be approved and announcements that need no approval. To meet this business need, you could create a new announcement content type based on the original content type, so that you get all the same functionality of the built-in announcement list and a workflow. Site owners can then choose to associate the new content type with their announcement list, so they are able to create the two types of announcements.

Note The three-state workflow needs a column to store the three states. All columns in a content type must be a site column; therefore, if you associate the three-state workflow with a content type, you must add a Choice site column to store the three states.

In the following exercise, you will create a new content type, add a site column to the content type, associate a workflow template with the content type, and configure its settings.

 SET UP Open the SharePoint Team site that you used in the previous exercise, if it is not already open.

BE SURE TO verify that you have sufficient rights to create a content type. If in doubt, see the Appendix at the back of this book.

1. Click **Site Actions**, and then click **Site Settings**. The Site Settings page is displayed.

2. Under **Galleries**, click **Site content types**, and then, on the **Site Content Types** page, click **Create**. The New Site Content Type page is displayed.

3. In the **Name** box, type **Team Announcements**, and in the **Description** box, type **Use this content type to create new lists where the team can create team announcements**.

4. In the **Select parent content type from** list, select **List Content Types**, and in the **Parent Content Type**, select **Announcement**, if it is not already selected.

5. In the **Group** section, select **New group** and type **WideWorldImporters**.

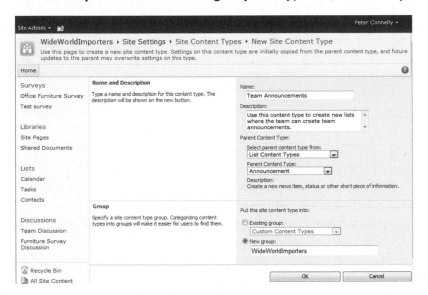

6. Click **OK**. The Team Announcements page is displayed.

7. In the **Columns** section, click **Add from existing site columns**.

    The Add Columns to Content Type page is displayed.

8. In the **Available columns list**, scroll down and select **Status**. Then click **Add**.

    The Status column appears in the Columns To Add list.

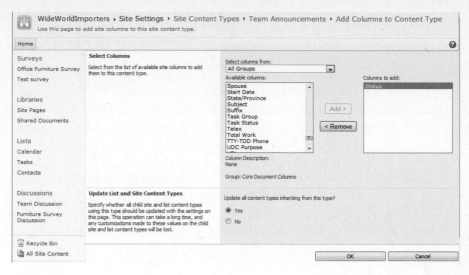

9. Click **OK**.

The Team Announcements page is displayed. Status is listed in the Columns section with the Source column blank. This indicates that the Status column was added to this content type and not inherited from a parent content type.

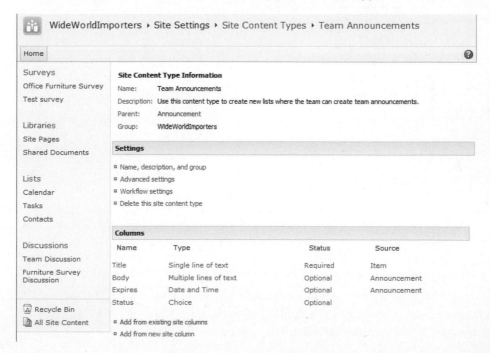

10. In the **Settings** section, click **Workflow settings**.

11. On the **Workflow Settings** page, click **Add a workflow**.

    The Add a Workflow page is displayed.

12. In the **Workflow** section, select **Three-state**, if not already selected. Then, in the **Name** section, type a new name for this workflow, such as **Announcement Approval**. Leave the other sections at their default settings and then click **Next**.

    The Customize the Three-state Workflow page is displayed.

13. In the **Workflow states** section, the site column that you added to the content type automatically appears with the three choices, **Not Started**, **Draft** and **Reviewed**, for the three states of the workflow. If this column does not appear, from the **Select a Choice field** list, click **Status** and enter the initial, middle, and final states in the three lists as needed.

14. Leave the other sections at their default settings, and then click **OK**.

    The Team Announcements page is displayed.

✖ **CLEAN UP** Close the browser.

Key Points

- Workflows can help to automate and track long-running, repetitive processes that require human interaction, after someone has defined exactly what form that automation will take.

- Plan your workflows and involve the people who will use the workflow.

- A workflow template is available only when a workflow feature is activated.

- Workflow templates can be associated with sites, lists, libraries, or content types.

- Each of the built-in workflow templates can be customized in a limited fashion to define the exact process necessary to meet your business needs.

- To maintain the status of a document through a three-state workflow process, you must create a Choice column that stores the three states of the workflow

- The workflow name is used as the name of a column; therefore, do not give the workflow the same name as an existing column.

- You cannot start two instances of the same workflow on a list item or document.

- A workflow's progress is recorded in a Workflow History list, and workflow tasks are assigned to participants by using a Tasks list.

- You can receive an email notification when a workflow task is created.

- Outlook 2010 serves as a place to receive workflow-related notifications and complete workflow tasks.

- Workflow templates can be associated with content types. This reduces the amount of rework you would otherwise need to complete to provide consistent workflows across multiple lists, libraries, and sites.

Chapter at a Glance

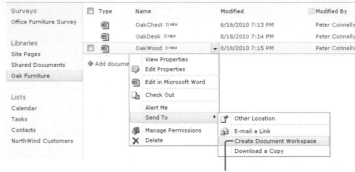

Create a Document Workspace, page 338

Publish a document back to a
document library, page 342

Create a Meeting
Workspace, page 344

Create a blog site, page 356

12 Working with Workspaces and Blogs

In this chapter, you will learn how to

✔ Create a Document Workspace.

✔ Access an existing Document Workspace.

✔ Publish a document back to a document library.

✔ Delete a Document Workspace.

✔ Create a Meeting Workspace.

✔ Understand the Home page of a Meeting Workspace.

✔ Add items to a Meeting Workspace.

✔ Customize a Meeting Workspace.

✔ Create a blog site.

✔ Create a blog post.

✔ Add a blog comment.

✔ Use RSS feeds.

Every company holds meetings. These meetings often have a specific agenda; if they don't, the company would benefit if they did. Sometimes participants need to prepare for a meeting by completing a task or two in advance. The task may be simply reviewing a document, assembling a list of questions, or perhaps creating a prototype of something to bring to the meeting. A meeting can become inefficient or even ineffective because the preparation tasks that participants are expected to complete are not communicated effectively. All too frequently, when participants do make preparations, they use an outdated version of a document or complete the wrong tasks because they are confused by the barrage of tasks sent through numerous emails. In addition, after the meeting is over, meeting notes or follow-up steps may need to be provided to the participants. Wouldn't it be nice if all the notes, documents, tasks, and other meeting details could be kept in a centralized location that was easy to find? A bonus would be if all the content in this centralized store could be searched.

Microsoft SharePoint Foundation provides a site template called a *Meeting Workspace* that helps improve communication before and after a meeting by supplying a common place to store information that is relevant to the meeting. By providing a single point of communication, Meeting Workspaces can help make meetings more efficient— something every organization, both large and small, can use.

Another template provided by SharePoint Foundation is the blog site template. Wikis and *blogs* are methods that enable anyone, including nontechnical users, to write web pages and publish them on Internet, extranet, and intranet websites for other users to see. Both allow users the freedom to publish content for broad consumption. Blogs are personal journals or observations, whereas anyone can contribute to content on a wiki. When making changes, wiki users are responsible for ensuring accuracy and relevance. In Microsoft SharePoint 2010, you can create a wiki on any site by creating a wiki library. To create a blog, you must create a blog site. Most wikis and blogs can use Really Simple Syndication (RSS) feeds to notify users when site content changes.

See Also For more information on wiki libraries refer to Chapter 5, "Working with Libraries." For more information on wiki pages, refer to Chapter 6, "Working with Web Pages."

In this chapter, you will learn how to work efficiently with Workspaces by both creating Document and Meeting Workspaces and accessing existing Workspaces. You will also learn how to publish a document back to a document library and delete a Document Workspace. After the Meeting Workspace is created, you will learn how to add items, such as objectives, agendas, and attendees, to the Workspace. You will also learn how to use blogs, as well as how to enable an RSS feed on a blog.

> **Practice Files** You don't need any practice files to complete the exercises in this chapter.

Important Remember to use your SharePoint site location in place of *http://wideworldimporters* in the following exercises.

Creating a Document Workspace

There are two ways to create a document library. The first method is to create it through the SharePoint web interface, and the second method is to create it using a Microsoft Office 2003 or Office 2007 application. When using either method, the resulting Document Workspace is the same; only the procedure that you use to create it differs.

Note You cannot create a Document Workspace from within an Office 2010 application.

A Document Workspace centers around one particular document. It is important to stress this fact. You want to have only one document per Document Workspace, because a Document Workspace is linked back to the original document when it is created from an existing document in an existing library. This enables you to copy the document easily from the Document Workspace back to its original source location. This unique feature of Document Workspaces is not shared by any other type of SharePoint site. In this way, you and your team members can work on the document without interfering with the main site or allowing others to read the document before it is complete.

In the following exercise, you will create a Document Workspace from an existing document by using the browser.

SET UP Open the SharePoint site that contains the document that you wish to collaborate on using a Document Workspace, such as the site you used to complete the Adding Documents exercise in Chapter 5.

BE SURE TO verify that you have sufficient rights to a Document Workspace. If in doubt, see the Appendix at the back of this book.

1. On the Quick Launch, click the document library that contains the document, such as **Oak Furniture**.

   The All Documents view of the document library is displayed.

2. Move your mouse over the document, such as **OakWood.docx**, and click the arrow that appears. Point to **Send To**, and then click **Create Document Workspace**.

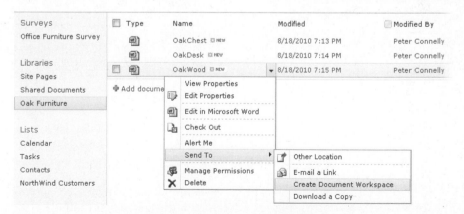

   The Create Document Workspace page is displayed.

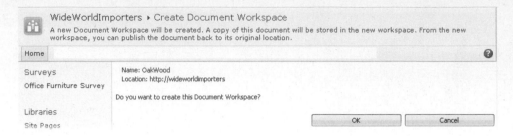

3. Click **OK**.

A new Document Workspace is created as a subsite below the original site and populated with the OakWood.docx document.

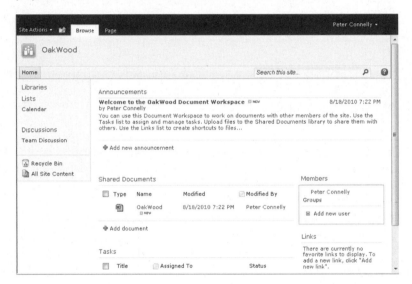

Note The Document Workspace does not inherit permissions from the parent site. Only the person who created the Document Workspace has access to the site. That person is mapped to the Full Control permission level and is listed on the home page of the Document Workspace under Members.

 CLEAN UP Close the browser.

Tip You can also create a Document Workspace using New Site on the Site Actions menu. However, this method does not provide the same integration with an existing document as does the process outlined in the previous exercise. To obtain the full benefits of a Document Workspace, you should create it from an existing document or from an Office 2003 or Office 2007 application.

Accessing an Existing Document Workspace

After creating a Document Workspace, you will need to navigate to it to work on the document. However, unless you know specifically where to look, it can be difficult to locate the Document Workspace once you have created it, especially if you created the Workspace several days or weeks ago and now don't remember exactly where it is. Moreover, if you create a large number of Workspaces, it can become problematic to remember the Uniform Resource Locator (URL) for each one.

Having a built-in method for finding Workspaces is very helpful when you need to return to them quickly and easily.

In this exercise, you will browse to the Document Workspace for OakWood.docx, which you created in the previous exercise.

 SET UP Open the SharePoint site from which you'd like to navigate to an existing Document Workspace.

BE SURE TO verify that you have sufficient rights to view the Document Workspace. If in doubt, see the Appendix at the back of this book.

1. Click **Site Actions**, and then click **View All Site Content**.

   The All Site Content page is displayed.

2. To the right of **View**, click **All Site Content**, and then click **Sites and Workspaces**.

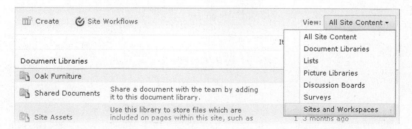

   The All Site Content Page redisplays, showing only sites and Workspaces.

3. Under Sites and Workspaces, click the Document Workspace that you would like to open, such as OakWood.

The OakWood Document Workspace appears. You can work with this site as you would any other SharePoint site.

 CLEAN UP Leave the browser open if you are continuing to the next exercise.

Publishing a Document Back to a Document Library

The ability to publish a document back to its original source document library is a unique feature of Document Workspaces. If the Document Workspace was created from a document in a document library, then the Publish to Source Location link will be available. If the Document Workspace was not created from a document in a document library, then the link will not be available. The reason that we use Document Workspaces is that we can keep the source document free of changes while we edit and update the document in the Workspace.

The Publish to Source Location link essentially copies the updated document from the Document Workspace back into the source library, thereby replacing the existing parent copy. It prevents you from having to recall the original location of the document while still keeping the source document up to date.

In the following exercise, you will publish a document from the Document Workspace back to the document library.

 SET UP Open the Document Workspace in which you'd like to publish a document from a document library back to the parent site, if it is not already open.

BE SURE TO verify that you have sufficient rights to write to the document library where you are going to publish the document. If in doubt, see the Appendix at the back of this book.

1. Move your mouse over **OakWood.docx**. When an arrow appears to the right of the document name, click the arrow, point to **Send to**, and then click **Publish to Source Location**.

The Publish to Source Location page appears.

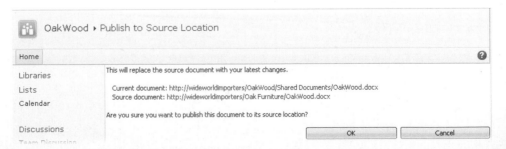

2. Click **OK**. The Operation Completed Successfully page appears.

3. Click **OK**. You are returned to the home page of the Document Workspace.

This action copies the latest version of OakWood.docx from the Document Workspace back to the document's original document library (in this case, Oak Furniture). Confirmation that the operation has completed successfully appears.

 CLEAN UP Leave the browser open if you are continuing to the next exercise.

Deleting a Document Workspace

You can think of a Document Workspace as a temporary SharePoint site. It is a collaborative environment for discussing, editing, and writing a single document, and it enhances content creation. The Document Workspace typically has a short life—several months at most—because its main purpose is to help with content creation. Once the document is finished, it should be stored in a document library for others to access and read. The Document Workspace for that specific document can then be deleted. Because the life cycle of a Document Workspace is short, you can expect to create and delete Document Workspaces fairly often. Deleting Document Workspaces will also save space on your server running SharePoint and reduce the clutter that numerous Workspaces can cause.

In this exercise, you will delete the OakWood.docx Document Workspace.

➡ **SET UP** Open the Document Workspace that you want to delete, if it is not already open.

BE SURE TO verify that you have sufficient rights to delete the Document Workspace. If in doubt, see the Appendix at the back of this book.

1. On the **Site Actions** menu, click **Site Settings**.

2. Under **Site Actions**, click **Delete this site**.

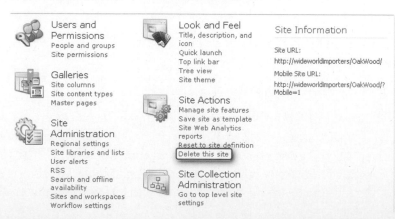

The Delete This Site confirmation page appears, informing you that everything in the site will be deleted.

3. Click **Delete**. A warning dialog box will appear.

4. Click **OK**. Your Document Workspace is now deleted.

 CLEAN UP Close the browser.

Creating a Meeting Workspace

There are three methods that can be used to create a Meeting Workspace:

- In the browser, select New Site from the Site Actions menu of a SharePoint site.

- Select the Meeting Workspace check box when you create a Calendar list.

   See Also The process of creating lists is detailed in Chapter 4, "Working with Lists."

- Click Meeting Workspace on a new meeting request in Outlook 2007 or Outlook 2010. When you create a meeting request in Outlook, you can create a Meeting Workspace site or link the meeting to an existing Workspace site.

The first method creates a Meeting Workspace, just like creating any other site. The power of a Meeting Workspace is revealed when you use either of the two other methods. You can then create recurring meetings to be managed by one Meeting Workspace, and, using Outlook, you can view attendees' schedules using your Microsoft Exchange Server installation and identify a time for the meeting that suits all attendees. Using Outlook to add or remove attendees will register the meeting in Exchange Server and automatically modify the site permissions of the Meeting Workspace.

See Also Chapter 13, "Using SharePoint Foundation with Outlook 2010," contains a section that creates a Meeting Workspace from an Outlook 2010 calendar appointment displayed on the Ribbon when inviting others to join the meeting.

When you create a Meeting Workspace by using the *Basic Meeting Workspace* template, three default lists are added automatically: Objectives, Agenda, and Attendees. A document library is also created to house meeting documents. These lists and the library function just like any other list or library. Each list has a Web Part on the front page of the Meeting Workspace, making it easy to interact with the information within any of them. In addition, the Attendees list identifies the user who created the Meeting Workspace as the meeting organizer.

In the following exercise, you will create a recurring event for a series of public workshops and associate a Basic Meeting Workspace with that recurring event. Many people are involved with the public workshops, and having details in a Meeting Workspace on a SharePoint site makes it easier to communicate information, including changes, to everyone involved. You will be adding information to this Workspace in the next several exercises.

SET UP Open a SharePoint site where you'd like to create, as a subsite, the new Meeting Workspace.

BE SURE TO verify that you have sufficient rights to create a Meeting Workspace. If in doubt, see the Appendix at the back of this book.

New Event

1. On the Quick Launch, under **Lists**, click **Calendar**.

   The Calendar view of the Calendar list is displayed for the current month.

2. On the **Events** tab, click **New Event** in the **New** group.

   The Calendar – New Item dialog opens.

3. In the **Title** box, type **Public Workshops**, and then, in the **Recurrence** section, select **Make this a repeating event**. When the page refreshes, select **Weekly**.

4. In the **Workspace** area at the bottom of the page, select the **Use a Meeting Workspace to organize attendees, agendas, documents, minutes, and other details for this event** check box, and click **Save**.

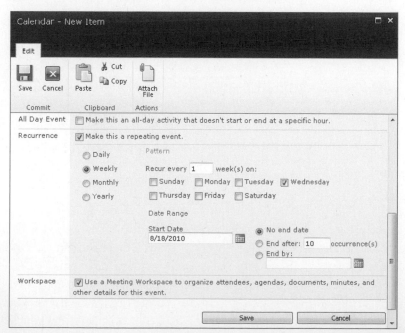

The New Meeting Workspace page is displayed. All of the information is already filled out for you. You might want to remove the spaces from the URL Name field or change the permissions to be unique, but neither action is required.

See Also See the sidebar entitled "Naming a URL," in Chapter 3, "Creating and Managing Sites," for details about good naming conventions for the URL Name field.

Title and Description

Type a title and description for your new site. The title will be displayed on each page in the site.

Title:

Public Workshops

Description:

Web Site Address

Users can navigate to your site by typing the Web site address (URL) into their browser. You can enter the last part of the address. You should keep it short and easy to remember.

For example, http://wideworldimporters/*sitename*

URL name:

http://wideworldimporters/ Public Workshops

Permissions

You can give permission to access your new site to the same users who have access to this parent site, or you can give permission to a unique set of users.

Note: If you select **Use same permissions as parent site**, one set of user permissions is shared by both sites. Consequently, you cannot change user permissions on your new site unless you are an administrator of this parent site.

User Permissions:

◉ Use same permissions as parent site
○ Use unique permissions

OK   Cancel

5. Click **OK**. The Template Selection page is displayed.

   Troubleshooting If the chosen URL name already exists in this scope, SharePoint takes you to an error page that explains that the website address <*NameOfTheChosenSite*> is already in use. Click the Back button in the browser to choose another URL name.

6. In the **Select a template** list, select **Basic Meeting Workspace**, if it is not already selected.

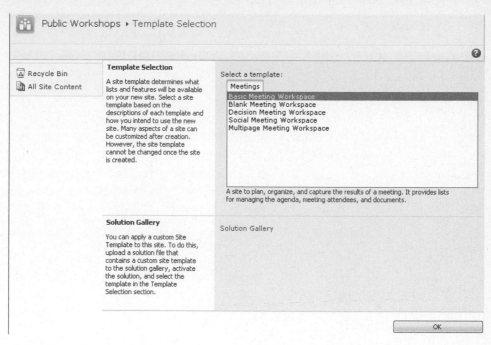

7. Click **OK**.

The home page, default.aspx, of the newly created Public Workshops site is displayed. In the left pane, there is a link for each recurrence of the event. Most Meeting Workspaces are used to manage one meeting date; however, with a recurring meeting, one Meeting Workspace manages all of the meeting dates. Additional events can then be linked to an existing Meeting Workspace, in which case, other event dates would also be displayed in the left pane. When no event is linked to a Meeting Workspace, the left pane is not displayed.

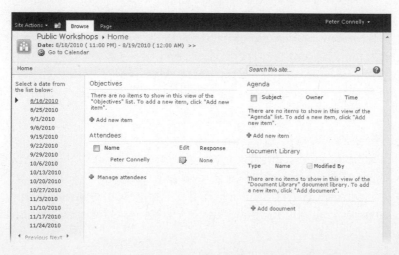

CLEAN UP Leave the browser open if you are continuing with the next exercise.

Understanding the Home Page of a Meeting Workspace

Once you have created a Meeting Workspace, you can familiarize yourself with the home page layout. The first obvious difference is that there isn't a Quick Launch, which means that you need to use the Site Settings page to find the links to the Recycle Bin and All Site Content, which are typically found at the bottom of the Quick Launch of a Team site.

Tip Clicking the title of any default Web Part (Objectives, Agenda, Attendees, or Document Library) takes you to that list's default list view. From any list view, you can find the familiar All Site Content and Recycle Bin links in the left navigation pane.

The home page of a Basic Meeting Workspace contains four Web Parts, one for each list or library created within the site:

- Objectives list
- Attendees list
- Agenda list
- Document Library

These four Web Parts contain information for each meeting that is managed by the Meeting Workspace. A meeting should typically have at least one *objective,* as well as an *agenda* to inform people about the meeting. The Meeting Workspace is organized in a way that makes it easy for the organizer to communicate the reason for holding the meeting. Also, there should typically be a list of meeting attendees. The document library does not necessarily need to be used, but it is a convenient place to store documents, such as information that attendees might need to read before the meeting, meeting minutes after the meeting concludes, or Microsoft PowerPoint presentations used during the meeting. At the top of the page, if the site was created from within Outlook or from a calendar event, the date and time of the meeting, as well as the location (if specified), is found.

If you create a Meeting Workspace from a *recurring event* using Outlook or a calendar event, additional information is provided on the Meeting Workspace page. On the left side of the page is located a list of dates that includes each instance of the recurring meeting. Each date has its own view of the home page, enabling you to establish different objectives, agendas, attendees, and documents for each specific instance of the meeting.

The Sync to SharePoint Workspace, New Page, and New Site options are missing from the Site Actions menu, which means that you cannot sync a Meeting Workspace with a SharePoint Workspace. The page structure is also different on a Meeting Workspace; therefore, there is no New Page link on the Site Actions menu. However, the Site Actions menu does have two new links: Add Pages and Manage Pages.

Tip Although you cannot create a site below a Meeting Workspace using the Site Actions menu or the Create page, you can still create a subsite by creating a Calendar list and creating a Meeting Workspace associated with an event. Only Meeting Workspace sites can be created in this manner.

In this exercise, you will add another page to the Meeting Workspace.

 SET UP Open the Meeting Workspace that you created in the previous exercise, if it is not already open.

BE SURE TO verify that you have sufficient rights to add a page. If in doubt, see the Appendix at the back of this book.

1. On the **Site Actions** menu, click **Add Pages**.

   The default.aspx page is displayed in Edit mode. Three Web Part zones, Left, Center, and Right, are displayed. The Pages tool pane opens.

2. In the **Page Name** box, type **More**. Leave **Appears for all meetings** selected.

   Tip Selecting Appears For This Meeting Only configures the new page to be displayed only for the current meeting occurrence.

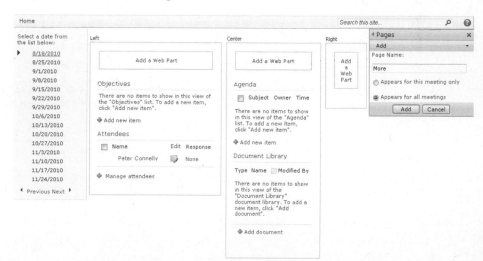

3. In the **Pages** tool pane, click **Add**. The Add Web Parts tool pane opens.

The new page is displayed in Edit mode, with three empty Web Part zones. In the left navigation pane, above the recurring meeting dates, there is a Pages link, under which there is a link to the new page.

Tip Although only one date is selected when you add a Web Part to a page in a Meeting Workspace, that Web Part will be displayed no matter what date you select. Similarly, when you add a list or library Web Part to a page, the list or library Web Part is displayed for each date. However, by default, only list items or documents relevant to a specific meeting date are displayed in the list or library Web Parts. If you want all list items in a list or all documents in a library to be displayed no matter which date is selected, navigate to the list's List Settings, navigate to the Advanced Settings page, and then, from the List Settings page, select the Share List Items Across All Meetings (Series Items) option. Note, however, that once items become series items for a list, you cannot change the setting back—so make sure that's what you want.

4. In the **Web Parts** tool pane, click **Text Box**. At the bottom of the **Add Web Parts** tool pane, leave **Left** selected in the **Add to** list, and then click **Add**.

The Text Box Web Part is displayed in the Left Web Part zone. A list that will hold the information presented by the Web Part is also created. This Web Part typically is used to take notes during the meeting.

Tip The Add Web Parts tool pane opens only when a page is first created. When modifying an existing page, click Add a Web Part, and then the Web Part pane opens at the top of the page.

 CLEAN UP Leave the browser open if you are continuing with the next exercise.

Adding Items to a Meeting Workspace

To get the most use from a Meeting Workspace, you must add information and relevant details to it so people are motivated to visit the Workspace.

Tip To associate a list item or document with a specific meeting date, you must select the date in the left navigation pane prior to creating the list item or uploading the document.

In this exercise, you will create an objective and four agenda items and add a new user as an attendee to the Meeting Workspace.

 SET UP Open the Meeting Workspace that you created in the previous exercise, if it is not already open.

BE SURE TO verify that you have sufficient rights to create items in the Objectives and Agenda lists and rights to add a new user to the Meeting Workspace. If in doubt, see the Appendix at the back of this book.

1. On the left side of the page, under **Select a date from the list below,** click the date of the next meeting. (In this example, the date is **8/18/2010**. The dates that are listed on the left side of the page are populated based on when you complete this exercise.)

   If you didn't use a repeating event, there won't be a list of dates from which to choose. Simply use the default instance.

2. In the **Objectives** Web Part, click **Add new item**.

   The Objective new item page is displayed.

3. In the **Objective** box, type the meeting objective, such as **How to efficiently sell imported items**.

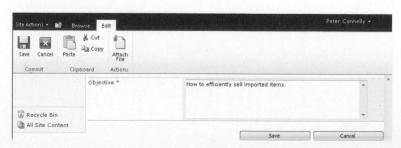

4. Click **Save**.

   The home page of the Meeting Workspace is displayed. The new objective appears in the Objectives Web Part. Because objectives are simply items stored in a list, you can create as many objectives as you want per meeting.

5. In the **Agenda** Web Part, click **Add new item**.

   The Agenda new item page is displayed.

6. In the **Subject** box, type a subject for the agenda, such as **Introduction**, and then, in the **Owner** box, type the name of a person who is responsible for this agenda item, such as **Todd Rowe**.

   Tip The person listed as the Owner does not have to be listed as an Attendee. The Owner box is simply a free-form text field.

7. In the **Time** box, type the time for this agenda item, such as **5:00-5:15 PM**, and then, if you want, enter some text into the **Notes** area (not illustrated in this exercise).

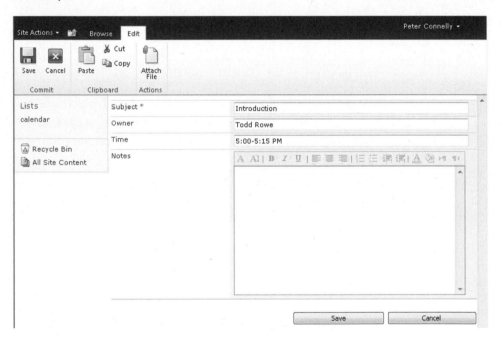

8. Click **Save**.

The home page of the Meeting Workspace is displayed. The new agenda item appears in the Agenda Web Part.

9. Repeat steps 5-8 to create three agenda items for the workshop using the information in the following table:

Subject	Owner	Time
Establishing an International Vendor	Todd Rowe	5:15-5:30 PM
Buying in Bulk	Olga Kosterina	5:30-5:45 PM
Questions and Answers	Olga Kosterina	5:45-6:00 PM

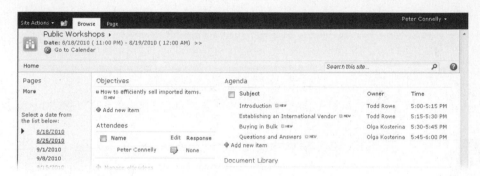

10. In the **Attendees** Web Part, click **Manage attendees**.

The Manage Attendees page is displayed.

New Item

11. On the **Items** tab, in the **List Tools** tab set, click **New Item** in the **New** group.

The Attendees – New Item dialog appears.

Check Names

12. In the **Name** box, type the email address or user name of the attendee, such as **Todd Rowe**, and then click the **Check Names** icon.

Troubleshooting If you enter a user name, SharePoint automatically prefixes the user name with a domain name, such as *wideworldimporters*\. If the user name is not recognized, SharePoint displays a "No Exact Match Was Found Click The Item(s) That Did Not Resolve For More Options" message below the Name box.

13. In the **Response** drop-down list, select **Accepted**, and in the **Attendance** drop-down list, leave the default set to **Required**.

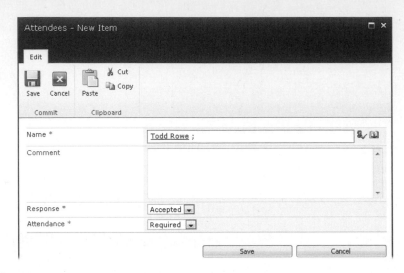

14. Click **Save**.

Todd is added as an attendee for this public workshop, and you are returned to the Manage Attendees view of the Attendees list. If you want, you can add other attendees by repeating steps 11-14.

Navigate Up

15. Using the **Navigate Up** icon, click **Public Workshops** to return to the home page of the Public Workshops Meeting Workspace.

Tip When you select a different date, under Select A Date From The List Below, than the one that you selected in step 1 of this exercise, the objective, the four agenda items, and the attendee Todd Rowe that you added in this exercise will not be displayed. To add Workspace items for other meeting dates, you must repeat this exercise, selecting the new meeting date in step 1.

 CLEAN UP Leave the browser open if you are continuing with the next exercise.

Customizing a Meeting Workspace

Now that you have added all the information to the default Meeting Workspace, you might want to add more information for the attendees. You can accomplish this by creating new lists and libraries and by adding Web Parts that display their contents to the Home page or other pages, if you have created them.

See Also For more information on Web Parts, see Chapter 6.

In this exercise, you will create a new list that you will use to tell attendees what they are expected to bring with them to the meeting. You will then add a Web Part to the Home page to display the contents of that list.

SET UP Open the Meeting Workspace that you created previously in this chapter, if it is not already open.

BE SURE TO verify that you have sufficient rights to create a list and edit the home page. If in doubt, see the Appendix at the back of this book.

1. Click **Site Actions**, and then click **More Options**. The Create dialog appears.

2. Under **Filter By**, click **Tracking**, and then, in the middle of the page, click **Things to Bring**.

3. In the **Name** box, type **Homework**.

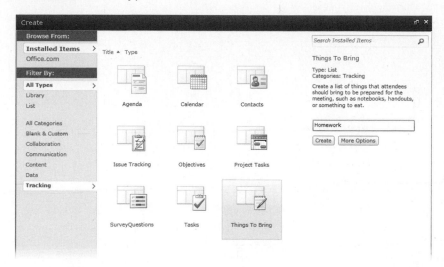

4. Click **Create**.

The All Items view of the Homework list is displayed.

New
Item ▾

5. On the **Items** tab, in the **List Tools** tab set, click **New Item** in the **New** group.

The Homework – New Item dialog appears.

6. In the **Item** text box, enter a value, such as **International Vendor List**. Leave the **Comment** and **Owner** fields blank, and then click **Save**.

The All Items view of the Homework list is displayed.

7. On the **Browse** tab, click **Home** to display the default page of the Meeting Workspace.

8. Click **Site Actions**, and then click **Edit Page**.

9. In the **Left** Web Part zone, click **Add a Web Part**.

The Web Parts pane is displayed at the top of the page.

10. Under **Categories**, click **List and Libraries**, and then, under **Web Parts**, click **Homework**.

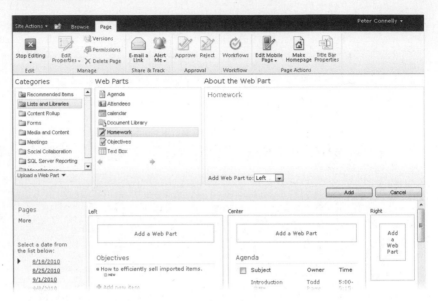

11. Click **Add**.

The Web Parts pane disappears, and the Homework Web Part is added to the Left Web Part zone, above the Objectives Web Part zone.

Stop Editing

12. On the **Pages** tab, click **Stop Editing**.

 CLEAN UP Close the browser.

Creating a Blog Site

A web log, known as a *blog*, is a personal journal or commentary shared on a website. *Blogging* refers to publishing thoughts, in formal essays or more informal formats, on a blog website; a person who does this is called a *blogger*. The thoughts shared on the blog website are called *posts* or articles. Each post or article is displayed in reverse chronological order, with the most recent additions featured most prominently and older items grouped in archives organized by the month in which they were created.

Blog posts can be categorized to help users find past conversations. Also, blogs are indexed so that a visitor can search through old blogs and learn from past conversations.

Bloggers write blogs frequently, often on a daily basis. Some allow visitors to comment on the blog, provide feedback, and ask questions.

Note When using SharePoint Server 2010, the logical location for a blog site is a user's personal site, or My Site, where a link exists that you can use to create a blog.

In this exercise, you will create a blog site and then establish categories for your blog posts.

 SET UP Open a SharePoint site where you'd like to create, as a subsite, the new blog site.

BE SURE TO verify that you have sufficient rights to create a site. If in doubt, see the Appendix at the back of this book.

1. From the **Site Actions** menu, select **New Site**. The Create page appears.

2. Under **Filter By**, click **Content**, and then click **Blog**.

3. In the **Title** box, type **Olga's Blog**, and then, in the **URL name** box, type **OlgaBlog**.

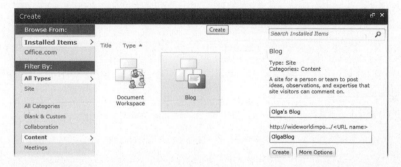

4. Click **Create**.

    The Operation in Progress page is displayed, which is then replaced by the home page of the Olga's Blog website, which consists of four Web Parts, called Posts, Blog Tools, About This Blog, and Links, each of which contains one link to a Photos picture library. You can use the Links list to add link items to point to other users' blogs. Two additional Web Parts can be found on the Quick Launch:

    ○ Categories, where three sample categories are listed: Category 1, Category 2, and Category 3.

    ○ Archives, which redirects users to the Archive view for the Posts list. This view displays only those posts that are approved.

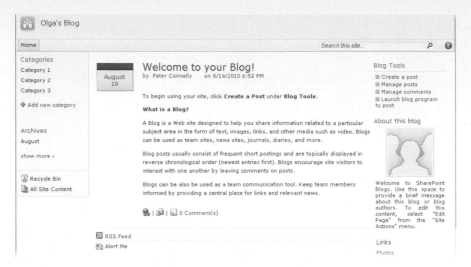

5. On the Quick Launch, click **Categories**.

   The All Categories view of the Categories list is displayed.

6. Click the **Edit** icon to the right of **Category 1** to display the **Categories - Category 1** dialog.

7. In the **Title** box, delete **Category 1** and type **Office**. Then click **Save**.

8. Repeat steps 6 and 7 to replace **Category 2** with **Bedroom** and **Category 3** with **Garden**.

9. Click the **Browse** tab, and then click **Home** to display the home page of the blog site.

   Under the Categories area are listed Bedroom, Garden, and Office.

10. Under **Categories**, click **Add new category**.

    The Categories - New Item dialog is displayed.

11. In the **Title** box, type **General**, and then click **Save**.

    Under the Categories area are listed Bedroom, Garden, General, and Office.

12. On the blog site's home page, in the **Blog Tools** Web Part, click **Manage posts**. The Posts list is displayed using the All Posts view.

Delete Item

13. Move the mouse over the **Welcome to your Blog** list item, and then select the check box that appears. On the **Items** tab, click **Delete Item**.

    A Message From Webpage dialog box appears.

14. Click **OK** to send the blog post to the Recycle Bin.

    The Posts list is redisplayed. The Welcome to your Blog list item is not listed.

✖ **CLEAN UP** Close the browser.

Creating a Blog Post

A blog post is the method by which you share your opinions and knowledge. You must remember that, as a blogger, you are responsible for the commentary you post and can be held personally liable if your posting is considered defamatory, obscene, proprietary, or libelous. Similar to posting information on a wiki, you should practice good manners and understatement.

You can create a blog post by using many tools, including Microsoft Word 2007 or Word 2010, Microsoft OneNote 2007 or OneNote 2010, Microsoft Live Writer, and the browser. On the blog website in the Blog Tools Web Part, there is a link that allows you to start a blog program, such as Word, quickly in order to create a blog post. The New SharePoint Blog Account dialog box appears. The web address of the blog site is listed in the Blog URL box.

A Word dialog box then opens, warning that when Word sends information to the blog service provider, it may be possible for other people to see that information, including your user name and password. If you choose to continue, another Word dialog box opens, stating that the account registration was successful.

Once a blog post is opened in Word, the Blog Post tab is active. The Blog group provides easy access to the home page of your blog site, where you can assign a category to the blog post, open an existing blog, manage accounts, and publish the blog. Any pictures that you insert into the post using Word are automatically copied to the Photos picture library when the blog post is either published or published as a draft.

In the following exercise, you will create and modify a blog post by using the browser.

SET UP Open the blog SharePoint site that you created in the previous exercise.

1. On the blog site's home page, in the **Blog Tools** Web Part, click **Create a post**.

   The Posts - New Item dialog is displayed. Notice that the Posts list has content approval enabled.

2. In the **Title** box, type **Welcome**, and in the **Body** box, type **Welcome to my blog! It will be devoted to furniture. Please use comments to provide feedback to posts.**

3. In the **Category** list, select **General**, and then click **Add**.

4. On the **Edit** tab, click **Publish**.

Publish

   The blog site's home page is displayed with the Welcome posting as the first posting on the page. The post states the time that the post was published, together with its category. Clicking the Category link on this line displays a page where all similarly categorized posts are listed. This behavior is the same as clicking a selection under Categories on the Quick Launch.

Tip If you include pictures on any of your posts, upload them into the Photos picture library on your blog website.

5. In the **Blog Tools** Web Part, click **Manage posts**. The Posts list is displayed using the All Posts view.

6. Move the mouse over the **Welcome** post, and then select the check box that appears. On the **Items** tab, click **Edit Item**. The Posts – Welcome dialog appears.

7. In the **Category** section, click **Bedroom**, and then click **Add**.

Tip Similar to other Microsoft programs, it is possible to add multiple categories in web pages by holding down the Shift key while selecting the categories between the first click and the second click. Holding down the **CTRL** key selects or clears categories.

8. Click **Publish**, and then, on the **Browse** tab, click **Home**.

The blog site's home page is displayed. Two categories are listed for the Welcome post: General and Bedroom.

✖ **CLEAN UP** Leave the browser open if you are continuing with the next exercise.

Adding a Blog Comment

To interact with a blogger, you can leave comments on a blog post. As a blogger, you must review comments left on your posts, not only to respond to comments, but also to delete comments that are either off-topic or are used to advertise websites or broadcast spam. If the aim of a blog post is to start a discussion and you receive virtually no responses, then you could use a comment to post a question to your own blog post.

In this exercise, you will add a comment to a blog post and then delete the comment.

 SET UP Open the blog SharePoint site that you used in the previous exercise, if it is not already open.

BE SURE TO verify that you have sufficient rights to add a blog post to the Posts list and to delete a comment from the Comments list. If in doubt, see the Appendix at the back of this book.

1. On the blog site's home page, below a post, click **0 Comment(s)**. The post is displayed with a Comments form.

2. In the **Title** box, type **Re: Welcome to your blog**, and, in the **Body** box, type **Welcome Olga!**

3. Click **Submit Comment**.

   The post is redisplayed with both a Comments and an Add Comment area. Below the post, 1 Comment(s) is displayed.

4. To the right of the **Re: Welcome to your blog** comment, click **Edit**.

   The Comments - Re: Welcome To Your Blog dialog is displayed.

Delete Item

5. On the **Edit** tab, click **Delete Item**. A dialog box appears.

6. Click **OK** to send the comment item to the Recycle Bin.

   The Comments page is displayed with no comments.

 CLEAN UP Leave the browser open if you are continuing with the next exercise.

Using RSS Feeds

An RSS feed is a data format that provides users with a means of keeping up to date with content that is added to a website. (Originally, the data format was known as RDF (Resource Description Framework) Site Summary, and then it became known as Rich Site Summary. Today, however, RSS is known as Really Simple Syndication.) By using SharePoint Foundation, you can decide to syndicate content. This means that you can create an RSS feed for any list or library, thereby allowing users to subscribe to it by using an RSS feed aggregator such as Outlook 2007 or Outlook 2010 and Internet Explorer 7.0 or later. The blog site and Blog Posts list are enabled by default to offer RSS support.

In the following exercise, you will view the RSS field for the blog posts in your browser and disable RSS support for a blog.

SET UP Open the blog SharePoint site that you used in the previous exercise, if it is not already open.

BE SURE TO verify that you have sufficient rights to manage the Posts list. If in doubt, see the Appendix at the back of this book.

1. On the blog site's home page, below all the posts, click **RSS Feed**. The RSS feed for the blog posts is displayed.

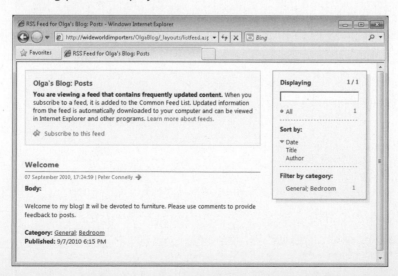

2. In the browser, click **Back**. The home page of Olga's Blog site is displayed.

3. In the **Blog Tools** Web Part, click **Manage posts**. The Posts list is displayed using the All Posts view.

List
Settings

4. On the **List** tab, in the **List Tools** tab set, click **List Settings**. The List Settings page is displayed.

5. Under **Communications**, click **RSS settings**. The Modify RSS Settings page is displayed.

Troubleshooting If the RSS Settings link is not available, then RSS support is not enabled either in the SharePoint 2010 Central Administration website or at the site collection level. See Chapter 3 for more information.

6. In the **List RSS** section, under **Allow RSS for this list**, click **No**.

7. Scroll to the bottom of the page, and click **OK**. The List Settings page is displayed.

8. Click **Home** to redisplay the blog site's home page. The RSS Feed link is no longer displayed.

 **CLEAN UP** Close the browser.

Key Points

- You can create a Document Workspace from an existing document in a document library so that you can use the Publish to Source Location feature to update the original document with the latest version.

- Meeting Workspaces communicate key information about a meeting.

- You can create a Meeting Workspace from a recurring event if you want to present different information each time that the meeting occurs.

- After the Meeting Workspace is created, add relevant information to the Objectives, Agenda, and Attendees Web Parts.

- Use the document library in a Meeting Workspace to store presentations, documents, pictures, meeting minutes, or other material relevant to the meeting.

- You can customize a Meeting Workspace by adding new pages, lists, and Web Parts.

- Blogs are personal journals or observations that are usually maintained by one person.

- Blog posts can be categorized to help users find past conversations.

- To interact with a blogger, you can leave comments on a blog post.

- Bloggers should review comments on their posts for objectionable or inappropriate content.

- The Blog Posts list is enabled for RSS support, thereby allowing users to syndicate content.

Chapter at a Glance

Connect a SharePoint Contacts list to Outlook, page 369

Move an Outlook contact to a SharePoint Contacts list, page 372

Copy SharePoint contacts into Outlook, page 374

Send an email using a SharePoint Contacts list, page 376

View SharePoint calendars and personal calendars in Outlook, page 377

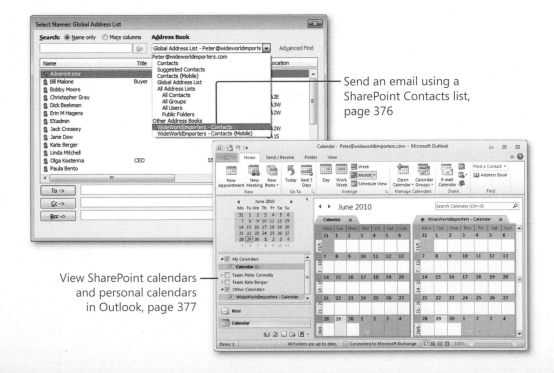

13 Using SharePoint Foundation with Outlook 2010

In this chapter, you will learn how to

- ✔ Connect a SharePoint Contacts list to Outlook.
- ✔ Move an Outlook contact to a SharePoint Contacts list.
- ✔ Copy SharePoint contacts into Outlook.
- ✔ Send an email using a SharePoint Contacts list.
- ✔ View SharePoint calendars and personal calendars in Outlook.
- ✔ Take SharePoint content offline.
- ✔ Manage SharePoint alerts in Outlook.
- ✔ Create Meeting Workspaces from Outlook.
- ✔ Configure an RSS feed.

Microsoft SharePoint Foundation 2010 integrates with Microsoft Outlook 2007 and Outlook 2010 to enable you to keep a local copy of your team's Calendars, Tasks, and Contacts lists, as well as libraries. Information can be synchronized in two directions for items in Contacts lists, calendars, Tasks lists, and discussion boards. A local copy of the Microsoft SharePoint data is then available offline when you are not connected to the network and can be synchronized with the SharePoint site manually or automatically when you next connect. You can aggregate and manage all your tasks in one place whether you created them within Outlook, in a SharePoint Tasks list, or within Microsoft OneNote.

When dealing with documents, Outlook 2007 and Outlook 2010 also provide a method of taking libraries or folders offline. In addition, documents held within SharePoint libraries or folders can be synchronized with their offline copies using the other applications in the Microsoft Office 2010 suite. Other types of standard lists—such as Issues, Link lists, Custom lists, or properties, such as views and metadata—are not supported in Outlook. Microsoft SharePoint Workspace 2010 should be used to synchronize these SharePoint resources with their offline copies.

Outlook supports Really Simple Syndication (RSS) feeds so that you can subscribe to and stay up to date with the latest news sites and blogs. You can manage your RSS feeds in Outlook just like other mail by flagging them for follow-up, assigning them a specific color, or automating any process by using rules.

By using other integration features, you can manage all your SharePoint alerts from one Outlook dialog box. By using Outlook meeting requests, you can create Meeting Workspace sites.

Note Like other Office applications, Outlook 2010 comes with the new Microsoft Office Fluent user interface (UI), which features a Quick Steps area and the backstage view. If you are new to Outlook 2010 and want to investigate the new features, a short video can be found on the Outlook product team blog at *http://blogs.msdn.com/b/outlook/archive/2009/07/14 /announcing-microsoft-office-2010-technical-preview.aspx*; and a Microsoft TechNet article, titled "Changes in Outlook 2010," can be found at *http://technet.microsoft.com/en-us/library /cc179110.aspx*.

In this chapter, you will learn how to copy and move Outlook contacts to and from a SharePoint Contacts list. You will also learn how to connect SharePoint Calendar lists to Outlook, view SharePoint calendars side by side with personal calendars, edit SharePoint calendar items offline, manage SharePoint alerts in Outlook, create Meeting Workspaces from Outlook, and subscribe to a SharePoint list's RSS feed.

Although you can complete the tasks documented in this chapter using Outlook 2007, the steps and screenshots in this chapter were created using Outlook 2010. If you use Outlook 2007, your steps and screenshots will be slightly different. See the book *Microsoft Windows SharePoint Services 3.0 Step by Step*, by Olga Londer, Bill English, Todd Bleeker, and Penelope Coventry (Microsoft Press, 2007), for detailed steps on using Outlook 2007.

> **Practice Files** Before you can complete the exercises in this chapter, you need to (1) download the Chapter 13 practice files from the book's catalog page to the following folder on your computer: Documents\Microsoft Press\SBS_SPF\Chapter13 and (2) install the Chapter 13 practice site using the Chapter13_Starter.wsp file. See "Using the Practice Files" at the beginning of this book for more information.

Important Remember to use your SharePoint site location in place of *http://wideworldimporters* in the following exercises.

Connecting a SharePoint Contacts List to Outlook

To initiate the integration between SharePoint lists and libraries and Outlook 2007 or Outlook 2010, you need to connect the list or library. You can connect most SharePoint lists, as well as all SharePoint library types, to Outlook. The following list and gallery types are not supported for connection to Outlook:

- Survey
- Issue Tracking
- Announcements
- Links
- Custom List
- Solutions Gallery
- List Templates Gallery
- Web Part Gallery

Once a list is connected to Outlook, you can modify that list within Outlook at any time whether you are online or offline. You can also share the connection with others: right-click the library name in Outlook, and then click Share This Folder.

SharePoint permissions carry over when using SharePoint resources in Outlook 2007 or Outlook 2010. For example, if you have permission to edit a document or list item on the SharePoint site, you can also edit the document or list item within Outlook.

When you modify a document from a library that you have connected to Outlook, you will be modifying an offline copy of that document, known as a *cached copy*, by default. You can choose to send to the SharePoint library when you have completed your modification. During your offline editing, another user could modify the same document, so it is recommended that you always check out your document before you edit it. You can turn off offline editing using Options in Microsoft Word 2010 backstage view.

Note In Outlook 2003, connecting to a SharePoint list was called *linking,* and you were allowed to link only to SharePoint Contacts and Calendar lists. Although you could see the contents of these SharePoint lists within Outlook 2003, both online and offline, the information presented was read-only. To edit the contents of these lists, you had to use the browser.

In the following exercise, you will connect to Outlook from a Contacts list on a SharePoint site. You can use the same technique to connect to other SharePoint lists or libraries.

Connect to
Outlook

SET UP Open a SharePoint site, such as one created from the practice .wsp file for this chapter. If you have not created a site based on this chapter's .wsp file, then you will need a Contacts list to complete this exercise. You can create a Contacts list by following the steps in the exercise in Chapter 4, "Working with Lists," that explains how to create a list.

BE SURE TO verify that you have sufficient rights to read the items in the Contacts list. If in doubt, see the Appendix at the back of this book.

1. On the Quick Launch, under the **Lists** section, click **Contacts**.

2. On the **List** tab in the **List Tools** contextual tab set, click **Connect to Outlook** in the **Connect & Export** group.

3. If a Microsoft Internet Explorer Security dialog box opens, stating: Do you want to allow this website to open a program on your computer?, click **Allow**.

4. If an Internet Explorer Security warning dialog box opens, stating: A website wants to open web content using this program on your computer, click **Allow**.

Outlook opens, and you might be asked to supply your user name and password.

An Outlook dialog box appears, stating: You should only connect lists from sources you know and trust.

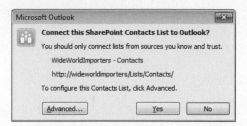

5. Click **Advanced** to open a **SharePoint Lists Options** dialog box.

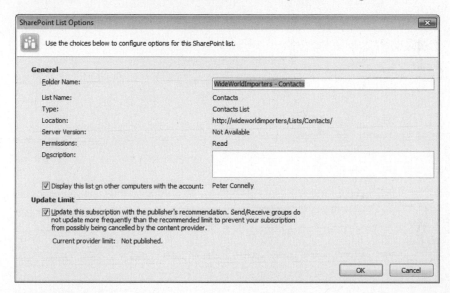

6. In the **Folder Name** text box, type **WideWorldImporters – Contacts**, and click **OK**.

7. In the **Microsoft Outlook** dialog box, click **Yes**. Outlook displays the WideWorldImporters Contacts list.

When you connect a list or library to Outlook, the list or library appears in the respective areas of the Outlook Navigation pane. Calendars appear in the Calendar pane under Other Calendars, tasks appear in the Tasks pane under Other Tasks, and Contacts lists appear in the Contacts pane under Other Contacts. Discussion lists and libraries appear in a folder in the Mail pane under SharePoint Lists.

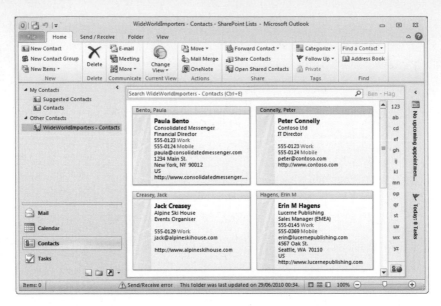

Tip To remove a connected SharePoint list or library from Outlook, select the folder in the Navigation pane and then, on the Home tab, click Delete in the Delete group. Alternatively, right-click the folder in the Navigation pane and then click Delete Folder. Removing connected lists or libraries from Outlook helps you to focus on current projects.

Deleting a connected SharePoint list folder from Outlook does not delete the SharePoint list or its data from the SharePoint server; however, the data in that list is no longer available offline from within Outlook. An alternative method of managing connected SharePoint lists or libraries is to click the File tab to switch to the backstage view of Outlook. Then, under Account Information, click Account Settings, and then click Account Settings in the drop-down menu to display the Account Settings dialog box. Click the SharePoint Lists tab, click the SharePoint list or library that you want to manage, and then click Remove or Change.

 CLEAN UP Close the browser. Leave Outlook open if you are continuing to the next exercise.

Moving an Outlook Contact to a SharePoint Contacts List

By connecting a SharePoint Contacts list to Outlook 2007 or Outlook 2010, you are creating an Outlook Contacts folder. You can then copy the contact information in your Outlook Contacts folder back into the SharePoint Contacts list. The new contacts within the Contacts folder are added to the SharePoint Contacts list the next time Outlook synchronizes with SharePoint, and you can then share the contact information with users who visit your SharePoint site. Any other users who also have connected the SharePoint Contacts list to their copy of Outlook will observe the new contacts within their Outlook Contacts folder, when they next synchronize with SharePoint.

In this exercise, you will move contact information from your Outlook Address Book to a Contacts list on a SharePoint site. You can use the same technique to move calendar items from a SharePoint Calendar list to your Calendar folder, as well as to move task and event items into their respective Outlook folders.

Troubleshooting You cannot move a recurring series of events by using the steps detailed in this exercise. Instead, open the recurring series or the individual occurrence from a recurring series within Outlook. Click the File tab to display the backstage, and then click Move to Folder.

SET UP Open Outlook, if it is not already open. You can use the Contacts list that you connected to Outlook in the previous exercise, or you can use another Contacts list.

BE SURE TO verify that you have sufficient rights to create new list items in a Contacts list. If in doubt, see the Appendix at the back of this book.

1. In the Outlook **Navigation** pane, under **My Contacts**, select **Contacts**.

2. Select the two or more users that you want to move by holding down the **SHIFT** or **CTRL** key while clicking the left mouse button.

   Tip Press **CTRL+A** to select all contacts.

Move

3. On the **Home** tab, click **Move** in the **Actions** group, and then click **Other Folder**.

4. In the **Move Items** dialog box, scroll down. To the left of the **SharePoint Lists** folder, click the green arrow icon and then select **WideWorldImporters – Contacts**.

Note When you connect external lists to Outlook, they are created in the SharePoint External Lists folder.

5. Click **OK**.

   A Microsoft Outlook dialog box appears, stating that any incompatible content will be removed during the next synchronization and that the original version of each affected item will be preserved in the "Local Failures" folder.

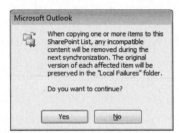

6. Click **Yes**.

   The Contacts folder is displayed; the contacts that you selected are not.

   Tip To move a single contact, select the contact and press CTRL+SHIFT+V to open the Move Items dialog box. Alternatively, while holding down the mouse button, drag the contact to WideWorldImporters – Contacts in the Outlook Navigation pane. You can also use these techniques to move more than one contact.

   ✖ CLEAN UP Leave Outlook open if you are continuing with the next exercise.

Copying SharePoint Contacts into Outlook

You can copy any single contact or event item from a SharePoint list to Outlook 2007 or Outlook 2010. Once the contact item is copied into the Contacts folder, the contact item in the Contacts folder and the contact item on the SharePoint Contacts list are independent of each other—that is, there is no link between them. Therefore, amendments made to the contact in the Outlook Contacts folder are not done to the version in the SharePoint Contacts list. To ensure that your contact information does not become out of date, you should assign a definitive location for a specific contact by maintaining it as a contact item on either a SharePoint Contacts list or in your Outlook Contacts folder. If contact information is to be shared among a team, then a SharePoint Contacts list is the preferred location.

Troubleshooting You cannot copy a recurring series of events by using the steps detailed in the following exercise. Instead, copy a recurring series or an individual occurrence from a recurring series by opening it within Outlook. On the Appointment Series tab, click Copy to My Calendar in the Actions group.

In the following exercise, you will copy contacts from a Contacts list in a SharePoint site into Outlook. You can also copy calendar, event, or task items by using the same technique.

 SET UP Open Outlook, if it is not already open. You can use the Contacts list that you connected to Outlook in a previous exercise, or you can use another Contacts list. Ensure that there are contact items added to the list.

BE SURE TO verify that you have sufficient rights to read items in the Contacts list. If in doubt, see the Appendix at the back of this book.

1. In the Outlook **Navigation** pane, under **Other Contacts**, select **WideWorldImporters – Contacts**.

2. Select the users that you want to copy by holding down the **SHIFT** or **CTRL** key when selecting the users.

   Tip Press **CTRL+A** to select all the contacts.

Move

3. Right-click one of the contacts that you selected, click **Move**, and then click **Copy to Folder**.

The Copy Items dialog box appears.

4. Scroll to the top of the dialog box and select **Contacts**, and then click **OK**. The contacts are added to your Outlook Contacts folder.

Troubleshooting If the name or email address of the contact already exists in your Outlook Contacts folder, the Duplicate Contact Detected dialog box is displayed so that you can resolve the conflict.

Tip An alternative method to copy contacts is to select one or more contacts and, while holding down the **CTRL** key and the mouse button, drag the contacts to the Contacts folder in the Outlook Navigation pane.

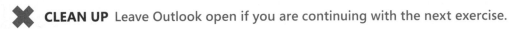 **CLEAN UP** Leave Outlook open if you are continuing with the next exercise.

Sending an Email Using a SharePoint Contacts List

You might occasionally move and copy contacts to a SharePoint Contacts list. You may also frequently use a Contacts list to look up specific contact details, such as a telephone number, or send the contact an email.

In this exercise, you will send an email by using a SharePoint Contacts list.

SET UP Open Outlook, if it is not already open. You can use the Contacts list that you connected to Outlook in a previous exercise, or you can use another Contacts list. Ensure that there are contact items added to the list.

BE SURE TO verify that you have sufficient rights to read list items in a Contacts list. If in doubt, see the Appendix at the back of this book.

1. In the Outlook **Navigation** pane, select **Mail**.

New E-mail

2. On the **Home** tab, click **New E-mail** in the **New** group. The Untitled – Message (HTML) dialog box opens.

3. Click **To**. The Select Names: Global Address List dialog box opens.

4. On the **Address Book** list, select **WideWorldImporters – Contacts**.

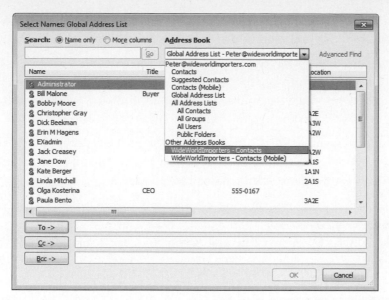

5. Double-click the name of the contact to whom you want to send a new email message, and then click **OK**.

6. Enter your email message subject and text, and then click **Send**.

 CLEAN UP Leave Outlook open if you are continuing to the next exercise.

Viewing SharePoint Calendars and Personal Calendars in Outlook

You can work with multiple calendars when using Outlook 2007 or Outlook 2010, thereby enabling you to create calendars for specific purposes, such as having one for work and one for your personal life. By using Outlook, you can view several calendars at the same time. When you view and scroll multiple calendars, they all display the same date or time period. This feature is particularly useful if you have connected a SharePoint Calendar list to Outlook. By doing so, you are creating an Outlook Calendar folder in which a copy of the data from the SharePoint list is stored locally. In this way, you can keep track of any calendar items in a SharePoint list from the Outlook Calendar folder, even if you are not connected to the network.

In the following exercise, you will connect to a SharePoint Calendar list and view your personal Outlook calendar and a connected SharePoint Calendar list side by side.

SET UP In the browser, open the SharePoint site where the Calendar list is located.

BE SURE TO verify that you have sufficient rights to read list items in a Calendar list. If in doubt, see the Appendix at the back of this book.

1. On the Quick Launch, under the **Lists** section, click **Calendar**, and then, on the **Calendar** tab, click **Connect to Outlook** in the **Connect & Export** group.

2. If an Internet Explorer Security dialog box opens, stating: Do you want to allow this website to open a program on your computer?, click **Allow**. Then, if an Internet Explorer Security warning dialog box opens, stating: A website wants to open web content using this program on your computer, click **Allow**.

   Outlook opens, and an Outlook dialog box appears, stating that you should connect only lists from sources you know and trust, and asking whether you want to connect this SharePoint Calendar to Outlook.

3. Click **Advanced** to open a **SharePoint Lists Options** dialog box, and then, in the **Folder Name** text box, type **WideWorldImporters – Calendar** and click **OK**. Then, in the **Microsoft Outlook** dialog box, click **Yes**.

   You might be asked to supply your user name and password. Your personal Outlook calendar appears side by side with the connected SharePoint Calendar list. The background color of the Calendar folder name matches the color on the displayed calendar so that you can discern between the two calendars.

Tip Once a Calendar list is connected to Outlook, use the check box to the left of the calendar name to control the number of calendars that you want to view side by side.

4. Click the arrow on the **WideWorldImporters – Calendar** tab.

   The two calendars are viewed in *overlay* mode, where the two calendars are merged; however, the two calendars remain color-coordinated as do the appointments in both calendars.

 CLEAN UP Leave Outlook open if you are continuing to the next exercise.

Taking SharePoint Content Offline

Connecting lists to Outlook enables you to aggregate all your list items in one place. For example, you can view all the calendar events in the Calendar window or all your tasks in the Tasks window, or you can view tasks assigned only to you on the To-Do Bar. When you connect a SharePoint list or library, including external lists, to Outlook, a local copy of the SharePoint content is stored locally on your computer. Connected SharePoint content can be used online or offline; however, it is important to understand the synchronization process for each.

- **Online** Once a list or library is connected, edits made in Outlook are synchronized automatically with the master content on the SharePoint site, dependent on the Send/Receive settings. The default, Send/Receive Group, All Accounts, is configured for your mail items, and it also controls the updates to subscribed RSS feeds and SharePoint lists. The All Accounts group schedules an update to occur every 30 minutes. You can force synchronization by using the Send/Receive All Folders command on the Send/Receive tab or by using F9. You can create new Send/Receive groups, which contain all or only a subset of your SharePoint connected lists or libraries, with their own synchronization schedules. Once the SharePoint list or library is updated, your changes are synchronized with other users who are connected to these SharePoint lists and libraries in Outlook. If those users have the list or library open in the Outlook detail pane, then they will not see the updates until the next synchronization schedule.

  Note When connected to Outlook, external lists (meaning that the data is external to SharePoint) are created in the SharePoint External Lists folder, which is not controlled by the Send/Receive settings. External lists are synchronized by default every 6 hours. When you right-click an external list in Outlook, you can find the Synchronization status and when the data was last refreshed from the external system. You can then force synchronization.

- **Offline** When you are offline, you can view and edit cached copies of the SharePoint content, but your modifications are not synchronized with the master content on the SharePoint site. To synchronize the content, you must go online. Data that is presented in an external list may or may not be available offline, depending on how the External Content Type for that external list is configured.

Tip The Archive feature in Outlook cannot be used with the SharePoint List folder, or with any connected lists or libraries.

In this exercise, you will make Calendar list content available offline, and then edit an appointment offline.

SET UP Open Outlook, if it is not already open, showing the Calendar list that you connected to Outlook in a previous exercise.

BE SURE TO verify that you have sufficient rights to modify list items in a Calendar list. If in doubt, see the Appendix at the back of this book.

Work Offline

1. On the **Send/Receive** tab, click **Work Offline** in the **Preferences** group.

   On the Outlook status bar, a red circle with a white cross and the text "Working Offline" appears.

   Troubleshooting If the Work Offline command does not appear in the Preferences group, verify that your account is configured for Cached Exchange Mode. This can be configured using the backstage by clicking Account Settings, and then, from the drop-down menu, clicking Account Settings. On the E-mail tab, select the relevant account, and then click Change. Select the Use Cached Exchange Mode option. You will need to close Outlook and reopen it for the changes to take effect.

New Appointment

2. Click the **WideWorldImporters – Calendar** tab, and then, on the **Home** tab, click **New Appointment**. A new, untitled appointment form opens.

3. On the form status bar, hover the mouse over the icon, or put it over the link to the right of **In Shared Folder**. A tooltip appears with the date that the Calendar list was last updated.

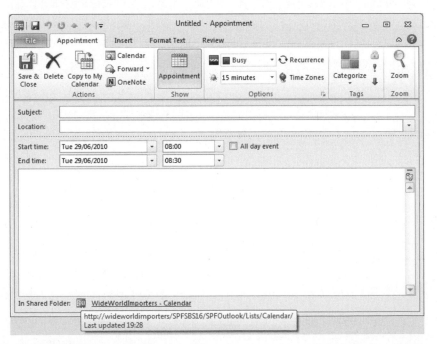

4. In the **Subject** box, type **SharePoint team meeting**, and then, on the **Appointment** tab, click **Save & Close**. If a **Reminder** dialog box opens, click **Dismiss**.

The new appointment appears in the detail pane.

Troubleshooting You may have to arrange the calendars to show the daily view to see the new appointment.

5. In the **Navigation** pane, under **Other Calendars**, right-click **WideWorldImporters – Calendar**, and click **Open in Web Browser**.

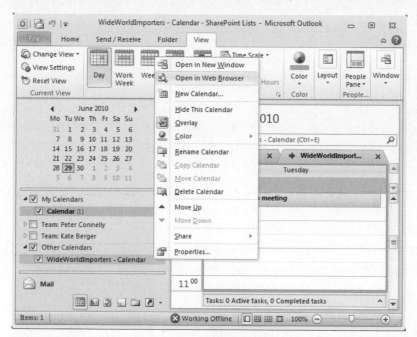

The SharePoint Calendar list is displayed. Notice that the appointment that you added in Outlook does not appear in the SharePoint Calendar list.

6. Close the browser.

Work Offline

7. On the **Send/Receive** tab, click **Work Offline** in the **Preferences** group.

The Offline icon disappears from the Outlook status bar.

8. Press **F9**.

Tip Synchronization between Outlook and SharePoint occurs periodically. Pressing F9 synchronizes all Outlook connections immediately.

9. In the **Navigation** pane, under **Other Calendars**, right-click **WideWorldImporters – Calendar**, and then click **Open in Web Browser**.

The SharePoint Calendar list is displayed. The appointment that you added in Outlook appears in the SharePoint Calendar list.

 CLEAN UP Close the browser and leave Outlook open if you are continuing with the next exercise.

Managing SharePoint Alerts in Outlook

When you create an alert for an item, such as a document, list item, document library, list, survey, or search result, you immediately receive a confirmation email message notifying you that the alert was created successfully. This message indicates that the alert process is working. The confirmation message also contains information about the alert and provides links to the SharePoint site where the item is located. When someone makes a change to the item, you receive an email message alert that indicates what was changed, who made the change, and when the change was made. You should create an alert when content has changed and you need (or want) to take notice of it.

To avoid alerts swamping your inbox, you should choose carefully the SharePoint content about which you wish to be alerted. Ideally, you should select only important content that you want to monitor. Consider subscribing to RSS feeds to monitor other SharePoint content that is not as important and does not need your close supervision.

By default, Windows SharePoint Services does not provide an alert aggregation capability for all your alerts across every SharePoint site. To manage your alerts by using the browser, you would have to visit each site that has an alert set. To help you manage your alerts, you could save the message notifying you that an alert was created successfully because it provides a link to the SharePoint site. You could then use the email message alert to navigate to those sites on which the alerts are set.

In an environment where many SharePoint sites exist, managing your alerts could be a daunting task if they were monitored and organized merely by the links in your email alert messages and by memory. When using Outlook 2007 or Outlook 2010, you can manage the email alerts received from all SharePoint intranet sites and trusted websites from one dialog box.

In the following exercise, you will use Outlook 2010 to create a new alert.

 SET UP Open Outlook, if it is not already open. The exercise will use the SharePoint Contacts list that you used earlier in this chapter, but you can use another Contacts list if you want.

BE SURE TO verify that you have sufficient rights to create an alert on the Contacts list. If in doubt, see the Appendix at the back of this book.

1. Click the **File** tab to display the backstage, and then click **Manage Rules & Alerts** in the middle pane. You may need to scroll down.

    The Rules And Alerts dialog box is displayed.

2. Click the **Manage Alerts** tab.

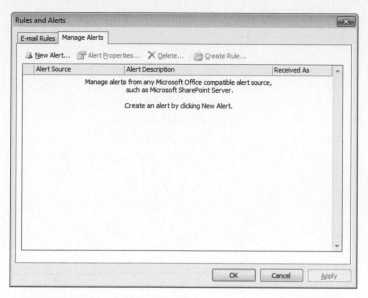

3. Click **New Alert**. The New Alert dialog box is displayed.

4. In the **Web site Address** box, type the Uniform Resource Locator (URL) of a SharePoint site that contains a Contacts list, and then click **Open**.

A browser window opens, displaying the New Alert page.

5. Select **Contacts**.

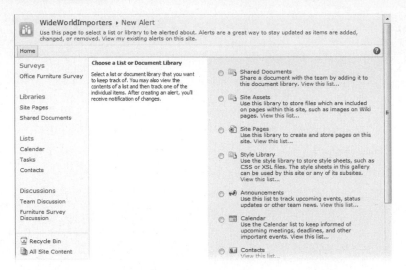

6. Scroll down and click **Next**. The New Alert page is displayed.

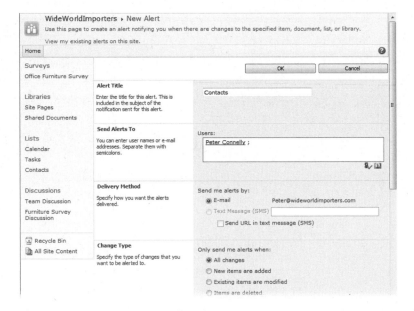

Tip The Send Alerts To section is visible only to users who are assigned the Manage Lists permissions for the list. This section allows users who manage the list to configure alerts for other users.

7. In the **Send Alerts To** section, type your email address if it doesn't already appear. Review the other settings, and then click **OK**.

Troubleshooting If your SharePoint server is not configured to send email, an Error page will display. Only a server administrator can configure email settings for a SharePoint installation.

The browser displays the My Alerts On This Site page. Under the Frequency: Immediate area, the alert named Contacts is listed.

8. Close all browser windows.

9. Switch to Outlook, where the **Rules and Alerts** dialog box should still be visible. A new alert, **Contacts: All items (All Changes)**, should be listed.

Troubleshooting If the alert does not appear in the Rules And Alerts dialog box, click OK and then click Manage Rules & Alerts. If the new alert still does not appear, then close Outlook. Restart Outlook, and then reopen the Rules And Alerts dialog box.

From the Rules And Alerts dialog box, you can do any or all of the following:

○ Alter the properties of an alert. The Alert Properties dialog box provides a link to the SharePoint site, buttons to "Modify Alert" and "View Item," and a link to the Alerts management page on the SharePoint site.

○ Select multiple alerts by using the **SHIFT** or **CTRL** key when you click an alert. You can then click Delete to delete all the alerts you selected. Click Yes in the Microsoft Outlook warning dialog box that appears, asking whether you want to delete the selected rows.

○ Use Outlook rules to manage your alerts so that a notification window pops up, a sound is played, the alert email message is moved to a specified folder, or some other action is performed on the alert message.

 CLEAN UP Close all Outlook 2010 dialog box windows, and leave Outlook open if you are continuing to the next exercise.

See Also Chapter 4, "Working with Lists," Chapter 5, "Working with Libraries," and Chapter 6, "Working with Web Pages," contain more information about managing alerts on lists and documents from the browser.

Creating Meeting Workspaces from Outlook

Every company holds meetings. These meetings often have a specific agenda; participants may need to prepare for meetings by completing a task or two prior to the meeting. The task may be simply reviewing a document, assembling a list of questions, or perhaps creating a prototype of something to bring to the meeting. A meeting can become inefficient, or even completely ineffective, because the preparation tasks that participants are expected to complete are not communicated effectively. In addition, after the meeting is over, meeting notes or follow-up steps may need to be provided to the participants and tracked.

SharePoint Foundation provides a site template called Meeting Workspace that helps improve communications before and after a meeting. Meeting Workspaces enable you to share your meeting agenda and objectives, publish documents and files, track tasks, and complete other collaborative activities through one central location. By centralizing this information, your meeting attendees have access to the latest information, and you avoid sending files through your email system. Three of the methods that can be used to create a Meeting Workspace are as follows:

- In the browser, select New Site from the Site Actions menu on a SharePoint site.
- Select the Meeting Workspace check box when you create a Calendar list.
- Click Meeting Workspace on a new meeting request in Outlook 2007 or Outlook 2010. When you create a meeting request in Outlook, you can create a Meeting Workspace site or link the meeting to an existing Workspace site.

Once you have created a Meeting Workspace, you should familiarize yourself with the site because it is slightly different from a Team site. It has no Quick Launch, and the pages are Web Part pages and not wiki pages. And if you create a Meeting Workspace from a recurring event, additional information is provided on the home page of the site.

Note Before you can create your first Meeting Workspace using Outlook, you must add the Meeting Workspace command to either the Quick Access Toolbar or the Ribbon, which you will do in the next exercise. You will need to do this only once because Outlook will remember your custom settings.

In this exercise, you will create a Meeting Workspace using Outlook.

SET UP Open Outlook, if it is not already open.

BE SURE TO verify that you have sufficient rights to create a site. If in doubt, see the Appendix at the back of this book.

New Items

1. On the **Home** tab, click **New Items** in the **New** group, and then click **Meeting**. A new, untitled meeting form opens.

2. Click the **File** tab to display the backstage, and then click **Options**.

   The Outlook Options dialog box opens.

3. Click the **Quick Access Toolbar**, and then, from the **Choose commands from** list, select **Commands Not in the Ribbon**.

4. In the list of commands, scroll down to **Meeting Workspace** and then click **Add**.

The Meeting Workspace command appears in the Customize Quick Access Toolbar list.

5. Click **OK** to close the Outlook Options dialog box. The untitled meeting form is displayed.

6. In the **To** box, type the email addresses of the people you want to invite to the meeting. In the **Subject** box, type **Product Review**.

Important SharePoint uses the Subject of the meeting request as the Meeting Workspace site name. If you create a Meeting Workspace site with a blank Subject line, Outlook will create a Meeting Workspace site with the name Untitled*XXX*, where *XXX* is a number based on the number of existing untitled sites.

7. In the **Location** box, type **Wide World Importers Main Office**.

Meeting
Workspace

8. On the **Quick Access Toolbar**, click **Meeting Workspace**. The Meeting Workspace Task pane appears to the right of the form.

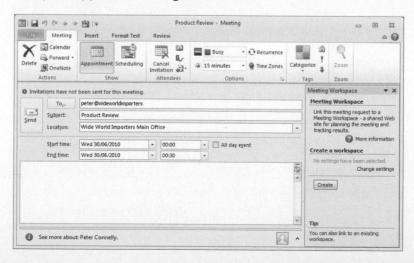

9. In the **Meeting Workspace** Task pane, in the **Create a workspace** section, click **Change settings**. The Meeting Workspace Task pane displays **Select a location**.

10. Click **Click to select**, and then select **Other**. The Other Workspace Server dialog box is displayed.

11. Type the URL of a SharePoint site. The Meeting Workspace site will be a subsite of the SharePoint site that you type here.

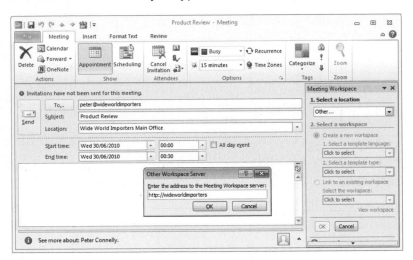

Important You cannot create a new Meeting Workspace site under an existing Meeting Workspace site. You must also be a member of a site group with the Create Subsites permission for the parent site.

12. Click **OK**.

Tip You can select a different language for your site if other language packs are installed on your SharePoint server. You can also choose a different Meeting Workspace template. By default, SharePoint installs five Meeting Workspace templates: Basic Meeting Workspace, Blank Meeting Workspace, Decision Making Workspace, Social Meeting Workspace, and Multipage Meeting Workspace. You can associate a meeting request with an existing Meeting Workspace by selecting the link to an existing Workspace option.

13. In the **Meeting Workspace** Task pane, click **OK**, and then click **Create**.

Outlook connects to the SharePoint website and creates the Workspace. A meeting request is placed in your Outlook Calendar that contains the details of the meeting and a URL to the Meeting Workspace. No corresponding entry exists in the Calendar list for the parent site. The Outlook meeting request and Meeting Workspace Task pane are updated.

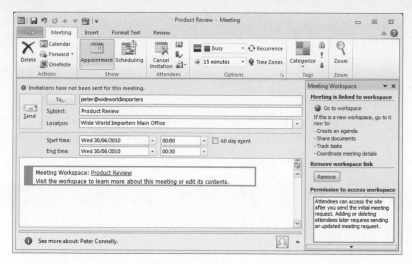

14. Click **Send**.

    Outlook attempts to add the attendees to the Meeting Workspace site in the
    Contributor site group. If you have entered an illegal email address, a Check
    Names dialog box opens, which you can use to choose a new name or add a new
    contact. If Outlook was unable to include the attendees to the site, a notification is
    displayed.

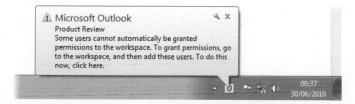

    Attendees can access the Meeting Workspace site that you created by clicking the
    link in the invitation email that they receive from you.

15. Click the **Product Review** link to display the **Product Review Meeting
    Workspace** site in the browser.

 CLEAN UP Close the browser and leave Outlook open if you are continuing with the
next exercise.

After creating the Meeting Workspace, you can add or remove attendees using the
meeting request in Outlook. When you send the meeting request, Outlook updates the
Meeting Workspace.

Important If you change the meeting request and click Save and then close the meeting
request instead of clicking Send Update, the updates will not be sent to the Meeting
Workspace site.

You can also add and remove attendees through the Meeting Workspace site by clicking Manage Attendees in the Attendees Web Part; however, this does not update the meeting request in Outlook, which you will need to do manually. For this reason, many users prefer to create and manage Meeting Workspaces from within Outlook.

When you delete a Meeting Workspace, the meeting request in your calendar contains a broken link pointing to the recently deleted site. Similarly, when you cancel the meeting or delete the meeting request in your Outlook calendar, the Meeting Workspace still exists and displays a message that this has occurred.

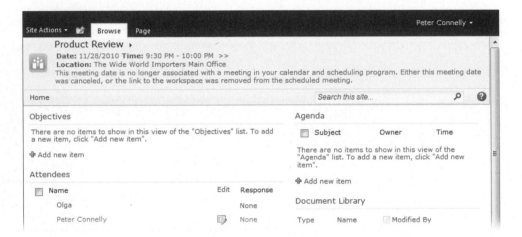

This is sometimes called an *orphan site*. Of course, you can still delete the site from the Site Settings page accessed through the Site Actions menu. However, you may not remember where you created the Meeting Workspace. Consequently, you should save a link to your Meeting Workspace, such as on a SharePoint link list, or delete the Meeting Workspace after saving any important information that the site contained. Therefore, do not cancel a meeting and send a new meeting request if you just want to change some details about a meeting. Instead, send an updated meeting request to attendees because this maintains the link between the meeting request and the Meeting Workspace.

Configuring an RSS Feed

In the previous section, you learned how to manage alerts, which are notifications received via email that notify you when content has changed in a SharePoint list or library. Alerts are a "push" method of notification. SharePoint pushes content to you based on specific criteria at predefined intervals.

Outlook 2007 and Outlook 2010 support RSS—the acronym previously meant Rich Site Summary—which is another method of notifying you when something has changed or new content is published within a SharePoint site. Outlook allows you to syndicate this information, and such programs are called *RSS readers*.

RSS is a "pull" method of notification. You decide when to use an RSS reader to read content exposed as RSS feeds; therefore, most people will use RSS for tracking content that is regularly updated. It is commonly used to stay up to date with the latest news on websites and blogs, but it can also be used to distribute pictures or audio or video content. Sites that expose their content via RSS are said to have an *RSS feed*. You can create an RSS feed on content stored in a SharePoint list. Therefore, very simple business processes can be handled by alerts. RSS suits ad-hoc queries or processes. More complex business processes can be managed using the built-in workflows or built using Microsoft SharePoint Designer 2010 or Visual Studio 2010.

See Also More information on the built-in workflows can be found in Chapter 11, "Working with Workflows."

In this exercise, you will add an RSS feed to Outlook 2010.

SET UP Open the browser and display the SharePoint list or library with which you would like to subscribe to the RSS feed. The exercise will use the *http:// wideworldimporters* site and the Shared Documents library, but you can use whatever site and list or library you want.

BE SURE TO verify that you have sufficient rights to the list or library. If in doubt, see the Appendix at the back of this book.

**RSS
Feed**

1. On the **Library** tab, click **RSS Feed** in the **Share & Track** group.

   The Team Site: Shared Documents page is displayed.

2. Right-click **Subscribe to this feed**, and then click **Copy Shortcut**.

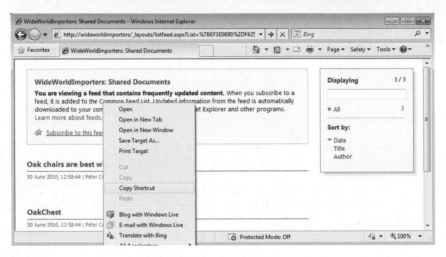

Tip   You can also copy the URL of the RSS feed from the browser address box.

3. Open Outlook 2010, if it is not already open. On the navigation bar, under your mail folders, right-click **RSS Feeds**, and then click **Add a New RSS Feed**.

The New RSS Feed dialog box opens.

4. In the **Enter the location of the RSS Feed** box, press **CTRL+V** to paste the shortcut that you copied in step 2.

5. Click **Add**.

The New RSS Feed dialog box closes, and an Outlook dialog box opens, warning that you should only add subscriptions from sources you know and trust.

6. Click **Advanced** to open the **RSS Feed Options** dialog box.

7. In the **General** section, in the **Feed Name** box, type **WideWorldImporters: Shared Documents**.

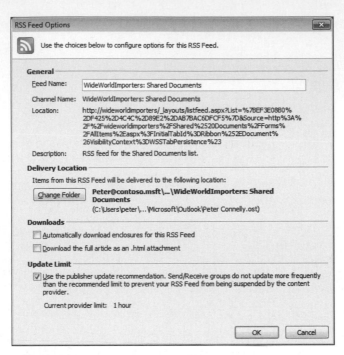

8. Click **OK** to close the **RSS Feed Options** dialog box, and then click **Yes** to close the **Microsoft Outlook** dialog box.

The RSS feed, WideWorldImporters:Shared Documents, appears as a folder. The detail pane displays an entry for each document in the Shared Documents library.

Note You can change the properties of the RSS feed as follows: Click the File tab to display the backstage, click Account Settings, and then, from the drop-down menu, click Account Settings to display the Account Settings dialog box. Click the RSS Feeds tab and then select the RSS feed whose properties you wish to modify. Click Change to display the RSS Feed Options dialog box, where you can change the RSS feed properties.

 CLEAN UP Close Outlook and any browser windows that may be open.

Key Points

- You can copy contacts listed in your personal Outlook Contacts folder both to and from a SharePoint Contacts list.

- You can copy and move SharePoint list items both to and from Outlook.

- You can connect any SharePoint Contacts list, Calendar list, Tasks list, or discussion board to Outlook. This action creates a folder in Outlook that you can synchronize with the SharePoint list or that synchronizes automatically every 20 minutes.

- In Outlook 2010 and Outlook 2007, you can view multiple calendars side by side. These calendars can be connected to SharePoint Calendar lists.

- You can aggregate and manage all your tasks in one place whether you created them within Outlook, in a SharePoint Tasks list, or within Microsoft OneNote.

- You can manage all your SharePoint alerts from the Rules And Alerts dialog box in Outlook.

- You can create a Meeting Workspace site from Outlook by using a meeting request. When using this technique, you create a Meeting Workspace as a subsite to a SharePoint website.

- You can manage your RSS feeds in Outlook just like your other mail by flagging them for follow-up, assigning them a specific color, or automating any process by using the rules.

Chapter at a Glance

Import data from an Excel spreadsheet to a list in SharePoint, page 398

Export an Excel table to a SharePoint site, page 404

Export data from an Access database to a list in SharePoint, page 408

Link a data-centric application to a SharePoint list, page 417

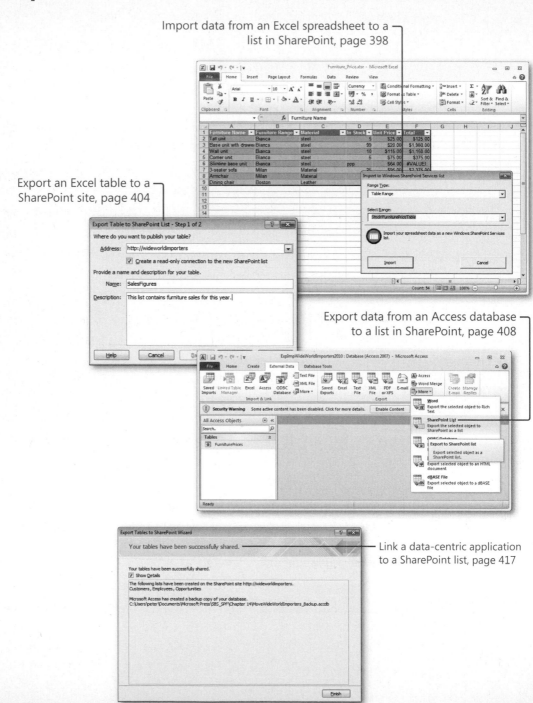

14 Using SharePoint Foundation with Excel 2010 and Access 2010

In this chapter, you will learn how to

- ✔ Import data from an Excel spreadsheet to a list in SharePoint.
- ✔ Export a SharePoint list to an Excel spreadsheet.
- ✔ Export an Excel table to a SharePoint site.
- ✔ Export data from an Access database to a list in SharePoint.
- ✔ Import a list to an Access database.
- ✔ Link an Access database to a SharePoint list.
- ✔ Link a data-centric application to a SharePoint list.
- ✔ Work offline.

Microsoft SharePoint Foundation 2010 provides the collaborative backbone to the Microsoft Office 2010 System. This chapter focuses on the integration of SharePoint Foundation with Microsoft Excel 2010 and Microsoft Access 2010.

Excel 2010, similar to Excel 2007, allows you to export and import data to and from SharePoint lists and provides one-way synchronization from SharePoint lists to Excel spreadsheets, so that you can take the data offline and then synchronize with the SharePoint lists when you reconnect.

The combination of SharePoint Foundation and Access 2010 makes it easy for you to build client–server databases against SharePoint Foundation. In doing so, users who do not possess the skills or privileges to be a Microsoft SQL Server database administrator can still obtain the manageability and stability benefits of storing data on the server while retaining the ease of use of Access 2010. The level of server functionality integrated into Access 2010 increases when used in combination with Access Services in SharePoint Server 2010 Enterprise Edition.

Access 2010, like Access 2007, Excel 2010, and Excel 2007, allows you to export and import data both to and from SharePoint lists. Access also provides two-way synchronization between Access databases and SharePoint lists, so that you can work with lists offline and then synchronize the changes when you reconnect.

Although you can complete the tasks documented in this chapter using Excel 2007 and Access 2007, the steps and screenshots in this chapter were created using Excel 2010 and Access 2010. If you use Excel 2007 or Access 2007, your steps and screenshots will look slightly different. See the book *Microsoft Windows SharePoint Services 3.0 Step by Step* by Olga Londer, Bill English, Todd Bleeker, and Penelope Coventry (Microsoft Press, 2007) for detailed steps on using Excel 2007 and Access 2007 with SharePoint.

> **Practice Files** Before you can complete the exercises in this chapter, you need to download the Chapter 14 practice files from the book's catalog page to the following folder on your computer: Documents\Microsoft Press\SBS_SPF\Chapter14. See "Using the Practice Files" at the beginning of this book for more information.

Important Install and activate the Office 2010 suite before beginning any of the exercises in this chapter. Remember to use your SharePoint site location in place of *http://wideworldimporters* in the following exercises.

Importing Data from an Excel Spreadsheet to a List in SharePoint

In many situations, you might already have data within a spreadsheet, but later you find that you need to share the data with other members of your team. SharePoint provides the ability to import data from an Excel 2010 spreadsheet into a SharePoint list. Those users who have appropriate permissions may read the SharePoint list, while others may even revise the list or enter additional data. You can choose to import all the data held on a worksheet, a *range* of cells, a *named range*, or an *Excel 2010 table*.

In the following exercise, you will use your browser to create a SharePoint Custom list that contains data imported from an Excel 2010 spreadsheet.

> **Practice Files** You will use the practice file Furniture_Price.xlsx, located in the Documents\Microsoft Press\SBS_SPF\Chapter14 folder.

SET UP Open the SharePoint site to which you would like to import data from the Excel spreadsheet. Remember to use your SharePoint site location in place of *http://wideworldimporters* in the exercises. If prompted, type your user name and password, and click OK.

BE SURE TO verify that you have sufficient rights to create a list. If in doubt, see the Appendix at the back of this book.

1. Click **Site Actions**, and then click **More Options**.

   The Create dialog is displayed.

2. In the left pane, under **Filter By** and then under **All Categories**, click **Blank & Custom**, and then, in the middle pane, click **Import Spreadsheet**. In the right pane, click **Create**.

   The New page is displayed.

3. In the **Name** box, type **FurniturePrice**.

   Tip Any Uniform Resource Locator (URL) in SharePoint is limited to 260 characters. The name that you type here is used to create both the URL and the title of the list. Later in this exercise, you will change the title to a user-friendly name.

4. In the **Description** box, type **This list contains the furniture items in stock together with their unit prices**.

   Important If you import a spreadsheet into a site based on the Meeting Workspace template, an option appears on the New page to share the same items for all meetings. If you choose not to share the same items for all meetings, then each meeting displays the list with only the items added for that date. Once items become series items for a list, you cannot change the setting back to list items for a specific date.

5. Click **Browse**.

   The Choose File To Upload dialog box appears and displays your Documents folder (or the last folder that you accessed).

6. If the **Documents** folder is not displayed in the **Choose File to Upload** dialog box, under **Libraries**, click the **Documents** icon. Navigate to the **Chapter14** practice folder, and then double-click the **Furniture_Price.xlsx** file.

   Troubleshooting If a dialog box opens, stating that the specified file is not a valid spreadsheet or contains no data to import, then add your SharePoint site as a trusted site or local intranet. If you are using Internet Explorer to add a site as a trusted site, click Tools and then click Internet Options. In the Internet Options dialog box that opens, click the Security tab. Click Trusted Sites, and then click Sites. In the Trusted Sites dialog box that opens, click Add and then Close. Click OK to close the Internet Options dialog box. Once you have added your SharePoint site as a trusted site, repeat this exercise from step 1.

   The Choose File to Upload dialog box closes.

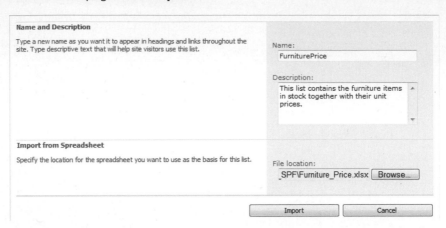

7. On the **New** page, click **Import**.

Excel 2010 opens Furniture_Price.xlsx and displays the Import to Windows SharePoint Services List dialog box.

8. From the **Range Type** drop-down list, check that **Table Range** is selected.

9. Click in the **Selected Range** drop-down list, choose **Stock!FurniturePriceTable**, and then click **Import**.

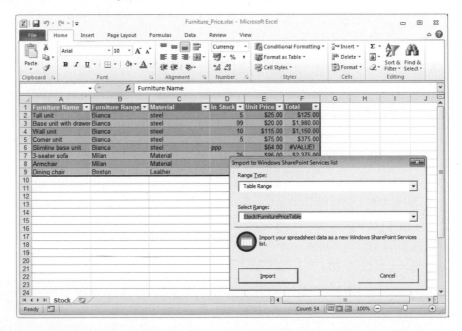

The All Items view of the FurniturePrice list is displayed, and the URL in the Address box is *http://<siteURLname>/Lists/FurniturePrice/AllItems.aspx*, where *<SiteURLname>* is the URL of your site, such as *http://wideworldimporters*.

Tip If you import a range of cells from an Excel 2007 spreadsheet and want the Excel 2010 column names to become the SharePoint list column names, you should first edit the spreadsheet and convert the range of cells to an Excel 2010 table.

List
Settings

10. To change the title of the list, click the **List** tab on the Ribbon, and then click **List Settings** in the **Settings** group. The List Settings page appears.

11. Under **General Settings**, click **Title, description and navigation**.

    The General Settings page appears.

12. In the **Name and Description** section, in the **Name** box, type a user-friendly name such as **Furniture Price List**.

13. In the **Navigation** section, click the **Yes** option to display this list on the Quick Launch.

14. Click **Save** at the bottom of the web page. The List Settings page appears.

15. On the breadcrumb, click the **Furniture Price List** link. The All Items view of the Furniture Price List appears.

    The title of the list has changed to "Furniture Price List," but the URL remains as *http://<siteURLName>/Lists/FurniturePrice/AllItems.aspx*.

 CLEAN UP Leave the browser open if you are continuing to the next exercise.

Exporting a SharePoint List to an Excel Spreadsheet

You can export the contents of SharePoint lists, results of a survey, or document libraries to an Excel 2010 spreadsheet. The exported list or library is a web query that stays updated with changes to the original list in your SharePoint site. The Excel 2010 spreadsheet maintains a connection to the SharePoint list and therefore becomes a *linked object*.

In this exercise, you will export a list from a SharePoint site to an Excel 2010 spreadsheet. You will add data to the spreadsheet and then synchronize the data in the spreadsheet with the contents of the list on the SharePoint site.

 SET UP In the browser, open the SharePoint site, if not already open, where you have a list whose contents you want to export to an Excel 2010 spreadsheet. This exercise uses the list that you created in the previous exercise.

BE SURE TO verify that you have sufficient rights to edit items in the list. If in doubt, see the Appendix at the back of this book.

1. In the Quick Launch, in the **Lists** area, click **Furniture Price List**.

   Tip The export process exports only the columns and rows contained in the list's current view; in this exercise, that is the All Items view. If none of the views contain the data that you want to export, then you must create a new view to meet your needs. Alternatively, you can choose one of the existing views, export the list to a spreadsheet, and then delete the unwanted data.

Export to
Excel

2. On the Ribbon, click the **List** tab, and then click **Export to Excel** in the **Connect & Export** group.

   SharePoint generates an Excel web query file, and the File Download dialog box opens.

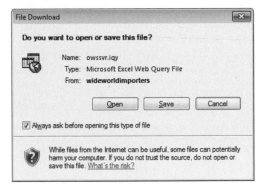

3. Click **Open**.

Excel 2010 opens a new workbook that contains one worksheet named owssvr(1). An Excel Security Notice dialog box is displayed, warning you that data connections have been blocked.

4. Click **Enable**.

The Excel 2010 query results are displayed in the owssvr(1) worksheet in an Excel 2010 table. Each column in the list contains an AutoFilter arrow in the header row, and the Design contextual tab is active. Excel 2007 names your table _owssvr_1.

Tip When you export a SharePoint library, Excel 2010 represents the documents in the list with hyperlinks that point to the documents on the SharePoint site. Similarly, attachments on list items are replaced with a hyperlink. In the Excel 2010 spreadsheet, click this link to open the file.

Tip You should make a habit of renaming your tables so that you recognize the data they contain. This helps make formulas that summarize table data much easier to understand. To rename your table, first ensure that the Design contextual tab is active, and then, in the Properties group, edit the value in the Table Name field.

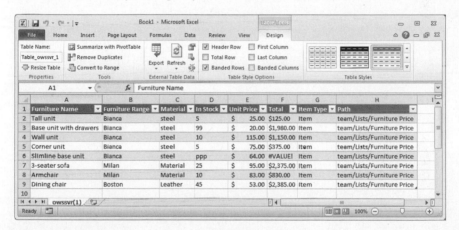

5. Click cell **A10**, type **Antique**, and press **TAB**. Type **Bi**, and press **TAB** again.

IntelliSense completes the word *Bianca* for you.

6. Type **wood**, and press **TAB**. Type **5**, and press **TAB**. Type **10**, and then press **ENTER**.

Excel 2010 places a dollar ($) sign before the number 10.

Tip The columns in Excel 2010 retain the data types from the exported SharePoint list; they do not retain the formulas of a calculated column.

Refresh All

7. Click the **Data** tab, and click **Refresh All** in the **Connections** group.

The spreadsheet is updated with a copy of the data from the Furniture Price List on the SharePoint website. Your changes to data in the Excel 2010 spreadsheet are lost, unlike what happens with Excel 2003. In Excel 2007 and Excel 2010, changes that you make to data in your Excel worksheet do not synchronize with the list on the SharePoint website; that is, only a one-way synchronization occurs from the SharePoint site to Excel 2010 or Excel 2007. When using Excel 2003, two-way synchronization is still available.

Properties

8. Click cell **A2**, and then, in the **Connections** group on the **Data** tab, click **Properties**. The External Data Properties dialog box appears.

   You can use this dialog box to alter the behavior of the refresh activity.

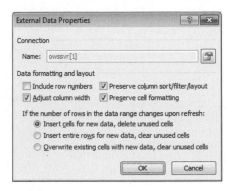

9. Click **Cancel**.

   See Also You can also initiate the exporting and linking of a SharePoint list to Excel 2010 by using the Access Web Datasheet task pane, which contains four options: Query list with Excel, Print with Excel, Chart with Excel, and Create Excel PivotTable Report. For more information on the Datasheet View and task pane, see Chapter 9, "Working with List and Library Views."

 CLEAN UP Close the browser and Excel 2010. You do not need to save the spreadsheet.

Exporting an Excel Table to a SharePoint Site

Creating a SharePoint list from within Excel 2010 or Excel 2007 is known as exporting an Excel table. In Excel 2003, this was known as publishing an Excel list. Once the table data is placed on the SharePoint site, users can see the Excel data without opening Excel. As in the first exercise of this chapter, you can maintain a link between the SharePoint list and the Excel data, but any changes in the Excel spreadsheet are not reflected in the SharePoint list. You can only synchronize changes in the SharePoint list to the Excel spreadsheet.

In the following exercise, you will export a spreadsheet to a SharePoint list by using Excel 2010 and a two-step wizard.

> **Practice Files** You will use the practice file Sales_Figures.xlsx, located in the Documents\
> Microsoft Press\SBS_SPF\Chapter14 folder.

SET UP Start Excel 2010 and open the Sales_Figures.xlsx document.

BE SURE TO verify that you have sufficient rights to create a list. If in doubt, see the
Appendix at the back of this book.

1. In Excel 2010, click any cell within the data.

> **Note** If you are using an Excel spreadsheet other than the practice file, and the data
> that you want to export is already found within an Excel 2010 table, skip to step 4.

Format as
Table

2. On the **Home** tab, in the **Styles** group, click **Format as Table**, and then choose a
table style.

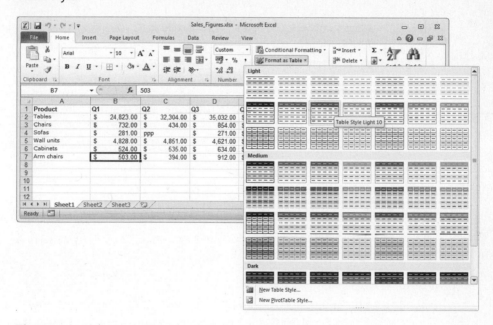

> **Tip** By selecting one cell in the data, Excel 2010 automatically selects a range of cells
> that contain data; however, you can select a different range of cells to use when creating
> a table. In addition, if your data does not contain headers, Excel 2010 creates them for
> you and labels them as Column1, Column2, and so on.

3. When the **Format As Table** dialog box appears, click **OK**.

Excel 2010 converts the data in the workbook into a table. Each column header contains an AutoFilter arrow and a black border surrounding the data, which means that the table is active on the worksheet.

The Design tab on the Table Tools contextual tab appears.

Tip If the table is not active on the worksheet, then the Design tab disappears. To export a table, it must be active on the worksheet. To make a table active, click any cell in the table.

Export

4. On the **Design** tab, in the **External Table Data** group, click **Export**, and then, from the drop-down menu, click **Export Table to SharePoint List**.

   The first step of the two-step Export Table to SharePoint List wizard is displayed.

5. In the **Address** box, type the name of the site where you want to export the data, such as **http://wideworldimporters**.

6. Select the **Create a read-only connection to the new SharePoint list** check box.

   Important If the Create A Read-Only Connection To The New SharePoint List check box is selected, the spreadsheet is linked to the SharePoint list and you can synchronize updates from the SharePoint list to the spreadsheet. However, once the SharePoint list is created, you cannot link the spreadsheet to the SharePoint list. Therefore, if you wish to synchronize updates between the list and the spreadsheet, be sure to select this check box now.

7. In the **Name** box, type **SalesFigures**, and in the **Description** box, type **This list contains furniture sales for this year.**

8. Click **Next**.

   Excel checks the data in each column to ensure that the data belongs to a data type supported by SharePoint Foundation. If it doesn't, Excel usually applies the Text data type to each column. Excel also checks whether each column contains only one type of data. If a column contains a mixture of data types, such as numbers and text, then Excel chooses Text as the data type. Once Excel completes its check, the second step of the two-step Export Table to SharePoint Site wizard is displayed.

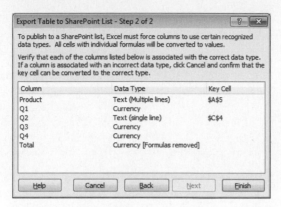

In the Key Cell column, notice that cell A5 in the Product column and C4 in the Q2 column contain a different data type from the rest of the cells in their columns. Also, the formulas are removed from the Total column. If you have the region and language format (also known as the date, time, or number format) of your operating system set to English (United States), then columns Q1, Q3, Q4 and Total have a data type of Currency; otherwise, they will have a data type of Number.

Tip At this point, you can click Cancel, correct the erroneous data, and then restart the export process. Also, because Excel removes formulas during the export process, you may consider deleting the Total column and creating a calculated column once you have completed the export process and the data is on your SharePoint site.

9. Click **Finish**. A SharePoint Foundation dialog box is displayed with the URL of your new SharePoint list.

   Important The new SharePoint list does not appear on the Quick Launch.

10. Click the URL of your new SharePoint list. A new browser window opens, displaying the new SharePoint list.

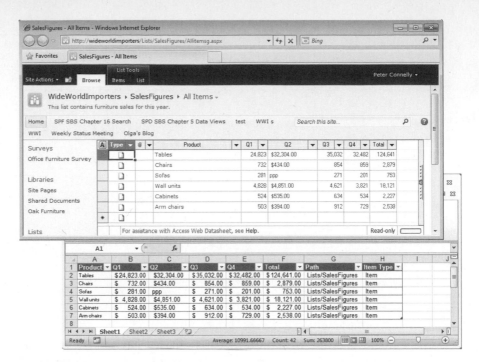

Important Before you close Excel, notice that the spreadsheet contains two extra columns. When you export a spreadsheet that is linked to a SharePoint list, Item Type and Path columns are added to your spreadsheet. On the Design contextual tab, use the External Table data group to alter the properties of a range of cells, open the connected SharePoint list in a browser, or unlink a list.

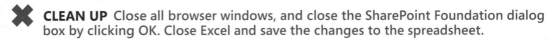 **CLEAN UP** Close all browser windows, and close the SharePoint Foundation dialog box by clicking OK. Close Excel and save the changes to the spreadsheet.

Exporting Data from an Access Database to a List in SharePoint

Traditionally, Access uses client database objects to manipulate and display data, tables, reports, and queries, where the Access database is stored on a file system or in a SharePoint library and requires the use of Access on the computer. When you create such a database with Access 2010, the same file format that was used with Access 2007 is created—an accdb file. However, Access 2010 has introduced a new database object—an Access web object where tables, queries, and reports are displayed with a browser using Access Services, a component of SharePoint Server 2010 Enterprise Edition.

See Also An Office visual instruction on creating web databases with Access 2010 and Access Services can be found at *http://msdn.microsoft.com/en-us/library/ff402351(office.14).aspx*.

Tip When creating new database solutions in Access 2010, use a web database template, and check that it is compatible with SharePoint Access Services. Therefore, should you want to create a Web Access service site from your Access database in the future, you will not need to convert your database.

When you integrate data between Access 2010 and SharePoint Foundation, you are limited to using similar methods that were used with Access 2007. However, Access 2010 contains SharePoint connectivity improvements and a wizard that allows you to use the new SharePoint 2010 list improvements, such as enforcing cascade delete and restricting the delete relationships between two lists.

See Also More information on changes in Access 2010 can be found at *http://technet. microsoft.com/en-us/library/cc179181.aspx*. Information on SharePoint connectivity performance improvements can be found at *http://blogs.msdn.com/b/access/ archive/2010/02/05/access-2010-performance-improvements-against-sharepoint-lists.aspx*, and details of data platform improvement can be found at *http://blogs.msdn.com/b/access/ archive/2010/02/15/data-platform-improvements-in-sharepoint-2010.aspx*.

Access 2010 consists of a number of tabs, many of which provide a quick way to work with SharePoint websites and lists, as summarized in the following table.

Tab	Group	Description
Create	Tables	Use the SharePoint Lists drop-down menu to create a list on a SharePoint site and a table in the current database that links to the newly created list.
External Data	Import & Link	Use the More drop-down menu to import from or link to data on a SharePoint list.
	Export	Use the More drop-down menu to export the selected object as a SharePoint list.
Database Tools	Move Data	Use the SharePoint command to move your tables to a SharePoint list and create links to those tables in your database.

Access allows you to export a table or other database objects to a number of formats, such as an external file, a dBase database, an Excel workbook, a Rich Text Format (RTF) file, a text file, a PDF or XPS file, an email attachment, an Extensible Markup Language (XML) document, an Open Database Connectivity (ODBC) data source, or a Hypertext Markup Language (HTML) document. Beginning with Access 2003, you can also export a table to a SharePoint site where a new list is created.

Tip Access 2010 does not support linking, importing, or exporting using the Installable Sequential Access Method (ISAM) for Lotus 1-2-3, Paradox, and Jet 2.*x*.

In the following exercise, you will export a table from within an Access 2010 database into a SharePoint site by creating a new SharePoint list.

> **Practice Files** You will use the practice file ExpImpWideWorldImporters2010.accdb, located in the Documents\Microsoft Press\SBS_SPF\Chapter14 folder.

SET UP Start Access 2010 and open the ExpImpWideWorldImporters2010.accdb database. Remember to use your SharePoint site location in place of *http://wideworldimporters* in the following exercise.

BE SURE TO verify that you have sufficient rights to create a list. If in doubt, see the Appendix at the back of this book.

SharePoint List

1. Under **Tables**, click **FurniturePrices**, if it is not already selected, and then, on the Access ribbon, click the **External Data** tab. In the **Export** group, click **More**, and then click **SharePoint List**.

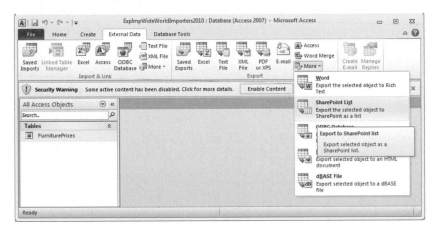

The Export – SharePoint Site dialog box is displayed.

2. In the **Specify a SharePoint site** area, choose the site where you want to export the table, such as **http://wideworldimporters**.

   Troubleshooting If the URL of your SharePoint site does not appear, type the URL in the text box.

3. In the **Specify a name for the new list** box, type **exportFurniturePrices**.

4. Leave the **Open the list when finished** check box selected.

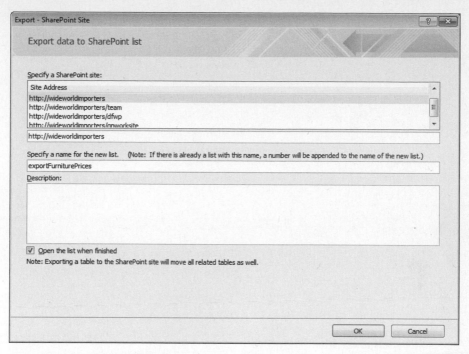

5. Click **OK**. The **Exporting Table to SharePoint List** dialog box opens, displaying the progress of the import.

   The browser opens and displays the newly created list, exportFurniturePrices, in All Items view.

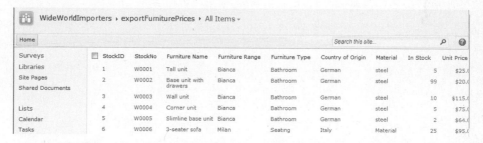

   Troubleshooting If you mistype the website name in the Site text box, Access 2010 displays a warning dialog box, stating that it can't find the website. If this occurs, verify the website address and try again.

6. Return to the **Save Export Steps** page of the **Export – SharePoint Site** dialog box in Access.

7. Select the **Save export steps** check box. The Save As and Description text boxes, as well as the Create Outlook Task areas, appear.

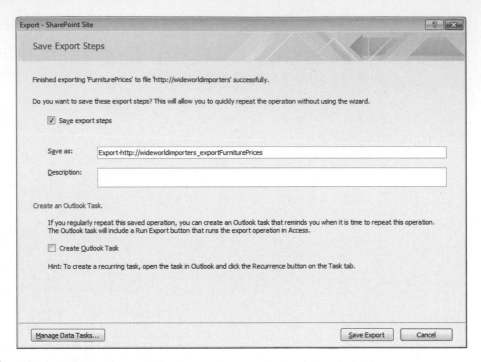

8. Click **Save Export**. The Export – SharePoint Site dialog box closes.

To export the data to a SharePoint list, Access queries the Access table for data, which it then copies to the SharePoint list. By saving the export query, you can now repeat the above steps without using the wizard. Your saved exports can be found under the External Data tab in the Export group. Similarly, you can save your export as a Microsoft Outlook task, which you can then configure to remind you to run the export query.

✖ CLEAN UP Close the ExpImpWideWorldImporters.accdb database and close the browser. Choose No if prompted to save the changes.

Importing a List to an Access Database

By using Access 2010, you can create a new table by importing data from an external data source, such as a dBase database, an Excel workbook, an Outlook or a Microsoft Exchange Server folder, an XML document, an ODBC data source, or a SharePoint website. The new table becomes an integral part of your database, and the data is not affected by subsequent changes made to the data source after it is imported.

In this exercise, you will import data from a SharePoint list.

> **Practice Files** You will use the practice file ExpImpWideWorldImporters2010.accdb, located in the Documents\Microsoft Press\SBS_SPF\Chapter14 folder.

SET UP Start Access 2010 and open the ExpImpWideWorldImporters2010.accdb database that you used in the previous exercise. You can also use your own list if you want. Remember to use your SharePoint site location in place of *http://wideworldimporters* in the following exercise.

BE SURE TO verify that you have sufficient rights to read list items. If in doubt, see the Appendix at the back of this book.

SharePoint List

1. On the Access ribbon, click the **External Data** tab. In the **Import & Link** group, click **More**, and then click **SharePoint List**.

   The Get External Data – SharePoint Site dialog box appears.

2. In the **Specify a SharePoint site** area, choose the site that contains the list with the data that you want to import into the database.

   Troubleshooting If the URL for the SharePoint site does not appear, type the URL in the text box.

3. Select the **Import the source data into a new table in the current database** option.

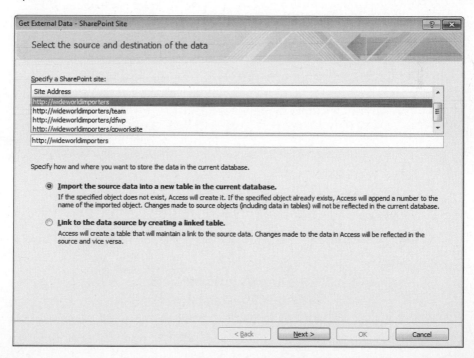

4. Click **Next**. The Import Data From List page of the Get External Data – SharePoint Site dialog box appears.

5. Select the check box to the left of the list from which you want to import the data, such as **exportFurniturePrices**.

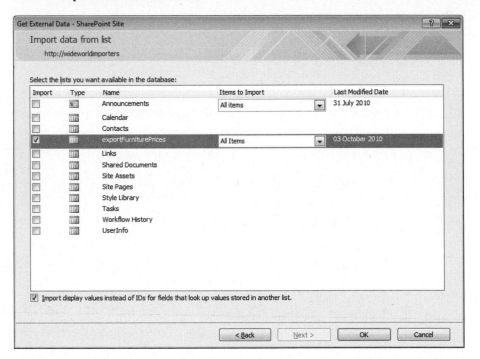

Tip When you import data from a SharePoint list, the imported data is based on a view, and only those columns and rows shown in the view are imported. You can select the required view from the Items To Import drop-down list.

The Import page displays values instead of IDs for lookup values stored in another list, and allows you to maintain the lookup relationship that this list may have with other SharePoint lists.

6. Click **OK**. The Save Import Steps page of the Get External Data – SharePoint Site dialog box appears.

7. Click **Close**. The Get External Data – SharePoint Site dialog box closes, and the exportFurniturePrices table appears under Tables in the Access navigation pane.

8. Double-click the **exportFurniturePrices** table. Access opens the exportFurniturePrices table in Datasheet view.

Troubleshooting If a table is not created from your SharePoint list, then a table called Web Compatibility Issues is created, which lists incompatibilities. Correct the issues and repeat this exercise.

You can now edit the value in the cells of the table. Such changes will not be reflected back in the expFurniturePrice list on the SharePoint website.

Important Changes to the SharePoint list are not copied to the Access table, nor are changes to the Access table reflected in the SharePoint list. A linked object is not created as part of this process.

 CLEAN UP Close the ExpImpWideWorldImporters.accdb database and any open browser windows.

Linking an Access Database to a SharePoint List

Data was copied in the previous two sections so that the same data could be stored in both an Access database and on a list on a SharePoint site. However, no data synchronization between these two data locations occurred. If you do not want to maintain two copies of that data but do need to refer to the data within Access, then Access provides methods of accessing external data that are physically located outside an Access database. The easiest way to reference a SharePoint list externally is to use linked tables, which were known as attached tables prior to Access 95. A linked table stores only a connection to the SharePoint list. You should use linking rather than importing if the data is maintained by either a user or a separate application on the SharePoint website.

Access 2010 contains improvements when the link table data is cached in local tables when online with SharePoint, thereby improving large list performance. When server connectivity is lost, the database automatically goes into offline mode. When connectivity is restored, Access automatically synchronizes data changes for you.

See Also Microsoft Business Connectivity Services (BCS), originally called the Business Data Catalog, is now available in both SharePoint Foundation and SharePoint Server 2010. The definitions that allow BCS to connect to the back-end applications can also be used to reveal external data in Office 2010 applications, including Access 2010, Outlook 2010, Microsoft Workspace 2010, Word 2010, Microsoft InfoPath 2010, and Excel 2010. Information on how to create a BCS definition and how to use the definition in Access 2010 can be found in Chapter 7, "Using Business Connectivity Services," in the book *Microsoft SharePoint Designer 2010 Step by Step,* by Penelope Coventry (Microsoft Press, 2011).

In this exercise, you will link a table to a SharePoint list.

> **Practice Files** You will use the practice file ExpImpWideWorldImporters2010.accdb, located in the Documents\Microsoft Press\SBS_SPF\Chapter14 folder.

 SET UP Start Access 2010 and open the ExpImpWideWorldImporters2010.accdb database that you used in the previous exercise. You can use your own Access database if you wish. Remember to use your SharePoint site location in place of *http://wideworldimporters* in the following exercise.

BE SURE TO verify that you have sufficient rights to edit items in the list. If in doubt, see the Appendix at the back of this book.

SharePoint List

1. On the Access ribbon, click the **External Data** tab. In the **Import & Link** group, click **More**, and then click **SharePoint List**. If an Access dialog box opens, stating that all objects must be closed prior to continuing this operation, click **Yes** to close the objects.

   The Get External Data – SharePoint Site dialog box appears.

2. In the **Specify a SharePoint site** area, choose the site that contains the list to which you wish to link.

   Troubleshooting If the URL for the SharePoint site does not appear, type the URL in the text box.

3. Check that the **Link to the data source by creating a linked table** option is selected, and then click **Next**.

   The Choose The SharePoint Lists You Want To Link To page of the Get External Data – SharePoint site dialog box is displayed.

4. Select the check box to the left of the list to which you wish to link, such as **exportFurniturePrices**.

5. Click **OK**.

   The Get External Data – SharePoint site dialog box closes. Access has a linked table: exportFurniturePrices1. To the far right of the Access status bar, the text "Online with SharePoint" is displayed.

6. Right-click the linked **exportFurniturePrices1** table, and then select **More options**.

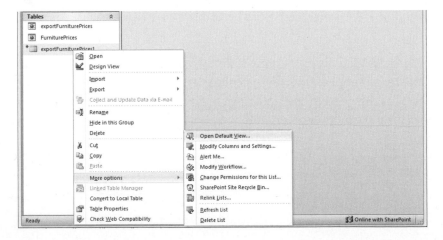

7. Click **Open Default View**.

   The browser opens and displays the exportFurniturePrices list in All Items view.

8. Switch back to Access. Under **All Tables**, in the **exportFurniturePrices1** group, double-click **exportFurniturePrices1** to open the linked table in Datasheet view, and then, click the cell in the first row under the **Furniture Name** column, and type **Base Unit**.

9. Click the cell in the second row under the **Furniture Name** column.

   Important By moving to another row, Access automatically synchronizes changes to the SharePoint list.

Refresh

10. Switch back to the browser, click **Refresh**, and then verify that the first row has been modified.

11. On the Ribbon, click the **Items** tab, and then click **New Item** in the **New** group.

   The exportFurniturePrices – New Item dialog is displayed.

New
Item ▾

12. In the **StockNo** box, type **W0033**, and then click **Save**.

   The W0033 item is added to the list.

   Tip To see the new item in the browser, you will need to scroll to the bottom of the list and click the right arrow to display the next page.

Refresh All

13. Switch back to Access. On the **Home** tab, click **Refresh All**.

   ✖ **CLEAN UP** Close the ExpImpWideWorldImporters.accdb database and any open browser windows.

Linking a Data-centric Application to a SharePoint List

Many Access applications grow from the need to manage and aggregate data. These data-centric applications often prove useful to more than one person in an organization, and thus the need to share them increases. However, Access is not truly meant for concurrent use. As Access database applications grow and become more complex, it is necessary to consider upsizing them to a data repository that can support more users while increasing availability, reliability, and manageability. Beginning with Access 2000, various tools and wizards have helped with this process. Starting with Access 2007, you can now upsize your Access database to SharePoint, which is known as moving your Access database.

Note In Access 2007, moving to and then storing a database in a SharePoint library was known as *publishing*. In Access 2010, publishing a database is used when moving to and storing your Access database in a special SharePoint site, which is known as a *web database site*. You can use web database sites only with SharePoint Server 2010.

When you move data from an Access database to a SharePoint site, this process creates a SharePoint list for each Access table. Data from Access tables is moved into these SharePoint lists, and each data row becomes a list item in a SharePoint list. Tables in the Access database are replaced with linked tables that point to the newly created SharePoint list or lists. The Access database now becomes a user interface to the data by retaining views, reports, and relationships between tables.

Tip Unlike in Access 2007, saving the Access database in a SharePoint library cannot be completed as part of the move process. When an Access database is saved to a SharePoint list, and users open the database in Access to make design changes, the last person who uploads the changed database back to the SharePoint library overwrites changes by other users. Therefore, use the checkout and check-in functionalities of SharePoint libraries when making database design changes.

Because the data is now in SharePoint, you can use SharePoint functionality. For example, you can restore deleted list items from the Recycle Bin and apply workflow rules to data items. If you choose to save the database in the document library, users who want to use the database can navigate to the document library in a browser, where the database can be opened in Access.

Prior to Access 2007, multiple users kept their own copies of an Access database and amended it separately, often not viewing others' amendments until they were included in official documents and the need to amalgamate the changes was recognized. To allow users to keep their own copy of a database, a business process would need to be introduced to maintain the data integrity of the database and distribute updates to the appropriate users. By using the process outlined here, Access 2007 and Access 2010 users can add and modify data by using either SharePoint or the linked tables within the Access database. New views, data relationships, and reports maintained in the Access database file can be managed as any other document when saved in SharePoint, including check-in and checkout facilities. Security on the data and the Access database can be maintained using SharePoint security. To take advantage of these new features, you must move your data from your Access database to SharePoint.

See Also More information on developing Access 2010 hybrid applications can be found at *http://blogs.msdn.com/b/access/archive/2010/07/20/the-access-show-developing-access-2010 -hybrid-apps-with-dick-moffat.aspx.*

In the following exercise, you will move data from within an Access database to a SharePoint site.

> **Practice Files** You will use the practice file MoveWideWorldImporters.accdb, located in the Documents\Microsoft Press\SBS_SPF\Chapter14 folder.

SET UP Start Access 2010 and open the MoveWideWorldImporters.accdb database. Remember to use your SharePoint site location in place of *http://wideworldimporters* in the following exercise.

BE SURE TO verify that you have sufficient rights to create lists. If in doubt, see the Appendix at the back of this book.

SharePoint

1. On the Access ribbon, click the **Database Tools** tab. In the **Move Data** group, click **SharePoint**.

   The Export Tables to SharePoint Wizard is displayed.

2. In the **What SharePoint site do you want to use?** text box, type the name of your SharePoint site, such as **http://wideworldimporters**.

3. Click **Next**.

   The Moving Data to SharePoint Site dialog box displays the progress of the move operation, eventually stating that the tables are shared successfully and noting whether any issues were encountered.

4. Select the **Show Details** check box.

   The Move to SharePoint Site Wizard dialog box displays the tasks that it completed during the move operation. Note that a backup of the database is made.

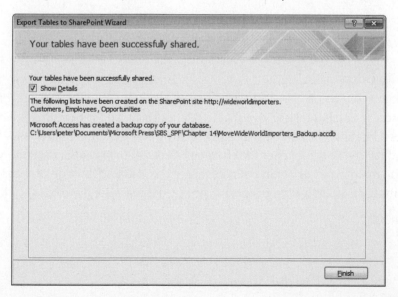

5. Click **Finish**. In the left navigation pane in the Supporting Objects group, the three Access tables—Customers, Employees, and Opportunities—are now linked tables.

6. Click **File** to display the backstage view of Access.

7. In the left navigation pane, click **Save & Publish**.

8. Under **File Types**, verify that **Save Database as** is selected and then, under **Save Database As**, select **SharePoint.**

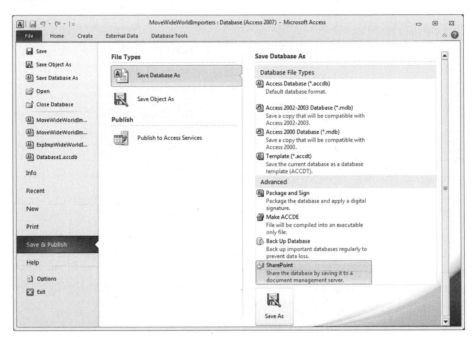

9. Click **Save As**. The Save to SharePoint dialog box is displayed.

Note Saving a database to a document library in Access 2007 is known as publishing the database. In Access 2010, the verb *publish* is used when publishing a database to Access Services, which is a function of SharePoint Server 2010.

10. In the **File name** box, type the URL of the SharePoint site that contains the document library where you wish to save your Access database, such as **http://wideworldimporters**, and then press **ENTER**.

The All Site Content of the SharePoint site is displayed in the Save to SharePoint dialog box.

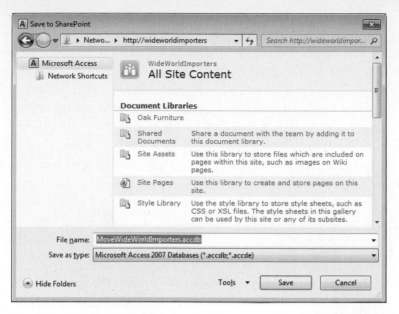

11. Double-click **Shared Documents**. The contents of the Shared Document library are displayed.

12. Click **Save**. The Saving dialog box displays the progress of the save operation. A yellow toolbar labeled Save Changes appears below the Ribbon.

 CLEAN UP Close the MoveWideWorldImporters.accdb database and the browser.

Working Offline

In the previous section, when you moved an Access 2010 data-centric application to a SharePoint site or imported data from a SharePoint list, you created linked tables where you can view and update the data using Access. In these tables, the data is stored outside Access. However, you might still like to access the data in a disconnected environment. When using Access 2007 or Access 2010, you are able to cache SharePoint list data locally in an offline mode. The data that is held locally is not independent of the data in the SharePoint list. You may synchronize changes back to the SharePoint site any time you want.

Tip When an Access database has many linked tables pointing to large SharePoint lists, it may be advisable for performance and storage reasons to create a Access database specifically for users who are constantly taking data offline and are required to synchronize that data over slow network connections.

In this exercise, you will synchronize data and a metadata column with a table linked to a SharePoint list when working offline. This exercise uses the linked tables that were created during the move operation in the previous exercise. You can also use your own tables that are linked to a SharePoint list if you want.

> **Practice Files** You will use the practice file MoveWideWorldImporters.accdb, located in the Documents\Microsoft Press\SBS_SPF\Chapter14 folder.

 SET UP Start Access 2010 and open the MoveWideWorldImporters.accdb database that you saved in the Shared Documents library in the previous exercise. Remember to use your SharePoint site location in place of *http://wideworldimporters* in the following exercise.

BE SURE TO verify that you have sufficient rights to edit items in the lists linked to the Access tables. If in doubt, see the Appendix at the back of this book.

Work Offline

1. On the Access ribbon, click the **External Data** tab, and, in the **Web Linked Lists** group, click **Work Offline**.

   The text "Offline With SharePoint" appears on the status bar. On the External Data tab, in the Web Linked Lists group, the Synchronize and Discard Changes commands are enabled. All data is cached within the Access database, and links to the SharePoint lists are cut temporarily.

   Important If you share this Access database, the data is then visible to users who do not have permissions to view it on the SharePoint site, which could be a security risk.

2. Under the **Supporting Objects** group, double-click **Opportunities**.

Access opens the linked Opportunities table in Datasheet view. The application behaves much as it did online.

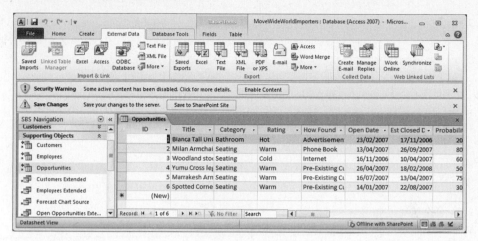

3. Right-click **Opportunities**, select **More Options**, and then click **Open Default View**. The browser opens and displays the Opportunities list in All Items view.

4. Switch back to Access. In the Datasheet view of the **Opportunities** table, click the cell in the first row under the **Title** column and type **Bianca Corner Unit**. Click a cell in the second row.

Troubleshooting If an Access dialog box opens, stating that a value must be greater than 1/1/1900, click OK to close the dialog box. Press the **ESC** key to discard your changes. On the External Data tab, in the Web Linked Lists group, click Work Online, and then repeat steps 1, 2, and 4.

Pencil Icon

A dimmed pencil icon in the first column of the first row indicates that you have made changes to this row. When you are online with the SharePoint website, moving out of the row that you are editing causes Access to synchronize changes. The dimmed icon indicates that this has not occurred here.

5. Switch back to the browser. Click **Refresh**, and then verify that the first row has not been modified.

6. In the browser, click the cell in the first row under **Title**, type **Woodland Bench**, and then click a cell in the second row.

Synchronize

7. Switch back to Access. On the **External Data** tab, in the **Web Linked Lists** group, click **Synchronize**.

Access temporarily connects to the SharePoint list to synchronize changes. The Resolve Conflicts dialog box appears.

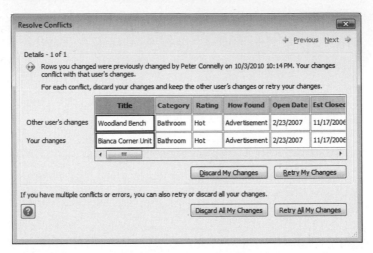

8. Click **Discard My Changes**. The Access database remains offline, and the Datasheet view of the Opportunities table closes.

9. Under **Supporting Objects**, double-click **Opportunities**.

   Access opens the linked Opportunities table in Datasheet view, and the Title column of the first row contains the text "Woodland Bench."

10. In the Datasheet view of the **Opportunities** table, click the cell in the first row under the **Title** column and type **Bianca Corner Unit**. Click a cell in the second row.

11. On the **External Data** tab, in the **Web Linked Lists** group, click **Work Online**.

    The text "Online with SharePoint" appears in the status bar, and the Datasheet view of the Opportunities table closes.

12. Switch back to the browser. Click **Refresh**, and then verify that the first row contains the text "Bianca Corner Unit."

Create Column

13. On the Ribbon, click the **List** tab, and then, in the **Manage Views** group, click **Create Column**.

14. In the **Name and Type** section, in the **Column name** box, type **Advertisement** and select the **Yes/No** option. Click **OK**.

    The Opportunities page is displayed with the Advertisement column at the end of the list.

15. Switch back to Access. Under **Supporting Objects**, right-click **Opportunities**, click **More options**, and then click **Refresh List**.

16. Open the **Opportunities** table, if necessary, and check that the **Advertisement** column is visible.

✖ **CLEAN UP** Close the MoveWideWorldImporters.accdb database and the browser.

Key Points

- You can create a custom list from the browser by importing data from an Excel 2007 or Excel 2010 spreadsheet.

- You can create an Excel 2007 or Excel 2010 spreadsheet from the browser and export data into it from a SharePoint list.

- From within Excel 2007 or Excel 2010, you can export data from an Excel table into a newly created SharePoint list.

- You can synchronize changes between a SharePoint list and an Excel 2007 or Excel 2010 spreadsheet. This is a one-way synchronization process.

- Integration with SharePoint Foundation makes Access 2010 a great collaboration tool, while also enabling data to be stored on enterprise servers for better manageability.

- Access 2010 allows you to export and import data to and from SharePoint lists. Data in the Access table is not affected by subsequent changes made to the SharePoint list because there is no synchronization process between Access 2010 and a SharePoint site.

- When using Access 2010, you should create a new table that's linked to a SharePoint list where data is maintained by users on the SharePoint website and you want Access 2010 to use the most current data. This functions well for data that are shared between people and enables you to take advantage of SharePoint features such as workflow, security, and searching.

- You can use linked tables in Access 2010 to enter data into SharePoint lists, where two-way synchronization is provided, and you can maintain a cache to use when working offline.

- In Access 2010, you can move a database to a SharePoint site. Data is moved into SharePoint lists, and then, if you want, you can save the Access database in a document library.

Chapter at a Glance

Create a form library from InfoPath, page 428

Modify a form library template, page 434

Create a custom document information panel, page 440

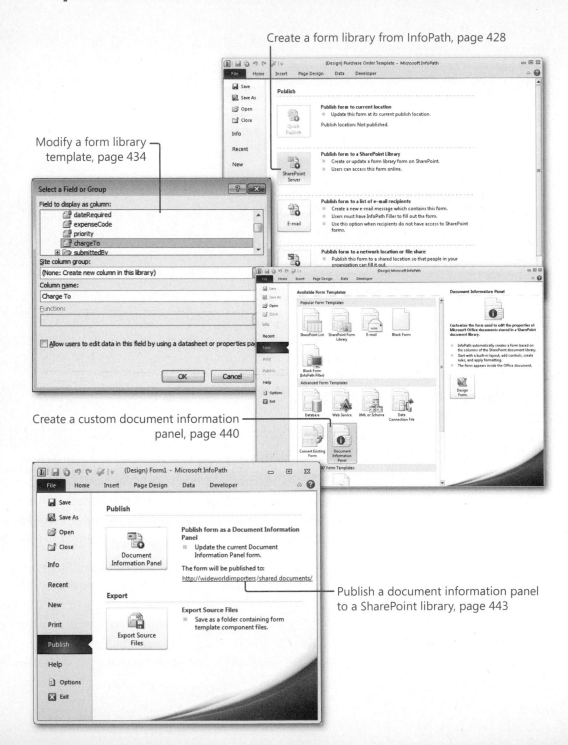

Publish a document information panel to a SharePoint library, page 443

15 Using SharePoint Foundation with InfoPath 2010

In this chapter, you will learn how to

- ✔ Create a form library.
- ✔ Modify a form library.
- ✔ Create a new form.
- ✔ Edit an existing form.
- ✔ Create and modify a custom Office document information panel in InfoPath.
- ✔ Edit custom document properties and view them in SharePoint document library.

Microsoft SharePoint Foundation 2010 provides many features that allow you to use Microsoft InfoPath Designer 2010 and Microsoft InfoPath Filler 2010 in a SharePoint context. In particular, SharePoint form libraries provide the primary integration point between SharePoint Foundation and InfoPath 2010. *Form libraries* allow you to use and share InfoPath 2010 forms. An *InfoPath form* collects information from a user in a structured way. InfoPath Designer 2010 allows you to design form templates, while InfoPath Filler 2010 allows you to fill out the forms. Form libraries provide a central location where users can fill out and store forms based on the same template. For example, you can use InfoPath Filler 2010 to fill out purchase orders and subsequently store them in a SharePoint form library.

In this chapter, you will learn how to use InfoPath 2010 to work with SharePoint form libraries and the forms stored within these libraries. You will create a SharePoint form library and modify an existing form library from InfoPath Designer 2010. You will then use InfoPath Filler 2010 to fill out new forms based on a form library's template, as well as edit existing forms stored in the form library. In addition, you will learn what a *document information panel* is and how to create and customize the document information panel based on an InfoPath Designer 2010 template. Finally, you will use the document information panel to view and edit properties of a Microsoft Word 2010 document.

See Also SharePoint Server 2010 includes InfoPath Form Services that provide more features and functionality for InfoPath integration than SharePoint Foundation 2010, such as browser-enabled form templates that enable forms to be displayed and filled out using the browser. For more information, refer to *http://technet.microsoft.com/en-us/library/cc303431.aspx*.

> **Practice Files** Before you can complete the exercises in this chapter, you need to (1) download the Chapter 15 practice files from the book's catalog page to the following folder on your computer: Documents\Microsoft Press\SBS_SPF\Chapter15 and (2) install the Chapter 15 practice site using the Chapter15_Starter.wsp file. See "Using the Practice Files" at the beginning of this book for more information.

Important Remember to use your SharePoint site location in place of *http://wideworldimporters* in the following exercises.

Creating a Form Library

A SharePoint form library stores forms that are based on the same form template. An *InfoPath form template* is a file that defines the appearance, structure, and behavior of an InfoPath 2010 form. Form templates allow form designers to create the look, feel, and functionality of the form. After the form template is created, users create new forms by filling out the fields provided by the template.

Tip Forms that are stored in SharePoint form libraries can be taken offline using SharePoint Workspace.

In Microsoft Office 2010, there are two separate InfoPath 2010 products: InfoPath Designer 2010 and InfoPath Filler 2010. InfoPath Designer 2010 allows designers to create form templates. For example, a template for purchase orders can be created in InfoPath Designer 2010. InfoPath Filler 2010 provides users with a familiar Office environment where they create new forms by filling out the fields provided to them by the form template. For example, a new purchase order can be created in InfoPath Filler 2010 based on the purchase order template.

In the previous two versions of Office, there was only one product—InfoPath. It had two different modes: Design mode and Fill Out A Form mode. Design mode was similar to InfoPath Designer 2010, and Fill Out A Form mode was similar to InfoPath Filler 2010. However, InfoPath 2010 provides more features and functionality than its predecessor, InfoPath 2007.

See Also To learn more about the differences between InfoPath 2010 and InfoPath 2007, refer to *http://blogs.msdn.com/b/infopath/archive/2009/07/15/what-s-new-in-infopath-2010.aspx*.

When you create a new SharePoint form library from InfoPath Designer 2010, you publish a form template into a newly created library. The library is then associated with this template, and every form in this library has the same appearance and structure.

See Also You can also create a form library from a SharePoint site. For detailed instructions, refer to Chapter 5, "Working with Libraries."

In the following exercise, you will use InfoPath Designer 2010 to create a new SharePoint form library named Purchase Orders.

> **Practice Files** You will use the practice file Purchase Order Template.xsn, located in the Documents\Microsoft Press\SBS_SPF\Chapter15 folder.

 SET UP Open InfoPath Designer 2010 before beginning this exercise. Close the Getting Started window if it appears.

BE SURE TO verify that you have sufficient rights to create a library in your site. If in doubt, see the Appendix at the back of this book.

1. In InfoPath Designer, on the **File** tab, click **Open**.

   Tip The File tab in InfoPath acts as a toggle that takes the user from the back view to the onstage view.

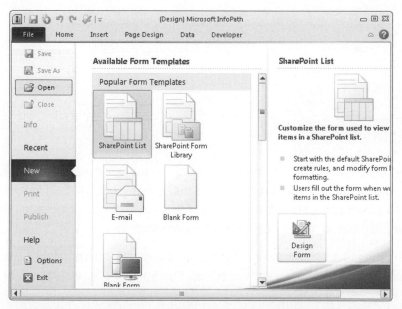

2. Navigate to the **Documents\Microsoft Press\SBS_SPF\Chapter15** folder, select **Purchase Order Template.xsn**, and click **Open**.

   The Purchase Order template opens in Design mode. Note the Fields pane that appears on the right of the InfoPath window.

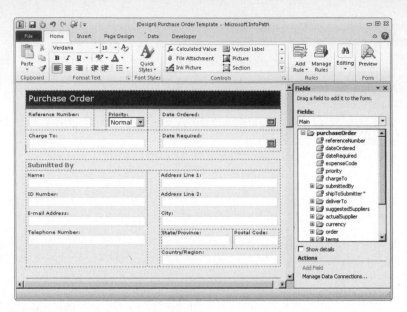

3. On the **File** menu, click **Publish**.

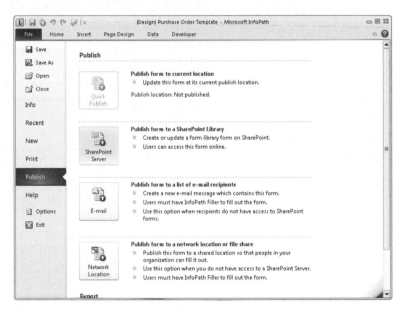

4. On the page listing the options for publishing location, select **SharePoint Server: Publish form to a SharePoint Library**. The InfoPath Publishing Wizard opens.

5. On the first page of the Publishing Wizard, in the **Enter the location of your SharePoint or InfoPath Forms Services site**, type the Uniform Resource Locator (URL) of the SharePoint site in which you want to create the form library, such as *http://wideworldimporters*. Click **Next**.

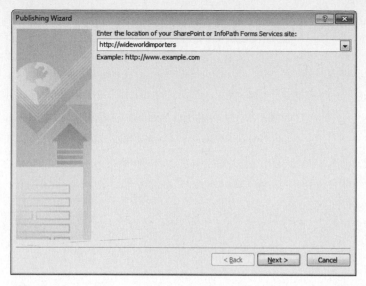

6. If prompted, type your user name and password for the SharePoint site, and click **OK**.

7. On the next page, select **Form library**, and click **Next**.

8. On the next page, select **Create a new form library**, and click **Next**.

9. On the next page, in the **Name** box, type the name for the form library, such as **Purchase Orders**. In the **Description** box, type a description of the information in the form library that you are creating, such as **Contains purchase orders**. Click **Next**.

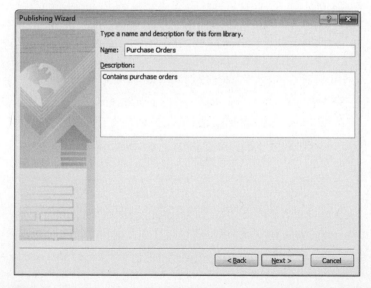

Tip You have to provide a name for your new library, but a description is optional.

10. The next page in the Publishing Wizard allows you to define the layout of the Form
Library page. The form library displays the form data in a table. Data in the table
columns comes from the form fields. This page of the Publishing Wizard allows you
to create the table layout by defining the form fields that you want to become the
columns in the table.

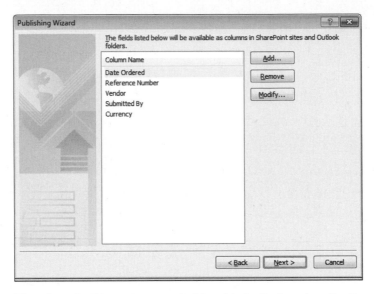

Tip After the library is created, this table is displayed on the Form Library page in the
library's default view.

The table columns for this form library are listed in the Column Name list. Five form
fields will become columns after the library is created: Date Ordered, Reference
Number, Vendor, Submitted By, and Currency. Because the majority of orders for
Wide World Importers use the same currency, the owner has decided not to display
the currency used in the purchase orders on the site.

11. To prevent the Currency column from appearing in the form library, select
Currency, and then click **Remove**.

The Currency column is removed from the Column Name list.

12. Click **Next**.

Tip Table contents on the Form Library page can be searched on a SharePoint site.
Therefore, if you want to make particular form data searchable, make sure the field that
contains this data becomes a table column.

13. On the next page, verify the form information that you provided and then click
Publish. The form library is created.

14. On the confirmation page, select **Open this form library**, and then click **Close**.

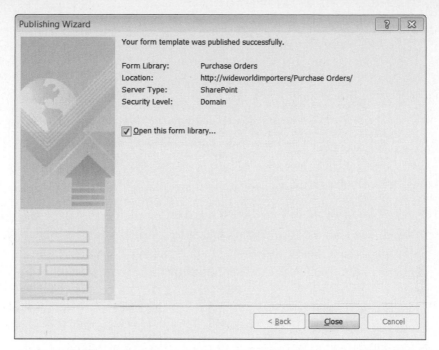

The Purchase Orders library page appears in the browser. The library is empty. Note that the name of the library appears on the Quick Launch, under Libraries.

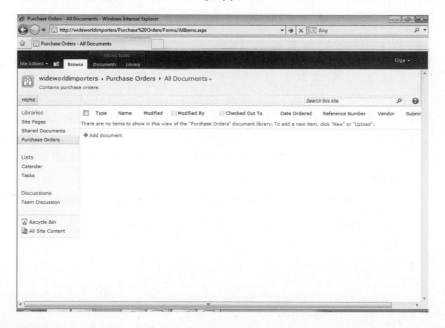

 CLEAN UP Close InfoPath Designer 2010 and close the browser.

Tip When the form template is published to the SharePoint library, it is stored in the Forms folder in this library with the default name Template.xsn. If you want to verify that your template has been published, start the browser and go to the site to which you published a template, such as *http://wideworldimporters*. Click All Site Content in the left navigation panel. Under Document Libraries, click the Purchase Orders library. On the Form Library page, from the Library Tools group on the Ribbon, select the Library tab, and in the Connect & Export group, click Open with Explorer. The Forms folder is displayed in Windows Explorer, and your form template is stored inside this folder. Double-click the Forms folder to verify that Template.xsn is inside this folder. After locating the form template, close Windows Explorer and then close the browser.

Modifying a Form Library

To modify an existing form library, you can change the form template on which the library is based. Care must be used when changing a form template because your changes might result in the loss of data within the existing forms in the library that are based on this template. For example, if you remove a field from a form template, this field no longer appears in the existing forms that are based on that form template; consequently, the data in this field is lost. However, if you are making additions to the form or changing its appearance, you shouldn't lose any data.

Tip If in doubt, do not modify the existing library. Instead, publish the changed form template to a new form library.

In this exercise, you will modify the existing form library from InfoPath Designer 2010. In the Purchase Orders form library template, you will change the form title to "Wide World Importers Purchase Orders," and then add the Charge To column to the table layout of the Form Library page.

 SET UP Open the SharePoint site in which your existing form library is located. If prompted, type your user name and password, and click OK.

BE SURE TO verify that you have sufficient rights to modify this library. If in doubt, see the Appendix at the back of this book.

1. On the Quick Launch, click the **Purchase Orders** library.

2. On the **Purchase Orders** form library page, from the **Library Tools** group on the Ribbon, click the **Library** tab.

3. In the **Settings** group, click **Library Settings**.

Library Settings

4. On the **Form Library Settings** page, in the **General Settings** section, click **Advanced settings**.

5. On the **Form Library Settings: Advanced Settings** page, in the **Document Template** section, under **Template URL**, click **(Edit Template)**.

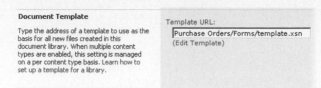

6. If prompted, type your user name and password for the SharePoint site, and then click **OK**.

7. If a dialog box appears that asks whether you want to continue, click **Yes**.

The Purchase Orders form template opens in InfoPath Designer 2010.

8. Position your cursor to the left of the **Purchase Order** heading. Type **Wide World Importers** so that the heading reads "Wide World Importers Purchase Order."

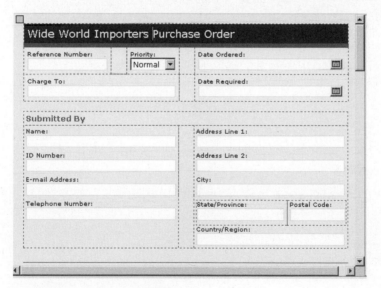

9. On the **File** tab, click **Publish**.

10. On the page listing the options for publishing location, select **SharePoint Server: Publish form to a SharePoint Library**. The InfoPath Publishing Wizard opens.

11. On the first page, in the **Enter the location of your SharePoint or InfoPath Forms Services site**, keep the URL of the SharePoint library that you want to edit the template for, such as *http://wideworldimporters/Purchase Orders*. Click **Next**.

12. On the next page, make sure that **Form Library** is selected, and then click **Next**.

13. On the next page, click **Update the form template in an existing form library**, and then select the **Purchase Orders** library from the list of existing libraries. Click **Next**.

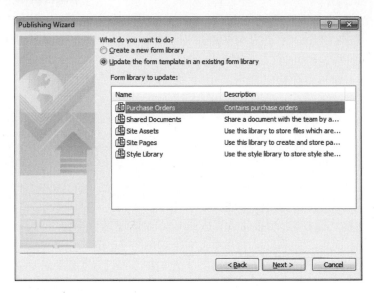

You will now modify the table layout for the Form Library page by adding a Charge To column.

14. On the page that lists column names, click **Add**. The Select A Field Or Group dialog box appears.

15. Select the **chargeTo** field. In the **Column name** box, edit the field so that it reads **Charge To**. Click **OK**.

Charge To is added to the list of column names.

16. Click **Next**.

17. On the next page, verify that the form information is correct, and then click **Publish**. The modified template has been published to the SharePoint site.

18. On the confirmation page, select the **Open this form library** check box and click **Close**. The browser opens the modified form library. Verify that the new Charge To column heading has been added and is displayed at the far right of the page.

 CLEAN UP Close InfoPath Designer 2010, and then close the browser.

Creating a New Form

After a form library is created, users can fill out new forms and edit existing forms in the library.

In the following exercise, you will create a new form and save it to the SharePoint form library.

➡ **SET UP** Open the SharePoint site in which the form library is located. If prompted, type your user name and password, and click OK.

BE SURE TO verify that you have sufficient rights to create forms in this library. If in doubt, see the Appendix at the back of this book.

1. In the left navigation panel, click **All Site Content**.

2. Under **Libraries**, click the **Purchase Orders** library.

3. On the **Purchase Orders** form library page, click **Add document**. Alternatively, in the **Library Tools** group on the Ribbon, click the **Documents** tab and, in the **New** group, click the **New Document** button.

InfoPath Filler 2010 opens and displays a new form based on the Purchase Order template. You will now fill out the form.

4. In the **Reference Number** field, type **12345**. Under **Vendor Information**, in the **Company name** field, type **Contoso**. Fill out other form fields with fictitious data.

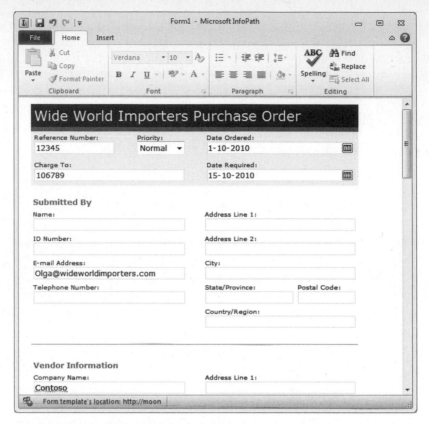

5. From the **File** menu, click **Save As**. The Save As dialog box appears.

6. In the **File Name** box, type **ContosoPO**.

7. Click **Save**. The form is saved to the Purchase Orders form library.

8. From the Windows taskbar, restore the browser that points to the Purchase Orders form library.

9. Refresh the browser and verify that the ContosoPO form is listed in the library.

 CLEAN UP Close InfoPath Filler 2010, and then close the browser.

Editing a Form

You might often find yourself in a situation in which you need to edit an existing form that is stored in the SharePoint form library, such as correcting mistyped data. The existing form is edited in InfoPath Filler 2010 and then saved to the form library.

In this exercise, you will edit the existing form and save it back to the form library.

SET UP Open the SharePoint site in which the form library is located. If prompted, type your user name and password, and click OK.

BE SURE TO verify that you have sufficient rights to edit forms in this library. If in doubt, see the Appendix at the back of this book.

1. Navigate to the **Purchase Orders** library.

2. On the **Purchase Orders** page, hover the mouse over the **ContosoPO** name so that the arrow appears to the right. Click the arrow, and then select **Edit in Microsoft InfoPath**.

   Tip You can also simply click the ContosoPO name. If the File Download dialog box appears, click Open.

3. The ContosoPO form opens in InfoPath Filler 2010. Change the **Reference Number** to **12346**.

4. In InfoPath, from the **File** menu, select **Save**. The form is saved to the Purchase Orders form library.

5. From the Windows taskbar, restore the browser that points to the Purchase Orders form library.

6. Refresh the browser and verify that the edited form with reference number 12346 is listed in the library.

You will now edit the ContosoPO form and save it under a different name.

7. On the **Purchase Orders** form library page, hover the mouse over the **ContosoPO** name so that the arrow appears to the right. Click the arrow and then select **Edit in Microsoft InfoPath**.

8. The ContosoPO form opens in InfoPath Filler 2010. Change the **Reference Number** to **12347**.

9. Under **Vendor Information**, change the **Company name** to **Northwind Traders**. Feel free to make other changes to the form data if you want.

10. In InfoPath, from the **File** menu, choose **Save As**. The Save As dialog box appears.

11. In the **File Name** box, type **NorthwindPO**, and then click **Save**. The form is saved to the Purchase Orders form library.

12. From the Windows taskbar, restore the browser that points to the **Purchase Orders** form library.

13. Refresh the browser and verify that the NorthwindPO form is listed in the library.

![CLEAN UP icon] **CLEAN UP** Close InfoPath Filler 2010, and then close the browser.

Creating a Custom Office Document Information Panel

Document properties, also known as *document metadata,* are specific details about a particular document, such as document title, author name, subject, date when it was last modified, whether the file is read-only, and other file characteristics. You can specify document properties from the File tab in Office 2010 applications, including Microsoft Word 2010, Microsoft Excel 2010, Microsoft PowerPoint 2010, and Microsoft Access 2010.

When an Office document is saved, you can view and modify properties for that document by right-clicking the file in Windows Explorer and selecting Properties. The collection of properties, or metadata, is displayed in the document information panel.

In SharePoint 2010, document properties are displayed as columns in a Document Library page. You can create a custom document information panel and modify an existing document information panel from within InfoPath Designer 2010. The custom document information panel is then used instead of the automatically generated document information panel in the SharePoint library. When you create a custom document information panel using InfoPath Designer 2010, you start with the automatically generated document information panel on which a SharePoint library is based, and then you modify it. The document information panel is an InfoPath 2010 form that provides a template for the metadata for the documents stored in this SharePoint library.

Tip You can create only one document information panel per content type.

See Also For more information about creating document information panels, refer to *http://msdn.microsoft.com/en-us/library/ms563688.aspx.*

In the following exercise, you will use InfoPath Designer 2010 to create a custom document information panel for a document library based on a default Document content type.

Important The exercises in the rest of this chapter use the default Document content type that the document libraries are based on. It is not recommended that you change this content type on the live site that already has documents stored in the libraries. Instead, you can create a practice site based on the site template provided in the Chapter 15 practice file folder and use the CustomDocument content type in place of the Document content type in the following exercise and the subsequent sections in this chapter.

SET UP Open InfoPath Designer 2010 before beginning this exercise. Close the Getting Started window if it appears.

BE SURE TO verify that you have sufficient rights to modify the library. If in doubt, see the Appendix at the back of this book.

1. In InfoPath Designer 2010, from the **File** menu, choose **New**, select **Document Information Panel**, and click **Design Form**. The Data Source Wizard opens.

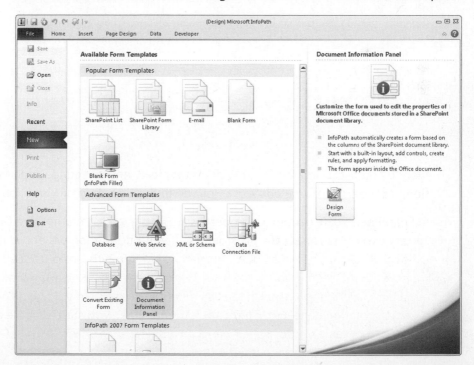

2. On the first page of the **Data Source Wizard**, in the **Enter the address location of the document library you want to modify**, type the URL of the SharePoint document library in which you want to create a custom document information panel, such as **http://wideworldimporters/Shared Documents.** Click **Next**. InfoPath connects to the library and obtains information about content types in this library and the columns that are configured to be displayed on the library page.

3. On the page listing the content types that are associated with the document library, select **Document**. Click **Next**.

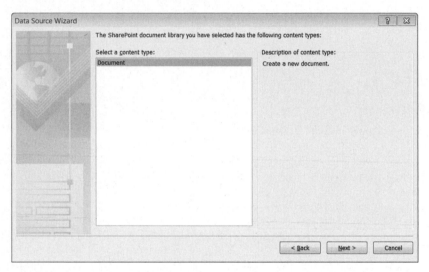

4. On the last page of the **Data Source Wizard**, click **Finish**.

5. InfoPath Designer 2010 opens the automatically generated document information panel.

6. You will now modify the panel. In the panel, above the **Title** box, type **My Custom Document Information Panel**.

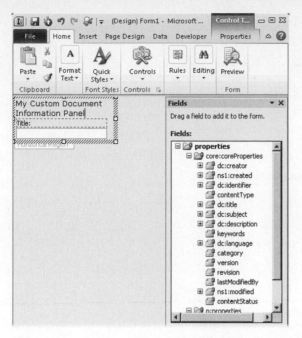

7. You will now publish the custom panel back to the library. On the **File** menu, click **Publish**, and then select **Document Information Panel**.

You are prompted to save the panel before you can publish it. To do this, click OK, and then browse to the location where you would like to save the panel and click Save. The Publishing Wizard opens.

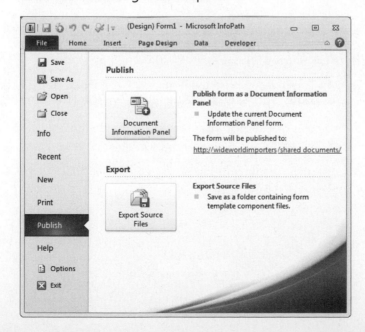

8. In the Publishing Wizard, click **Publish**. The document information panel is published to the SharePoint library.

9. On the confirmation page, click **Close**.

 **CLEAN UP** Close InfoPath Designer 2010.

Viewing and Editing Custom Document Properties

You can view and edit properties of Office documents that are stored in a SharePoint library based on a custom document information panel using the Office applications that created these documents, such as Word 2010, Excel 2010, and PowerPoint 2010.

See Also SharePoint 2010 allows you to display any document property in a table column in a document library through a mechanism called *property promotion/demotion*. For more information about promotion and demotion of document properties, see *http://msdn.microsoft.com/en-us/library/aa543341.aspx*.

In the following exercise, you will create a new document from the SharePoint library, edit a property of this document in Word 2010, save the document back to the library, and then view the document in a Document Library page.

 SET UP Open a SharePoint site where you'd like to view and edit the properties of a document. If prompted, type your user name and password, and then click OK.

BE SURE TO verify that you have sufficient rights to edit documents in this library. If in doubt, see the Appendix at the back of this book.

1. Navigate to the **Shared Documents** document library.

2. In the **Library Tools** group on the Ribbon, click the **Documents** tab. In the **New** group, click the **New Document** button. Word 2010 opens.

3. In Word, open the **Document Information Panel** by going to the **File** tab, selecting **Info**, clicking **Properties**, and then selecting **Show Document Panel**.

   In the **Document Information Panel**, notice the text that you added using InfoPath Designer 2010 in the previous exercise.

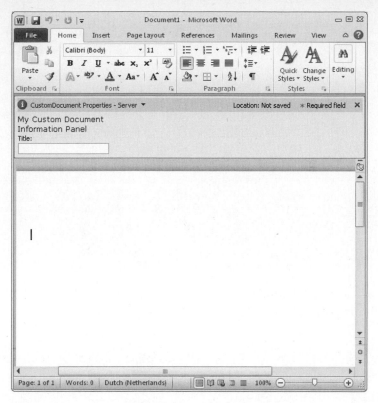

4. You will now fill out the document information panel with the property for this document. In the **Document Information Panel**, in the **Title** box, type **My Title**.

5. On the **File** tab, click **Save**.

6. From the Windows taskbar, restore the browser that points to the **Shared Documents** library.

7. Refresh the browser and verify that there is a document called "My Title" listed in the library in the **Title** column.

 CLEAN UP Close Word 2010, and then close the browser.

Editing a Custom Document Information Panel

If you need to change a custom document information panel that you created earlier, you can edit it in InfoPath Designer 2010. Doing this in SharePoint Foundation requires several steps: locating the existing document information panel file in the SharePoint library, manually opening it in InfoPath from the file system, editing it in InfoPath, and finally publishing it back into the SharePoint library.

Tip Editing the document information panel is much easier in SharePoint Server. All you need to do is click a link called Document Information Panel Settings on the content type settings page. This allows you to either create a new document information panel or edit an existing one.

See Also For more information about changing a document information panel, refer to *http://msdn.microsoft.com/en-us/library/ms494347.aspx*.

In this exercise, you will locate and edit the document information panel that you created in the previous exercise.

SET UP Open the SharePoint site in which the document library based on the existing document information panel is located. If prompted, type your user name and password, and click OK.

BE SURE TO verify that you have sufficient rights to modify this library. If in doubt, see the Appendix at the back of this book.

 Open with Explorer **1.** Navigate to the library where you want to edit the document information panel, such as **Shared Documents**. Click the **Library** tab on the Ribbon, and in the **Connect & Export** group, click **Open with Explorer**. The Shared Documents library opens in Windows Explorer.

2. Navigate to the **Forms\\Document** folder and locate a file called *[GUID]***customXsn.xsn**, where *GUID* (Global Unique Identifier) is a hexadecimal prefix that appears before *customXsn* in the file name of the document information panel for this library. In this example, *GUID* is 638295263359396b.

3. Right-click *[GUID]***customXsn.xsn**, and select **Properties.** From the Properties window, make a note of the name of the file (*[GUID]*CustomXsn.xsn) and its location. You will need this information later in the exercise. For example, you can copy and paste the file name and location from the Properties window into Notepad.

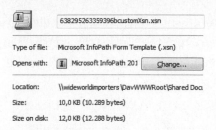

	638295263359396bcustomXsn.xsn
Type of file:	Microsoft InfoPath Form Template (.xsn)
Opens with:	Microsoft InfoPath 201 Change...
Location:	\\wideworldimporters\DavWWWRoot\Shared Docu
Size:	10,0 KB (10.289 bytes)
Size on disk:	12,0 KB (12.288 bytes)

4. Open InfoPath Designer 2010.

5. On the **File** tab, click **Open**. The Open in Design Mode window appears.

6. Browse to the *[GUID]*customXsn.xsn, using the file name and location that you saved in step 3, such as **\\wideworldimporters\DavWWWRoot\Shared Documents\Forms\Document\638295263359396bcustomXsn.xsn**. Click **Open**.

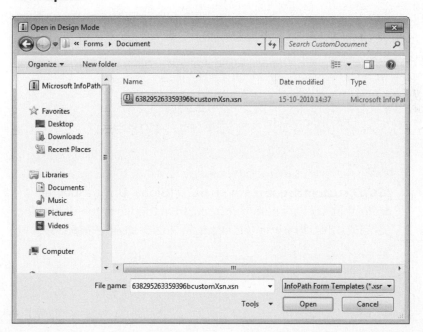

7. The document information panel opens in InfoPath Designer 2010.

8. You can now edit the document information panel in InfoPath Designer 2010. Make one or more changes to it.

9. On the **File** menu, click **Publish**, and then select **Document Information Panel**.

   You will be prompted to save the document information panel before you can publish it. Click **OK**, and then click **Save**. The Publishing Wizard opens.

10. In the Publishing Wizard, click **Publish.** The modified panel has been published back to the Shared Documents library.

11. On the confirmation page of the Publishing Wizard, click **Close**.

12. Optional: using the previous exercise as a guide, create a new document from the Shared Documents library, fill out the modified document information panel in Word 2010, save the document back to the library, and view the changes on the library page in the browser.

✖ CLEAN UP Close Windows Explorer, close InfoPath Designer 2010, and then close the browser. In addition, close Word 2010 if you have it open.

Key Points

- SharePoint form libraries provide the primary integration point between SharePoint Foundation 2010 and InfoPath 2010.

- Form libraries can be created from within InfoPath Designer 2010, as well as from the SharePoint site.

- When you create a new SharePoint form library from InfoPath Designer 2010, you publish a form template into a newly created library.

- You can define a table layout on the Form Library page when you publish the form template into this library.

- After the form library has been created, you can modify its template by using InfoPath Designer 2010.

- You can fill out a new form in the form library using InfoPath Filler 2010.

- To edit an existing form, click the form on the library's page. The form opens in InfoPath Filler 2010. Edit the form data, and then save the form to the library.

- A document information panel contains properties of an Office document. InfoPath Designer 2010 allows you to customize a document information panel for a content type in a SharePoint library. The custom properties are displayed as columns on a library page.

Chapter at a Glance

Execute a simple search query, page 454

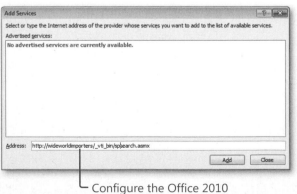

Execute a complex search query, page 455

Search a SharePoint site from within Office 2010, page 459

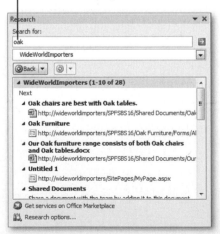

Configure the Office 2010 Research pane, page 458

16 Finding Information on the SharePoint Site

In this chapter, you will learn how to

✔ Search the SharePoint site.

✔ Search for files across multiple document libraries from within Microsoft Office 2010.

Two basic methods are available to find information in Microsoft SharePoint Foundation 2010. The first method is to browse a hierarchical structure of links and pages to find the information that you need. The second—and often faster—method of finding information is to search for it.

Searching for information is the process of entering one or more words in the search box to form a search query that is executed against the index built on the SharePoint servers by your system administrators. The servers process your *query* and return a set of *content items* that match your query. These content items contain links to the list items, documents, lists, libraries, or sites that you want to find.

This chapter introduces the basic concepts of how to execute search queries.

> **Practice Files** Before you can complete the exercises in this chapter, you need to (1) download the Chapter 16 practice files from the book's catalog page to the following folder on your computer: Documents\Microsoft Press\SBS_SPF\Chapter16 and (2) install the Chapter 16 practice site using the Chapter16_Starter.wsp file. See "Using the Practice Files" at the beginning of this book for more information.

Important Remember to use your SharePoint site location in place of *http://wideworldimporters* in the following exercises.

Searching the SharePoint Site

Before discussing the execution of a search query, certain basic concepts must be covered. A search query contains one or more words that represent the content that you are trying to find. When executing a query, SharePoint returns a set of content items that form a result set. Your queries are executed against a summary of the content, known as an *index*, which enables SharePoint to respond quickly. You can think of the search index as similar to the index you find at the end of this book. The index is updated periodically. By default, it is refreshed once every hour, but the frequency can be configured differently by your SharePoint administrator. Therefore, when you create new data in your SharePoint site, such as a new announcement, it may not appear immediately in your result set. Similarly, if you delete a document from a document library, it still may appear in the result set, but when you click the link for the document, an error message, "The webpage cannot be found," displays. The link to the document in the result set is called a *broken link*.

Troubleshooting If you query to locate information that you know exists and it doesn't appear in your result set, check the spelling of your search query, wait the length of time set by your SharePoint administrator, and repeat the search query. If it still does not appear in the result set, then the index has not been updated, so contact your SharePoint administrator for assistance.

To find information, you may need to enter more than one query term. The more query terms you enter, the more discriminating your query becomes, thereby producing a more focused result set. Search queries can comprise any of the following items:

- A single word
- Multiple words
- A single phrase in quotes
- Multiple phrases in quotes

Note The search box is limited to a maximum of 255 characters.

SharePoint does an implicit *AND* when you search for multiple words or multiple phrases. For example, when you search for the multiple, separate words "oak" and "furniture," the result set contains only those content items where both words occur. Those words do not have to be side by side, but they do both need to be in the content item somewhere. If a document contains the words "oak" and "chest" but not "oak" and "furniture," that document will not appear in the result set. When you search for the complete phrase "oak furniture," the result set contains only those content items where the two words "oak furniture" appear together.

Note Links to files that are attached to list items do not appear in the result set; however, if an attachment contains the words or phrases you are searching for, then a link to the list item appears in the result set.

When you use two words or two phrases in your search query and separate them by the word *OR*, then when either word or phrase appears in a document, that document appears in the result set. You can create complex search queries, such as *(chest OR furniture) AND oak*. This will return content items that contain the words "oak" and "chest" or the words "oak" and "furniture," but will not return content items that contain the words "chest" and "furniture."

In earlier chapters in this book, you used columns on lists and libraries to save list item and document property values, also known as metadata. You can use some of these *metadata properties* to help you create powerful search queries, thereby creating a more focused result set. Some of the default metadata properties are listed here. For those metadata properties that store text, in the search box, use the syntax *property:value* where *value* is a word or phrase.

- **author** Use this to find all content items authored by a particular person or persons, such as author:peter.

- **filename** Use this to find all documents based on their file name, such as filename:"oak furniture".

- **filetype** Use this to find specific file types, such as filetype:docx.

- **title** Use this to find content items based on the value entered in the title column, such as title:"oak chest".

- **description** Use this to find content items based on the value entered in the description column, such as description:oak.

- **contenttype** Use to find content items of a particular type, such as document, announcement, task, or wiki.

- **Size** Use this to find files according to their size. For example, size>45000 will find all files greater than 45000 bytes.

When you enter a search query on the home page of your site, the result set will return content items from the current site and any subsites below it. When you use a view to display the contents of a list or library and you enter a search query in the search box on those pages, the result set will contain only content items from that list or library. On the Search Results page, you will see a Search Scope drop-down list to the left of the search box, which displays the scope of your result set. For example, if you entered a search query on the home page of your site, then in the scope list, *This Site* is selected. When you enter a search query on a list or library view, then the *This List* scope is selected on the Search Results page. You can then use the scope list to broaden your search query to *This Site*.

Note Other SharePoint products include enhanced search capabilities; for example, SharePoint Server 2010 and Search Server 2010 Express include additional scope and metadata property options and enhancements to the Search Results page, such as the ability to sort the result set by result type, site, or modified date and the ability to subscribe to the search query as a Really Simple Syndication (RSS) feed or by creating an alert and links to data external to SharePoint websites.

In this exercise, you will familiarize yourself with the interface and enter a query phrase to observe how the results are more focused when multiple phrases and properties are entered in the search box.

 SET UP Open the SharePoint site. This exercise will use the *http://wideworldimporters* site, but you can use whatever SharePoint Team site you want. If prompted, type your user name and password, and then click OK.

BE SURE TO verify that you have sufficient permissions to execute a query in the site you are using. If in doubt, see the Appendix at the back of this book.

1. In the upper-right corner of the home page, in the search box, type a query term that can be found in at least one document in your site, such as **oak**, and press **ENTER**.

   Troubleshooting If you cannot see the search box, click the Browse tab.

   The result set contains items that match your query term, including documents and folders. If more than one page of content items matches your query, the total number of pages in the result set appears, with each page number representing a link to that page of the overall result set.

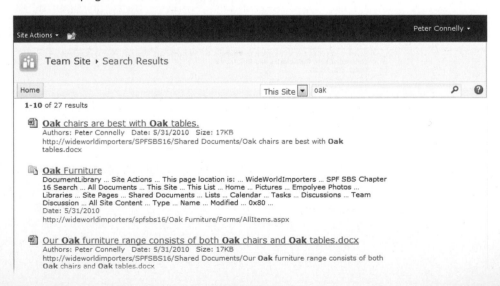

2. In the search box, type a phrase in quotation marks, such as "**oak chairs**", and press **ENTER**.

The number of items returned in the result set is less than what was returned in step 1.

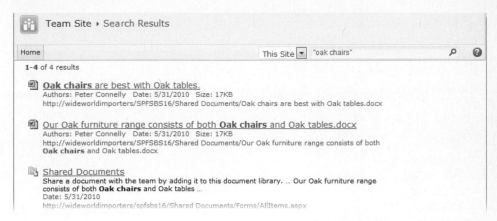

3. Add another phrase, such as "**oak furniture,**" to help make your query more specific.

Now the result set is more focused, containing only content items in the site that contain both phrases.

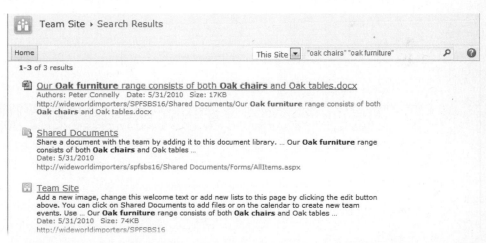

4. Separate the two phrases with the **OR** operator, and then press **ENTER**.

The result set contains items that include either the phrase "oak chairs" or the phrase "oak furniture".

5. In the search box, type a search query for two types of file types that can be found in your site that are authored by a specific person, such as **(filetype:docx OR filetype:jpg) author:peter**.

The result set contains only items authored by Peter that are either Microsoft Office 2007 or Office 2010 files or .jpg files.

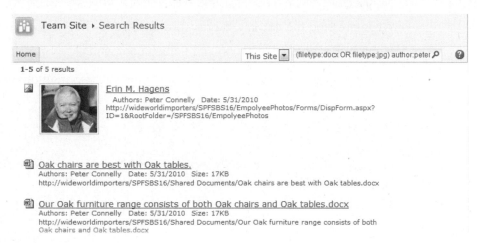

CLEAN UP Close the browser.

Searching for Files Across Multiple Document Libraries from Within Office 2010

When you are using an Office application, you often need to search for information to include in your document. Office 2003, Office 2007, and Office 2010 suites include the Research pane specifically for this reason. The Research pane can display information from local and online thesauruses, translation services, search engines, and business and financial sites. You can also configure the Research pane to retrieve information from other sources, such as SharePoint websites.

Note The Research pane is not available with Microsoft Access 2010, Microsoft InfoPath Designer 2010, Microsoft InfoPath Filler 2010, Microsoft SharePoint Workspace 2010, or Microsoft SharePoint Designer 2010.

The Research pane organizes the sources of information into categories. By default, queries are performed against the All Reference Books category. When you search for information, you can specify an entire category or a single service. Once you have typed a word or phrase into the Research pane search box, the results of the search query are displayed, organized by service in collapsible sections. To view or hide the results for a particular service, use the + or - button in the section header for that service. The Research pane stores the results of previous searches for the duration of the session and provides Back and Forward buttons to navigate through the search result history.

The Research pane can be opened using one of the following methods:

- On the ribbon Review tab, click Research in the Proofing group.

- While pressing the **ALT** key, click a word or selection in the document.

- Right-click a word or selection in the document, and click Look Up.

When you open the Research pane using one of the last two methods in this list, the word or phrase that you click is used as the search query and immediately executed against the default research category to produce the search results.

In this exercise, you will configure the Research pane to connect to a SharePoint site, and then you will use the Research pane to search for content on that SharePoint site.

SET UP Open Microsoft Word. This exercise will use the *http://wideworldimporters* site, but you can use whatever SharePoint Team site you want. If prompted, type your user name and password, and then click OK.

BE SURE TO verify that you have sufficient permissions to execute a query in the site you are using. If in doubt, see the Appendix at the back of this book.

Research

1. On the **Review** tab, click **Research** in the **Proofing** group.

The Research pane opens.

2. At the bottom of the **Research** pane, click **Research options**.

The Research Options dialog box opens.

3. Click **Add Services**.

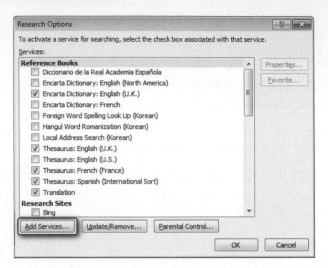

The Add Services dialog box opens in front of the Research Options dialog box, which remains open.

4. In the **Address** box, type the Uniform Resource Locator (URL) of the SharePoint site that you would like to search, and then append **/_vti_bin/spsearch.asmx** to the end of the URL, such as **http://wideworldimporters/_vti_bin/spsearch.asmx**.

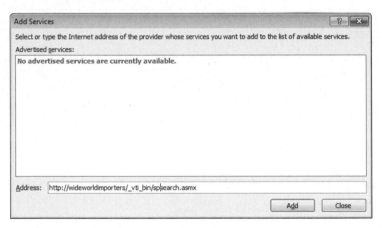

5. Click **Add** to close the **Add Services** dialog box. If prompted, type your user name and password, and then click **OK**.

The Microsoft SharePoint Foundation 2010 Search Setup dialog box automatically opens.

6. Ensure that the check box to the left of your SharePoint site is selected, and then click **Install**.

The Microsoft SharePoint Foundation 2010 Search Setup dialog box closes.

7. Click **OK** in the **Add Services** dialog box that appears.

In the Research Options dialog box, in the Services box, your SharePoint site is added under the Intranet Sites and Portals category. You may need to scroll to find this category.

8. Click **OK** to close the **Research Options** dialog box.

9. In the **Search for** box, in the **Research** pane, type **oak**, and then, from the list, select your SharePoint site, such as **WideWorldImporters**.

Tip You can use the same search queries in the Research pane as you use in the search box when you display your SharePoint site in the browser.

The result set from searching your SharePoint site and the subsites below it is displayed in the search result section of the Research pane.

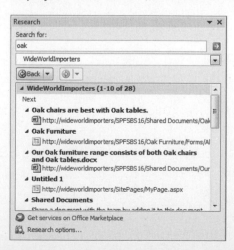

> **Tip** If the text "This service did not respond" appears and no search results are displayed, contact your server administrator.

 **CLEAN UP** Close the browser.

Key Points

- You can find information by searching for it actively instead of browsing for it.
- Enter any combination of words and phrases to help you find the content of your choice.
- Use metadata properties to create powerful search queries to produce a more focused result set.
- Use the Research pane in Office applications to search for content on SharePoint sites.

Appendix

SharePoint Foundation Permissions

Microsoft SharePoint Foundation 2010 includes 32 user permissions that determine the specific actions that users can perform on the site. Permissions are grouped into permission levels. In essence, each permission level is a named collection of permissions that can be assigned to SharePoint users and groups. Five default permission levels are available on every site: Read, Contribute, Design, Full Control, and Limited Access. Table A-1 lists default permission levels along with their corresponding permissions in Microsoft SharePoint Foundation.

Table A-1 **Default Permission Levels**

Permission Level	Description	Permissions Included by Default
Limited Access	Allows access to shared resources in the website so that users can access an item within the site. Designed to be combined with fine-grained permissions to provide users with access to a specific list, document library, item, or document without giving users access to the entire site. Cannot be customized or deleted.	View Application Pages, Browse User Information, Use Remote Interfaces, Use Client Integration Features, Open
Read	Allows read-only access to the website.	View Application Pages, Browse User Information, Use Remote Interfaces, Use Client Integration Features, Open, View Items, Open Items, View Versions, Create Alerts, Use Self-Service Site Creation, View Pages

Permission Level	Description	Permissions Included by Default
Contribute	Allows users to create and edit items in existing lists and document libraries.	View Application Pages, Browse User Information, Use Remote Interfaces, Use Client Integration Features, Open, View Items, Open Items, View Versions, Create Alerts, Use Self-Service Site Creation, View Pages, Add Items, Edit Items, Delete Items, Delete Versions, Browse Directories, Edit Personal User Information, Manage Personal Views, Add/Remove Personal Web Parts, Update Personal Web Parts
Design	Allows users to create lists and document libraries, as well as edit pages in the website.	View Application Pages, Browse User Information, Use Remote Interfaces, Use Client Integration Features, Open, View Items, Open Items, View Versions, Create Alerts, Use Self-Service Site Creation, View Pages, Add Items, Edit Items, Delete Items, Delete Versions, Browse Directories, Edit Personal User Information, Manage Personal Views, Add/Remove Personal Web Parts, Update Personal Web Parts Manage Lists, Override Check Out, Approve Items, Add And Customize Pages, Apply Themes And Borders, Apply Style Sheets
Full Control	Allows full control.	All permissions

You can create new permission levels that contain specific permissions, as well as change which permissions are included in the default permission levels, with a few exceptions. While it is not possible to remove permissions from the Limited Access and Full Control permission levels, your SharePoint administrator can make specific permission levels unavailable for the entire web application by using SharePoint Central Administration. If you are a SharePoint administrator and want to do this, do the following: In SharePoint Central Administration, from the Application Management page, select Manage Web Applications, choose your web application, click the Permission Policy button on the Ribbon, and then delete the permissions levels that you would like to disable.

Depending on the scope, user permissions in SharePoint Foundation can be grouped into three categories: list permissions, site permissions, and personal user permissions. Table A-2 lists user permissions in SharePoint Foundation in alphabetical order, detailing their scope, permission dependencies, and the permission levels that they are in by default.

Table A-2 **User Permissions**

Permission	Description	Scope	Dependent Permissions	Included in These Permission Levels by Default
Add And Customize Pages	Add, change, or delete Hypertext Markup Language (HTML) pages or Web Part pages; edit the website by using a SharePoint Foundation– compatible editor.	Site	View Items, Browse Directories, View Pages, Open	Design, Full Control
Add Items	Add items to lists, documents to document libraries, and web discussion comments.	List	View Items, View Pages, Open	Contribute, Design, Full Control
Add/Remove Personal Web Parts	Add or remove personal Web Parts on a Web Part page.	Personal Permissions	View Items, View Pages, Open	Contribute, Design, Full Control
Apply Style Sheets	Apply a style sheet (.css file) to the website.	Site	View Pages, Open	Design, Full Control
Apply Themes And Borders	Apply a theme or borders to the entire website.	Site	View Pages, Open	Design, Full Control
Approve Items	Approve minor versions of list items or documents.	List	Edit Items, View Items, View Pages, Open	Design, Full Control
Browse Directories	Enumerate files and folders in a website by using Microsoft SharePoint Designer and Web DAV interfaces.	Site	View Pages, Open	Contribute, Design, Full Control
Browse User Information	View information about users of the website.	Site	Open	All

Permission	Description	Scope	Dependent Permissions	Included in These Permission Levels by Default
Create Alerts	Create email alerts.	List	View Items, View Pages, Open	Read, Contribute, Design, Full Control
Create Groups	Create a group of users that can be used anywhere within the site collection.	Site	View Pages, Browse User Information, Open	Full Control
Create Subsites	Create subsites such as Team, Meeting Workspace, and Document Workspace sites.	Site	View Pages, Browse User Information, Open	Full Control
Delete Items	Delete items from a list, documents from a document library, and web discussion comments in documents.	List	View Items, View Pages, Open	Contribute, Design, Full Control
Delete Versions	Delete past versions of list items or documents.	List	View Items, View Versions, View Pages, Open	Contribute, Design, Full Control
Edit Items	Edit items in lists, documents in document libraries, and web discussion comments in documents; customize Web Part pages in document libraries.	List	View Items, View Pages, Open	Contribute, Design, Full Control
Edit Personal User Information	Users can change their own user information, such as adding a picture.	Site	Browse User Information, Open	Contribute, Design

Permission	Description	Scope	Dependent Permissions	Included in These Permission Levels by Default
Enumerate Permissions	Enumerate permissions in the website, list, folder, document, or list item.	Site	Browse Directories, View Pages, Browse User Information, Open	Full Control
Manage Alerts	Manage alerts for all users of the website.	Site	View Items, View Pages, Open	Full Control
Manage Lists	Create and delete lists, add or remove columns in a list, and add or remove public views of a list.	List	View Items, View Pages, Open, Manage Personal Views	Design, Full Control
Manage Permissions	Create and change permission levels on the website; assign permissions to users and groups.	Site	View Items, Open Items, View Versions, Browse Directories, View Pages, Enumerate Permissions, Browse User Information, Open	Full Control
Manage Personal Views	Create, change, and delete personal views of lists.	Personal Permissions	View Items, View Pages, Open	Contribute, Design, Full Control
Manage Web Site	Perform all administration tasks and manage content for the website.	Site	View Items, Add and Customize Pages, Browse Directories, View Pages, Enumerate Permissions, Browse User Information, Open	Full Control
Open	Open a website, list, or folder to access items inside that container.	Site	None	All

Permission	Description	Scope	Dependent Permissions	Included in These Permission Levels by Default
Open Items	View the source of documents with server-side file handlers.	List	View Items, View Pages, Open	Read, Contribute, Design, Full Control
Override Check Out	Discard or check in a document that is checked out to another user without saving the current changes.	List	View Items, View Pages, Open	Design, Full Control
Update Personal Web Parts	Update Web Parts to display personalized information.	Personal Permissions	View Items, View Pages, Open	Contribute, Design, Full Control
Use Client Integration Features	Use features that start client applications; without this permission, users must work on documents locally and then upload their changes.	Site	Use Remote Interfaces, Open	All
Use Remote Interfaces	Use Simple Object Access Protocol (SOAP), Web DAV, or SharePoint Designer interfaces to access the website.	Site	Open	All
Use Self-Service Site Creation	Create a website by using Self-Service Site Creation.	Site	View Pages, Browse User Information, Open	Read, Contribute, Design, Full Control
View Application Pages	View forms, views, and application pages; enumerate lists.	List	Open	All

Permission	Description	Scope	Dependent Permissions	Included in These Permission Levels by Default
View Items	View items in lists, documents in document libraries, and web discussion comments.	List	View Pages, Open	Read, Contribute, Design, Full Control
View Pages	View pages in a website.	Site	Open	Read, Contribute, Design, Full Control
View Versions	View past versions of list items or documents.	List	View Items, Open Items, View Pages, Open	Read, Contribute, Design, Full Control
View Web Analytics Data	View reports on website usage.	Site	View Pages, Open	Full Control

Index

A

About the Authors

Olga Londer is an architect at Microsoft, where she works across countries and geographies to help Microsoft's technical audiences, such as developers and IT Professionals, to take the best advantage of Microsoft's products and technologies. She has written several books on Microsoft SharePoint and Microsoft Internet Information Services (IIS), she has won the British Computer Society IT Trainer award, and she has been a frequent speaker at numerous conferences and a technical content lead for many international Microsoft conferences, including TechEd. Before joining Microsoft in 2004, Olga was a Microsoft Most Valuable Professional (MVP) for SharePoint and IIS and worked for QA Ltd, a leading IT training and consulting company in the UK, where she led many SharePoint implementation projects for blue-chip clients. Olga lives in London.

Penelope Coventry is a Microsoft Most Valuable Professional (MVP) for Microsoft SharePoint Server and an independent consultant based in the UK, with more than 30 years of industry experience. She currently focuses on the design, implementation, and development of SharePoint-based solutions, and she has worked with SharePoint since 2001. Penny has written a number of books, including *Microsoft Office SharePoint Designer 2007 Step by Step, Microsoft SharePoint Designer 2010 Step by Step, Microsoft SharePoint Server 2010 Administrator's Companion, Office SharePoint Server 2007 Administrator's Companion, Microsoft SharePoint Products and Technologies Resource Kit*, and two editions of *Microsoft Windows SharePoint Services Step by Step*. Penny is frequently seen at TechEd, either as a Technical Learning guide or on the SharePoint Ask-the-Experts stand. She also speaks at the SharePoint Best Practices conferences, the European SharePoint Evolution Conference, Swedish SharePoint and Exchange Forums, UK SharePoint User Group meetings, and SharePoint Saturdays.

Penny lives in Hinckley, Leicestershire, England, with her husband, Peter, and dog, Poppy.

What do you think of this book?

We want to hear from you!

To participate in a brief online survey, please visit:

microsoft.com/learning/booksurvey

Tell us how well this book meets your needs—what works effectively, and what we can do better. Your feedback will help us continually improve our books and learning resources for you.

Thank you in advance for your input!

Microsoft® *Press*

Stay in touch!

To subscribe to the *Microsoft Press*® *Book Connection Newsletter*—for news on upcoming books, events, and special offers—please visit:

microsoft.com/learning/books/newsletter